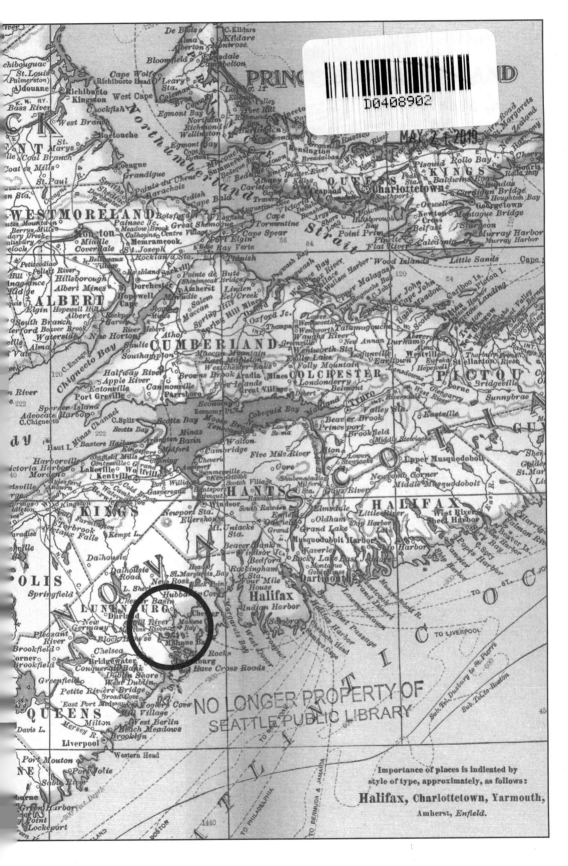

Importance of places is indicated by
style of type, approximately, as follows :

Halifax, Charlottetown, Yarmouth,

Amherst, Enfield.

To Gabriel and Grace,
whose searches, I hope, will all lead to discoveries.

THE CURSE OF
OAK ISLAND

Also by Randall Sullivan

The Price of Experience

Untouchable

LAbyrinth

The Miracle Detective

THE CURSE OF OAK ISLAND™

The Story of the World's Longest Treasure Hunt

RANDALL SULLIVAN

Atlantic Monthly Press

New York

Page 1: *The Oak Island Mystery*, Courtesy of the Estate of R. V. Harris. Randall Sullivan. Aerial map, Courtesy of OakIslandTreasure.co.uk; page 2: William Kidd, Courtesy of the Library of Congress. Henry Morgan © Bridgeman Images; page 3: William Phipps, State House Portrait Collection, Courtesy of the Maine State Museum. Samuel de Champlain, Samuel Ball © Bridgeman Images; page 4: *Collier's Magazine* excerpt, Public Domain/University of Michigan Library; page 5: *Collier's Magazine* excerpt, Public Domain/University of Michigan Library; page 6: Frederick Blair, Courtesy of D'Arcy O'Connor. William Chappell, Courtesy of the Beaton Institute, Cape Breton University; page 7: Melbourne Chappell, Courtesy of Beaton Institute, Cape Breton University © Prometheus Entertainment. Franklin Delano Roosevelt, Courtesy of the Nova Scotia Archives. page 8: Excerpt from *True Tales of Buried Treasure*, Courtesy of the Estate of Edward Rowe Snow. Gilbert Hedden, Courtesy of D'Arcy O'Connor; page 9: William Shakespeare, Public Domain. Title page of *Novum Organum Scientarum*, Francis Bacon © Bridgeman Images; page 10: David Tobias, Courtesy of Ovagim Arslanian. Robert Dunfield, Courtesy of the Estate of Robert Dunfield; page 11: Fred Nolan, Courtesy of Ovagim Arslanian. Nolan's cross © Prometheus Entertainment; page 12: Both images of Dan Blankenship, Courtesy of D'Arcy O'Connor. "G Stone," Courtesy of Charles Barkhouse; page 13: Robert Restall top, Courtesy of The Chronical Herald Library © Prometheus Entertainment. Robert Restall, Courtesy of the Restall Collection © Prometheus Entertainment; page 14: Reprinted newspaper, Courtesy of Delaware County Daily Times. Robert Restall and family, Courtesy of the Restall Collection © Prometheus Entertainment; page 15: Dan Henskee, Courtesy of Dan Henskee. Marty Lagina, Rick Lagina, Courtesy of A&E Television Networks, LLC; page 16: All images courtesy of A&E Television Networks, LLC.

FIRST EDITION

Printed in Canada
Published simultaneously in Canada

First Grove Atlantic hardcover edition: December 2018

ISBN 978-0-8021-2693-1
eISBN 978-0-8021-8905-9

Library of Congress Cataloging-in-Publication data is available for this title.

Atlantic Monthly Press
an imprint of Grove Atlantic
154 West 14th Street
New York, NY 10011

Distributed by Publishers Group West

groveatlantic.com

19 20 21   10 9 8 7 6 5 4

Introduction

Thirteen years ago, I began an article for *Rolling Stone* magazine with these lines:

> Can what's buried beneath the ground on Oak Island possibly be worth what the search for it has already cost? Six lives, scores of personal fortunes, piles of wrecked equipment, and tens of thousands of man-hours have been spent so far, and that's not to mention the blown minds and broken spirits that lie in the wake of what is at once the world's most famous and frustrating treasure hunt.

Still a pretty strong opening, I'd say, and the question remains a valid one. The article was published in the magazine's January 22, 2004, edition, and every comment I heard about it was positive. I was not entirely satisfied with the piece, however, especially as time passed. I knew I'd left things out; magazine deadlines force one to work fast and the limited space in the pages of any periodical compels writers to make tough choices and sharp cuts—or to let editors make those choices and those cuts for them. It was the nagging thought that I'd accepted the semiofficial legend of Oak Island without sufficient examination, though, that truly bothered me.

In the summer of 2010, I was working as the host of a show being produced for the Oprah Winfrey Network. Early on, Joe Nickell of the *Skeptical Inquirer*, perhaps the best known naysayer in the country, was brought in to be my on-camera adversary. Nickell had written an article that attempted to debunk certain "myths" surrounding Oak Island, and when we spoke briefly about this off camera, I was acutely aware that I wasn't confident enough in what I knew about the historical record to refute some of what he was saying. That troubled me.

It also troubled me that I might have given some preposterous theories about what had taken place on Oak Island more than their fair due, while dismissing as outlandish at least one hypothesis that I had come to believe deserved serious consideration.

Oak Island had long been a Rorschach test for dozens of historical loose ends and broken threads, most of the major conspiracy theories and a good many of the minor ones, and just about every tale of lost treasure out there. The island drew obsessive-compulsives, crackpots, and the sincerely curious to it like no place on Earth. None of this changed the fact, though, that Oak Island was a genuine enigma and quite arguably the most mysterious spot on the planet. I wanted another shot at the place.

I got one in the late spring of 2016 when I received a telephone call from the producers of the astonishingly successful cable television series *The Curse of Oak Island*, inviting me to spend a month or so on the island while the show was shooting its fourth season in Nova Scotia that summer.

It wasn't getting back on television that I looked forward to as much as getting back on Oak Island. That tiny dot of land off the coast of Nova Scotia haunted my imagination like no other place I've been. That July I headed back there for the first time since the autumn of 2003. I didn't delude myself into believing I was about to solve the mystery. All I aimed for was to tell the island's story in a more comprehensive and entertaining way than any who had gone before me. But of course, I told myself, one never knew what one might find when one started looking.

CHAPTER ONE

Oak Island sits off the coast of Nova Scotia just north of the 45th parallel, the halfway point between the equator and the North Pole, about forty-five miles southwest of Halifax. It's almost a mile long and not quite a half mile wide at its broadest point, narrowing to only a little more than a thousand feet at its sunken center, which is filled mostly with swamp and marsh. The island is commonly described as peanut shaped, but when I've looked at it from above I've always seen a baby elephant, mainly because of the curve of an incipient trunk that protrudes from its east end, wrapping around the southern shore of a compact, crescent-shaped bay that was once known as Smuggler's Cove. Small hills of glacial drift, known geologically as drumlins, rise to about 35 feet above sea level on both ends of the island. The composition of the island's two sides is very different: on the east layered with limestone, gypsum, and sandstone, on the west mainly quartzite and slate. Because the geologic structures of the island's east and west ends are so dissimilar, and because the swamp divides them, some theorists think Oak Island was once two islands, very close together that may or may not have been joined by the work of men.

While there are more than 350 other islands in the churning silver-gray waters of Mahone Bay, it's not difficult to imagine why this one would have stood out to the mariners of the sixteenth, seventeenth, and eighteenth centuries. It is larger than most of the other dots of land in those waters and very close to shore, barely two hundred yards from a protrusion of the mainland that's been known for the past two and a

half centuries as Crandall's Point. What most impressed the first Europeans to live in the Mahone Bay area, though, was that the island was
covered with a magnificent forest of mature oak trees, with deep roots
and stout trunks that supported massive, spreading limbs, leaving most
of the ground in the shadow of their canopy. It may have been the only
island in Mahone Bay where oak trees grew, and certainly it was the
only island covered with them. Those trees were what gave the island
its eventual name, though it was designated simply as Island No. 28
by Charles Morris, the surveyor general of the province, who between
1762 and 1765 conducted the first survey of the island and divided it
into thirty-two four-acre lots. In 1776, a British cartographer named
Des Barres attempted to name it Glouster Isle, but he was overruled by
the locals' insistence on calling it Oak Island.

The island's oaks, growing so close to the mainland, were an especially attractive feature to the settlers who in 1759 accepted pieces of
the hundred-thousand-acre Shoreham Grant that brought hundreds
of men and dozens of families to the south shore of Nova Scotia from
New England. They were mostly English and Welsh, with names like
Monro, Lynch, and Seacombe, and populated a village they called
Chester Township. On the south end of the bay, a mostly German and
Swiss population was in the process of creating the great seagoing and
shipbuilding town of Lunenburg, famous for the Georgian mansions
topped with five-sided dormers that were the homes of sea captains in
that epoch of tall ships. The settlers in the Chester area, though, were
mostly farmers, plus a few ambitious souls who prospered by building
and operating lumber mills. Most of the trees on the other islands of
Mahone Bay and on the mainland as well were evergreen softwoods—
spruce and pine predominated—making the island a primary source of
hardwood timber. That a single island among the dozens in Mahone
Bay should be covered with oak trees was for a period of sixty years or
so the principal mystery of the place. The first to describe the island in
print and to remark on its impressive forest of oak trees was a French
nobleman named Nicolas Denys, who had helped establish LaHave,

the settlement at the entrance to Mahone Bay, in 1632. Denys could conceive of no explanation for how the oaks had gotten there.

AMONG THE POINTS DRIVEN HOME by a study of Oak Island is how much of what we call history is hearsay and supposition, conflation and apocrypha. Even revisionists go back to the earliest written sources, created by men who were putting to paper what they'd heard from people who were themselves often repeating stories they'd been told by someone else. Historians since the time of Herodotus and Thucydides have been deciding what version of events to include and what version to leave out; readers can only hope they've chosen wisely.

If one person is identified as the first to discover the works on the island, the name Daniel McGinnis is almost unanimously put forward. As the story is told, McGinnis was sixteen years old in the late spring of 1795 when he rowed to Oak Island one fine morning to explore it, all alone. It was still early in the day, the story goes, when the teenager stumbled upon an unusual saucer-shaped depression in the earth, about 13 feet in diameter, on the elevated ground of the island's east drumlin. The forked limb of a giant oak extended over the clearing, cut off at a point where its two branches were still almost as thick as a man's thigh. Attached to the limb, about 15 feet above the ground, was a weather-worn wooden tackle block that was held in place with a wooden peg or "treenail" of the type used in the construction of wooden ships. Taking all this in, young Mr. McGinnis surmised that he had happened upon the hiding place of a pirate treasure.

During the seventeenth and early eighteenth centuries, when buccaneers terrorized shipping lanes across the globe, Mahone Bay had been one of the world's great pirate havens. Tales of buried treasure were endemic to the region, but the legends that surrounded Oak Island were particularly ominous. According to several of Nova Scotia's numerous amateur historians, the citizens of nearby Chester Township had for years shared stories of "strange lights" that glowed on the island after dark. Author Edward Rowe Snow, who embraced this bit of apocrypha as historical fact, wrote that a number of fishermen claimed to have seen on the island human figures "silhouetted against bonfires," as one local chronicler put it. Eventually, Snow had written, two men overcome with curiosity had ventured out to Oak Island to investigate. They never returned.

Daniel McGinnis did make it back to Chester, according to the story, where he recruited two young friends, also teenagers—John Smith and Anthony Vaughan—to help him dig for the treasure he was certain must have been buried at this mysterious spot on Oak Island. The first thing the three did was attempt to remove the tackle block hanging from the forked limb of the oak tree. But it slipped off the treenail and fell to the ground, where it shattered into powdery fragments, suggesting to the boys that it must be very old. They went to work on the ground then, armed with pickaxes and shovels. They had reached a depth of only 2 feet, though, when they hit a tier of carefully laid flagstones. (They would later decide after some investigation that the rocks were not from Oak Island but instead had been moved there from Gold River, about two miles north on the mainland.) Eagerly tossing the stones aside, McGinnis and his friends found themselves at the entrance to a large shaft. The sides were made of hard, packed clay, but the earth inside was loose and easy to shovel. Driven by the excitement of discovery, the three dug within a few days to a depth of 10 feet, where they struck solid wood. Assuming they had hit the top of a treasure chest, the teenagers shoveled feverishly, only to discover that what they had found was a level platform of oak logs, all about 6 to 8 inches in diameter, the ends of which had been embedded in the walls of the shaft. Removing these, the boys kept digging over the next few days, clearing out the loose soil with a pickaxe, two shovels, a rope, and a bucket. When they hit solid wood for a second time at 20 feet, the three again dug feverishly, convinced that his time they really *had* found the top of the treasure chest. What they had struck with their shovels, though, was another tier of oak logs, with their rotting ends embedded in the sides of the shaft exactly as the logs at 10 feet had been. At that point, the three looked up at the walls of clay towering above them and realized that even a partial collapse would bury them alive. It was agreed that they needed to mount a much more substantial operation, involving both a far larger workforce and more expensive materials and equipment if they were to go deeper into the shaft.

The three youngsters bought land on Oak Island, as the story goes, where they supported themselves as farmers while making regular trips to nearby towns, seeking out men of means who might help them recover what they were calling Captain Kidd's treasure.

I HAD RETURNED TO NOVA SCOTIA determined to test every major theory and to question all received wisdom about Oak Island. After four weeks of research, assisted by, among others, the Nova Scotia Archives, the South Shore Genealogical Society, and local historian Charles Barkhouse, I was convinced that the tale was mostly true. This is not to say entirely true. There were a number of details in the narrative that I either doubted or was convinced couldn't be right, and several others that I believed might be embellishments added as the story was told and retold.

For the moment, I was leaving aside the deeper mystery of who was behind the works on Oak Island and concentrating instead on the story of how those works had been discovered. Even then, the best answers I could find to my questions about who, what, and when were so unclear that nebulousness may have been their most defining feature. At least I didn't have much doubt that the first to find the massive hole in the ground, now world-famous as the Money Pit, *had* been the young man Daniel McGinnis. While McGinnis himself was dead by the time the treasure hunt on Oak Island hit high gear in the mid-nineteenth century, his former partners, Vaughan and Smith, had been alive to describe what took place on the island in the early days—dating back to the discovery of the Money Pit—to those who produced the earliest

written accounts. Both said there was no question Daniel was the first
to spot the features that had inspired the three of them to start digging.
Who Daniel McGinnis had been, though, was still a puzzle with a lot
of missing pieces to me.

McGinnis was described as "an enigma" by R. V. Harris, the
lawyer whose 1958 book *The Oak Island Mystery* had made the Money
Pit story known outside Nova Scotia: "His age in 1795 is unknown.
His origin and parentage is unknown." So where had the story of the
sixteen-year-old boy who discovered the Money Pit come from? From
Anthony Vaughan, mostly, it seemed. Vaughan, an old man by the time
his memories were recorded for posterity, had been a main source for
the first published account of what had taken place on Oak Island,
which appeared in the October 16, 1862, edition of the *Liverpool Transcript*, a now-defunct weekly newspaper that was distributed throughout
southwestern Nova Scotia during the mid- and late nineteenth century.
Vaughan had actually told his story at length more than twelve years
earlier, in an 1849 interview with a devout Presbyterian named Robert
Creelman, who was a member of a treasure-hunting group known as
the Truro Company. The author who made use of the Creelman interview for the *Transcript* article was Jothan (sometimes called Jotham) B.
McCully, who had been part of both the Truro Company and the Oak
Island Association, separate treasure-hunting groups that had worked
on Oak Island between 1849 and 1865. McCully may also have written
the second and far more detailed published account of the discovery
of the Money Pit, which appeared in three consecutive editions of a
Halifax triweekly called the *Colonist* in January 1864, although the
author was identified only as a "member" of a team that had searched
for treasure on Oak Island in 1861. The *Transcript* and *Colonist* articles
each had relied on interviews with John Smith (who died in 1857) as
well as those Creelman had conducted with Anthony Vaughan, but
Smith apparently had been more taciturn than his old friend. Not so
Smith's daughter, Mary, who worked as the housekeeper for Judge
Mather Byles DesBrisay, the county magistrate and local eminence

who authored *History of the County of Lunenburg* (originally published in 1870), which included a two-page account of the discovery of the Money Pit that was the first to appear between hard covers. Mary Smith, apparently quite voluble, had told Judge DesBrisay the story from her family's perspective on multiple occasions.

Those three accounts, published sixty-seven, sixty-nine, and seventy-five years after the putative date of the Money Pit's discovery, were the core versions of the Oak Island story before Harris's book was published. There were of course various documents and records dating back to the early nineteenth century that related to the assorted treasure-hunting companies that had formed to attempt the recovery of whatever might be buried on Oak Island. And the scene at the Money Pit had been briefly described in an 1863 volume titled *Rambles among the Blue-Noses*, written by British author Andrew Learmont Spedon, whose aim was to amuse the people back home with tales from the provincial wilds of eastern Canada. There was also an account of the discovery of the Money Pit written in 1866 by one Israel Longworth, but his work, "History of the County of Colchester," had never been published. And only a fragment remained of a manuscript written in 1863 by another early treasure hunter, James McNutt, that described the early search for treasure on Oak Island.

So the early story of the treasure hunt on the island was based largely on the recollections of Anthony Vaughan and Mary Smith, along with various others who claimed to have heard it from Daniel McGinnis and John Smith. This paucity of sources and questions about their reliability have fueled rampant speculation about what *really* happened on Oak Island in those early days, everything from the allegation that the three young men cooked up a story to cover their tracks after finding a huge treasure trove on Oak Island to the claim that McGinnis, Smith, and Vaughan were the front men for a conspiracy of Yankee loyalists operating a smuggling operation out of Oak Island during the Revolutionary War. The evidence offered to back up these and the dozens of other alternative theories of what took place on Oak Island in the last years of the eighteenth century is of course even more meager than the evidence that supports what has become the more or less official version.

R. V. Harris wrote in *The Oak Island Mystery* that most of what could be actually known about Daniel McGinnis's background had to be derived from "the origins and lineages" of Vaughan and Smith, whose family histories were much easier to find in Nova Scotia's early public records. In my opinion, no one was in a better position to make such an assertion than Harris, who had served as the attorney to the two men who drove the treasure hunt on Oak Island for seventy years between 1895 and 1965 and who had inherited and relied on the vast collection of records and documents that now made up the bulk of the huge Oak Island file at the Nova Scotia Archives in Halifax. So I took his advice.

I began with Vaughan. Government and church records established that he was the son of an Anthony Vaughan Sr., who had come to Nova Scotia from Massachusetts in 1768 to claim his piece of the British Crown's Shoreham Grant: two hundred acres on the mainland almost directly across from Oak Island. Anthony Vaughan Jr. was thirteen years old in 1795, which offered at least some tangential confirmation that his friend Daniel McGinnis probably had been a teenager also. Judge DesBrisay, in his book, described Vaughan and his family as living on the mainland in 1795 and that jibes with what other early writers up to and including R. V. Harris have maintained. But there was little question in my mind that the boy's family owned land on Oak Island well before the discovery of the Money Pit. There are deeds that show Anthony Vaughan Sr. acquired lots 15 and 17 on Oak Island in 1765 (which wouldn't seem possible if he had emigrated to Canada in 1768) and lot 14 in 1781. One of Vaughan Sr.'s brothers bought lot 13 in 1781. It is also clear that the Vaughans were operating a lumber mill on the mainland directly across from Oak Island. In 1788 they petitioned the Surveyor General of Woods in the province of Nova Scotia for permission to cut down "Sundry Pine Trees" on nine hundred acres of land for the purpose of farming the land and milling the trees. So there seems little doubt that by 1795 the Vaughan brothers were using or intended to use the trees on their Oak Island properties as timber for their mill and that Anthony Vaughan Jr. must have had some familiarity with the island.

John Smith was almost certainly living on Oak Island in 1795. In fact, he may have been born there, but it appears more likely that he moved to the island in 1786 at the age of eleven. Born on August 20, 1775, he would have been nineteen years old in the spring of 1795 (more support, in my mind, that Daniel McGinnis really was sixteen years old or so at that time). Smith's family, like Vaughan's, had come to Mahone Bay as part of the Shoreham Grant immigration. An Edward Smith, who was most likely (though not certainly) an uncle of John Smith's father, had acquired the title to Oak Island's lot 19 on March 8, 1768. John Smith himself made a first appearance in the public record on September 28, 1790, when he married (at age fifteen!) one Sarah Floyd. He next publicly registered his existence on June 26, 1795, when he purchased lot 18 on Oak Island from a Chester merchant named Casper Wollenhaupt for £5. It was the plot of land where the Money Pit was located. That purchase seems to have been the main basis for the claim that the Money Pit had been discovered in the late spring of 1795, the assumption being that Smith had bought the property to secure access to the presumed treasure. Not unreasonable, but far from conclusive.

But back to Daniel McGinnis. I was distracted briefly by the claims of a handful of amateur historians (and the subject of Oak Island is beset by literally thousands of amateur historians) who doubted that such a person as Daniel McGinnis had actually ever existed, their claim being that the Smith and Vaughan families had used this fictional character as a front to cover their own secretive activities on the island. Judge DesBrisay had described Daniel McGinnis as one of the earliest settlers on Oak Island, but there is no record of anyone named McGinnis owning property on the island prior to 1795. Some of the doubters pointed out that there was no Daniel McGinnis listed in the records of the poll tax imposed on Nova Scotians by the British Crown in 1791, but that merely suggested to me again that McGinnis probably *had* been a teenager, because only those over the age of twenty-one were required to pay the poll tax and therefore would be listed in the Crown records. Others who questioned whether McGinnis was a real person also pointed out that no grave marker with his name had ever been found in Lunenburg County. The early newspaper accounts, though, had described McGinnis as having been buried on Oak Island, and there is to this day a collection of rocks on the drumlin where the Money Pit is located that could very well mark his final resting place. A shard of broken stone from that pile was found to have letters and numbers that could have been consistent with the name, the date of birth, and the date of death of a Daniel McGinnis. On top of that, records existed of various McGinnises living on Oak Island throughout the 1800s. And on the southwest end of the island were the remains of the foundation for a home that had been described since the beginning of the twentieth century as the "McGinnis place."

Finally, I consulted a volume titled *Families of Western Shore*, recommended to me by the South Shore Genealogical Society as the most accurate source available. There was a lengthy section in the most recent edition of the book on the "McInnis-McGinnis" clan that began in the late eighteenth century and ended in the late twentieth, when the book was published. The first entry described the arrival in Nova Scotia of a Donald Daniel McInnes, a "Planter" of Welsh descent, who came to Chester from New England with, among others, "the Vaughan Brothers" in or around the year 1772. McInnes (whose family name became McGinnis at some point before the end of the eighteenth century) was described as having "settled on Oak Island." The only confusing entry was one showing that McInnes had been awarded a Crown grant of one hundred acres near Chester in 1784, which suggested that was when he came to Nova Scotia, rather than with the Shoreham Grant immigrants who had arrived in 1772.

My bearings were further shaken when Karlie Morash, who runs the museum on Oak Island, gave me a copy of a document that had been prepared by "the McGinnis family" that she said showed Daniel McGinnis had been thirty-six years old at the time of the Money Pit's discovery. These family members had relied mainly on three documents: an "Application for Compensation for losses" suffered during the American Revolutionary War that was dated April 7, 1785; a related submission "To the Honourable Lord Commissioner of his Majesty's Treasury" dated February 17, 1785; and the application for a memorial to Donald McInnes, "Captain of the North Carolina Militia." On the basis of those, the family had created a time line for Donald Daniel MacInnes (yes, yet another spelling) that followed him from his birth in Scotland in 1759 through his immigration to America in 1770, his residence with his parents in North Carolina, his enlistment in the ranks of the loyalists in 1776 when the revolution broke out, his service under General Angus McDonald and then with Lord Charles Cornwallis, his command of a gunboat in Charleston, South Carolina, and his eventual relocation to Nova Scotia (in or around the year 1785). The final event listed on the time line was the man's attendance of the baptism for his grandson Johan James MacInnes in Chester in 1795.

I was flummoxed. When I went back to *Families of the Western Shore*, however, I found that the genealogy in that volume passed from Donald Daniel McInnes, to a "Daniel Jr." who had "found 'The Money Pit Site' in 1795." The only explanation I could come up with was that either Karlie or the McGinnis descendants had confused Daniel McGinnis, discoverer of the Money Pit, with his father. But what about the claim that family records showed "Donald MacInnes" attending the baptism of his grandchild in Chester in 1795? That might be accounted for by the other available eighteenth-century document relating to either Donald or Daniel McInnes in Nova Scotia (found in the archives of the Church of Jesus Christ of Latter-day Saints), a copy of the record of the marriage of Donald Daniel McGinnis to Maria Barbara Saller at St. James' Anglican Church in Lunenburg on September 8, 1795. Daniel Jr. was supposed to have been sixteen when he found the Money Pit a few months before that date, but a marriage later that year hardly seemed out of the question, given that his friend John Smith had been only fifteen when he married. But what about the alleged baptism of the grandson of Donald MacInnes? I went back to *Families of the Western Shore*, where, with both a sense of relief and a conviction that I could be done chasing the ghost of Daniel McGinnis, I discovered a reference to a document recording the baptism of one James Johan McGinnis, son of Daniel and Maria Barbara, in Chester on July 26, 1797.

I was satisfied that I had a working model of who Daniel McGinnis had been and where he had come from: the son of a Scottish or Welsh father who came to America as a boy, lived with his family in North Carolina, joined the loyalist side in the Revolutionary War and emigrated to Canada after the British surrender, accepting the grant of one hundred acres near Chester that he worked as a farmer. If Donald Daniel Sr. had been born in 1759, then it made sense that Donald Daniel Jr. might have been born twenty years later in 1779, which would have made him sixteen years old in 1795. The story held up, but only to a point.

It seemed clear that the tale of young Daniel McGinnis rowing out to a mysterious uninhabited island where he was startled by the discovery of a weird depression in the ground was not exactly how things had really happened. In 1951, the Nova Scotia Bureau of Information (a government agency that no longer exists) published the first official account of the Oak Island story. The document's concise summary of the Money Pit's discovery reads as follows: "Anthony Vaughan, Jack Smith and Dan McInnes, on a shooting trip to Oak Island from the neighboring mainland, found an aged oak with a sawed short limb from which dangled a stout line and pulley. Under the tree was a depression in the ground, apparently man made."

Among the many problems with that account is that Oak Island was inhabited in 1795 by John Smith and his family among others. It was possible Smith already owned lot 18 on Oak Island when the Money Pit was discovered at some date after June 26, 1795. (One account of the Pit's discovery placed the year as 1799.) Daniel McGinnis might have rowed out to the island—almost certainly *had* rowed out to the island, if he wasn't already living there—but it could have been for the purpose of visiting his friend John or doing some work for John's family.

Or maybe he *was* tracking game; Frederick Blair, the dominant figure in the Oak Island treasure hunt from the late nineteenth century through the middle of the twentieth and the greatest researcher of the Oak Island story, wrote that McInnes had been "partridge hunting" when he found the Money Pit. Other accounts say that he was cutting trees for either Smith or Vaughan when he stumbled on the anomaly that would launch what has become the longest treasure hunt in human history.

What exactly that anomaly had been was yet another question for which a variety of answers had been offered.

The account of the discovery in Judge DesBrisay's book read:

> McInnes one day discovered a spot that gave evidence of having been visited a good many years earlier. There had been cuttings away of the forest, and oak stumps were visible. One of the original oaks was standing, with a large forked branch extending over the old clearing. To the forked part of this branch, by means of a treenail connecting the fork in a small triangle, was attached an old tackle block. McInnes made known his find to his neighbors.

No mention of a large circular depression. Also, DesBrisay's account made it sound as if McGinnis was living on the island at the time, as were "his neighbors" Smith and Vaughan. Only when all three went back to the spot the next day did they notice that the ground beneath the tackle block had "settled and formed a hollow," according to DesBrisay, who wrote that the three "cleared away the young trees, and removed the surface soil for about two feet" before finding the tier of flagstones and the entrance to a shaft.

The first newspaper account written by McCully for the *Liverpool Transcript* also described McGinnis as initially being curious about the stumps of old oak trees crowned with thick mats of moss and then noticing that the trees growing among the stumps were younger than the other oaks in the forest. The descriptions of "oak stumps" and "young trees" seemed especially significant to me, because, if true, they almost certainly ruled out a number of the theories of Oak Island that had been offered over the years, some of them dating back a thousand years or more. There was no way (and arborists hired by *The Curse of Oak Island* have confirmed this) that McGinnis would have noticed either the oak stumps or the young trees if the "cutting away of the forest" had occurred centuries earlier. To me, that almost certainly meant that whoever was responsible for the original excavation in that spot had done the work no earlier than the seventeenth century. This considerably shortened the long list of candidates who had been proposed by literally dozens of theorists.

The *Colonist* articles of 1864, also possibly written by McCully, made less of the oak stumps than of three remaining oak trees that grew in an equilateral triangle around the Money Pit. The articles make it clear that those three trees were what marked the ground between them. The *Colonist* articles also state that after observing the triangle of trees, McGinnis noticed that the bark of each trunk had letters and symbols carved into it. This description appears in no other early account of the Money Pit's discovery.

Among the many questions raised by these early accounts is this: just what kinds of oak trees were growing on Oak Island back in 1795? The original trees are long gone, mostly killed off by an infestation of black ants during the nineteenth century. R. V. Harris had noted that a number of his sources "apparently with a view to adding more mystery to their stories, have stated that this species of oak does not grow elsewhere in Nova Scotia, that they are southern trees found no farther north than Louisiana." Also, at least two historians who authored books on the subject of piracy and mentioned Oak Island in their works (one being Charles B. Driscoll, whose *Doubloons* is regarded in Canada as a classic work) had written that the trees on the island were the species known as live oak (*Quercus virginiana*), an evergreen oak found only in the southern United States. Harris, though, asserted that the trees on the island were "undoubtedly" red oaks, which do grow on the Nova Scotia mainland. He cited the autopsy of one of the last surviving old oaks on the island, a wounded tree that had been cut down in 1931 "and examined critically with a view to determining its age and the cause of the injury." Embedded deep in the tree's trunk, those who cut it open found the tip of a thick knife blade that had broken off inside it. When the rings of the tree were counted outward from the blade, it was determined that at least 183 years had passed since the wound was inflicted, which Harris claimed as support for his theory that "the 'Pit' was constructed between 1650 and 1750." Some later investigators would point out that those who had identified the trees on the island not as red oaks but as live oaks "had the benefit of seeing them in person," as one put it. The last account concerning the oaks written while some of them were still standing on the island was in the pamphlet published by the Nova Scotia Bureau of Information, whose anonymous author had visited the island by motorboat during the summer of 1951. "The bare branches of three large, dead oaks tower above the evergreens east of Pirate Cove, and there are a few standing large dead oaks around the corner on the southern side [of the island]. There are a few other oaks in leaf, but all much smaller."

Those who insist the trees on Oak Island were brought north in wooden ships and planted there make much of the fact that the recovered fragment of the McNutt manuscript asserted that the first thing Daniel McGinnis had noticed that caused him to stop and consider the Money Pit location was a circle of red clover growing in the spot, a variety of clover that was not native to Nova Scotia. This claim about the red clover and other nonnative plants growing around the Money Pit was repeated in T. M. Longstreth's *To Nova Scotia*, published in 1935.

What most confused me about the nineteenth-century descriptions of the Money Pit's discovery was the part about the tackle block. When I'd first heard the story of the old wooden pulley fixed to the oak tree branch that hung over the Money Pit, I'd reflexively dismissed it as apocrypha. If some group of people had gone to the massive effort of performing the extraordinary work on Oak Island for the purpose of concealing a treasure (for which, obviously, they planned to return at some later date), it did not make sense that they would have been so careless as to leave an obvious tell. And yet the story of the tackle block attached to the forked branch of the oak by a treenail had been repeated in every early account of the discovery of the Money Pit. I had a sense it must be true. But if it was true, this meant that whoever had dug the Money Pit in the first place had wanted it to be found. That seemed even more certain if one accepted as accurate an early account attributed to Anthony Vaughan that there were carved "marks and figures" on the trunk of the oak near its base.

WHAT MCGINNIS, SMITH, AND VAUGHAN DID after they gave up digging in the Money Pit by themselves is easier to know than what happened earlier, because the three young men were by then intent on involving others in their treasure hunt. First, though, they took precautions to protect their find. Before they went in search of a partner or partners who would help them mount a more extensive excavation, the three teenagers marked the depth their dig had reached, loosely refilled the bottom of the pit with dirt, surrounded it with oak sticks driven into the mud, then covered those over with branches from young trees they had felled.

They also searched the island. Their most significant find was what was left of an "old road" (which is Judge DesBrisay's description; another writer called it a "rough path") that led to the Money Pit site. In DesBrisay's account, the three actually found the road before they started digging and that discovery seems to have been what convinced Smith and Vaughan that their friend McGinnis really had found something. Besides the road or path, the discovery that seems to have most excited the three was a large iron ringbolt they found at low tide on an eastern cove of the island, embedded in a rock. The three assumed it was where the ship had tied up while the pirates had buried their treasure. Though there is no clear record of when McGinnis purchased his property on Oak Island, it seems clear from the recollections of others that McGinnis, after marrying, built himself a house on the southwestern part of the island and farmed the land. Smith, already married and the owner of lot 18, built himself a house near the Money Pit and proceeded to acquire lots 16, 17, 19, and 20, giving him ownership of the entire twenty-four-acre eastern end of the island. Vaughan, by every account, lived on the mainland even after marrying. This is perhaps why, after an intervening period of seven or eight years, it was Vaughan who found the partner who would organize the first well-financed assault on the Money Pit.

The early accounts offer multiple explanations of why it took so long. Only those willing to work twelve-hour days could make a life on Mahone Bay during that time, and neither the young men nor their neighbors had the time, the energy, or the money to reopen the Money Pit and try digging deeper into it. Others have argued that people were afraid of Oak Island. Word that McGinnis, Smith, and Vaughan claimed to have found a spot where pirate treasure was buried had produced an oft-repeated local legend that the buccaneers killed a black slave and left his ghost to guard their treasure. There were also stories that a witches' coven met on the island and cast curses on anyone who dared to visit. But the simplest (and therefore most likely) explanation was that the three young friends kept their mouths closed about what they had found and waited for an encounter with a person of means they believed could help them find the treasure.

In retrospect, what seems most remarkable is that McGinnis, Smith, and Vaughan never seem to have wavered in their belief about who had buried that treasure.

CHAPTER TWO

From the perspective of what we know about the world today, it might seem absurd that the belief it was Captain Kidd's treasure buried on Oak Island should persist for more than a hundred years. Even when the second edition of his *History of the County of Lunenburg* was published in 1896, Judge DesBrisay referred to the Money Pit as the burial place of "the Kidd Treasure." From the point of view of the people living in Mahone Bay in the late eighteenth century, however, this notion was perfectly reasonable.

The coastlines of Nova Scotia and Newfoundland had been pirate havens all during the seventeenth century and well into the eighteenth. In Nova Scotia, there was hardly a bay, cove, or inlet that did not have some legend of pirate treasure associated with it. And no part of Nova Scotia was more steeped in such lore than Mahone Bay. According to R. V. Harris, "the name '*Mahone*' itself is derived from the French word *mahonne* which in turn is derived from the Turkish word *mahone*, which means a low-lying craft, propelled by long oars, called sweeps, and much used by pirates in the earlier days of the Mediterranean." There's some question about whether the bay's name actually *is* an allusion to pirate boats, though most believe so. "Mahone Bay" first appeared on a chart of the Nova Scotia seacoast drawn by a Captain Thomas Durell in 1736, but Durell left no indication of where he got the name. It is clear, though, that pirates had been making use of the bay for more than a hundred years by then, and the reasons why it was so attractive to them are obvious. Twenty miles long by twelve miles wide, surrounded by thickly forested hills and protected from view by the Tancook Islands, Mahone Bay provides an ideal location to scan what are today the main shipping lanes running along the southern coast of Nova Scotia. And Oak Island might be the most protected body of land in the entire bay, with outer islands blocking sight of it until one sails very close to the mainland. A ship anchored on the south shore of Oak Island is about as well hidden from the open sea as it is possible to be and remain afloat, in a spot where it would take five minutes to row a boat to a mainland, which back in the seventeenth century was heavily populated with white-tailed deer, black bear, and moose, along with plenty of pheasant and grouse. The bay was then and remains today the summer home of hundreds of thousands of ducks and geese, not to mention the haddock, mackerel, and scallops that also fill its waters. During the warm season, it's difficult to imagine a better place for a ship's crew to fatten up, lay in provisions, and make repairs.

Henry Howard Brownell, in his 186_ work *The English in America*, observed not only that pirates had been "quite numerous all along the Atlantic coast of America" during the previous two centuries, but also that the freebooters made LaHave, at the entrance to Mahone Bay, "their depot." In 1700, the French governor of Arcadia actually invited the pirates of Nova Scotia to make LaHave their base of operations, in order to keep the fort there out of British hands. The buccaneers happily obliged, mainly because the fort "was favorably situated for committing depredations on the trade with Massachusetts," as Thomas Chandler Haliburton put it in volume 1 of his *An Historical and Statistical Account of Nova Scotia*, published in 1829.

This sort of cozy relationship between pirates, government officials, and financial interests was common in the years between 1600 and 1750. Those who worked under the sponsorship of the British Crown were called privateers, and there were any number who alternated between collecting bounties for the ships they captured and simply seizing the loot and sailing off on the high seas. I found it remarkable that the greatest of all the privateers who turned pirate—the most successful and powerful buccaneer in history, in my estimation—is so little known. Perhaps this is because the career of Peter Easton (1570–1620) came so early in the history of English piracy. He was the scion of a family that was admired and respected for its service to the Crown, not only for having fought in the Crusades under Richard the Lionheart, but also for having distinguished themselves in the defeat of the Spanish Armada. Peter Easton himself was still a loyal servant of Queen Elizabeth in 1602, when she commissioned him as a privateer and gave him command of a convoy that was to protect the British fishing fleet in Newfoundland. His commission from the Queen gave Easton the legal right to press local fishermen into his service and to attack enemy ships and wharves with impunity; he was actually encouraged to capture any Spanish ship that he could. Aboard his flagship *Happy Adventure*, with what had once been the Crusader flag, the St. George's Cross, at its masthead, Easton enjoyed immediate success. His career as a privateer was short-lived, however, because when Elizabeth died in March 1603 her successor, James I, promptly sued for peace with Spain. Easton's continued attacks on Spanish ships turned him into the first notorious British pirate, a role he played with remarkable dash and vigor. For the next decade, he and his fleet captured Spanish ships from the West Indies to the Mediterranean, taking enormous wealth in gold, while at the same time extorting protection money from English ships throughout the Atlantic Ocean. In 1610, his convoy successfully blockaded Bristol Channel, which gave Easton control of all shipping that came and went from British ports in the west of England. Throughout this time, Easton maintained his headquarters in Newfoundland, where his home base was an island in Placentia Bay called Oderin. Horseshoe-shaped and composed mainly of high hills, Oderin's sheltered harbor not only had room for all of Easton's ships, but it also concealed them from virtually every approach. (Placentia Bay was also the protected body of water where Franklin D. Roosevelt and Winston Churchill met aboard a ship to draft the Atlantic Charter as they prepared to join forces in World War II.) In Newfoundland, Easton continued to fill his ranks with men from English fishing vessels. Many were pressed into service, but it was widely reported that most of the fifteen hundred fishermen who joined Easton's crews did so voluntarily.

The British captain Sir Richard Whitbourne, in his work *Discourse and Discovery of Newfoundland*, recalled that in late 1611 he had met "the famous pirate, Peter Easton, who then commanded ten stout ships." Whitbourne's encounter with Easton was more than a meeting. In fact, the pirate captured and plundered all of the thirty ships under Whitbourne's command at St. John's (today the largest city in Newfoundland) and took Whitbourne himself prisoner. The captain was not released until he pledged to obtain a pardon for Easton upon his return to England.

Even after turning Whitbourne loose, though, Easton remained unrelenting. In June 1612, by Whitbourne's account, Easton sailed into Harbour Grace, where he stole five ships, a hundred cannons, and "goods to the value of £10,400"—millions of dollars in today's money. The pirate also "induced" an additional five hundred English fishermen to join his crews and robbed assorted French, Flemish, and Portuguese ships of their cargos and provisions. On the mainland, his crews robbed settlers, burned their forests, and murdered those who resisted.

Easton's behavior was not entirely malign, Whitbourne would point out when he submitted his request that the pirate be pardoned. Easton, then in near-total control of Canada's Atlantic coast, had permitted the first man appointed by the Crown as proprietary governor of Newfoundland, John Guy, to form the island's founding British colony at Cuper's Cove. He would not allow Guy to form a second colony, however.

By the time Easton's pardon was granted by King James I, he was working the Barbary Coast, where he took a number of Spanish ships. From there he sailed to the Caribbean, where it was reported he had breached the purportedly unassailable fort at San Felipe del Morrow in Puerto Rico (which had previously withstood a siege by Sir Francis Drake). Whether that is true or not, Easton certainly captured the treasure-laden Spanish ship *San Sebastian*, which he hauled back to Newfoundland. On discovering that his pardon had been granted, Easton retired to Villefranche on the French Riviera with two million pounds of gold, wealth that permitted him to acquire the title marquis of Savoy and live out the remainder of his days in splendor.

It's difficult to think of another outlaw in history who made crime pay better than Peter Easton. Among his admirers is Marty Lagina, one of the two brothers who have driven the treasure hunt on Oak Island since 2007. It was Marty who first suggested to me that Easton might be the man behind the works on Oak Island: "This was a very smart guy, and he wouldn't have just sailed off with all his wealth and risked losing it on the sea or on land. He would have kept something in reserve, hidden. Why not on Oak Island?"

While Easton may have had motive and opportunity, there's absolutely no evidence that connects him with Oak Island. Placentia Bay is more than a thousand miles from Mahone Bay. The idea that Easton was responsible for what took place on the island certainly can't be dismissed, but that's about the extent of the theory's viability.

Of course, the evidence is even thinner for the numerous other famous pirates who have been linked to Oak Island. Those who propose Edward "Blackbeard" Teach (1680–1718) as the man behind the Money Pit like to cite his famous boast that "I've buried my money where none but Satan and myself can find it, and the one that lives longest takes all," but that's about all they have. There's nothing to indicate that Teach was ever anywhere near Nova Scotia. Henry Morgan (1635–1688) is another candidate who has been suggested. Those who back Morgan note that after sacking the city of Panama in August 1670, the famous pirate captain and his crew sailed away with spoils of gold, silver, and gemstones worth well over $100 million in today's values. Just six months later, Morgan, suspecting a mutiny among his men, slipped away during the night. Aside from the fact that the treasure of Panama has never been found or accounted for, however, there's nothing that connects Morgan to Nova Scotia, let alone to Oak Island.

A slightly more plausible case might be made for Sir William Phipps (1650–1694). Phipps was a privateer who managed to remain in the good graces of the Crown, in large part because of a spectacular early success. In 1687 and 1688 Phipps led a pair of expeditions that recovered the *Concepcion*, an *almiranta* or "flagship galleon," of the Spanish fleet that had foundered on a reef along Hispaniola's Ambrosia Bank more than forty years earlier and was still loaded with a fantastic thirty-four-ton treasure of silver coins, silver bullion, gold doubloons, gemstones, and Chinese porcelain that was worth well over a $1 billion in today's money. When Phipps hauled his prize back to London, he became a wealthy man and a national hero. He was knighted and made a Sheriff of New England, where he eventually rose to the position of Massachusetts governor. While most of the other famous pirates and privateers of his time sailed the waters of the Caribbean, Phipps was quite familiar with the North Atlantic, and in fact he was almost as celebrated for his sacking of the Acadian city of Port Royal on Nova Scotia's Bay of Fundy as he was for the capture of the *Concepcion*. Phipps was proposed as the originator of the Money Pit in a book titled *Oak Island and Its Lost Treasure*, put out by Formac, a Halifax house that has created a significant-sized cottage industry devoted to publishing works that champion doggedly researched but often weakly supported theories of Oak Island. The suggestion that Phipps kept a huge part of the treasure recovered from the *Concepcion* and buried it on Oak Island is something that can't be simply shrugged off, but that's about as much as can be said for it.

THE PEOPLE LIVING IN THE MAHONE BAY of the late eighteenth and early nineteenth centuries had just one pirate in mind when they spoke of the Oak Island treasure, however, and that was William Kidd (1645–1701). This singular focus on Captain Kidd was, I believe, largely a function of time and place. His rise to prominence came three-quarters of a century later than Peter Easton's and took place only after

he had settled in New York City. The unquestionably political circumstances of Kidd's trial and execution by the British Crown, though, were
what made him a pirate legend.

Kidd was "of obscure origin" according to the *Encyclopedia Britannica*,
though the man himself testified before the High Court of Admiralty in
London that he had been born in Greenock, Scotland, in 1645. His father
may have been a ship's captain who was lost at sea, but some historians
have made the case that the famous pirate was sired by a Church of Scotland minister. Historians also have made claims that in his youth Kidd
served as an apprentice on a pirate ship, that he commanded a privateer
in the wars of William III and fought the French, and that he performed
"brave service" for the Crown in the American colonies. It can be stated
with a bit more confidence (but no real certainty) that by 1680 Kidd, then
thirty-five, had prospered well enough from his life at sea that he was
able to resign from the British navy and purchase his own ship. What we
can be sure about is that in 1689, Kidd attempted to settle in New York
and to establish himself there as a person of means. This early effort at
making a life on land was cut short the same year, though, when Kidd
was dispatched by British authorities to the Caribbean. There is yet more
disagreement about whether he went there as the captain of a privateer
or as a member of the French and English crew of a pirate ship that
mutinied, renamed the ship *Blessed William*, and made Kidd their new
captain. Either way, the *Blessed William* became part of the small British
fleet that defended the island of Nevis from the French; Kidd and his
crew were instructed that they could collect their pay from any French
ships or towns they captured and looted.

By 1691, Kidd had made it back to New York, where he married
a wealthy young widow named Sarah Oort and began to join society,
becoming acquainted with at least three governors and contributing to
the construction of Trinity Church in Manhattan. At the behest of the
British Crown, he was still employed off and on as a privateer, serving
during the Nine Years' War (1688–1697) off the coasts of Massachusetts and New York and in the Caribbean. In December 1695, New

York's new governor, Richard Coote, the 1st Earl of Bellomont, tasked the "trusty and well-beloved Captain Kidd" with taking command of a British privateer that was to attack both pirates and ships of the enemy French. Kidd could not refuse without destroying his reputation and so sailed to London to prepare for the voyage that would cost him his life and make him a legend. In England, he was given a new ship named the *Adventure Galley*, along with command of thirty-four cannons and a handpicked crew of 150. He carried a letter of marque signed by William III that licensed him as a privateer obliged to surrender 10 percent of his booty to the Crown. The *Adventure Galley*'s voyage got off to a bad start, though, when Kidd and his crew failed to salute a British navy yacht as they sailed down the Thames. When the yacht fired a shot across the bow to demand what was considered a proper show of respect, the *Adventure Galley*'s crew replied by presenting to the navy their backsides. Such unprecedented impudence resulted in the navy pressing virtually the entire crew of Kidd's ship into its service. The *Adventure Galley* made it shorthanded back to New York, where Kidd was compelled to pick up a new crew, this one made up mostly of former pirates and hardened criminals.

By the autumn of 1696, the *Adventure Galley* was sailing off the coast of Madagascar, where a third of the crew died of cholera. The new ship began to spring leaks and Kidd failed to find any of the pirate ships he had told both his backers and his men would be there. With an increasingly discontented crew aboard the *Adventure Galley*, Kidd sailed to the entrance to the Red Sea, another popular pirate refuge, but again found no prizes to capture. Under pressure to deliver rewards to his backers (among them Governor Bellomont) and increasingly menaced by an unruly crew that regularly threatened mutiny, Kidd still refused to cross the line into piracy. That refusal would lead to a confrontation with a ship's gunner named William Moore, who on October 30, 1697, was sharpening a chisel on the deck of the *Adventure Galley* when a Dutch ship appeared on the horizon. Moore demanded that they attack the Dutchman, but Kidd said he would not do it, knowing that to do so would infuriate Dutch-born King William. Kidd called Moore a lousy dog. Moore replied, "If I am a lousy dog, you have made me so," and he accused the captain of bringing him and the rest of the crew "to ruin." An enraged Kidd picked up an ironbound bucket and threw it at Moore, fracturing the skull of the gunner, who died the next day.

At his eventual trial, two members of Kidd's crew would accuse him of savage abuses that included hoisting rebellious men and drubbing them with the dull edge of a cutlass. Others, not called to testify, said later that Kidd had punished his men only after they ransacked the trading ship *Mary* while he and the *Mary*'s captain were speaking in his quarters, and that this punishment consisted mainly of forcing the crew to return what they had taken. Only those who refused were beaten.

It was not until January 1698 that the *Adventure Galley* finally took a great prize. This was the four-hundred-ton *Quedagh Merchant*, an Indian ship under hire to Armenian merchants, loaded with gold, silver, and a rich assortment of East Indian merchandise that included silks, satins, and muslins. The captain of the captured ship was an Englishman carrying passes from the French East India Company promising him the protection of the French crown. When Kidd learned that the captain was English, he attempted to persuade his men to return the ship and its cargo, but the crew refused and Kidd, who at that point maintained only tenuous control over his men, backed down and agreed to keep the prize. That decision made him a criminal in the eyes of the British navy, which ordered its commanders to "pursue and seize the said Kidd and his accomplices" for having committed "notorious piracies." Kidd kept the *Quedagh Merchant*, as well as the captain's French passes, hoping the latter would justify his capture of the ship. It was a calculated risk, as Kidd knew that British admiralty courts in North America frequently turned a blind eye to the trespasses of English-licensed privateers, especially if those trespasses were committed against the French.

Renaming the seized ship *Adventure Prize*, Kidd set sail again for Madagascar, where he encountered an old nemesis, the pirate Robert Culliford, who years before had stolen a ship and crew from Kidd. This time, Culliford stole only the crew—or most of it, anyway. With just thirteen men remaining, Kidd ordered the worm-eaten *Adventure Galley* to be burned at sea, then sailed the *Adventure Prize* across the Atlantic. Upon arrival in the Caribbean, Kidd discovered he was a wanted man and that at least four English men-of-war were hunting him. He abandoned the *Adventure Prize* in a concealed location and sailed a sloop toward New York. Avoiding apprehension by a series of clever maneuvers, Kidd came to his downfall by trusting Governor Bellomont, who lured him to capture in Boston. Kidd seems to have convinced himself that Bellomont and the various other Whig politicians (advocates of constitutional monarchy) who had backed him would come to his defense in the end, but the governor and the others were far more concerned about protecting themselves from the accusations of their rivals. Bellomont kept Kidd confined in Boston's Stone Prison (often having him held in solitary confinement in the prison's dungeon) and also ordered that Kidd's wife, Sarah, be imprisoned in New York. After more than a year of that misery, Kidd was returned to England to be questioned before Parliament. The accused pirate quickly discovered that the newly elected Tory ministry was determined to use the now-infamous Captain Kidd as a tool to discredit his Whig sponsors. Kidd, though, was apparently still convinced that Bellomont and his other backers would come to his aid and refused to name names. Realizing Kidd was of no use to them, the Tories sent him to stand trial at the High Court of Admiralty in London on charges that included the murder of William Moore. While awaiting his trial, Kidd was lodged in the hellhole of Newgate Prison, where he busied himself by writing letters to King William pledging loyalty to the Crown and pleading for clemency.

The accused still imagined that his backers would help him at trial, but in fact Bellomont and the others withheld both the money and the evidence (including the French passes taken from the *Quedagh Merchant*) that might have helped him avoid being condemned to death. On the testimony of two former crewmen who had been granted pardons if they helped the prosecution, Kidd was convicted of murder and five counts of piracy. While awaiting execution, he wrote a letter to the speaker of the House of Commons in which he claimed that on the way back to New York from the Caribbean he had "lodged goods and Treasure to the value of one hundred thousand pounds." This sum (equivalent to approximately $20 million in today's money) he would happily surrender to the Crown if he were permitted to lead a ship to the spot where it had been buried, Kidd added. The request was refused and on May 23, 1701, he was hanged at Execution Dock in Wapping. Afterward, Kidd's body was displayed over the River Thames at Tilbury Point inside a gibbet (a metal cage affixed to a gallows) where it was left to rot for three full years as a warning to those who might contemplate following the dead man into piracy.

A broadside song about Captain Kidd called "Farewell to the Sea, or, the Famous Pirate's Lament" became enormously popular in the weeks and months after his execution and spread the false notion that he had confessed to his crimes. The broadside also popularized the story that Kidd had buried treasure on his way back to New York from the Caribbean. "Two hundred bars of gold, and rixdollars [silver coins] mani-fold, we seized uncontrolled," was the song's most oft-repeated line. The legend of Captain Kidd's buried treasure would make its way into the works of Robert Louis Stevenson, Washington Irving, and Edgar Allan Poe, among others. It would also lead to treasure hunts that stretched from Grand Manan Island on the Bay of Fundy (between Nova Scotia and Newfoundland) to the Vietnamese island of Phú Quốc.

What cemented the idea that Captain Kidd's treasure was on Oak Island, however, was the story of a confession made by an old sailor with his dying breaths. By the nineteenth century, the tale had become apocryphal to the point of cliché, but it seems to have originated in the story of Captain Kidd's treasure that spread up the Atlantic coast of North America around the middle of the eighteenth century. On his deathbed, the story went, this sailor confessed to having been a member of Captain Kidd's crew and claimed that he and the others had buried a treasure worth two million pounds on "an island." In fact, a treasure buried by William Kidd on his return from the Caribbean already *had* been found on an island.

Gardiners Island (which still belongs to the Gardiner family and is today the only US real estate still intact as an original royal grant from the British Crown) is a six-by-three-mile piece of land standing just offshore from the town of East Hampton on New York's Long Island. In 1701, shortly after learning that William Kidd had been arrested for piracy and was to face trial in England, John Gardiner contacted Governor Bellomont to tell him that Captain Kidd had anchored off his island in June 1699, when he had come ashore to say he wished to bury a chest filled with treasure and two boxes, one filled with gold and the other filled with silver. In the treasure chest were diamonds, rubies, Spanish coins, and candlesticks. The treasure was intended for Lord Bellomont, Kidd told the Gardiners, who agreed that the privateer might cache the two boxes and the chest on their property. In thanks, Kidd gave Mrs. Gardiner a length of gold cloth and a bag of sugar.

It was more than a year later when John Gardiner read that Captain Kidd was on trial for piracy in England. Gardiner contacted Bellomont and told him of the buried treasure. British soldiers were immediately dispatched to retrieve it. Once it was delivered to him, Bellomont shipped the loot to England to be used against Kidd at trial. During the proceedings at the Old Bailey, the value of what Kidd had cached on Gardiners Island was placed at around $1 million in today's money—far less than the value of the booty Kidd was believed to have accumulated during his three years as a rover on the high seas. (The coins and effects Kidd had with him when he was captured were sold for £6,471—nearly $15 million in current value—in 1701, and used by the Order of St. Anne to establish Greenwich Hospital in London.)

So there was a not entirely unreasonable basis in the minds of eighteenth-century North Americans for the widespread belief that there remained a hidden Captain Kidd treasure on an island somewhere off the Atlantic coast. And that lent enough credence to the tale of the old sailor's deathbed confession to let it take hold in the popular imagination.

Jothan McCully in his 1862 article for the *Liverpool Transcript* observed that the early settlers of Mahone Bay had brought this story with them from New England and that Daniel McGinnis, John Smith, and Anthony Vaughan were all quite familiar with it. So it was no wonder that the three young men told prospective partners that they believed they had found the spot where Captain Kidd's treasure was buried.

There is one other outstanding description of the connection between Captain Kidd, Oak Island, and the discovery of the Money Pit. In 1939, a ship's captain named Anthony Vaughan, the grandson of the Anthony Vaughan who had been the friend of Daniel McGinnis and John Smith, gave an interview in which he added elements to the story that were previously unknown. Captain Vaughan, who was ninety-nine years old at the time of this interview—meaning his memories went back before the middle of the nineteenth century—said that the story of the Money Pit's discovery he had heard started with a trip to England around 1790 made by a sailor who was a member of either the Smith or McGinnis family. While in England, this sailor had befriended an old fellow who claimed he had been a member of Captain Kidd's crew and, out of gratitude for help he had been given, confirmed the story that Kidd had buried a huge trove of booty on an island in "New Anglia" that was "covered with oaks." Months later, the younger sailor stopped over in Nova Scotia and related this story to family members there, whose excitement had led to a search of Oak Island and the discovery of the Money Pit.

The story may not be true, but it certainly doesn't lack appeal. And that alone has been enough to keep it in circulation.

CHAPTER THREE

It was the spring of 1804 when a distant relative of Anthony Vaughan's named Simeon Lynds became the first of many who have financed the search for treasure on Oak Island. Two versions of how this happened were published in the nineteenth century. According to the more colorful of the two accounts, John Smith's wife, Sarah, was pregnant and refused to give birth to her child on Oak Island because of superstitions associated with the place. Instead she traveled to Truro, the largest nearby town, about seventy miles distant, to have the child delivered by a "Dr. Lynds." Her husband, John, came along, of course, and immediately sized up the physician as the partner he had been hoping to find. After hearing Smith's story, this version goes, Lynds visited Oak Island and was so excited by what he saw that he returned immediately to Truro and formed a company to finish the job that Smith and his two young friends had started. Among the problems with this account is that it seems in places to imply that the child delivered by "Dr. Lynds" was the Smiths' first. Church records in Chester, though, show that the couple's first child was christened on April 15, 1798, years before Lynd joined the probe of the Money Pit.

What R. V. Harris called the "more plausible version" of the story was that Simeon Lynds was a merchant, not a doctor, and he was in Chester to do business in early 1804 when he spent an evening with Anthony Vaughan's father and heard the story of what Vaughan's son and two other young men had found on Oak Island. The next day, Lynds went with the younger Vaughan to take a look at the Money Pit and was so impressed by what he saw that he hurried home to Truro to find other investors.

Whichever version is accurate (and almost certainly it's the second), what can be known for sure is that Simeon Lynds quickly assembled an impressive collection of partners in this enterprise. Lynds's first and more important get was Colonel Robert Archibald, the government surveyor who had first laid out the township of Onslow in 1780 and now served as the justice of the peace and town clerk there. Once Archibald had agreed to accept a position as director of operations for what was now being called the Onslow Company, he recruited his nephew Captain David Archibald, whose brother was about to become the speaker of the assembly in Nova Scotia and later would serve as attorney general of the province. Also added to the roster of investors was Thomas Harris, the sheriff of Pictou County. That men of such standing in their communities were willing to invest their time, their money, and their reputations in the Onslow Company says something about how convinced they were that a treasure of enormous value had been buried on Oak Island. And what had convinced them, clearly, was what they saw when the Money Pit was reopened. What they found when they dug deeper, though, is truly extraordinary, so extraordinary that it has driven men to follow after them for more than two centuries so far.

IN JUNE 1804, the company's investors set sail from Onslow aboard a sloop loaded with tools and provisions, following a southwesterly course along the twisting shoreline that took them past the mouth of the Bay of Fundy. A passage of some 350 miles ended when the sloop anchored off Oak Island in what was then known as Smuggler's Cove (today it is called Smith's Cove). They were met onshore by McGinnis, Smith, and Vaughan, along with a crew of local workmen who were mostly farmers looking to earn wages and hoping for a small piece of the Oak Island treasure, if there was one. After unloading their cargo and setting up a camp, the entire group went to inspect the Money Pit. They found that the Pit had caved in on top and formed "the shape of a sugar loaf resting on its apex," as R. V. Harris paraphrased one early account, and that an enormous pile of mud had settled to the level of the log platform 20 feet deep. After their crew had cleared away the debris and mud, Lynds and his partners were delighted, according to the early accounts based on interviews with the members of the Onslow Company, to find that the sticks McGinnis, Smith, and Vaughan had driven into the ground around the Money Pit back in 1795 (if that was the actual year) were still in place, meaning that no one had disturbed the spot. Thus encouraged, the men began to work the ground with picks, shovels, and crowbars, building a wooden box cribbing that protected them from a collapse by reinforcing the surrounding walls as they descended, employing the same rope-and-bucket method McGinnis, Smith, and Vaughan had used years before to empty the pit, only with more rope, several buckets, and the best block-and-tackle system money could buy.

After removing the log platform that had stopped McGinnis and his two friends at 20 feet, the Onslow Company crew continued digging. At 30 feet, their shovels clanged against wood. Just like the three young men who had struck the tier of oak logs at 20 feet years before them, the workmen were certain that they had hit the top of a treasure chest. But it was another platform of oak logs, their rotting ends embedded in the sides of the shaft just as the tiers of logs at 10 feet and 20 feet had been. The Onslow Company crew members showed one another the pick marks in the hard clay walls of the surrounding shaft and were certain these had been made by the men who first dug it out. The workmen and their employers asked one another what could compel men to dig deeper than 30 feet to bury a treasure. Only a cache of incredible riches could possibly explain it.

They were asking the same question after they struck another log platform at 40 feet, this one covered with a thick layer of charcoal. The Onslow Company's investors agreed that the only reasonable explanation for the charcoal was that there had been a smithy set up on this platform to sharpen the tools of the men who had opened the Pit originally.

There was another platform at 50 feet. According to the McNutt manuscript, this tier of logs was covered with a layer of smooth beach stones with "figures and letters" cut into them. At 60 feet, according to McNutt, the platform of logs was spread with a mat of manila grass and "the rind of coconut." Well aware that coconut fiber had been commonly used as dunnage to protect cargo that had originated in the Caribbean, this find fed the idea that what had been hidden so deep underground must be a fantastic treasure of Spanish gold captured by pirates in the seventeenth century. There was yet another platform of logs at 70 feet, this one covered with a blue-tinted clay "putty" (later used to seal the windows of twenty buildings on the mainland).

According to the McNutt manuscript, what became known as the "inscribed stone" was found at 80 feet. Adams A. Tupper, a mining engineer who had joined the treasure hunt more than a decade before McNutt did, said that the stone had been found at 90 feet. (It should be mentioned that there are also accounts that suggest the log platforms were not so exactly spaced, which is to say they were only more or less, not exactly, 10 feet apart.)

What McNutt and Tupper agreed on was that the slab was unmarked on its upper side when the Onslow crew first uncovered it. Only when they flipped the stone over did the workers discover that some sort of message had been etched into it.

Descriptions of those carvings (which may have been more like scratchings) and of the stone itself have varied in a number of respects. "Three feet long and one-foot square, with figures and letters cut into it," was how McNutt described the slab, "and being freestone, being different than any on that coast." However, in his *Transcript* article (reprinted in the *Halifax Sun and Advisor*), McCully had described "a stone cut square, two feet long and about a foot thick, with several characters cut on it."

Judge DesBrisay's account has to be given weight because it was based mainly on what he was told by the daughter of the man who took possession of the stone and kept it on display in his home for more than forty years. What the Onslow crew had found ("farther down" than the charcoal and putty, in DesBrisay's telling) was "a flagstone about two feet long and one wide, with a number of rudely cut letters and figures upon it," according to the judge's *History of the County of Lunenburg*. "They were in hope that this inscription would throw some valuable light on their search, but unfortunately they could not decipher it, as it was too badly cut, or did not appear in their own vernacular."

Anthony Vaughan, who told Creelman the stone was found at 90 feet, said it was 3 feet long and 16 inches wide. There were no letters carved into the stone, the way Vaughan told it, just strange "figures."

One eyewitness described the stone as yellow-tinged Swedish granite. Another thought it was porphyry and said it was olive colored.

What all accounts agree on is that after the stone was lifted from its place and removed from the Pit, a slow seep of water began to soften the dirt beneath the workmen's feet. This quickly became a problem. According to the *Colonist* article: "At 93 feet [the water seepage] increased and they had to take out one tub of water for two of earth. Still they had no idea that anything was wrong." It was dusk by then and, as they did each evening, the men finished their workday by probing the bottom of the Pit with a long crowbar. This time, according to the *Colonist* account, "they struck a hard impenetrable substance bound by the sides of the pit. Some supposed it was wood, and others called it a chest. They left for the night to resume operations in the morning, when they fully expected to solve the mystery."

What the men found when they reported for work the next day was that the Pit had filled with water to the 65-foot level. According to all of the early accounts, the Onslow crew bailed that entire day and into the night, but could not lower the water level by more than a few inches. Frustrated and baffled, they sat among the heaps of dirt and debris that surrounded the rim of the shaft, wondering what to do next. The farmers among the workmen told Colonel Archibald that haying season was upon them and that they would have to leave the island to return home in time to cut, dry, and store their grass. Archibald ordered

a temporary suspension of work while he and the other investors came
up with a new plan of attack.

In October, the Onslow Company sent "a committee" to Hants
County to meet with a "Mr. Mosher" who was reputed to be the best
authority in the entire province on how to remove water from a shaft.
Mosher was paid the princely sum of £80 to rig a special pump that
was transported to Oak Island and lowered into the Money Pit. There,
in a preview of things to come, the pump promptly burst. By then, the
weather was growing wet and cold with the approach of winter. Colonel
Archibald decreed that they should adjourn the expedition until the following spring, in hope that a better plan might be arrived at before then.

The Onslow Company did return to Oak Island in the spring of
1805 with a new strategy, developed by Colonel Archibald, for emptying
the water from the Money Pit. Fourteen feet southeast of the Pit, they
sank a shaft to a depth of 110 feet, planning to tunnel under the bottom
of the original shaft and approach the treasure from below. When the
diggers got within 2 feet of the original Pit, though, water began to ooze
through the end of the tunnel. The bank of clay suddenly collapsed in
front of them and water surged through. The men in the tunnel barely
made it out alive, and within two hours the new shaft was also filled
with water to the 65-foot level.

One more attempt was made at bailing, but the crew could not
lower the water in the new shaft either. By then, the Onslow Company's
investors had spent themselves nearly into bankruptcy and surrendered
their effort on Oak Island.

NEARLY HALF A CENTURY WOULD PASS before another serious
effort was made to bring up whatever was at the bottom of the Money
Pit. By then, the Onslow Company's two most significant members
were dead: Colonel Robert Archibald died in 1812 and Captain David
Archibald went two years after that. McGinnis, Smith, and Vaughan
lived on for some time after.

McGinnis built his family home on the opposite end of the island from the Money Pit, where generations of his descendants lived. Daniel's grandson John McGinnis, for instance, was born on Oak Island in 1865 and remained there all his life. Smith, who took possession of the mysterious stone that the Onslow Company crew had pulled from deep in the Money Pit, built it into the backing of his fireplace, "strange characters outermost, so that visitors might see and admire it," as Charles Driscoll wrote. Hundreds of people trooped through the modest Smith home to examine the curiosity over the next few decades. Vaughan returned to the mainland to work with his increasingly prosperous family.

The first of the three to die was the Money Pit's original discoverer, who passed sometime in early 1827. The only exact dates known are the ones on which Daniel McGinnis's will was dated, January 4, 1827, and the date it was probated, February 27, 1827. Anthony Vaughan was one of two executors and John Smith was a witness. So was a man whose role in the early discoveries made on Oak Island remains a mystery, one Samuel Ball.

I was startled to learn during my return visit to Oak Island, thirteen years after going there to research the *Rolling Stone* article, that in the first edition of *History of the County of Lunenburg*, the one published in 1870, Judge DesBrisay had identified the three who discovered the Money Pit as Daniel McGinnis, John Smith, and Samuel Ball. Ball was not replaced by Vaughan until the second edition of DesBrisay's book was published in 1896. There was no explanation for the change offered. Ball was still in the book, described as one of the "early residents" on Oak Island, "a coloured man, who came from South Carolina where he had been a slave to a master whose name he adopted." DesBrisay added only that Ball was remembered as "a good man."

A bit more information than that was available. Samuel was born (probably in 1764) and grew up on a plantation in South Carolina. On November 14, 1775, fearing the revolutionary fever that was sweeping through the colonies, John Murray, 4th Earl of Dunmore and governor of Virginia, issued the Proclamation of Kemps Landing, in which he declared free men any black males who would join His Majesty's forces in the battle against rebel forces. Based on this promise, Ball escaped the plantation shortly after the Revolutionary War broke out and joined the troops commanded by Lord Charles Cornwallis, but he was quickly transferred to the army marching on New York under the command of General Henry Clinton, then assigned to the command of a Major Ward and stationed at Bergen Point, New Jersey. At Bergen Point, Ball worked for the British army as "a woodcutter" until Cornwallis surrendered at Yorktown, then fled along with many of the other loyalist freemen to Canada.

Records show that Ball arrived in Shelburne in 1783 and remained there three years before moving to Chester. Based on an 1809 petition (called a memorial in those times) that Ball submitted to a justice of the peace named Thomas Thompson in Chester, we know that Ball had by then been living on Oak Island for twenty-three years. In his petition, Ball requested the allotment of land promised to black slaves who had joined the loyalist cause. Thomas stated Ball's case in writing:

> Your Memorialist Ball has no lands but, what he has purchased, never having got any from government, and there is a four-acre lott vacant, No. 32, on Oak Island, joining a lott purchased by your Memorialist. Your Memorialist therefore prays, Your Excellency well be pleased to grant, or otherwise order to have said Lott. Your Memorialist has but one son living. Chester, 9th September 1809.
>
> This day the above named Samuel Ball came before me and made oath on the Holy Evangelist, that what is stated in the above memorial is strictly true, which I verily believe to be so.
>
> I do hereby further certify that I have known said Samuel Ball, above twenty years, and I believe he is an honest, sober and industrious settler, worthy of encouragement.
>
> Thos. Thompson, Jus'Peace.

The lot Ball requested was granted, and eventually he acquired others, gradually becoming the owner of nine four-acre lots on Oak Island, which made him for a time the landowner with the most real estate on the island. Ball had paid £8 for the first lot he purchased on Oak Island according to the deed dated September 22, 1787. This was a considerable sum at the time and evidence, as shown by the records in the Lunenburg County Book of Deeds, that acre for acre Oak Island was the most expensive land in Mahone Bay. How Ball was able to afford to purchase another seven lots in addition to the one he was awarded by the British Crown and also to acquire an additional hundred acres on the mainland and on Hook Island is something of a mystery. In various poll tax registries, Ball was listed as a farmer who raised cattle and sheep, also working as a logger and fisherman. Somehow, though, Ball and his wife, Catherine, were able to afford a servant named Isaac Butler who remained with them until Ball's death on December 14, 1845, at the age of eighty-one. Ball's will, probated on January 5, 1846, shows that his hundred acres on the mainland adjoined "lands owned by Daniel McGinnis."

For more than a century and a half, there have been accusations that the young men who discovered the Money Pit (along with Samuel Ball, who was not so young but may have been part of that original discovery) did in fact find a treasure there, which explained their apparently "sudden prosperity" in the early nineteenth century. The story that the young men found three chests of treasure about 20 feet deep in the Money Pit and took one each surfaced in 2007. That year, a local historian named Danny Hennigar spoke to a woman descended from McGinnis who showed him a heavy cross of braided gold that was clearly hammered and hand formed, claiming she had inherited it as part of the treasure passed down through the generations from Daniel McGinnis. The cross, the woman said, had been examined by experts who said it was six hundred years old. That same woman, Joyce McGinnis, also showed up on the island in 2015 with her two sisters and repeated the tale of the three

chests—which made for a dramatic story for the season three finale of
The Curse of Oak Island. According to her, this cross was the one part of
his treasure that Daniel McGinnis had held on to, insisting that it be
handed down through the generations from oldest son to oldest son.
Her brother had received it from her father, Joyce McGinnis said, but
when he was about to die without a male heir, he had given it to her,
making her promise to "never let this out of your sight." Joyce McGinnis
said she'd taken it to several jewelers who had told her "it could be as
old as five hundred years." In the summer of 2016, the producers of *The
Curse of Oak Island* arranged for the cross to be examined by Dr. Lori
Verderame, a former professor of art history at Penn State who had built
a business identifying ancient artifacts. She reported that the cross was
rose gold, between twenty-two and twenty-four carats in weight, and
was of Spanish colonial design and manufacture, probably cast in a mold
in either Mexico or Peru sometime between 1550 and 1700. The tiny
holes in the cross had originally held emeralds, she said.

Others have focused their suspicion on John Smith, who not only
fathered fourteen children and supported his brood comfortably, but
also came to own 19 percent of Oak Island, all of nearby Frog Island,
and pieces of several other islands. How had that been possible, this
faction of amateur investigators has demanded. They point to John
Smith's grandson Murdock Smith, who in the late nineteenth century
donated the funds for the construction of the library at Port Williams,
Nova Scotia, suggesting that he was using a portion of the "treasure" he
had inherited to relieve his familial guilt. In fact, Murdock Smith was a
successful dentist in Massachusetts and might very well have been able
to pay for the library out of his own savings. As for the real estate holdings of John Smith, those could have been amassed by a combination
of hard work, thrift, and shrewd investment.

The stories of the Vaughan family coming into "sudden wealth"
around the end of the eighteenth century are both the most numerous and the most compelling. These stories seem to go back to two of
Anthony Vaughan's brothers, John and Daniel, who in the early 1800s

became wealthy shipyard and mill owners in New Brunswick. The story that they got their start with a pile of gold coins received from their nephew Anthony Jr. might have something to do with the fact that, according to *Families of the Western Shore*, the Vaughans established their business in New Brunswick in 1796, within a year of the Money Pit's putative discovery. Those tales of the Vaughans and the mysterious source of the family's wealth have stayed alive for more than two centuries. In 1991, an eighty-one-year-old man named Carl Mosher who was living in the veterans' unit of the Fishermen's Memorial Hospital in Lunenburg, told one of those stories to a local reporter. Back in 1925, Mosher said, his grandmother Lucy Vaughan, a descendant of Anthony Vaughan, showed him "a wooden trunk containing about twenty-five white canvas bags of gold." Not long after this, according to Mosher, Lucy's brother Edward Vaughan "took the trunk and disappeared, leaving his property, business, wife and family."

In August 2016, I spoke to a woman named Anna Frittenburg, the great-great-granddaughter of Ennis Joudrey, for whom one of the two major inlets on Oak Island, Joudrey's Cove, was named. Her grandfather (Ennis Joudrey's grandson) Harris Joudrey, who was born on Oak Island in 1889, had spoken often of the Vaughans and his suspicions about their wealth, Frittenburg told me.

He said there were four Vaughan brothers living in the area when he was growing up, and that they lived very well, even though they never seemed to work. They had this little schooner that they sailed to the States two or three times a year. My grandfather had been friends with one of the brothers when they were young. He said one time this boy got ill and my grandfather went to visit him. He said the boy was so happy to have a visitor that he sent him to a closet in his room and said, "Move that board." When my grandfather did, behind the board, in between the wall studs, was a bag filled with gold coins. And the Vaughan boy told him, "You could take some." My grandfather said he put the board back without taking any of the coins, but that he never forgot that day. He said that later when the Vaughan boy who had been his friend was grown up and was sailing off to Massachusetts or Rhode Island with his brother on their schooner, he became convinced they were making these trips in order to sell some of their gold.

I rejected (although, I must admit, not categorically) the idea that McGinnis, Smith, and Vaughan had found the treasure back in 1795, for pretty much the same reasons I scorned the theory that the story the three had told of the Money Pit had been a clever fraud. The fraud hypothesis was mainly the product of one Richard Joltes, a colleague of Joe Nickell's at the *Skeptical Inquirer*. Joltes's assertion is that Smith and Vaughan and, possibly, McGinnis (if he actually existed) had cooked the whole thing up as a for-profit scam. The main thing wrong with this argument is fairly obvious, though Joltes seems not to have noticed it. There were only two ways that McGinnis, Smith, and Vaughan could have made money from a manufactured story about treasure buried on Oak Island. One would have been to sell the property on which the Money Pit was located, and Smith—the actual owner of lot 18—not only made no effort to do this, but also refused all offers that came his way and held on to all of his Oak Island property until the end of his life. The other way in which Smith and his two friends could have profited from a fraud would have been to demand payment from those who wanted to search for treasure on Oak Island. It's clear, though, that the deal the three made with the Onslow Company was to permit the excavation of the Money Pit in exchange for a percentage of whatever treasure was found. There's not even a slight basis for doubt that all three of the Money Pit's discoverers believed there was a treasure buried on Oak Island. McGinnis was so convinced—and so convincing about it—that he inspired the succeeding generations of his family not only to hold on to their Oak Island properties, but also to continue the treasure hunt, as both Daniel's son and grandson did after he was gone.

That McGinnis, Smith, and Vaughan believed there was a treasure buried in the Money Pit also mitigates strongly against the story
that the three found the treasure back in the beginning. Why, if they
had, would they have continued searching for the treasure years afterward? Joyce McGinnis would explain more than two hundred years
later that her ancestor and his two friends had found only "a small
treasure" and believed the greater treasure was deeper down in the
Money Pit. This story had been told by others in previous decades,
the claim being that those who originally dug the Money Pit used the
three small chests of gold and silver found by McGinnis, Smith, and
Vaughan as a distraction to prevent searchers from probing deeper
into the Pit and finding the "real treasure." Some added that the three
chests were only there to stop the *wrong* searchers from going deeper,
so that only those worthy of a treasure much greater than gold and
silver would eventually find it.

Curious notions both, I didn't believe either. But I also wasn't
willing to completely dismiss them, because once I had confirmed to
my satisfaction that the early descriptions of the Money Pit's original
discovery and of the Onslow Company's search of the Pit were fundamentally accurate, I found myself convinced that the only explanation
for such fantastic underground works on Oak Island was that something
equally fantastic must have been buried down there.

That was the essential mystery of the place. But there were other
smaller mysteries that seemed to demand attempted solutions, and
Samuel Ball's role was one of them. The only way I could conceive of
approaching that particular problem was to try locating Ball's descendants to see if perhaps they, like the descendants of Daniel McGinnis,
had passed down a story through the generations. It turned out there had
been a descendant of Samuel Ball (eight generations removed) named
Frank Stanley Boyd who had posted some biographical notes and com-
mentaries on the blog of an organization called We Stand on Guard,
which had dedicated itself to "the elimination of Racism in Canada."
Boyd had died in Halifax in October 2010, however. I found his obituary,

which led me eventually to his son, John-David Boyd, a plumbing contractor in Quispamsis, New Brunswick.

My first contact with John-David was promising. Two or three days after I left a message on the voice mail at his business, Boyd called me back and seemed intent on impressing me. He repeated at least twice that he was "the head of the family" and the only one in a position to speak for the descendants of Samuel Ball. John-David also told me that when his father was near death, Frank Stanley Boyd had summoned him to his bedside to tell "the rest of the story," then had said, "don't give it away." I took this to mean John-David Boyd was looking to get paid for what he knew, if he knew anything. I could have been wrong about that, and I wasn't going to pay a source anyway, so I asked Boyd for his email address, which he gave me. The next day I sent a description of my background and intentions, then received a brief but cordial reply from Boyd that he would look it over and get back to me. Days passed, so I sent a second email letting Boyd know that my time in Nova Scotia was growing short. He answered two days later that he was busy with "a project" and that my request was "not a priority" for him. When he did not reply to the email I sent a couple of weeks after returning home, I passed his contact information along to the producers at *The Curse of Oak Island*, who, unlike me, *were* prepared to pay Boyd for his time. They told me a month later that he had not replied to any of their emails or phone calls. I sent one more email myself and got no answer.

If there was any light to be shed on Samuel Ball's role in the discovery of the Money Pit and the early days of the treasure hunt on Oak Island, it wasn't going to be shined by me. My frustration was one more reminder, as if I needed any at this point, that Oak Island has long produced more questions than answers.

CHAPTER FOUR

What the Onslow Company's investors had told family and friends about their experiences on Oak Island mostly has to be inferred from who joined the next excavation of the Money Pit. The Truro Company was formed in 1845, although it would not begin operations on Oak Island until four years later. This time there really was a "Dr. Lynds" among the investors (most likely Dr. David Barns Lynds, who lived and worked on Queen Street in Truro). Sheriff Thomas Harris was the only holdover from the Onslow Company's investors to acquire stock in the new venture, but Anthony Vaughan, now sixty-seven, joined the Truro Company also. The most significant contributions to the Oak Island legend, though, may have been made by four other men: Jothan McCully, who was appointed director of operations and wrote the first newspaper articles about the events on Oak Island; Robert Creelman, who interviewed Vaughan and John Smith and passed their recollections on for posterity; Adams A. Tupper, who would leave the most detailed account of the Truro Company's operations; and James Pitblado, another mining engineer who was appointed foreman of the crew that reopened the Money Pit in the summer of 1849 and would become one of the most mysterious figures in the annals of Oak Island.

John Smith had filled in both the Money Pit and the second hole dug 14 feet away by the Onslow Company, which has become known over the years as shaft no. 2. It was Anthony Vaughan, though, who helped the Truro team locate both shafts and then identified which was the Money Pit. The Truro crew had dug to a depth of only 6 feet in the Pit when they hit the top of the Mosher pump that had been abandoned by the Onslow Company back in 1804. Twelve days later, they had reached a depth of 86 feet, where some of the Onslow Company's cribbing was intact.

The *Colonist* article (probably McCully's) described what happened next:

> When Saturday night arrived . . . all further work was postponed until Monday morning. Sabbath morning came and no sight of water, more than usual, appearing in the Pit, the men left for church at Chester village with lighter hearts. . . . At two o'clock they returned from church, and to their great surprise found water standing in the Pit to the depth of sixty feet. . . .
>
> The next morning they set vigorously to work bailing, and had not been long engaged until the result appeared as unsatisfactory as taking soup with a fork.

For reasons that were not explained in either the *Colonist* or *Transcript* articles, McCully and Pitblado decided that they should proceed by probing the pit with a primitive drill called a pot auger, commonly used to prospect for coal. Curiosity with a whiff of desperation, along with a vague hope that they might bring up clues from below on the drill's tip seems to have motivated the decision, though that is inference and no more. Under the direction of McCully and Pitblado, five holes were bored to the maximum depth the pot auger could reach, 106 feet, on both the west and the east of the Money Pit's center. Mud and stone was all the pot auger brought up from the first two holes.

McCully's account in the *Transcript* described what happened when the drill was sent down a third time:

> The platform was struck at 98 feet, just as the old diggers [of the Onslow Company] had found it, when sounding with the iron bar. After going through the platform, which was five inches

THE CURSE OF OAK ISLAND

thick, and proved to be spruce, the auger dropped 12 inches, and then went through four inches of oak; then it went through 22 inches of metal in pieces; but the auger failed to bring up anything in the nature of treasure, except three links resembling the links of an ancient watch chain. It then went through eight inches of oak, which was thought to be the bottom of the first box and the top of the next; then 22 inches of metal, the same as before; then four inches of oak and six inches of spruce, then into clay seven feet without striking anything.

Those "links" have become gold in subsequent tellings, and they may have been, but McCully did not describe them so in his 1862 article. It was "the metal in pieces" that interested the Truro Company's investors, several of whom were present, including Dr. Lynds and the company's largest shareholder, John Gammel.

McCully and Pitblado moved the auger a few feet away to bore a fourth hole. The drill again struck the spruce platform at 98 feet, and as McCully told it:

Passing through this, the auger fell about 18 inches and came in contact with (as supposed) the side of a cask. The flat chisel revolving close to the side of the cask gave it a jerky and irregular motion. On withdrawing the auger, several splinters of oak (believed to be from the bilge of a cask) such as might come from the side of an oak stave, a piece of a hoop made of birch and a small quantity of a brown fibrous substance, closely resembling the husk of a coconut, were brought up.

Pitblado had instructed the men operating the pot auger to remove whatever was brought up on the chisel as carefully as possible, so that it might be examined under a microscope. Pitblado and McCully then directed the men to drill a fifth and final hole a few feet from the fourth. When the auger was brought up that last time, according to Gammel, he saw Pitblado wait until he thought no one was watching him to quickly pinch something from the chisel, wash it clean, then examine it closely before putting it into his pants pocket. He asked Pitblado to show him what he had removed from the auger, but the man refused, Gammel said, insisting that he would show it to all of the investors at the next meeting of the company's directors.

The only person Pitblado is known to have showed what he pulled from the auger that day, though, is one Charles Dickson Archibald, who was the manager of the Arcadian Iron Works in Londonderry, Nova Scotia. And all we really know is that Archibald then made a determined effort to purchase the eastern part of Oak Island from John Smith, offering considerably more than the property was worth and raising the offer when Smith refused. Smith would not sell, though. Archibald never made any known statement about what he had seen that had made him want so desperately to purchase the Smith prop-erties on Oak Island, and he would be recalled by his company to England by the time McCully thought to seek him out and ask. Pit-blado disappeared from the Mahone Bay area the same night he had pocketed whatever it was from the pot auger. According to that 1951 Nova Scotia Bureau of Information report, the "local legend" was that Pitblado had removed "a jewel" from the auger's blade. All that can be said for certain is that Pitblado never returned to Oak Island after that day and that the speculation about what he took with him has been endless. But my reading of the record is that it has never been more than that, speculation.

THOUGH THEY COULDN'T HAVE KNOWN IT at the time, in the spring of 1850 the Truro Company established a pattern of failure that was to be repeated by one group after another over the next century and a half. Each new search team would prepare for success in the belief that a new strategy combined with more advanced machinery would solve the puzzle of Oak Island. And each time they were defeated, the mess they left behind complicated the problem for the next group of treasure hunters.

The equipment the Truro Company barged out to Oak Island in 1850 included a pair of "two-horse gins," cast-iron engines powered by workhorses, which could be used for everything from milling grain to pumping water. It was the latter capacity that the treasure hunters of 1850 intended to employ. First, though, they sank a new shaft, the third on the drumlin where the Money Pit was located, digging through red clay so unyielding that at times it seemed they were trying to shovel through bricks. The density of that ground was in and of itself convincing evidence to the Truro Company that whatever channel was delivering water to the Money Pit had to be man-made; water was not going to find a natural course through clay that impenetrable.

The intent of this exhausting excavation was to create a new shaft (no. 3) they would fill with the water diverted from the Money Pit. They thought they could drain the Pit. Shaft no. 3 stayed dry down to a depth of 109 feet, at which point the Truro Company crew drove a tunnel toward the Money Pit. The result was the same as that achieved by the Onslow Company forty-six years earlier: as the diggers neared the Pit, the end of the tunnel collapsed under a surge of water that nearly drowned the men inside. The two-horse gins were put to work in both the new shaft and in the Money Pit, and the crew worked in bailing teams that kept at it twenty-fours a day for a solid week. The lowest water level they ever managed to attain in the Money Pit was 80 feet.

The Truro Company's defeat, though, led them to discoveries that have become a significant part of the Oak Island story. The first of these came when the crew realized that both the Money Pit and the new shaft had filled with saltwater, indicating that it had come from the bay. This meant that the best hope for success was to interrupt the flow of water at its source—or at least somewhere between its source and its point of entry into the Pit. Another reason it couldn't be a natural watercourse, the Truro Company's principals reasoned, was that if the water were already flowing underground where the Money Pit had been dug, it would have been impossible to excavate the Pit in the first place. So they had to be dealing with an artificial channel created by drawing from an inlet on the shoreline of the island. And there had to be gates somewhere along its path to permit the original depositors to stop the water and retrieve their treasure.

For the Truro Company, this was a staggering realization. It meant that the works on Oak Island were not only more sophisticated than anything they had ever seen, but also more than anything they had ever heard about. Exploring what had been done on the island and then figuring out a way to solve the problems this work had created would be a fantastically complex engineering problem, and McCully was only one of a number who were excited about taking it on. The company began what it knew would be a mammoth project by leaving the Money Pit to investigate the south shore of the island, focusing first on Smith's Cove, which seemed by its proximity the most likely place for an artificial channel of seawater to have been started.

They began with an examination of the Smith Cove's beach, situated about 520 feet from the Money Pit, with obvious advantages for channeling water with a tunnel. The company noticed almost immediately that all of the large stones had been removed from a considerable expanse of the beach. Then, when high tide began to ebb, the men observed that this section of the beach "gulched forth water like a sponge being squeezed," as McCully described it. The men stared at the water bubbling up through the surface and realized this couldn't be happening naturally. They began to shovel away the sand and stones. At a depth of 3 feet the Truro crew found a 2-inch-thick layer of a brown stringy material they believed (correctly) to be coconut fiber. Below that was a thicker layer of decayed eelgrass or kelp (there was and still is some debate which). Tons of coconut fiber and (most likely) eelgrass were pulled away and piled in heaps all along the shoreline until the workers revealed a compact and remarkably clean mass of beach rocks, protected from the sand and gravel on the surface of the beach by the 6-inch-thick mat of coconut fiber and eelgrass. The men of the Truro Company could only guess how many tons of sand and clay had been removed from the surface of the beach to make room for both the filter and the rocks beneath, but it had to be a hundred thousand pounds at least. The work that had gone into this was stupefying to contemplate, because what had been created was a giant insulating sponge spread out for a length of 145 feet along the shoreline between the high and low tide marks.

When they recovered from their astonishment, the Truro men agreed that this must be connected somehow to the tunnel that was flooding the Money Pit. To investigate more thoroughly, they decided to build a cofferdam to hold back the tide and enclose this portion of Smith's Cove while they excavated further. When that had been done and the men removed the layer of beach rocks, they were more astounded still, because what lay beneath were five remarkably well-made box drains constructed from flat stones, each about 8 inches wide, that fanned out from the edge of the high-water mark like the fingers of an open hand.

As the *Colonist* article described it:

> In investigating the drains, they found that they connected with one of larger dimensions, the stones forming which had been prepared with a hammer, and were mechanically laid in such a way that the drain could not collapse. There were a number of tiers of stones strengthening the higher part of the drain, on the top of which was also found a coating of the same sort of grass as that already noticed. Over it came a layer of blue sand, such as before had not been seen on the Island, and over the sand was spread the gravel indigenous to the coast.
>
> Having laid bare the large drain for a short distance into the bank, they found it had been so well made and protected that no earth had sifted through the arch to obstruct water passing through it.

The Truro men attempted to follow the drain into the island, but the surrounding soil became so soft and saturated with water that continuing was "impracticable," as the *Colonist* article put it. In the alternative, the men excavated half of the shoreline where the sponge of coconut fiber and eelgrass had been torn away, then calculated that whoever had done this work had removed the original beach to a depth of 5 feet. According to Robert Creelman, who was there with the Truro men, the only significant discovery made during this dig was "a partially burned piece of oak wood," the purpose of which no one could imagine.

At that point, the labors of the Truro men were interrupted by a fierce storm that rose up on Mahone Bay, creating an unusually high tide that poured over the top of the cofferdam and gradually washed it away, leaving the exposed box drains covered with sand. The company retreated to high ground, where it was agreed the fan of box drains must be the starting point of the tunnel that was flooding the Money Pit, which meant the only possible way forward was to find a way to block the tunnel or locate and close the gate that had to be somewhere within it. A plan was formed to sink a new shaft between the shore and the Money Pit, on the line between the box drains and the Pit. A spot 140 feet from the Pit was selected.

The Truro men had estimated that the flood tunnel would be about 25 feet deep, but they dug to a depth of 75 feet without locating either a tunnel or a flow of water. They moved 12 feet south and dug to a depth of 35 feet before encountering a large boulder. As they worked to pry the boulder loose, a rush of water poured into their shaft, within minutes filling it to the tide level with saltwater. They labored for days driving heavy timbers, called spiles, into the shaft, but this failed to stop the flow of water.

CONFLICTING ACCOUNTS of what took place after the Truro Company's failure to block the flood system have created some confusion about who and what was responsible for the most cataclysmic event in the history of the Oak Island treasure hunt up to that point: the collapse of the Money Pit. R. V. Harris, long considered the most authoritative chronicler of the early work on the island, attributed this disaster to the Truro Company and placed its occurrence in 1850. A majority of subsequent investigators—and I stand rather tentatively among them— believe it took place eleven years later in 1861, under the auspices of the newly formed Oak Island Association. I should caution the reader that this conclusion is based almost entirely on an article published in the September 30, 1861, edition of the *Novascotian* newspaper that relied on the eyewitness account of a man identified only as "the digger Patrick."

What we know with relative certainty is that the Truro Company dug one more shaft close to the Money Pit, down to a depth of 112 feet before the workmen drove a tunnel east toward the Pit and, one more time, had to flee for their lives when water and debris burst through the area where they were digging. At this point, funds exhausted and spirits broken, the men of the Truro Company packed up their gear and went home.

CHAPTER FIVE

In the years between 1850 and 1865, probably the most interesting development in the chronicle of Oak Island was the way word began to spread after the discovery of the artificial beach and the drain system. The story reached first across Nova Scotia, of course, then throughout the rest of Eastern Canada, and eventually across the national border into New England and New York.

The first mention of the treasure hunt on the island to appear in print was not actually in any of the newspaper articles or books mentioned earlier but in an 1857 report to the provincial government of Nova Scotia written by one of its geologists, Henry S. Poole, who was principally interested in the structural formation of Oak Island:

I crossed to Oak Island and observed shale all the way along the main shore, but I could not see any rock in situ on the Island. I went to the spot where people had been engaged for so many years searching for the supposed hidden treasure of Captain Kidd. I found that the original shaft had caved in, and two others had been sunk alongside. One was open and said to be 120 feet deep, and in all that depth no rock had been struck. The excavated matter alongside was composed of sand and boulder rocks and though the pit was some two hundred yards from the shore, the water in the shaft (which I measured to be within thirty-eight feet of the top) rose and fell with the tide, showing a free communication between the sea and the shaft.

We know from Anthony Spedon, whose *Rambles among the Blue-Noses* was published in 1863, that there was another attempt at excavating the Money Pit about a year after Poole's visit. "Up to the present moment," Spedon wrote, "the work [on Oak Island] has been resumed and relinquished a dozen times. Companies have been formed again and again, numerous experiments tried, and no less than fifteen different pits have been dug, at a cost of many thousands of dollars; and yet the *mysterious box* appears not to have been found." Given that there were nowhere near fifteen shafts on Oak Island at the time, Spedon's account has to be considered with some suspicion. He had at first regarded the story of the treasure hunt on Oak Island as "only a fictitious tale, or a chimerical infatuation," Spedon informed his readers, but then he met with Jothan McCully, who persuaded him to visit the island in the summer of 1862. During that visit, he had confirmed that "the operations [on the island] have been immense," Spedon reported. "The great obstruction and difficulty has been the inexhaustible quantity of water in the Pit. It appears to come from the sea, but no experiment as yet has been enabled to remove it, or stem the current." During the summer of 1859, Spedon wrote, a new iteration of the Truro Company "had no less than thirty horses employed at the pumps, but all efforts have proved abortive. . . . In the fall of 1861, at great expense, pumps were erected to be driven by steam power, but scarcely had the works been commenced when the boiler burst, causing operations to be suspended until another season."

Spedon's is the only description extant of the 1859 operations on the island and his description of the burst boiler in 1861 was also the first. Strangely, though, Spedon did not mention the most significant thing about that particular catastrophe, which was that it cost the life of the first man to die during the Oak Island treasure hunt. On the Oak Island Memorial that has greeted visitors to the island since 1995, he is listed simply as "Unknown." The first mention of his death did not come until seven years after it happened, in an account written by E. H. Owen of Lunenburg:

The boiler of one company burst, whereby one man was scalded to death and others injured. The water was pumped out by a large barrel-shaped tube made of thin materials, and reaching to some distance into the Pit. The stream of water was conducted from this into the sea by means of a long wooden trough, which extended down to the shore.

Owen also was the first to suggest an idea that I would find persuasive during my return visit to Oak Island in 2016, almost a century and a half after his account was written: "It appears that in digging the Pit in which [Captain Kidd] deposited his gold, he connected with it a subterraneous passage, leading towards the shore, by which means he might be enabled to recover his gold, without having to excavate the Pit, which he had filled up with such substance as would render it almost impenetrable to the enemy, if discovered." That there must be what R. V. Harris called a walk-in tunnel somewhere on the island seems certain to me, but as Marty Lagina's brother, Rick, pointed out to me during one of our conversations, "People have been looking for that tunnel a long time, and no one's ever found it." I still think it's there.

A handful of Oak Island investigators have speculated that the walk-in tunnel was found long ago by someone who took full advantage of this hidden entrance to the treasure chamber, then eradicated all trace of it. The name mentioned most often in this regard is Anthony Graves, who assumed ownership of most of Oak Island in 1857. In 1853, John Smith, in the name of what he called "natural love and affection," had conveyed all the property he owned to his two sons, Thomas E. and Joseph Smith. Shortly after their father's death four years later, the Smith brothers sold the property to one Henry Stevens, who promptly sold it to Graves. The new owner appeared to have little interest in the treasure hunt. He built his home and barns on the north side of Oak Island, above the shoreline along Joudrey's Cove (where pieces of the house's foundation can still be seen) more than 1,500 feet from the Money Pit and lived there until his death in 1887.

Stories that Graves regularly paid for his supplies in Mahone Bay with old Spanish coins are the basis of the claim that he found at least part of the Oak Island treasure, and these have been buttressed by the discoveries of such coins near the spot where Graves's house once stood, including one coin dated 1598. What undercuts the claims about Graves is that his two daughters clearly did not inherit any significant wealth from their father beyond his land. One of them, whose married name was Sophia Sellers, worked the ground on Oak Island with her husband as farmers who struggled to support their family.

The only involvement Anthony Graves seems to have had with the treasure hunt on the island was the deal he made with a new group from Truro that called itself the Oak Island Association. Graves was to receive one-third of any treasure recovered in exchange for permitting the new company to make yet another attempt to get to the bottom of the Money Pit, but he was due no cash payment.

A number of those who had been part of the Truro Company were members of the Oak Island Association, most notably Jothan McCully and James McNutt. McNutt kept a diary of the Association's efforts. The new company's proposal to investors was that with the right equipment and a sufficient workforce it would be able to drain the Money Pit and bring up the treasure. That this was essentially the same claim that had been made by the Truro Company did not dissuade the one hundred people who purchased the first $20 shares of the Oak Island Association that were offered to the public.

Money in hand, the Association in the spring of 1861 barged sixty-three workmen (being paid the then-considerable wage of $18 per month), thirty-three horses, four 70-gallon bailing casks and the most powerful pump to be found in all of Nova Scotia onto Oak Island. The workmen first cleared out the Money Pit and recribbed it to a depth of 88 feet before going to work on a new shaft about 25 feet to the east of the Pit. This shaft (now known as no. 6) was excavated to a depth of 118 feet, before yet another tunnel was driven toward the bottom of the Money Pit, the plan being pretty much the same as the one that had failed for the Truro Company back in 1850: divert the water in the original Pit into a new shaft.

According to a letter written by McCully one year later, the new tunnel "entered the old Money Pit a little below the lower platform, where [we] found the soft clay spoken of in the [1849] boring. The tunnel was unwisely driven through the old pit until it nearly reached the east pipe, when the water started, apparently coming from above the east side."

The man whom McCully was implicitly accusing of this unwise decision was the Oak Island Association's superintendent of works, George Mitchell. And while Mitchell's story does seem to be one of escalating desperation combined with increasingly poor decisions, the man has to be given credit for his relentless effort. What Mitchell ordered his men to do after the 118-foot shaft flooded was set up the big pump next to it while the men and the horses went to work around the clock with the bailing casks, not only attempting to lower the water level in no. 6 but also in the shaft on the west side of the Money Pit (no. 3) and in the original Pit itself. By McCully's account, the crew and the horses worked nonstop from two o'clock in the morning on Tuesday until late in the afternoon on Thursday and were able to lower the water level to a depth of 82 feet. At that point, the tunnel between shaft no. 3 and the Money Pit became clogged with soft clay that caused the water to begin rising. According to the accounts of McCully and McNutt, the Association crew worked to clear the tunnel until seven o'clock Friday morning, when another massive flow of soft clay out of the Money Pit replaced what they had just spent more than twelve hours hauling to the surface. As they worked to remove this new mudflow, the men recovered a number of curious items. In the *Novascotian* article, "digger Patrick" reported that these included pieces of wood, blackened with age, that had been "cut, hewn, chamfered, sawn and bored, according to the purpose for which it was needed." He and the others also pulled out "part of the bottom of a keg," Patrick recounted. McNutt, writing in 1867, described a "piece of juniper with bark on, cut at each end with an edge tool" and "a spruce slab with a mining auger hole in it" that were removed from the mudflow out of the Money Pit. McCully wrote that there were also oak chips, manila grass, and coconut fiber found in the mud, along with two large stones that he believed had been brought down from the surface of the island.

The Oak Island Association's work in the tunnel between shaft no. 6 and the Money Pit continued until five o'clock Saturday afternoon, when yet another rush of clay surged into the tunnel. The men working nearest to the Pit (among them Adams A. Tupper) reported that the bottom of the shaft had sunk by several feet and that the cribbing inside had shifted. Tupper can't have been the only one who recognized that sinking yet another shaft in the vicinity of the Money Pit—which made a total of six deep, broad holes and at least as many tunnels within a circle 50 feet wide—might have destabilized the Pit to a point of collapse. Perhaps there was some discussion about it when the men took a break for supper that Saturday evening. All we know for certain is that the men had just begun to eat when they heard a "tremendous crash" as McCully described it and hurried back to the Money Pit only to discover that water in it was "boiling like a volcano." The bottom had literally fallen out of the Pit, pulling down with it all of the cribbing and tools in the original shaft, along with tons of mud that flowed into the new tunnel.

In a letter written June 15, 1895, Samuel C. Fraser, who had worked as the foreman of operations for the Truro Company and had returned to the island as part of the Association, laid the blame on Mitchell:

> He finished the sinking of the 118 foot shaft through which the water was [to be] taken away, while the Money Pit was to be cleared out to the treasure. . . . I was sent down to clean out the Money Pit, but before going into it I examined the 118 foot pit and tunnel, which was then nearly finished. At the end of the tunnel I saw every sign of the cataclysm that was about to take place and I refused to go down [again] into the Money Pit . . . When

the pit fell down I was there, and I, with George Mitchell, threw a line down as far as it was open from the top when the subsidence ended: it was open 113 feet from the top. . . . There went down 10,000 feet of lumber, board measure, the cribbing of the old Money Pit.

This would prove to be the greatest disaster in the history of Oak Island not involving the loss of life, leaving the Money Pit an all but impenetrable jumble of mud, lumber, and equipment. The treasure, if there was one, was believed to have fallen either into a tunnel or deeper into the Pit.

The former Truro Company foreman Samuel Fraser believed the latter:

The pirates sank the shaft at first 155 feet deep, put part of the treasure there with a branch drain into it. Then working upon the older superstition that "treasure runs away from the seekers" . . . put another portion at 100 feet, with a drain into it.

This meant, Fraser wrote to his friend in 1895, that whatever was buried in the Money Pit had dropped into an open space that was, he estimated, 155 feet deep. On what basis Fraser supposed this he never stated in the letter.

Those who believed the treasure had slid into the tunnel seemed to have based much of this opinion on the fact that J. W. Publicover, the last man out of the 188-foot shaft no. 6 and its adjoining tunnel, had come to the surface with a yellow-painted wooden disk about the size of a barrelhead that had landed at his feet in the tunnel when the Money Pit collapsed. The men who examined it agreed that it must be part of an old keg or cask that had dropped out of the Money Pit's treasure chamber as the bottom fell out.

Whatever was true about that, the collapse of the Money Pit ended the efforts of the Oak Island Association in the summer of 1861. Yet, remarkably, most of the same men were back on the island in the spring of 1862. George Mitchell had been replaced by one J. B. Leedham as director of operations, but what Leedham did was little more than a duplication of all that had failed during the previous sixty years. He began by ordering the men to sink yet another shaft (no. 7) just west of the Money Pit. At 90 feet, the workmen found tools left behind by the Truro Company and at 100 feet tools that had been abandoned by the Onslow Company, evidence that they were digging through sections of the collapsed Money Pit.

When the new shaft reached a depth of 107 feet and no sign of the flood tunnel had been found, Mitchell ordered his men to dig a new shaft (no. 8) right next to the no. 6 shaft, then dig laterally until they struck the flood tunnel. When this effort, too, failed, Leedham sent his crew to Smith's Cove, ordering them to seal the "filter bed" beneath the man-made beach with packed clay. That didn't succeed either, of course. Leedham, whose frantic determination seems to have been a match for Mitchell's, then ordered the men to dig yet another shaft (no. 9) about 100 feet east of the Money Pit and 20 feet south of where the flood tunnel would be if it was dug on a straight line. When shaft no. 9 had been excavated to a depth of 120 feet, Leedham instructed his men to dig a series of exploratory tunnels to try to locate the flood channel. Given how unstable the ground around the Money Pit must have been by that point, it's a wonder Leedham found men willing to do such work, but apparently he did.

One of the exploratory tunnels was driven all the way to the Money Pit, which it entered at a depth of 108 feet. According to the Oak Island Association's records, the workmen were successful in draining the Money Pit to the level of the tunnel. Leedham descended to make an inspection, and in his notes he reported that while the walls on one side of the Pit were rock hard, they were so soft in other places that he could plunge a crowbar into them with relatively little effort.

The Association's records show that yet another tunnel was dug between the Money Pit and shaft no. 2, the one dug by the Onslow Company in 1805, but that the men found no sign of either the flood tunnel or the treasure chests they were looking for. At that point, operations were suspended while the Association's members returned to Truro to raise more money. They apparently succeeded, because on August 24, 1863, the *Novascotian* published a report that the Oak Island Association had resumed operations on the island and that "men and machines are now at work pumping the water from the pits previously sunk, and it is said that they are sanguine that before the lapse of the month they will strike the treasure."

Sanguinity aside, the Association did perform an astounding series of digs that summer, the most remarkable being a circular tunnel at a depth of 95 feet that went around the entire circumference of the Money Pit. They encountered two of the previous shafts that had been sunk in the vicinity but no sign of the flood system, and yet each time they dug down to a depth below 110 feet, their tunnels filled with seawater.

IN THE SUMMER OF 1864, at a depth of 110 feet, the Oak Island Association finally did find the flood tunnel, according to Samuel Fraser, who described this event in his 1895 letter to friend A. S. Lowden: "As we entered the old place of the treasure we cut off the mouth of the tunnel. As we opened it, water hurled around rocks about twice the size of a man's head with many smaller, and drove the men back for protection. . . . The [flood] tunnel was found near the top of our tunnel."

The Association's crew confirmed that they had in fact found the fabled flood tunnel by dumping cartloads of clay on the man-made beach in and around the box drains; when the water in the Money Pit was muddied just a short time later, the Association's investors were certain that they had indeed located the tunnel that men had been searching for since the early nineteenth century. Their sense of accomplishment was short-lived, however; every attempt they made at shutting off the flow of water failed, and they could not find the gate that they were certain must be somewhere inside the tunnel.

By the late summer of 1864, its funds exhausted and its investors discouraged, the Oak Island Association was winding down. The constant churn of seawater in the Money Pit was softening the walls of the shaft to the point that more and more of the workmen were refusing to enter it. To reassure their crew, the Association's members voted to hire a mining engineer to inspect the Pit. When the engineer declared the original shaft "unsafe" and advised that it be condemned, however, the Association accepted defeat and withdrew from the treasure hunt.

At least a couple of the Association's members insisted that the discovery of the flood tunnel was a victory they could build on, and they refused to give up. The evidence that men had gone to extraordinary—even incredible—lengths to bury something on Oak Island was now simply too overwhelming to doubt. A new treasure-hunting company would be formed, these diehards declared, and this one would find its way to the treasure.

THE DISASTERS WROUGHT by the Oak Island Association ensured that any future treasure hunters would be working on two fronts, not only wrestling with the puzzle of the original engineering project on the island, but also working through the jumble of failed efforts left behind by the searchers who had gone before them. The existence of nine or ten shafts and several dozen tunnels dug all around the Money Pit, combined with the collapse of the Pit in 1861, made further work in that location not only dangerous but also probably futile. In terms of the larger investigation of what had taken place on Oak Island, though, there was at least one positive result: prospective treasure hunters were forced to back up and look at the big picture beyond the drumlin on the east end of the island where the original Pit had been dug.

In March 1866, with the consent of Anthony Graves, the directors of the Oak Island Association assigned their rights on the island to a new company that was being formed in Halifax. It initially called itself the Oak Island Eldorado Company, but eventually became better known as the Halifax Company. Proposing to raise $4,000 in capital to begin operations, the Halifax Company incorporated in May 1866 by offering two hundred shares at $20 apiece. By June, these had been sold on the basis of a "Plan of Operations" that would begin in Smith Cove with the construction of "a substantial wood and clay dam seaward to extend out and beyond the rock work, so as to encompass the whole [cove] within the dam [and] pump out all the water within the area, and so block up the inlet from the sea." The cost of this work would be no more than £400 (about $2,000 in US currency at the time), promised the new company's directors, who added that "there cannot be any doubt but this mode of operation must succeed and will lead to the development of the hidden treasure, so long sought for."

Nearly all of what we know about the operations of the Halifax Company comes from James McNutt, who continued the search with the third enterprise that had employed him on Oak Island during the past sixteen years, and Samuel Fraser, who worked as a foreman for the Halifax consortium. It is from Fraser that we have a description of the cofferdam the company constructed, 12 feet high by 375 feet long off the shoreline of Smith's Cove, 110 feet below the high-water mark. Fraser does not describe the labor that went into this project, but it had to have been tremendous; nor does he remark on what must have been the company's devastation when the dam not only failed to stop the flow of water into the Money Pit, but also was fairly rapidly broken apart by tidal surges.

What the Halifax Company did next was both sad and predictable: they returned to the Money Pit. One more time, the Pit was cleared out, this time to a depth of 108 feet, 10 feet below the oak platform that had been struck by the Onslow Company in 1805. That platform, though, was gone, having fallen in the 1861 collapse. There were various speculations about where the platform—and the supposed treasure that had rested on it—were now. It was generally agreed that the Money Pit contained a cavity that went to a depth of perhaps 155 feet (Fraser insisted that this was how deep the original excavation had gone) and that the treasure could have dropped all the way to the bottom or into one of the tunnels to the Pit dug by various search groups. Believing that the treasure would have fallen in the direction of the tunnel that caused the Pit's collapse, the Halifax group dug into the south side of the Money Pit. Once again, though, the water in the Pit stopped their progress. In a letter written in 1898 by a man from Pictou, Nova Scotia, there is a description from the worker ("Mr. Robinson") who was at the front of the tunnel:

> After going a few feet he felt the earth give under his feet a little; he told the men to give him a pick and he drove it down and through and the water came up. He took a crowbar and put it down and his arm to the shoulder with it and says that he could swing the bar around in the Pit [below him] but the water was coming so fast he had to give it up.

The Halifax Company's crew then built a platform at the 90-foot level in the Pit, from which they would carry on what they called "boring operations." The day-to-day journal of the work kept by McNutt tells us that a drill inside a pipe was sent in various directions between November 26, 1866, and January 7, 1867. At a depth of 110 feet the drill went through spruce wood, then coarse gravel, then soft clay and blue mud to an additional depth of 20 feet, when water began to flow up through the tube, carrying with it wood chips, coconut fiber, and charcoal. At a depth of 134 feet from the surface the drill brought up oak borings, then some chips of either spruce or poplar from a plank it seemed to be running alongside of. Between 155 feet and 158 feet, the drill brought up a material that was dry and reddish brown. In other words, they found nothing new.

The company at that point decided on a radical departure, this being a move to solid ground 175 feet south of the original works to sink a new shaft (now no. 10) on a line between Smith's Cove and the Money Pit. They went down 175 feet, the deepest penetration of the island since the treasure hunt had begun, then used the shaft to drive tunnels laterally at depths of between 95 and 110 feet, the hope being that they would find the flood tunnel and divert it into the new shaft. The utter failure of this effort not only bankrupted the Halifax Company, but it also stopped the treasure hunt on Oak Island for more than a quarter century.

Still, stories of what had been discovered continued to spread, told and retold by men who had been part of the Truro Company, the Oak Island Association, and the Halifax Company. Among those who heard these stories, none seem to have been so thrilled by them as a boy named Frederick Leander Blair, born a year after the Halifax Company abandoned its efforts. Blair would not only revive the treasure hunt on Oak Island and sustain it for more than fifty years, but he would also become the best student of the island's history there has ever been.

CHAPTER SIX

That the story of "pirate treasure" buried on Oak Island could endure so long—well into the late nineteenth century—was much easier for me to understand when I learned that buried caches of gold coins were regularly being discovered in Nova Scotia during those years. People all across the province were thrilled by tales of treasure finds being made in nearby towns and villages. In Pictou County, the largest public gathering of 1876 had been generated by a story that swept through the town of New Glasgow, where, as the *Eastern Chronicle* reported it, "throngs of people, not less than a thousand" had rushed to the southwest corner of the Riverside Cemetery after hearing that a "group of individuals" had been seen "lurking about during the night." There, they discovered that "a spruce tree upwards of 40 feet had been uprooted, and a hole of considerable size dug," the newspaper reported. "When first seen after the digging, the place alleged to have all the appearance of a box of some size, having been exhumed, hauled across the tracks with sleepers and planks and dragged down the steep bank to the East River, where it was supposed the box of treasure was placed in a boat and carried away." Only a little more than a year later, the December 15, 1877, edition of the *St. John Daily News* splashed the discovery of more than sixty thousand "three spade guineas" that had washed out of a muddy bank at St. Martins on the Bay of Fundy. The estimated value at the time was more than $300,000, about $36 million in today's U.S. dollars.

It was not until the late nineteenth and early twentieth centuries that some in Nova Scotia began to suggest that what was buried on Oak

Island might not be pirate booty after all. The alternative theories these people offered arose from the century-and-a-half-long conflict between the French and the British for control of Canada's Atlantic coast.

The English had first claimed the northern reaches of the New World in 1497, when John Cabot landed on Cape Breton Island, now part of Nova Scotia. The French soon followed, though, with an eye to the establishment of settlements that defied British rule. The fort and town that Samuel de Champlain constructed at Port Royal on the Bay of Fundy was the first solid foothold the French made in what would become Nova Scotia. The British answered with a warning that they owned the entire province, as well as Newfoundland and New Brunswick, from the moment that Cabot planted the English flag at Cape Breton. Resulting wars large and small for control of the disputed territories were waged between the French and the British until deep into the eighteenth century.

The French, after losing what would be known as the War of the Spanish Succession and signing the Treaty of Utrecht in 1713, surrendered all of their holdings on the Canadian mainland, retaining just four islands along the Atlantic coast: Prince Edward, Cape Breton, St. Pierre, and Miquelon. King Louis XIV and the great-grandson who in 1715 succeeded him, Louis XV, moved vigorously to protect what France had been left with. On Cape Breton, government engineers, private contractors, craftsmen, and French soldiers would labor for more than a quarter century to construct the immense fortifications that enclosed the fifty-acre settlement at Louisbourg. The costs were enormous and what were known as "Louisbourg pay ships" regularly delivered a fortune in gold and silver coins from the French treasury to pay for men and materials. Two of those pay ships disappeared en route to Cape Breton. No survivors ever surfaced to explain what had happened and the ships themselves have never been found. In the late nineteenth and early twentieth centuries, it would begin to be whispered that to protect their wealth from an eventual British attack on Louisbourg, the French had hidden the gold and silver from those missing pay ships in an underground vault they had created in some remote part of Nova Scotia. Oak Island gradually became the favored location of those who spread this story.

A rival but related theory involving Louisbourg also emerged during this period, the story in this case being that a high-ranking French official had colluded with a corrupt contractor to funnel much of the gold and silver bound for Louisbourg into a secret hiding place, which again became Oak Island.

Neither theory was entirely implausible, but as I would find was the case with most of the possible answers to who was behind the works on Oak Island, the fact that they might *possibly* be true was the principal evidence that supported them. The same could be said of the third popular theory of who was responsible for works on Oak Island that began to spread in the late nineteenth century, this one involving the famous fleet of the Duc d'Anville. In 1746, a year after losing the fortress at Louisbourg to the British, France had assembled an armada of sixty-five ships carrying more than three thousand troops that set sail across the Atlantic to take back Louisbourg. The ocean crossing seemed damned from the beginning as storm after storm struck the fleet until the final and by far the most powerful tempest struck as the ships sailed past the "graveyard of the Atlantic," Sable Island, about ten miles off the southern tip of the Nova Scotia mainland.

Just twenty miles long, one mile wide, and made mostly of sand, Sable Island has been described as "the fastest moving island in the world" because of the shifting plates beneath it. Combined with the rough waters and thick fogs that surround it, this has created treacherous conditions for passing ships and also for planes that fly too close to the island. Four hundred seventy-five shipwrecks have been recorded around Sable Island since the seventeenth century, and it is believed the true number might be at least twice that. How many of these were from the d'Anville fleet is not possible to know precisely, but certainly more than half of the French armada at least was lost in the Sable Island storm, while the rest of the ships were scattered and separated. Most of the fleet that remained made it eventually to what would become Halifax Harbour (it was called Chebucto Harbour at that time), where d'Anville himself and many of his men died of the diseases that had broken out on their ships during the ocean crossing.

The story that connected this doomed expedition to Oak Island was that one of the ships separated from the fleet off Sable Island was a pay ship that found its way into Mahone Bay, where the captain decided to create an underground vault to store his cargo of gold and silver until he was certain it could be transported safely. The pay ship then sailed off toward Chebucto Harbour, the story continued, but was wrecked by yet another storm along the way, and the treasure the crew had buried on Oak Island remained there. Again, the theory could not be entirely dismissed, but there was nothing truly evidentiary to support it. And when the records of the d'Anville fleet were reviewed, historians noted that there was no mention of any of the ships carrying a cargo of "specie or bullion."

In retrospect, it seems rather remarkable that there was little mention, even in the early twentieth century, of an explanation for Oak Island rooted in the history of Nova Scotia that was far more credible. This theory involves the removal of the Acadians.

The Acadians had been French originally, back in 1605 when their first sixty families were settled by Champlain at Port Royal. Even as their numbers grew into the thousands, most of the Acadians remained on the Bay of Fundy, though a good number made their way to Mahone Bay, where they established small communities at LaHave and at what is today Lunenburg (called Merligueche back then). The Acadians gradually began separating from their French roots in an attempt to establish themselves as a unique population. This was a matter of sheer pragmatism, as it became increasingly clear that the Acadians' best hope for survival lay in refusing to take sides in the long struggle between France and England for control of the land they called home. Theirs was an ethos of labor and thrift. The Acadians worked as farmers, tradesmen, artisans, and small business owners and thrived in Nova Scotia. They also controlled much of the smuggling trade in the province and were reputed to be the main suppliers of provisions to pirate ships.

After the Treaty of Utrecht was signed, the English demanded that the Acadians swear an oath of loyalty to the British Crown that included a promise to bear arms against the French if called upon to do so. The Acadians resisted so successfully that the British eventually inserted a clause in the oath that permitted them to remain neutral during military conflicts. The Acadians' independent stance became impossible, however, after Edward Cornwallis was appointed the first governor of Nova Scotia in 1749 and created the city of Halifax to serve as his provincial capital. Governor Cornwallis (the uncle of Charles Cornwallis, who led the British armies against the Americans in the Revolutionary War) insisted that the Acadians' oath of loyalty be reconsidered in light of changing circumstances. The French had retaken Louisbourg and the rest of Cape Breton, and Cornwallis saw the ten thousand Acadians living in Nova Scotia as a potential threat to British control of the mainland. If he evicted them from the province, Cornwallis reasoned, the Acadians would almost certainly resettle on Cape Breton, substantially increasing the French presence on Canada's Atlantic coast. First the governor insisted that the Acadians retake the loyalty oath, this time without the clause that permitted them to remain militarily neutral. When the Acadians again refused to sign the oath, tensions with the British rapidly escalated beyond their ability to manage them. Still, most of them were caught off guard when, in 1856, Cornwallis ordered that the Acadians be rounded up at gunpoint, stripped of their land and possessions, then loaded aboard ships that would drop them off at ports spread along the American coast between Maine and Georgia. There was a rush among the Acadians to conceal their assets; they liquidated as much of their property as possible, then buried the coins in safe places.

When the Treaty of Paris was signed in 1763, the edict expelling the Acadians from Nova Scotia was revoked and a good many of them returned to the province. (Most of those who did not made their way to the bayous of Louisiana, where they became the Cajuns.) Few of the

Acadians were permitted to reclaim their former homes in Nova Scotia, however, which made it difficult if not impossible to gain access to the places where they had cached their fortunes before the expulsion of 1756. What resulted during the nineteenth century was story after story of some lucky plowman or merchant of British or German or Swiss origin discovering a stash of Acadian coins in a cellar, a well, or a farm field. In 1879, for example, just ten miles south of Oak Island, the discovery by a farmer named William Moser of more than two hundred French écus and Spanish escudos while digging up the floor of his barn had been front-page news in the local newspaper.

It was inevitable that someone would suggest, eventually, the underground vault on Oak Island was a kind of bank where the most prosperous of the Acadians had deposited their wealth before being rounded up by the British in 1756. It made a good deal of sense, except that there were very few if any truly wealthy Acadians.

On the other hand, Nova Scotia had been home to many rich Huguenots in the eighteenth century. Most of the Huguenots (Protestants, as opposed to the mostly Catholic Acadians) who left France for the New World because of religious persecution in the late seventeenth and early eighteenth centuries were upper class. Many were members of the French nobility and nearly all of the others were part of what historians have called an affluent artisan class.

In 1685, when the Edict of Nantes (which since 1598 had protected French Protestants from persecution by the Catholics) was revoked by Louis XIV, fifty thousand Huguenot families fled the country. Nova Scotia was among their primary destinations.

The theory that linked the Huguenots to Oak Island, though, seems to be most solidly founded in an early twentieth century report by the historian (and William Kidd biographer) Dunbar Henrichs. In 1928, Henrichs was living on Mahone Bay in the town of Chester. It was there that Henrichs was visited by a Frenchman who had come to Nova Scotia to investigate a family legend involving a group of wealthy Huguenots (including one of his ancestors) who had escaped from France aboard two ships immediately after the Edict of Nantes was revoked. The family story was that the ships had sailed together from La Rochelle across the Atlantic to the island of Saint-Domingue (in what is now Haiti), where the engineer accompanying them had supervised the construction of a complex of underground vaults protected by flood tunnels. Some but not all of the families had deposited their wealth in these vaults, then boarded one of the ships, which sailed off to New York. The second ship, carrying passengers who still held their wealth onboard, had sailed farther north to Nova Scotia, making its way eventually to Mahone Bay, where the leaders of this group selected an uninhabited island on which the same engineer supervised construction of a second system of vaults, also protected by flood tunnels. These vaults could be accessed either by a secret tunnel from the surface of the island or by closing a gate that had been installed in the flood tunnel system, as the Frenchman told the story, Henrich said.

Henrich admitted he hadn't taken the tale seriously until he heard that in 1947, nineteen years after his conversation with the mysterious Frenchman, a system of tunnels and vaults very similar to what had been described were found by an engineer named Albert Lochard in Haiti.

The Huguenot theory became quite a compelling one in his mind after that, Henrich said. There was one major problem with it, however. The Huguenots had not arrived in Nova Scotia in any numbers until after the Acadians were expelled in 1756, by which time the Mahone Bay area was populated by a good many New Englanders and Germans who had moved there on the promise of free land from the British government. It is doubtful that the Huguenots or anyone else could have created the works on Oak Island at that late date without people noticing.

The main objection to both the Acadian and the Huguenot theories of Oak Island, though, was the same one made in answer to those who suggested that whatever treasure had been buried in the Money Pit had long since been removed by the original depositors. If the people who placed the treasure there had returned for it, the reasoning went, they certainly wouldn't have bothered to close the Money Pit up so neatly as it was found to be by McGinnis and the others back in 1795. "They would have just left the dirt piled up and hole open—why not?" as Marty Lagina put it to me in a conversation over our breakfasts one morning in August 2016. That the platforms inside the Pit were still intact and the massive hole in the ground still filled in with soil all the way to the surface, along with the fact that there was no obvious sign of any point of entry anywhere else on the island, proved in the minds of Oak Island's treasure hunters that whatever had been buried down there remained. A young man who believed as much would incorporate the next company that conducted operations on Oak Island.

Frederick Leander Blair was a twenty-six-year-old insurance salesman working out of an office in Boston, Massachusetts, when he formed the Oak Island Treasure Company in 1893. Over the next fifty-eight years, as his interest grew into an obsession, Blair would not only become the driving force in the search for the treasure on the island, but he would also become the most relentless seeker in the search for answers as to how it got there and why. It is largely because of him that we know as much as we do about what happened during the first century after the discovery of the Money Pit, as the fascination with Oak Island crossed out of Canada to spread worldwide.

CHAPTER SEVEN

Frederick Blair was living and working in Massachusetts, but he had grown up in Nova Scotia: born in Thomson Station and reared in Amherst. He was a young child when he first heard stories of Oak Island, told by his uncle Isaac Blair, who had been part of the Oak Island Association and Halifax Company crews that had worked on the island during the 1860s. As Isaac Blair summed up his position in a letter to his nephew written in 1896: "I saw enough to convince me that there was treasure buried there and enough to convince me that they will never get it." Frederick Blair agreed with his uncle that the treasure was there, but for more than a half century refused to accept that it could not be gotten.

What distinguished Blair right from the beginning was his commitment to research. He began by interviewing his uncle Isaac and Isaac's friend Jefferson McDonald, from whom he had also heard tales of the treasure hunt on Oak Island as a boy. From those two, Blair moved on to the other men who had worked on Oak Island with the Truro Company and the Oak Island Association, focusing on those he considered most authoritative, among them James McNutt, Jothan McCully, Samuel Fraser, and Robert Creelman. Still working out of his office on Boston's Liberty Square, Blair collected every available document, including the journals and letters that chronicled the labor, the discoveries, and the failures of those who had gone before him. Many if not most of those documents would have been lost if not for the fact that Blair maintained them in his personal archives. He sought out everyone still living who had heard firsthand the stories of the three discoverers, McGinnis, Smith, Vaughan, and of the Onslow Company's leader, Dr. Lynds, and he made extensive notes of those interviews. Blair not only interviewed Adams A. Tupper, the former mining engineer for the Truro Company, but he also recruited him as a partner in his new Oak Island Treasure Company. Tupper, drawing extensively on his conversations with Anthony Vaughan during the middle of the nineteenth century, assisted Blair in writing the prospectus of the Oak Island Treasure Company, which began with a detailed account of the discovery and the attempted excavations of the Money Pit. Tupper also attached an affidavit in which he declared that he was "familiar with the various reports and traditions concerning the work done there before my own personal knowledge" and that his account of what he had been told was "to the best of my knowledge and belief, absolutely true."

Blair also spoke to Anthony Graves's daughter, Sophia Sellers, whose accidental discovery of what became known as the Cave-in Pit had been the biggest event on Oak Island in the years since the collapse of the Halifax Company. In the spring of 1878 she had been plowing with oxen about 350 feet from the Money Pit, Sellers told Blair, near what she knew was the supposed line of the famous flood tunnel. Suddenly one of the oxen disappeared into a "well-like" hole about 6 to 8 feet in diameter that had caved in under the animal's weight. She and her husband, Henry, had needed help to pull the animal out of the hole, and after that they had simply filled it in with boulders and worked around the area. Blair, though, decided that investigating this new discovery should be among his new company's first tasks.

"It is perfectly evident," he explained in his prospectus, "that the great mistake thus far has been in attempting to 'bail out' the ocean through the various pits. The present company intends to use the best modern appliances for cutting off the flow of water through the tunnel at some point near the shore, before attempting to pump out the water." This had been tried before, by both the Oak Island Association and the Halifax Company, as Blair certainly knew, but he apparently believed his "modern appliances" would make the difference. With them, he wrote, "there can be no trouble in pumping out the Money Pit as dry as when the treasure was first placed there."

In late 1893, one thousand shares in the Oak Island Treasure Company were offered at $5 apiece to undertake the work. Blair indirectly but skillfully exploited the widespread publicity that had attended the reported treasure finds at New Glasgow and St. Martins and the even greater sensation that had been created when a boatswain's whistle made of ivory or bone and said to be of "an ancient and peculiar design" was found on Oak Island at Smith's Cove. In a second edition of the Oak Island Treasure Company prospectus he published in early 1894, Blair proclaimed, "We are happy to state that the stock is selling quite rapidly and only a few hundred shares remain to be sold, of the one thousand shares sufficient to complete the work." It was "worthy of note," Blair added in this edition of the prospectus, "that with very few exceptions every man whom we have met that has ever worked on Oak Island has expressed his intention of taking stock in this Company."

It was true that Robert Creelman, Samuel Fraser, and Jefferson McDonald had already joined the company. What Blair didn't mention in the new prospectus was that a majority of the Nova Scotia shareholders were demanding that the planned work on Oak Island be overseen by a local committee, not by directors sitting in Boston offices. They organized a meeting in Truro on April 4, 1894, at which Creelman, McDonald, and Jothan McCully were among those who spoke. McDonald was unanimously elected to represent the Nova Scotia shareholders, and five other men were named to the committee that would be in charge of the operations on Oak Island. One of them, a lumberman from Amherst named William Chappell, would become almost as important in the story of the island as Blair himself. Adams A. Tupper was appointed by the committee to perform the hands-on supervision of the work, beginning in June 1894.

We know virtually every move the Oak Island Treasure Company made because Frederick Blair was just as scrupulous about recording the new company's activities as he had been about researching the past work on the island. The Treasure Company crew began with an exploration of the Cave-in Pit. When the boulders were removed to a depth of 18 feet, the new company's workmen found themselves standing in a shaft almost 8 feet in diameter that was nearly perfectly circular, with well-defined walls that convinced them they were looking at a piece of the original work on Oak Island. The miners among them agreed that the Cave-in Pit was an air shaft, essential for ventilation in a tunnel more than 500 feet long. They did not even need to use picks to clear the shaft, it was reported back to Boston, because while the earth inside was soft, the walls containing it were smooth and solid, made of clay so hard it was nearly impossible to sink a spike into them anyway; the labor of the men who had dug this shaft was unimaginable.

Blair would declare that he believed the Cave-in Pit might be the key to solving the entire problem of Oak Island. Eventually the stones and the loose soil inside the shaft were removed to a depth of 52 feet, and box cribbing was built that stretched from the bottom to several feet above the surface. An auger bored another 16 feet deeper into the Cave-in Pit without encountering any resistance. The next morning, though, water broke into the Cave-in Pit from shaft no. 4, dug by the Truro Company more than forty years earlier. When the cribbing grew unstable, it was agreed that working in the Cave-in Pit had become unsafe for the men.

Blair, Tupper, McDonald, and the committee overseeing the work agreed they would sink yet another shaft (no. 12), this one right next to the "pirate tunnel" (as the members of the company referred to the original tunnel that flooded the Money Pit), going deep enough to undermine the old tunnel from below, then destroy it with dynamite, thereby, they hoped, cutting off the flow of water to the Money Pit. The excavation of shaft no. 12 reached a depth of only 43 feet, though, before water from shaft no. 4 burst into it. They bailed this out, but then a seep of stagnant water, almost black, began to fill the new shaft. This was from the Money Pit, the men agreed, and they bailed that out also. Eventually they were able to dig to a depth of 55 feet, then strike a tunnel from the bottom of no. 12 toward the surface, in hopes of finding the flood tunnel. When they were just 25 feet from the surface, though, the tunnel had not been found.

James McGinnis, the grandson of Daniel McGinnis, claimed that one of the last things the Halifax Company had done was to build a stout platform in the Money Pit, just above the high-water mark, then fill the Pit in with loose soil from the platform to the surface. Henry Sellers also insisted there was such a platform. When the Treasure Company excavated what they believed to be the Money Pit to look for this platform, however, it could not be found. James McGinnis insisted they had looked in the wrong place. Winter was coming on, though, so the Treasure Company adjourned until the following spring.

As I studied the notes of the Treasure Company's attempt to reform itself in 1895, the familiar vows of previous searchers recurred yet again in a way that was both poignant and absurd. One A. S. Lowden had been named by the directors in Boston to serve as the new general manager of the company, and after a meeting of the stockholders on April 2, 1895, Lowden laid out a two-part plan that was long on effusion but short on originality in every respect:

ONE: "To make another effort to cut the tunnel off at or near the scene of last year's operations." There *had* to be a gate in the flood tunnel, Lowden wrote, repeating the conclusions of men who had preceded him by almost half a century. He proposed to locate it by tunneling from shaft no. 12 at the 49-foot level toward shaft no. 5.

TWO: "To attack the Money Pit direct, nothing having been done there last year, the exact conditions are not known."

Not surprisingly, Lowden's efforts to raise the money to purchase a larger and more expensive pump through a new stock issue failed utterly. The Nova Scotia stockholders met again in Truro on November 26, 1895, and appointed a new board of management that included William Chappell, with Frederick Blair to serve as treasurer. Blair, who had moved his insurance office from Boston to Amherst, Nova Scotia, to be closer to Oak Island, helped prepare a new version of the Treasure Company's prospectus that helped raise the $2,000 needed to purchase a top-of-the-line steam pump and boiler. This took almost a year, but in the late autumn of 1896 Blair's Amherst friend Captain John Welling was chosen to mount yet another new effort to get to the bottom of the Money Pit.

Blair received daily reports that tracked the work on Oak Island during the winter of 1896 to 1897. Shaft no. 2 had been doubled in width, while shaft no. 12, now 123 feet deep, was used to collect the water pumped out of no. 2. The failure of this effort is implied in reports to Blair during the spring of 1897 that the work had moved to the excavation of a new shaft (no. 13) 25 feet north of the Cave-in Pit. At a depth of 82 feet, the workmen began to tunnel toward the Cave-in Pit. They got within 4 feet before being driven out by water pouring through the tunnel's leading wall. Within a couple of weeks, the diggers struck what they at first believed was the Pirate Tunnel. It was 4 feet wide by 6 feet tall, well timbered, and connected to the Cave-in Pit. What they had found, however, turned out to be a tunnel dug by the Halifax Company crew in 1866. After considerable discussion, it was agreed that the Pirate Tunnel was likely not more than 5 feet below and they began to search for it.

This effort ended on March 26, 1897, when a workman named Maynard Kaiser was sent into one of the shafts (probably no. 13) to retrieve a cask that had fallen in. Rather than bring up the empty barrel, Kaiser for some reason chose to fill it with water, then ride atop the bucket as it was raised to the surface. The weight of the water and the man was more than the hoist could bear, and when the rope slipped off the gear both the cask and Kaiser plunged to the bottom of the shaft. He was dead by the time a crew of rescuers found him. Immediately, nearly the entire Treasure Company crew refused to continue working underground. As the April 13, 1897, edition of a Halifax newspaper reported it: "Captain Welling who is in charge of the work of excavating for the Oak Island treasure reports that all his men have quit the job. They became suspicious after the death of poor Kaiser last week and will not continue to dig. One of the men had a dream in which the spirit of Captain Kidd appeared and warned him they would all be dead if they continued the search."

Welling must have had some force of personality, because within a week he had assembled a new crew that on April 22 discovered yet another tunnel leading into the Money Pit. It was 9 feet square and solidly cribbed, with saltwater percolating into it from beneath. They excavated upward into the Money Pit from there, and at the 30-foot level found the platform built by the Halifax Company, exactly as James McGinnis had described it. After correcting the misalignment of the cribbing (with planks they attached as a skid), the crew began to once again probe deeper into the Pit. At 111 feet they found what they thought must be the flood tunnel. It was a sharply cut rectangular channel 2.5 feet wide that was floored with a layer of beach stones, gravel, and sand, in that order from the bottom up. Saltwater was flowing with great force through the tunnel. The horizontal ceiling was clear evidence this tunnel was man-made.

Yet another celebration was cut short, though, when the valve stem of the Treasure Company's prized steam pump broke. Within an hour the Money Pit was filled with seawater to tide level, leaving the flood tunnel under almost 50 feet of water.

After calculating the expense of repairing the pump and the cost of keeping it going, the Treasure Company's directors determined that yet another effort must be made to intercept the Pirate Tunnel near the shore of Smith's Cove and cut it off. To locate the flood channel, the crew began a series of boreholes about 50 feet from the high tide mark at the cove, following a perpendicular line across the approximate path the Pirate Tunnel must follow. They drilled five such holes, each 5 inches in diameter at varying depths between 80 and 95 feet. Sticks of dynamite were lowered into each of these holes, then ignited. The only apparent results of the subsequent explosions were the spumes of seawater that rose 100 feet and more into the air. An enormous charge of dynamite—more than 160 pounds—was then placed into the center borehole and detonated. There was no gush of water from the hole this time, but the water in both the Money Pit and in the Cave-in Pit boiled and foamed for almost a minute. The men agreed that they were in or next to a tunnel carrying water from the shore to the Money Pit.

There was contention among the crew, though, about what it meant that no saltwater had been found in this middle hole before a depth of 80 feet. Those who insisted the flood channel must now be blocked won the day and they agreed to return to the Money Pit and continue the boring operations there. The results of this decision would include what is arguably the most remarkable discovery in the history of the treasure hunt on Oak Island.

EARLY INTO MY WORK on *The Curse of Oak Island* I began to be convinced by what I knew about human nature that it was not a treasure of gold and silver that had been buried on the island. What had been done on Oak Island could only have been done by a large workforce, and there was no way I believed a group of even half a dozen people could or would have kept it a secret that a fortune in precious metals was concealed on an island off the coast of Nova Scotia.

There were answers to that, of course. One, obviously, was that whoever had buried the treasure on the island had already returned to retrieve it. That wasn't a possibility anyone who had hunted for treasure on Oak Island wanted to embrace and, as mentioned earlier, there was a standard response to this suggestion. The fact that we still don't know who hid whatever is hidden there, more than 250 years (at least) after it was likely buried, might also be explained in other ways. If the people who had done the actual labor were slaves, as many supposed, they might have been silenced by a mass execution immediately after their work was done. Or, if the work was done by soldiers or a ship's crew, they might have all gone down on the return voyage to wherever they were from, taking their secret with them to the bottom of the ocean.

THE CURSE OF OAK ISLAND 85

I conceded these points, then said that what I really believed was that it would be impossible to motivate men to do what had been done on Oak Island simply to hide a treasure of gold, no matter how great it might be. More than that would be required in my opinion. What had been concealed on the island had to be something of incalculable value, something that meant more than money ever could. I think Marty Lagina thought that was more than a little naïve. His brother, Rick, though, was inclined to agree with me.

Only a single piece of tangible evidence has ever been brought up from belowground to support my side of this argument, however, and it is not only of unknown origin, but preposterously tiny to boot. Infinitesimal some might say. It was found right around the first of September in 1897 during the boring operations of the Oak Island Treasure Company in the Money Pit.

A sketch drawn by Frederick Blair in February 1898 shows where the boreholes were drilled in a circular pattern around the rim of the Pit. The water had been pumped out to the 100-foot level, where a new platform was built and the drill mounted. William Chappell was one of those who operated the drill; he would describe in a sworn statement what the bit and the pipe that surrounded it brought back up to the platform. The first hole was bored to a depth of 122 feet before a piece of oak wood was penetrated. At 126 feet, the drill was stopped when it struck iron. A second hole was bored a foot away, and again the drill struck iron and was stopped. Chappell and the others decided to try a smaller drill, just 1.5 inches in diameter. This drill deflected off the iron and went around it, passing first through "puddled clay" then striking "soft stone or cement" at a depth of 153 feet, 8 inches. The drill worked its way through the "soft stone" and then went through 5 inches of solid oak, which proved to the men on the platform that they had not yet reached bedrock.

The drill was raised slowly and carefully. T. Perley Putnam, who was on the platform with Chappell and Captain Welling, had been placed in charge of removing, collecting, cataloguing, and preserving the borings from the drill's auger bit. He panned out the dirt from the auger in direct sunlight, then meticulously gathered everything that floated in the water. There were oak chips and coconut husks, Putnam reported, plus a small piece of—well, he was not sure what it was, he admitted. On instructions from Welling, Putnam several days later carried the borings he had collected in envelopes to the offices of Dr. A. E. Porter, a physician who was then practicing in Amherst. They had chosen Porter as a consultant, Frederick Blair would explain later, because the doctor owned the most powerful microscope to be found in Nova Scotia at that time.

On September 6, 1897, Porter examined the borings from the Money Pit in the presence of between thirty-five and forty men, including Putnam and Blair. Almost immediately his attention was attracted to the ball of "strange fiber" that Putnam had not been able to identify. It was only about the size of a grain of rice, as Porter would describe it, with some sort of fuzz or short hair on its surface. Using his medical instruments under the magnifier, Porter worked at this ball of fiber for several minutes, until it slowly began to unfold. After another few minutes, the doctor had it flattened out, whereupon he described it as being, to all appearances, a tiny piece of parchment paper with a fragment of writing in black ink that appeared to be parts of either the letters *ui* or *vi* or *wi*.

Blair insisted on an examination by experts in Boston associated with Harvard and the Massachusetts Institute of Technology. They reported back that the item most certainly was a piece of parchment that had been written on with a quill pen and India ink.

THE DISCOVERY OF THE PARCHMENT FRAGMENT was the real beginning of consideration of the possibility that what was buried on Oak Island might not be chests of gold buried by pirates but rather something of real—perhaps even profound—historical value. In a 1930 interview with the *Toronto Telegram*, Blair declared that the day the Oak

Island Treasure Company found the piece of parchment had provided "more convincing evidence of buried treasure than a few doubloons would be. I am satisfied that either a treasure of immense value or priceless historical documents are in a chest at the bottom of the Pit."

The 1897 borings in the Money Pit produced a great deal of evidence beyond the parchment. At 171 feet into one borehole, the chisel point that had replaced the auger bit struck solidly against iron. The drillers said they knew it from the sound. They continued to push the drill against this barrier for more than forty minutes and could make no deeper penetration than a quarter-inch. Chappell, Putnam, and Welling then withdrew the drill, pumped the loose material from the hole, and ran a magnet through it, collecting about a thimbleful of fine iron cuttings. What was regarded as an even more exciting discovery was made in a borehole where a tremendous spout of water rose out of the pipe when the drill was at 126 feet. They measured the flow with their pumps and determined it to be 400 gallons a minute. This had to mean there was a second flood tunnel, also coming from the south shore of the island, most likely from a location closer to the Money Pit than Smith's Cove.

The oak splinters, charcoal, and coconut fiber that came out of the boreholes were also saved for examination, but the greatest interest was in the soft stone struck by the drill at 153 feet, eight inches. The drillers believed this might be a kind of early cement and sent it for analysis to A. Boake, Roberts and Company in London. The report back from the London chemists was that this material did indeed seem to be a primitive sort of cement, composed of lime, carbonate, silica, iron, alumina, and magnesium. "From the analysis it is impossible to state definitively, but from the appearance and nature of the samples, we are of the opinion that it is a cement which has been worked by man."

The jubilation of the Treasure Company's principals soon gave way to a debate about whether they should issue new stock for sale in order to expand the operations on Oak Island. In the end, the stockholders voted unanimously that there would be no "outside" sale of shares in the company and that the current shareholders should finance any future work and split the proceeds only among themselves when the treasure was finally retrieved.

A new round of work began in October 1897. The plan this time was to sink one more shaft (no. 14) to a depth of between 175 and 200 feet, then drive a tunnel to the Money Pit, in hopes of draining it into the new shaft, which would be octagonal in shape, 13 feet across and 40 feet from the original Pit. Why the Treasure Company imagined they would produce a different result than had been found in previous attempts to do pretty much the same thing is not clear, but what happened was quite predictable: at 112 feet into the new shaft it began to fill with seawater at a rate that made continuing impossible. The company's response was to attempt yet another shaft (no. 15) about 35 feet southwest of no. 14. The diggers were encouraged when at 105 feet they came to an abandoned tunnel that had been dug by the Halifax Company and found it dry. At 160 feet, though, water began to pour into no. 15 from the Money Pit, where the water level briefly dropped by 14 feet, then rose again, until both it and the new pit were filled to sea level. Pumping was attempted until the plunger rod broke. Water quickly poured into the new shaft from the Money Pit and within a few hours both the tunnel and no. 15 were destroyed.

"Nothing daunted," as Frederick Blair's man R. W. Harris would put it, the Treasure Company sank four more shafts (nos. 16, 17, 18, and 19) to depths of between 95 and 144 feet. Each was abandoned when the diggers encountered quicksand, impenetrable boulders, or an overwhelming surge of water.

In the spring of 1898, however, the Treasure Company did perform a series of tests that gave them new and deeply unsettling news about what they were up against. First, they pumped shaft no. 18 full of water to well above tide level in the hope that they would force the muddy water in the new shaft out onto the beach at Smith's Cove. The muddy water *did* soon appear on the south shore of the island but not at Smith's Cove. Three different sections of the shore of the south beach showed evidence of the muddy water escaping from no. 18. To make certain of what this suggested, Welling and Chappell agreed that they should pump the Money Pit full of water above sea level, then drop red dye into it, hoping the dye would drain through the flood tunnel as it receded. As they hoped, the dye began to seep into the bay a short time later; again this was not at Smith's Cove but rather on the south end of the island in the same places where the muddy water had been seen earlier.

What it meant, almost certainly, was that there was at least one flood tunnel that ran toward the Money Pit from the south shore but not from Smith's Cove and that there could be as many as three such tunnels. Finding a way to drain the Money Pit had become an exponentially more complex problem. Yet what the Treasure Company chose to do next was return to the Pit itself.

For reasons that were not explained in the journal kept by Blair, the company's crew spent months on work that essentially doubled the size of the Money Pit. This was done by sinking a new shaft (no. 20) right next to the original Pit. A double wall of cribbing was constructed to divide the two halves of what was otherwise now a shaft measuring 10 feet by 8 feet. The excavation of the new shaft became increasingly difficult as the crew descended into rock-hard clay and was stopped at 113 feet by a surge of seawater that poured in with more force than the pumps could handle. The work continued, though. On April 2 the crew's foreman, a man named Burrows, told Blair that his men were 3 feet below the flood tunnel from Smith's Cove and that they were confident they could reach a depth of 126 feet within a couple of weeks and would there locate the tunnel from the south shore. Only a few days later, though, Burrows reported that most of his men had left the island to join fishing crews and that they were running out of coal to run the pumps and the boiler.

Creditors were literally standing at the Treasure Company's door. The county sheriff showed up on the island in May 1898 with a court order obtained by a Halifax machinery firm that forced the sale of every bit of equipment that could be carried off. Captain Welling had invested $4,000 of his own money and was at risk of losing his home. Putnam was in far worse shape, having put in $20,000; within a few months he had no choice but to declare a bankruptcy from which he never recovered. Blair proposed a new stock issue, based on the discoveries of the Treasure Company, but the other directors and shareholders, many of whom had already borrowed money to make their investments, turned him down. In December 1900, Blair used his own money to buy out all of the other shareholders and took complete control of the Treasure Company, vowing to continue the work on his own.

Blair summarized his position in a draft prospectus:

> When we went to work at the Island two years ago, we knew comparatively nothing about the conditions as they existed. We supposed at that time that the Money Pit was not over 120 feet deep and that the treasure was not over 110 feet down. Our work has since proved that the Pit is not less than 180 feet deep, that there are two tunnels instead of one, and that one of them is not less than 160 feet down, and that there is treasure at different points in the Pit, from 126 feet down to 170 feet, without a doubt. We have also found out that the work done by the Halifax Company is a greater hindrance to the procuring of the treasure than is the original work.
>
> We now claim that there is nothing that can prevent us getting the treasure.

All that was really certain was that the treasure hunt on Oak Island that had begun in the eighteenth century would continue into the twentieth.

CHAPTER EIGHT

Nothing proved the depth of Frederick Blair's commitment to Oak Island better than the years he spent negotiating his way through the thicket of government bureaucracy that was threatening to strangle the treasure hunt during the first part of the twentieth century. The root of the problem Blair had to wrangle with went all the way back to the year 1276, when England, under the reign of Edward I, had enacted the Law of the Treasure Trove. This statute required that "treasures found hidden or concealed without any known owner belong to the King." The royal prerogative had passed to the provincial governments in Canada, and J. W. Longley, the attorney general of Nova Scotia, declared in September 1895 that "any treasure discovered at Oak Island will, as far as I am concerned, belong to Her Majesty as represented by the Government of Nova Scotia. "

Blair moved to protect himself by applying for a lease under Nova Scotia's recently passed Mines Act that would permit him to search for and claim gold and silver on Oak Island within an area that was 450 feet by 500 feet and contained not only the Money Pit but all the other shafts that had been sunk on the east end of the island. After a decade-long campaign that involved hiring various agents to buffer him from the bureaucrats in Halifax, Blair acquired the Mines Act lease in late 1905. This document had a life span of forty years, but it only protected the precious metals Blair might find on Oak Island. Convinced at this point that the island's treasure might be something quite different than chests of coins, Blair (through his agent) negotiated a deal with the province that gave him the exclusive right to search for an undefined "trove" on Oak Island, as long as he agreed to pay the government 2 percent of the value of whatever he found. That agreement was not signed until 1909. To secure his position more firmly, Blair also signed an agreement with Henry Sellers that allowed him to conduct operations that included "digging or excavating" on the east end of Oak Island for a fee of $100 a year.

Finally in a position to proceed with the treasure hunt, what Blair needed now was a partner with the means to mount another onslaught against the Money Pit. Within just a few weeks, he teamed up with a man who appeared to fit the bill in every way.

Captain Henry Bowdoin certainly did not lack a flair for self-promotion. The news that the famous adventurer had joined the Oak Island treasure hunt was announced in the March 18, 1909, edition of the *New York Herald*. Bowdoin, at that time living at 44 Broadway in Manhattan, was described in the preface to his *Herald* interview as "a mining, mechanical and marine engineer, a Master and Pilot [with] a license as a submarine driver. He has dredged harbours and built bridges for the government and for corporations and says that modern machinery and engineering science will solve in a jiffy the difficulties Captain Kidd made to guard his treasure."

He had reached an agreement with Frederick Blair "for the apportionment of [the] ten million dollars" he estimated the Oak Island treasure would be worth, Bowdoin told the *Herald*, "and has ordered such machinery as he will need." He would start with a crew of six handpicked men who would leave for Nova Scotia by rail on May 1, Bowdoin said, after sending his machinery ahead by schooner. The cost of the operation he estimated at $15,000.

"Any competent engineer could clear up that affair in no time," Bowdoin told the newspaper. "And I don't want more than two weeks for the work, after I get my machinery and crew on the ground. It will be a vacation, and about all I stand to lose is the wages of the men and my own time, for the machinery will be valuable in my business afterward."

In another, shorter interview published the same day in the *New York Times*, Bowdoin admitted that "he had not yet decided how he will get at the treasure," but he did not think he would have much difficulty in choosing the right approach after an up-close look at the situation. "He says he may sink a caisson down around the place where the treasure is supposed to be," the *Times* reported, "or may build another jetty [coffer-dam?]. He may even send a diver down in one of the holes, equipped with a pick-axe. He has never been on Oak Island, so he will have to decide on that when he gets there." A bold fellow indeed.

The biggest news in the *Times* piece, though, was Captain Bowdoin's claim that what was buried on Oak Island was not the Captain Kidd treasure at all, but rather the crown jewels of France.

The crown jewels were almost certainly the most fantastic collection ever kept by a single family (the Bourbons) in human history. The regalia—the assortment of ceremonial accoutrements that were used during the coronations of French kings—was alone of unimaginable value. Along with the sword, scepter, chalice, and robe brooch, the regalia included as many as eight crowns, among them the one worn by Louis XV, in which the 141-carat Regent diamond (valued today at more than $100 million) was set in the lower part of the fleur-de-lis at the front of the crown, with the magnificent 56-carat Sancy diamond seated in the upper petal above, surrounded by eight of the famous Mazarin diamonds set between double rows of pearls and smaller diamonds. During the nineteenth century, newspapers in Europe and the Americas had carried many articles that catalogued not only the regalia, but also the many other pieces of the crown jewels, including the 136-carat Ruspoli sapphire, the 28-carat Topaze, and the 17-carat Great Emerald of Louis XIV.

The disappearance of the crown jewels during the French Revolution had spawned dozens of stories and legends that captivated and diverted the reading public. One commonly repeated version (which has appeared in any number of books about Oak Island, including R. V. Harris's otherwise reliable *The Oak Island Mystery*) was that in June 1791 Louis XVI and Marie Antoinette had fled the revolutionary mob in Paris, headed for Austria with crown jewels loaded in their luggage. Yet when the two were captured in Varennes, this account goes, the jewels were no longer with them and apparently had been spirited out of the country by an accomplice.

In fact, the crown jewels were being kept the whole time at the Royal Storehouse, where they remained until September 11, 1792, when they were stolen during looting at the height of the revolution's chaos. Nearly the entire collection was recovered a short time later when the thieves were captured, and eventually it became the property of Napoleon Bonaparte. Two extraordinary items, however, were not found with the thieves. One was the Sancy diamond, a huge pale-yellow stone that had been cut in the shape of two back-to-back crowns. The Sancy, which had been removed from the king's crown, would resurface in 1828, when it became part of the collection of Count Anatoly Nikolaievich Demidov, whose family eventually sold it to an Indian prince. The prince permitted its public display in Paris at the Exposition Universelle of 1867, offered at a price of one million francs.

The other and more significant missing item from the crown jewels was the French Blue, also known as the King's Jewel, a legendary gem that has become the most storied stone in human history. The French Blue was never seen again after it was taken from the Royal Storehouse in 1792.

The Blue was believed to have been mined in India's Golconda kingdom sometime during the sixteenth century. All anyone can say for certain is that the crudely cut stone, approximately 115 carats in size, had come into the possession of a French gem dealer named Jean-Baptiste Tavernier in the middle of the seventeenth century and that Tavernier sold it to Louis XIV around 1668. The king had the diamond recut into a 67.125-carat stone that was fabled for its strange luminescence, the way the gem reflected bluish-gray light on the one hand yet appeared to pulse with a brilliant red phosphorescence when a room was darkened. This effect may have been the beginning of the claim that the diamond was cursed. The king wore it on a ribbon around his neck during ceremonies and made it the centerpiece of a subcollection within the crown jewels called the Order of the Golden Fleece.

It was believed that the French Blue had been smuggled out of France to London sometime between being taken from the Royal Storehouse and Louis XVI's beheading on January 21, 1793. A story spread that the Blue had been broken into two pieces. The larger of the two, it was said, had been recut into a 42.52-carat stone the size and shape of a pear-shaped pigeon egg and would become known as the Hope Diamond. This was at the very least a disputed claim and there were many stories that the French Blue, along with other pieces of the crown jewels, were held in secret somewhere outside Europe. So back in 1909 there was a place in the popular imagination for the idea that this clandestine location where the Blue was hidden might be Oak Island. Not until 2005 did the claim that the Hope Diamond had been cut from the fractured Blue become more or less official. That was the year scientists at the Smithsonian Institution's National Museum of Natural History announced that they had used computer modeling that involved both the original Tavernier stone, the French Blue, and the Hope Diamond to determine that "the evidence very much supports the theory" that the Hope had been cut from the Blue. Even today, though, there are those who doubt it.

THERE'S NO KNOWN BASIS beyond his say-so for Captain Bowdoin's announcement that the French crown jewels were hidden on Oak Island, but the claim certainly captured public attention. Bowdoin moved quickly to take advantage. Less than two months after the articles in the *Herald* and the *Times*, Bowdoin used the *New York Sun* to announce that "he had decided that it's too big a job to tackle without selling a little stock first." To that end, he had formed a corporation in the Arizona Territory that he called Old Gold Salvage and Wrecking Company. Bowdoin himself wrote the new company's elaborate prospectus.

"Over one hundred years ago a treasure, estimated to be over ten million dollars, was buried on Oak Island, in Mahone Bay, Nova

Scotia, supposedly by pirates, who took such pains to safeguard it that, although numerous attempts have been made to recover it, it lies undisturbed to this day," the prospectus began. "These failures were due to lack of modern machinery and ignorance; each expedition being stopped by water and lack of funds." Technological advances would make the recovery of the treasure on Oak Island "easy, ridiculously easy," wrote Bowdoin, who explained that he would first locate the treasure in the Money Pit with a newly invented drill that was capable of bringing to the surface a core 2 inches in diameter. Once he and his team knew exactly where the treasure was, they would use the same drill to locate the flood tunnel from Smith's Cove and seal the tunnel off with sheet piling. Then, "a centrifugal turbine pump, capable of lifting 1,000 gallons per minute—one hundred and fifty feet vertically—will be lowered into the pit from a derrick and the water pumped out. If the tunnel plugs have done their work, the pump will clear out the water; the treasure be easily recovered, and all underground workings explored."

There was a small possibility that "the tunnel *not* be located; the pump *not* be able to keep out the water, and the bucket *not* bring up all of the treasure," the prospectus conceded, and if that should be the case, the company would respond by placing one of "Bowdoin's Air Lock Caissons" into the Money Pit. These watertight chambers were already being used to sink foundations through water and earth all over the planet, Bowdoin explained in his prospectus, and could clearly be applied to the problem of the Money Pit: "Compressed air keeps out all water and allows men to work at the bottom and send any articles up and out through the air lock. . . . THE TREASURE CAN POSITIVELY BE RECOVERED BY ITS USE."

Captain Bowdoin offered 250,000 shares of Old Gold Salvage and Wrecking Company stock in lots of ten shares at $1 a share. Promising a dividend of "4,000 percent," Bowdoin wrote that "operations would begin in May or June and be completed in three or four weeks," meaning investors would receive their returns before the end of summer.

Even with all the free advertising provided by New York's daily newspapers, Bowdoin was able to sell only five thousand shares (2 percent) of the Old Gold stock offering during the next three months. Among those who did invest in the company, though, was the most illustrious treasure hunter in the history of Oak Island, Franklin Delano Roosevelt. The future four-term US president was then a twenty-seven-year-old graduate of Harvard Law School working as a clerk at the Wall Street firm of Carter, Ledyard and Milburn. He had grown up hearing tales of Nova Scotia's buried treasures during the summers he spent with his family at their summer home on Campobello Island in the Bay of Fundy. In 1896, when he was fourteen, Roosevelt and a classmate from the Groton School had sailed from Campobello to nearby Grand Manan Island, where they spent four days digging for a chest said to have been buried there by Captain Kidd. All the two found was a plank in which some joker had carved "W. K." Roosevelt was nevertheless captivated by the stories of Oak Island's Money Pit, and when he read about Captain Bowdoin's planned expedition to Mahone Bay, he not only purchased ten shares of Old Gold Salvage and Wrecking Company stock, but he also persuaded three friends to do the same. The four young men made a pact that they would join the dig on Oak Island that summer for as long as they could get away from their jobs in New York.

Though vastly undercapitalized, Captain Bowdoin sailed with his men for Nova Scotia on August 19, 1909. It is only from the records kept by Frederick Blair (Old Gold's vice president) that we know Bowdoin made almost no effort to keep the promise to his investors about locating and blocking the flood tunnel to the Money Pit. The story that the crown jewels of France were hidden in the Money Pit also was abandoned. Almost immediately after arriving on Oak Island, Bowdoin had moved his men and his machinery to the east-end drumlin, where they set up what they called Camp Kidd. What confronted Bowdoin were two open pits side by side. One, assumed to be the Money Pit, measured 5 feet by 7 feet and was heavily cribbed to a depth of 110 feet, most of this being underwater. Right next to this Pit was the shaft dug by the Oak Island Treasure Company in

1899. According to Blair's notes, the presumed Money Pit was "floored over" at a depth of 30 feet, just above the water that filled it to tide level. Bowdoin's crew set immediately to opening the Pit by dropping charges of dynamite down the shaft, then used a steam-powered "orange peel" bucket to drag the shattered timbers to the surface. Once the Pit was cleared out down to the waterline, the crew began to rebuild the cribbing as they descended. At a depth of 107 feet, the captain sent a diver down to examine the bottom of the Pit. When the diver returned to the surface, he reported that the cribbing down below was badly damaged and that various planks and timbers were sticking up in all directions from the bottom of the Pit—perhaps a result of the 1861 collapse combined with the dynamite charges Bowdoin had exploded in the shaft.

The captain then commanded that the core drill be put to work. The first borehole went through 17 feet of sand and gravel, then 16 feet of blue clay before striking cement at 149 feet, exactly as Blair had predicted in a letter sent to Bowdoin the previous spring. After passing through 6 inches of cement, the Old Gold crew anticipated that they were about to drill into a treasure chest. Instead, the drill passed through 18 feet of yellow clay before reaching a bedrock composed of gypsum and quartz at 167 feet. Bowdoin and his crew would drive more than two dozen boreholes into the area around the Money Pit, going as deep as 171 feet, but encountered nothing more interesting than layers of cement that ranged between six and ten inches in thickness. (Twenty-two years later, in 1931, one witness to the Bowdoin borings, a man named J. B. Thomson, would claim that he had seen a thin, bright metal disk embedded in one of the core samples, but there's no mention of it in Blair's journal of the Old Gold operations.)

By November 1909, Bowdoin had exhausted Old Gold's scant finances and informed Blair that he could not continue the work. He made an agreement with Blair to resume operations on Oak Island the following summer, but then just a few months later he wrote from England that his business there would make it impossible for him to get back to Nova Scotia before the end of 1911.

If Bowdoin had simply abandoned the project at that point, his attempt would have been merely another failed expedition to Oak Island, memorable mainly for the captain's grand but empty boasts and because a future US president had made several brief trips to Oak Island during the late summer of 1909 to join the Old Gold crew. However, he was not satisfied "to quit without another try," Bowdoin wrote to Blair, "and knowing now the exact condition, would get to the bottom and clean things up next time."

Blair, who was far from impressed by what he had seen of the Old Gold Salvage and Wrecking Company, wrote back that he would be willing to consider a revised proposal from Bowdoin, but only if the captain could demonstrate "that he had sufficient funds on hand, or at his disposal, to complete the work in a proper manner."

Blair was startled by Bowdoin's reply:

I believe you had better see us if you come to New York this winter. Advise me ahead. If, however, we cannot get together on the time extension, it will be necessary for me to go to Oak Island and sell the machinery, etc., and when finished, the Company will want a full report which one of our people, a newspaper man, will want to publish. The report that I would have to give them would not help in getting further investments in Oak Island.

Blair, furious, wrote back:

Your letter almost conveys a threat that if we do not permit you to make further tests at Oak Island you will publish such information as would probably prevent the possibility of raising funds for exploration there in the future. Let me say that anything that can be said against Oak Island has already been written, and the publication of any article you might be able to bring forth would not in the least jar those of us who own the lease.

Blair *was* jarred, though, by what Bowdoin did next. No matter how abjectly Bowdoin might have failed in his probe of the Money Pit, the captain would make a powerful demonstration in the summer of 1911 of how effectively vindictive a man could be when he commanded good connections in the press. Bowdoin's article "Solving the Mystery of Oak Island" was published in the August 18 edition of *Collier's* magazine, one of the most widely read publications in North America. The piece began with the assertion that there had never been any treasure in the Money Pit or on Oak Island, then followed by ridiculing the notion that a 600-foot flood tunnel had been dug from Smith's Cove to the Pit, when it would have been so much easier to dig a 150-foot tunnel from other parts of the island's south shore. The water in the Money Pit was not arriving via a tunnel, Bowdoin asserted, but by "percolating" through the soil from the south shore. The captain disputed the story that a ringbolt had been in a boulder on the beach at Smith's Cove, pointing out that it would have been much easier to tie a line to an oak tree than to drill a hole in rock. Bowdoin also dismissed the claim (made by more than a dozen men who had witnessed it) that links of a chain or anything else of value had been brought up by the pot auger in 1849, because none of it would have stuck to a chisel being raised through 120 feet of water. For good measure, Bowdoin added that he did not believe there were any characters on the stone that had been found in the Money Pit by the Onslow Company in 1805.

Frederick Blair did not have access to a publication as widely read as *Collier's*. He replied at length to Bowdoin's article with one of his own, however, published in the February 23, 1912, edition of Nova Scotia's *Amherst Daily News*. Blair first pointed out that Bowdoin had refused to avail himself of the advice offered by any number of men who had been part of previous expeditions to Oak Island and had done almost no exploration before he began to blindly throw dynamite into the Money Pit, destroying most of the cribbing and leaving the rest of the timbers even more out of alignment than they had been when the Old Gold crew arrived. Bowdoin's pipes and rods had reached into only a small area of the bottom of the Pit, Blair asserted, and most of his borings had been into areas outside the Pit, where of course he had encountered natural formations. In his *Collier's* article, Captain Bowdoin had not only failed to explain the work done on the beach at Smith's Cove, in particular the five man-made drains, but he had also failed to mention their existence at all, Blair pointed out. Bowdoin also had not mentioned the various tests ranging from dynamite blasts to dye drops that had clearly established a man-made connection between the Pit and the south shore or the existence of the air shaft that Sophia Sellers's oxen had stumbled into back in 1878. Blair noted that on multiple occasions and in the presence of dozens of witnesses it had been shown that water did not "percolate" into the Money Pit, but rather it poured in at the rate of 500 gallons per minute (a hundred more than had been previously measured) and that the water level in the Pit rose and fell with the tides. He wasn't present—or for that matter even alive—back in 1849 when the links of chain and oak borings had been brought to the surface by the pot auger, Blair admitted, so he could offer only the testimony of those who *had* been there as evidence. Based on his personal experiences, though, he found the story entirely plausible, because he had seen personally the slivers of oak wood and other items that had come up out of the Money Pit, stuck to the clay on various drill bits. Bowdoin had also failed to mention the copious amounts of coconut fiber and charcoal that came out of the Money Pit and did not even try to explain the log platforms that had been found at 10-foot intervals in the Pit when it was first excavated. Blair seemed especially incensed by Bowdoin's suggestion that the Money Pit had been "salted" with that famous scrap of parchment. If he or anyone else had wanted to plant evidence of treasure in the Pit, they would have chosen gold or silver, Blair wrote. And it was ridiculous of Bowdoin to suggest that the Treasure Company's largest investor, Mr. Putnam, had spent himself into bankruptcy in a pointless hunt for a treasure he knew was not there.

Blair was particularly incensed that Bowdoin's article had relied heavily on a report by three professors associated with Columbia University that described the "so-called cement" as "natural limestone pitted by the action of the water." Captain Bowdoin was well aware that

A. Boake, Roberts and Company, arguably the finest analytical firm in Great Britain, had examined the cement taken out of the Money Pit and produced a report stating that it was almost certainly "man-made," yet Bowdoin had not mentioned this fact anywhere in his article. That article, Blair closed, had been nothing more than the sour grapes of a man who wanted to continue his exploration of the Money Pit and had been denied by Blair and the other leaseholders.

In spite of Blair's reply, Bowdoin's "report," as he had threatened, indeed made it difficult to obtain "further investments in Oak Island." Exactly how much negative impact the captain's *Collier's* article made is debatable, but we know for certain that the effort by a Wisconsin professor named S. A. Williams to raise money for a company he called the Oak Island Salvage Company in the summer of 1912 failed miserably. Professor Williams had proposed to solve the problem of the Money Pit by using what was known as the Poetsch method. He would sink a circle of thirty-five holes, each 5 inches in diameter and 3 feet apart, to a depth of 160 feet, Williams wrote in his prospectus. The holes would be lined with metal casings and sealed at the bottom with cement, then pumped dry. He would then drop pipes filled with a solution of calcium chloride chilled to a temperature of 35 degrees below zero (Fahrenheit) into each of the casings and in this way create a ring of ice around the Money Pit that would prevent the flood tunnels from reaching the shaft. It had worked at Anzin, France, and would work on Oak Island, the professor asserted, promising that neither he nor any other officers of the company would accept a salary and that every cent raised by the Oak Island Salvage Company's stock issue would be spent on machinery, labor, and supplies until a "satisfactory sample" of the treasure had been obtained. The prospectus was met by resounding indifference, and Williams was unable to raise enough money to arrange even a visit Oak Island.

THOUGH HIS MOTIVES WERE DESPICABLE and his argument dishonest, Captain Bowdoin had pioneered what would become the main line of attack on the Oak Island "legend." Eighty-eight years after its publication, Joe Nickell would cite the *Collier's* article as a primary source in his own "investigation" of Oak Island. "In 1911 an engineer, Captain Henry Bowdoin, who had done extensive borings on the island, concluded that the treasure was imaginary," Nickell wrote in his article for the March/April 2000 issue of the *Skeptical Inquirer*. "He questioned the authenticity of various alleged findings [such as the cipher stone and piece of gold chain], and attributed the rest to natural phenomena."

Nickell made many of the same factual omissions that Bowdoin had, failing to account for the work on the beach at Smith's Cove, including the five man-made finger drains. The one solid piece of scientific evidence upon which Nickell relied was a 1911 geological report commissioned by Bowdoin that noted the "numerous" sinkholes on the mainland opposite Oak Island, which Nickell cited as "strong evidence" to indicate that the supposed man-made works on the island were "really but natural sinkholes and cavities." Nickell cherry-picked the work of various Nova Scotia investigators (every one of whom had concluded that the evidence overwhelmingly supported the story of the Money Pit that had been passed down since the eighteenth century) to support his argument that the Pit was a natural formation. Nickell had been less than straightforward, to say the least, in the ways he attempted to obviate the accounts of those who had been present when the Money Pit was excavated during the early nineteenth century. Those log platforms found in the Pit? Some of the accounts suggested the platforms had been found at "irregular" intervals, rather than at every 10 feet, Nickell noted, then leapt from this to the assertion that "fallen trees could have sunk into the pit with its collapse, or 'blowdowns' could periodically have washed into the depression, later giving the appearance of 'platforms' of rotten logs." Nickell simply ignored the accounts of those who were there when the Money Pit was opened and who had found the platforms to be perfectly level and obviously man-made. He similarly dismissed their descriptions of the pick marks on the walls of the shaft.

Most far-fetched was Nickell's contention that the enormous quantity of coconut fiber pulled from the Money Pit could be accounted for by the "sinkhole theory," which would explain how the fiber might have worked its way into the deep caverns under the island.

Nickell's explanation for how the coconut fiber had made its way into the Pit was essentially a regurgitation of the contention at the core of the most detailed argument for the sinkhole theory, an article published in the *Atlantic Advocate* magazine's October 1965 issue. "Over many thousands of years debris, washed in by high tides and heavy seas, could have accumulated in this fault," wrote the author, Betty O'Hanlon. She added that "the tropical fiber could have come from the Gulf Stream which passes very near Nova Scotia. Strong gales could have blown the fiber onto the shore, where it would have become trapped in the fissure."

The main problem with this theory is that the Gulf Stream runs east more than three hundred miles south of Oak Island. And neither Nickell nor O'Hanlon had offered any sort of explanation for how Oak Island, out of more than three hundred other islands in Mahone Bay, along with the hundreds of miles of coastline on Nova Scotia's south shore, had become the spot where this aberration of nature had taken place. Perhaps the most striking quality of both the Nickell and O'Hanlon articles was that a pair of writers who had attempted to debunk the "will to believe" among Oak Island's treasure hunters appeared oblivious to the will not to believe that distorted their own work. Their articles and others that have followed are evidence of how thoroughly Captain Henry Bowdoin's malice infected the Oak Island narrative.

Bowdoin's attempt to debunk Oak Island apparently made little impact on his investor Franklin Delano Roosevelt, whose fascination with the place continued throughout his life, even during the years when, as US president, he was consumed with lifting the United States out of the Great Depression and preparing for the country's entry into World War II. Roosevelt maintained contact with those who had been and were still part of the treasure hunt on Oak Island for more than thirty years and seemingly savored every bit of new information about the island that was produced during that period. On August 31, 1938, during his second presidential term, Roosevelt would reply (on White House stationery) to a letter from Gilbert Hedden, who was leading the current expedition on Oak Island, thusly:

> Your note came while I was on my cruise in the Pacific. I wish much I could have gone up the Coast this summer and visited Oak Island and seen the work you are doing—for I shall always be interested in that romantic spot. I hope that you will let me know how you have been getting on with modern methods—ours were, I fear, somewhat antiquated when we were there more than a quarter of a century ago.
>
> Very sincerely yours,
>
> Franklin D. Roosevelt

FDR's interest notwithstanding, the two decades after Captain Bowdoin's *Collier's* article were marked by one aborted attempt after another to mount a new expedition to Oak Island. The situation was complicated when Frederick Blair was compelled to move his insurance business to Calgary. Even at a remove of three thousand miles, though, Blair maintained his hold on the Money Pit, negotiating a new eight-year lease with Sophia Sellers that lasted until 1921, when Blair signed a revised agreement that gave him control of the Pit and the area around it until 1931.

In 1915, Blair made a new partnership agreement with a syndicate based in Rochester, New York, headed by an engineer named William S. Lozier. The Rochester Group, as it was known, conducted a series of drilling operations at the Money Pit and three other locations during the summer of 1916, but surrendered the effort upon "failing to make any new discoveries," as Blair's notes had it. After the Rochester Group left the island, the Money Pit fell into a state of neglect. In November 1920, Blair informed a prospective partner that "the Pit caved in and more or less filled up with the cribbing, the timbers being in every imaginable shape. The ground surrounding the Pit has also caved in more or less and the spaces in and around the Pit are full of water."

Impenetrable as the Pit had become, there were still those who proposed to make a run at it. In August 1921, Blair signed an agreement with another engineer, Edward Brown of Newark, New Jersey. His plan was to sink a shaft 6 feet by 6 feet about 15 feet from the Money Pit, Brown told Blair. The new shaft would be strongly cribbed and an air lock installed at the top. Brown had concluded based on the available records that there were three treasure boxes in the Money Pit, and he intended to locate them by "sounding with an iron rod," then tunneling directly to the locations. Brown and his crew went to work on July 4, 1922, but their operations were a comedy of equipment failures and other minor catastrophes. When Blair paid a visit and found that Brown's drill had never gone deeper than 7 feet, he stopped the work and terminated their agreement.

The detailed record of his ideas and activities that Frederick Blair left behind leaves no doubt that he never stopped believing something of exceptional value had been buried on Oak Island. His fervency was nearly religious and his dealings consistently honorable. During the decade after the Captain Bowdoin fiasco, however, Blair's behavior suggests at least a whiff of desperation and even, perhaps, a slight degree of hucksterism. Exhibit A in this regard is the advertisement Blair placed in the *Boston Journal of Commerce* on December 7, 1922, under the heading "Buried Treasure":

> Speculative venture, partly proven, requires $50,000 for half interest. If Successful will produce millions within one year; otherwise possible eighty per cent loss. Satisfactory credentials, proofs partially successful efforts [*sic*], will prove good sporting effort for party financially able to take chance. Full frank details at interview. 228 F. Journal of Commerce.

The advertisement was straightforward, typical of Blair. The accompanying article, though, written with Blair's help, was quite a departure. CAN BURIED TREASURE LURE WALL STREET? read the headline above the text:

Two hundred years ago the Welsh buccaneer, Sir Edward [Henry] Morgan, descended on the town of Panama and relieved its inhabitants of as much of their wealth as he could take away. Some years later, when he died Governor of Jamaica, a rich and respected gentleman, the treasure he took from the Spanish Main had disappeared.

The rest of the world apparently has forgotten about this, but there is a man in New York who now says he is certain that this or some other treasure is buried 150 feet deep at a certain spot on Oak Island, near Nova Scotia. Oak Island is one of the 365 islands in the neighborhood, which are not inhabited regularly. This man, a native of Nova Scotia, is here to 'find men with imagination enough' to risk some funds in a venture based upon records he possesses, which he believes will conclusively prove that treasure exists at a spot of which he has secured control from the Canadian government.

The story goes back to 1795, when three partridge hunters on Oak Island discovered in the solitary wilderness a place which showed the work of man. To this spot there have come successive parties of treasure hunters, who have dug deeply and have worked out a well-defined pit. After over one hundred years of digging, there has been brought out of this pit cement, timber, salt water, metal, and a piece of parchment about half a square inch in area. However the individual interested, whose announcement appears in this paper, declares he now knows just where the suspected treasure is situated and thinks he can prove he does to any individual interested.

While Blair certainly attracted some attention with this rather overblown pitch, it was not until 1931 that he found the sort of partner he was looking for, who also turned out to be a person he already knew. William Chappell not only had been a member of the Oak Island Treasure Company during its operations on Oak Island in the last years of the nineteenth century, but he was also the man operating the drill that brought the scrap of parchment out of the Money Pit in 1897. In the years since, Chappell and his brothers had prospered as the owners and operators of a string of lumber and sawmills across Nova Scotia. He had never tired, however, of recalling the summers he spent on Oak Island, and over the years he infected his son Melbourne Chappell with what these days is called Oak Island fever. Mel was a member of the Engineering Institute of Canada, William Chappell informed Blair, and he had consulted with the finest mining engineers in the country about how best to recover the cement chamber they had struck with the drill back in 1897. He was advised that a strongly cribbed shaft sunk down to the chamber in which a 450-gallon-per-minute electric pump was employed to keep the work dry should do the trick, and he was prepared to provide financial backing for his son's plan.

"A man of sterling qualities and character" was how R. V. Harris would describe William Chappell, who like Frederick Blair was "religiously inclined" and fastidious in his habits. Blair was so impressed by the knowledge, ability, and determination of Chappell and son that he closed his insurance office for the summer of 1931 and took up full-time residence on Oak Island to be involved in the day-to-day operations.

William Chappell was quick to identify the crib work in the Money Pit that he said he had helped build back in 1897. Blair disagreed, insisting the Pit lay some distance away. The problem for both men was that the exact location of the Money Pit had become lost during the previous decade, as both it and several of the surrounding shafts had collapsed. After considerable discussion, Blair and William Chappell agreed to sink their new shaft (no. 21) just southwest of the Money Pit and to make it the broadest hole dug on Oak Island to date—12 feet by 14 feet—and to drive it deeper than any previous shaft had gone.

The excavation unearthed a fascinating variety of articles, beginning with an anchor fluke found at 116 feet. (Blair kept this item in his home for the next twenty years, until it disappeared after his death in 1951.) A few feet below the anchor fluke, they discovered an axe head that closely resembled one he had seen on an Acadian axe at the museum in Annapolis Royal, said Blair, who estimated it was 250 years old. A pick was found at 127 feet, as were parts of a miner's seal-oil lamp. According to Blair's notes:

> From 116 feet 6 inches to 155 feet, the earth in over half of the shaft was much disturbed. How these articles reached a depth of from ten to seventeen feet lower than any searcher ever reached is a question that must be answered. These tools, I believe, belonged to the searchers who worked there many years ago, and had fallen from a much higher level to where found.

Blair wrote that this was evidence to him of an open space beneath what previously had been thought to be the bottom of the Money Pit and into which he believed the treasure chests had fallen. At a depth of about 150 feet, in the softer part of the new shaft, "we commenced to uncover broken up pieces of stone," Blair went on, that had "the appearance of the so-called cement." These appeared to have been "dropped or dumped from a higher point," further convincing him that the treasure had plunged somewhere deeper into the earth when the Money Pit collapsed in 1861.

> The question now is, where is the wood and treasure—metal in pieces—which dropped from 100 feet, the iron struck at 126 feet by drillers, the cement and wood drilled into between 153 and 157 feet, and the iron at 171 feet? It appears as if we had

gone past them. They certainly must be somewhere in the near vicinity of our Pit.

The Chappell crew believed they might have made a major discovery at 155 feet below the surface, when, as William Chappell's nephew Claude Chappell recalled it, "we came to a short seam of shale rock and more water started coming in. It was coming in from three or four feet on one side; it wasn't just coming in from one little hole. It was a round, clearly defined tunnel." Several of the diggers said this must be the flood tunnel from the south shore.

At a depth of 163 feet, 6 inches, the company began to send tunnels in all directions, "but without locating foreign material," as Blair put it. "Although the conditions did not appear natural."

As the summer faded into autumn and the weather worsened, the Chappell expedition started to be bedeviled by a series of near catastrophes. The electrical system running the pump was damaged repeatedly by storms, and the pump's subsequent failures almost cost men their lives. The nearest miss involved Chappell's foreman, George Stevenson, who was in the tunnel at the 157-foot level when suddenly rising water caused the earth to soften and the walls of the tunnel to collapse. Stevenson was nearly entombed before his men pulled him out—covered head to toe in mud and gasping for breath—by the rope attached to his waist. Subsequent accidents over the next few days resulted in two other men suffering broken ribs. Finally, on October 29, 1931, bowing to the weather, the Chappell crew suspended work. Blair was "more convinced than ever—if that be possible—that there is treasure there," he wrote in his journal two days later. He and the Chappells agreed that work would resume in the spring of 1932. William Chappell's brothers, though, were unhappy that he had spent $40,000 without anything tangible to show for it other than some old artifacts. The Great Depression was finally hitting home even in Nova Scotia, and their receipts were dwindling, the Chappell brothers said. They could not agree to support further efforts on Oak Island.

William Chappell's counterargument became moot when Sophia Sellers died that year and Blair was unable to persuade her heirs to let him renew his lease on the Money Pit. Early in 1932, a New York engineer named John Talbot showed up in Nova Scotia and said he was representing a "financial interest" headed by the wealthy heiress Mary B. Stewart. Talbot apparently offered the heirs enough to gain their permission to spend seven weeks on Oak Island drilling in and around the Money Pit. He found nothing of note and abandoned the effort when his drill broke at a depth of about 50 feet just northwest of what had become known as the Chappell shaft. In the end, the most notable result of the New York concern's foray on Oak Island was the disappearance of the famous ivory boatswain's whistle that had been found in 1885. It was delivered to Mary B. Stewart in Manhattan in August 1932 and has never been seen since.

"If we had that whistle, and could date it, we might know who did the original work on Oak Island," Rick Lagina would tell me sorrowfully in August 2016.

"Might" and "know," I found myself thinking, could be the two most fraught words in the history of Oak Island.

CHAPTER NINE

It was the year 1933 that the erstwhile treasure hunter Franklin Delano Roosevelt became the thirty-second president of the United States, and also about when Oak Island historians began to turn decisively away from the Captain Kidd theory.

Thomas Nixon of Victoria, British Columbia, was the man running the operations on Oak Island during the early part of Roosevelt's first term in office. Nixon's place in the chronicle of the island would be just one more chapter consisting of grand announcements, elaborate plans, and less elaborate implementation, ending in an abysmal but familiar failure, except for the theory he brought to the treasure hunt and the method by which he had arrived at it. If Nixon proved anything, it was that the Oak Island story could and would get stranger.

Like Captain Bowdoin, Nixon would use the New York newspapers to announce his bold and thrilling claim about what it was that had been buried on Oak Island. His Canadian Oak Island Treasure Company was "equipped with the latest engineering apparatus," according to the story Nixon planted in the October 15, 1933, edition of the *New York Herald Tribune*. This redundant boast would likely have attracted little attention if not for the claim that the works on Oak Island had been completed by "a tribe of Incas" who had fled their homes hundreds of years earlier "carrying jewels and precious metals," as the *Herald Tribune* article put it. "The legend says the Indians landed on Oak Island and buried their riches in a deep tunnel running from the Atlantic Ocean to the centre of the island, and then vanished."

What the article didn't say was that this "legend" was the product of what at the time was known as "spirit rapping." This was a method of alleged communication with the souls of the dead that involved messages tapped out, most commonly on a tabletop. It had become a kind of craze in the United States during the years immediately before and after the Civil War, owing in large part to the public fascination with a pair of young teen sisters from New York State named Maggie and Kate Fox, whose supporters included Horace Greeley and Arthur Conan Doyle.

In the context of the era, it was perhaps understandable that Frederick Blair might form a partnership with a man who claimed to have learned during a séance that it was Inca treasure buried on Oak Island. And it couldn't have hurt that Nixon's psychic was referencing perhaps the richest lost treasure ever known to have existed.

Certain elements of the story of the so-called treasure of Tumbes are foggy conflations, but many others are as solid and certain as anything we call history can be. This story begins in the early sixteenth century, when an aspiring conquistador named Francisco Pizarro joined a colonization expedition to the New World. Pizarro, seeking to become as wealthy and famous as his distant cousin Hernán Cortés, the conqueror of the Aztec empire, distinguished himself in several battles with native tribes and by the year 1526 had risen to the position of second in command of the Spanish army in the region of Darien, in what we now know as Peru and Ecuador. In 1527 and 1528, Pizarro and his troops twice visited the city of Tumbes, where the people we today call the Incas lived (actually "Inca" was a term that could only be used by their king), and each time were stunned by the wealth and splendor of a place where even weapons and tools were made of silver and gold, and heaps of enormous emeralds filled vases and jars surrounding statues made entirely of precious metals.

Lacking the force to challenge the natives, Pizarro retreated all the way back to Spain, where he entreated King Charles to finance a military expedition that would claim the fabulous treasures of Tumbes.

Charles agreed and even stipulated that Pizarro would be governor of any lands he conquered.

Pizarro and his troops marched back into Tumbes in the autumn of 1532, but found the city in ruins and its treasures gone. There is a claim based on some historical evidence that the two priests Pizarro had left behind to minister to the natives instead warned the Incas of Pizarro's intentions and helped them move and conceal the treasure of Tumbes. Whether that is so, it is a certifiable fact that from Tumbes, Pizarro marched his men to the Inca city of Cajamarca, home of the newly crowned Inca king Atahualpa. With a force of just 160 men (but also several cannons that they used to devastating effect), the Spaniards routed an Inca honor guard of some six thousand and captured Atahualpa. The king quickly promised Pizarro that he would fill a room 24 feet long by 18 feet wide by 8 feet tall with gold and give him twice that amount of silver if his life was spared. Pizarro agreed and during the next two months the Inca began to deliver the promised precious metals. The gold and silver came slowly, though, and Pizarro and his men began to believe that the natives were using the time to assemble their eighty thousand men into an enormous army to rescue Atahualpa and destroy the Spanish. Pizarro's response was to announce in August 1533 that Atahualpa would be burned at the stake for his supposed crimes against humanity. The Inca king converted to Christianity to spare himself such a fate, but Pizarro then ordered that Atahualpa be garroted, and he was. The general of the Inca army responded by ordering that the 750 tons of gold he was bringing to secure his king's release now be hidden from the Spanish. The hiding place is most often said to be a cave in the Llanganates, a remote and misty mountain range between the Andes and the Amazon, in what is now central Ecuador.

Other stories and legends about what happened to the fabulous Inca treasure began to emerge even before the beginning of the seventeenth century. One often-repeated story was that the priests Pizarro left behind had aided the Incas in moving the treasure to the Isthmus of Darien (today the Isthmus of Panama), where the priests helped the Inca either obtain or build the ships they would use to transport the treasure to one of the Windward Islands (stretching from Dominica to Trinidad and Tobago). Eventually, the story became that the boats carrying the Inca treasure had been swept up and away by a series of enormous tropical storms and hurricanes that struck the Caribbean (the historical record suggests that the tempests that struck the region in the year 1530 were of astounding and terrifying force) and were swept north to some distant location, where the treasure of Tumbes was cached. Not until the advent of Thomas Nixon, though, was that location identified as Oak Island.

It was perhaps because he had no other offers at the moment that Blair reached an agreement with Nixon that would allow the British Columbia man to work on Oak Island between April and November 1934 on the condition that half of any treasure he found would go to Blair. His plan, Nixon had told both Blair and his backers, was to drive interlocking pilings around the Money Pit until he created a steel circle with a diameter of between 50 and 75 feet. He would then excavate the entire contents of this enormous enclosure as deep as he needed to go to recover the treasure. Instead, Nixon and his crew arrived on Oak Island in June 1934 and did no digging at all. What Nixon did do was bore fourteen holes that went as deep as 170 feet in the vicinity of the Money Pit. The most interesting things he brought up were bits of old oak timbers and fragments of gold-and-blue china. On November 1, 1934, Blair refused Nixon's request for an extension and terminated their relationship. Nixon threatened legal action, but in the end simply withdrew and disappeared from the Oak Island story.

The theory that it was Inca treasure buried on Oak Island, though, did not vanish with him. It would be revived by at least one self-appointed investigator in every decade that followed. So in his fleeting way, Thomas Nixon might be said to have pioneered the proliferation of theories about who or what was responsible for the work on Oak Island. Thus it might also be fitting that Nixon was about to be succeeded by the man who was the first to recognize that the answers to his questions might be written in the very topography of the island.

CHAPTER TEN

By the time Gilbert Hedden joined the Oak Island treasure hunt in 1935, he was as apparently well set financially as anyone who had preceded him. After graduating from the Rensselaer Polytechnic Institute in 1919, Hedden had become, at age twenty-two, the vice president and general manager of his family's business, Hedden Iron Construction Company of Hillside, New Jersey, fabricators and erectors of structural steel. He pocketed a tidy sum as his share of the company's sale to Bethlehem Steel in 1931 and earned a significant annual salary as plant manager of what Bethlehem was now calling its Hedden Works division. There was an independent spirit in the young man that chafed against corporate constraints, though, so in 1932 he walked away from Hedden Works to try the auto industry. By 1934, he was the owner of a thriving dealership in Morristown, New Jersey. In nearby Chatham, where he lived, Hedden was elected mayor that same year.

The dreamer in Hedden was not satisfied with this sort of conventional prosperity, however. That part of him had responded powerfully to an article about Oak Island that was published in the May 28, 1928, edition of the *New York Times Magazine*, an article that he carried with him and read repeatedly. The engineering challenge was what fascinated him, Hedden would say initially. In early 1934 he made a trip to Nova Scotia to take a look at the Money Pit area of Oak Island and make a close inspection of the problem it posed. Like Frederick Blair, Hedden was methodical, collecting all the available data that went back to 1795, studying every expedition to the island in the years since. He was all about separating fact from fiction, Hedden told Blair and his lawyer, R. V. Harris. He interviewed William Chappell and at least a dozen other men who had been part of previous treasure-hunting companies and began to assemble his own journal, one that rivaled Blair's in length and detail. "Investigation of the Legend of Buried Treasure at Oak Island, Nova Scotia," Hedden titled his thirty-one-page monograph, to which he attached an assortment of old surveys, charts, and aerial photographs of the island. Blair, effectively Hedden's partner by virtue of his continued hold on the treasure trove license, shared all of his records, letters, and plans. Only after completing a thorough study of those as well was Hedden prepared to state with conviction that he believed something extraordinary had taken place on Oak Island, something singular in the history of the world. He might not have known it yet, but Hedden was hooked for life.

Blair was pleased to hear Hedden's opinion, but he wanted to know what the man proposed to do about it. Blair might have lost his lease on the Money Pit area after failing to reach a deal with Sophia Sellers's heirs, who were demanding far too "fancy" a price for their property as he wrote Harris, but he still held the treasure trove license, which made him indispensable to any further Oak Island operations. On March 1, 1935, Blair and Hedden signed a deal that guaranteed each of them a share of any treasure recovered on the island, with Blair to lend his experience and expertise and Hedden to finance the work.

There was an immediate threat of complication when the province political leadership proposed that the Nova Scotia Mines Act should be amended to give the Minister of Mines the same authority over treasure troves that the office had over ores and minerals. The bill was explicitly targeted at Oak Island, and this stirred much controversy. The Mines Act amendment was ultimately killed in committee, but the heirs of Sophia Sellers had had their inflated sense of the value of the land affirmed and refused to sell for even two or three times what it was worth. Hedden was so determined to acquire the Sellers's Oak Island lots that he eventually agreed to pay the heirs $5,000, close to ten times the land's appraised value. He and the Sellers heirs signed their deed of sale in July 1935.

Hedden immediately impressed Blair with his seriousness by bringing electricity to the island by an underwater cable, building a wharf at
Smith's Cove, having the island surveyed, and building himself a cabin
not far north of the Money Pit. Blair was not happy, though, when Hedden announced that he had hired Sprague and Henwood, the Scranton,
Pennsylvania, company that had previously worked on Oak Island for
the Rochester Group in 1916, to "de-water" and excavate the Money
Pit and most of the other shafts surrounding it, then to drill laterally at
depths between 125 and 160 feet. "There does not appear to be anything
very decisive about the work outlined," Blair groused in a letter to Harris, "it being more along the lines of previous operations and open to
failure without definite results."

Hedden had money to spend, however. The man he selected to
lead his operation was Frederick Krupp, an engineer who had headed
major drilling operations on Africa's Gold Coast and in Persia. Blair
had to admit some satisfaction in seeing men who knew what they were
doing, equipped with the finest machinery that had ever been brought to
Oak Island, including turbine pumps fed by a 7,500-watt hydroelectric
power line that would empty the Money Pit and the other shafts at a
rate of 1,000 gallons per minute.

Based on what he had learned from William Chappell, Hedden instructed his crew to open and drain the Chappell shaft (no. 21),
strengthen the cribbing on its walls, then send drills in all directions.
The work began in June 1936 and before the end of the month the
men were working on a platform 90 feet deep in the shaft. When their
drills brought up oak splinters from a depth of 150 feet, both Blair and
Hedden agreed the wood must have come from either a box of some
kind or the platform that had fallen during the 1861 collapse. Below
165 feet, the drills struck granite boulders that had to be dragged to
the surface one at a time. The shaft was then retimbered to a depth of
170 feet, the deepest the cribbing had ever gone on Oak Island. At the
bottom, they found the earth "much disturbed," as Blair put it, but no
sign of treasure chests.

After adjourning for the winter, the Hedden crew was back on Oak Island in May 1937, when the men began work on the shaft that would become no. 22, determined to make it twice the size of the Money Pit, 12 feet by 24 feet. They dug into an old shaft cribbed with double pieces of 3-inch planking that was in fair shape and believed they had encompassed the Money Pit. By the end of June, the workmen were at a depth of 50 feet, where they found nearly a dozen 2-inch drill casings and several 6-inch casings. At 65 feet they found an old tin miner's lamp partially filled with whale oil and a piece of unexploded dynamite that Hedden decided had been left behind by the Oak Island Association in 1867. At 93 feet, they found what they were certain must be one of the original flood tunnels, mostly collapsed. Close by, the men discovered what appeared to be primitive putty. Hedden matched this against the putty that had been used to seal the windows of an old shack left by the Onslow Company and decided it was the same stuff.

At 106 feet, the Hedden crew found a tunnel 3 feet, 10 inches wide by 6 feet, 4 inches high, lined with 5- and 6-inch planks of hemlock timber. Following the timbering of the tunnel, the men reported that it passed through the Money Pit in an arc, as if part of a circle. They had found part of the Fraser tunnel from the 1860s, Hedden decided, which meant they were very close to the original shaft. At 124 feet, the crew stopped digging down and began to bore lateral 42-foot-long holes from the floor of the shaft. When oak fragments were brought up from five of the holes, Hedden and his men were jubilant, believing they must have hit the treasure. Winter was coming on hard by then, however, so Hedden ordered his men to seal things up tight so they could resume work in the spring of 1938.

This decision was "a grievous disappointment" to Frederick Blair, as his attorney, Harris, put it. The discoveries made by Hedden's people convinced Blair that they had confirmed the location of the Money Pit and he was tremendously excited. The drill casings, the unexploded dynamite and, especially, the old lamp filled with whale oil were all solid evidence they were in the original shaft, but what he found most convincing, Blair said, were the oak borings brought up from below 125 feet, just as they had been by the pot auger back in 1866 and again in 1897.

Hedden concurred, writing to Blair's lawyer, Harris, that he was convinced an unknown number of treasure chests were buried on Oak Island at a depth of between 160 and 175 feet and that they were encrusted with hardened blue clay. He believed the original chests had rotted and the treasure itself was embedded in that belt of blue clay. It must be a fantastic treasure, Hedden added, given the precautions that had been taken to protect it.

What neither Blair nor Hedden knew at that moment, however, was that Hedden was done digging on Oak Island. By November 1937, the New Jersey man had sunk more than $51,000 into the Oak Island search and from a financial standpoint his timing couldn't have been worse. The US Internal Revenue Service had filed a civil lawsuit against him that month, claiming back taxes related to the sale of his father's steel business in 1931. Years of litigation and attachments would follow. Suddenly desperate for cash, Hedden decided on a rapid expansion of his auto dealership back in New Jersey.

In March 1938, Hedden wrote to Blair's attorney, Harris, that because of the demands of his business, "I shall have to postpone my activities on the Oak Island adventure rather indefinitely." He asked the lawyer "to correspond with Blair and inform him of the present condition and of the fact that I will be unable to proceed any further this summer and possibly next."

Blair, unaware of Hedden's financial circumstances, was crestfallen and bitter. He was seventy-one years old, convinced that his last best chance to bring the Oak Island treasure up from below was evaporating before his eyes. Hedden's withdrawal was "nothing more or less than a downright betrayal," Blair wrote to Harris.

Those who followed after him, though, would eventually credit Gilbert Hedden as perhaps the most visionary treasure hunter ever to set foot on Oak Island, and as a man who made some of the most significant findings in the entire history of the endeavor. During the summer of 1936, while Frederick Krupp directed the work in the Money Pit area, Hedden had spent most of his time exploring the rest of Oak Island. In July 1936, he had been combing the beach at Joudrey's Cove when a granite rock about the size of two fists caught his attention. He dug it out and discovered the Roman numeral *II* carved into one of the rock's flat surfaces and below that the letters *GIN*, which looked to be a fragment of a word. The name McGinnis came to mind immediately. Locals who had worked on the island in previous decades told Hedden that the rock was part of a much larger boulder that had been blasted apart with dynamite back in the 1920s so that the crew could dig beneath it. Nothing was found, and afterward a number of men had carried away pieces of the boulder as souvenirs. That particular boulder had been of some interest, the former workmen told Hedden, because of the inscriptions etched into it. Some appeared to have been made during the nineteenth century, but there were other "strange symbols" that seemed much older.

To the exasperation of Blair and the amusement of the men on his crew, Hedden pulled them out of the Money Pit to spend two days searching the shoreline at Joudrey's Cove. Two more large inscribed rocks were discovered by the men, one etched with the letter *W* and another reading "S.S. Ross 1864," marks made, Hedden assumed, by a man who had worked with the Oak Island Association. But then a fourth and much larger inscribed rock was found, and the symbols carved into this one appeared to be much more weathered—and therefore much older than those on the other rocks—and were utterly indecipherable to Hedden and his crewmen. Hedden had the four slabs of rock rafted around the island to his dock at Smith's Cove, then hauled by a team of horses to his cabin near the Money Pit. When he attempted to fit the pieces together, though, nothing matched, which to Hedden meant he was missing many pieces of the original boulder that must indeed have been taken by the men who had blasted it apart back in the 1920s. Convinced that at least the most weathered of the inscriptions on the largest rock predated the discovery of the Money Pit, Hedden began to consider the possibility that the solution to the mystery of the island might have been left behind on the ground by the men who first dug the Pit and did the rest of the original work on Oak Island.

Hedden also studied the south shore during the summer of 1936, and in the process became convinced (as would later be proven accurate) that the shoreline there was eroding at the rate of 2 feet every forty years, which meant that much of the land trod upon by those who did the original work on Oak Island was now underwater. This made him curious about what might be found at low tide on Smith's Cove, and Hedden was soon rewarded with the discovery of two large timbers protruding from the rocks well inside the cofferdam that had been constructed by the Oak Island Association back in 1863. Hedden at first believed he was looking at a skidway built during the construction of the cofferdam, but he realized this was not so when he studied the two timbers more closely. They were each about 15 inches in diameter at the base and notched for a quarter of their circumference every 4 feet, where they had been fitted with cross members that had been attached with wooden pins. Suddenly Hedden realized that he was looking at the remnants of a much older structure, something that had been built back in a time when wooden pins were easier to make than iron bolts or champs, something, that is, that predated the early eighteenth century.

It would be almost forty years before anyone realized the full significance of what Hedden had discovered at Smith's Cove, but there is no question that the man himself understood the importance of the features he found during the following summer in 1937. Foremost among these was what has become known as the stone triangle. The process by which Hedden rediscovered the triangle (first spotted by Captain Welling in 1897), though, may have been as significant as the discovery itself, and it is certainly more captivating.

In June 1937, shortly after Hedden returned to Nova Scotia to spend his second summer on Oak Island, R. V. Harris, who had become Hedden's attorney as well as Blair's, showed him a recently published book titled *Captain Kidd and His Skeleton Island*, written by the English author Harold T. Wilkins. There was a map of an island used as an illustration in the book that bore remarkable similarities to Oak Island. Hedden was immediately fascinated, noting that the configurations of the shoreline of the mapped island in Wilkins's book, along with its offshore water depths and shoals were indeed similar to those of Oak Island. Even more striking, though, was that the island depicted on the map featured two mountains on its east and west ends, along with a sunken lagoon between them, correlating closely to the two drumlins and the swamp on Oak Island. On the Wilkins's map, there was also an X to mark the spot that was situated almost exactly where the Money Pit stood on Oak Island.

The Wilkins map bore a legend that read "W.K. 1669" and below that a handwritten list of distances and bearings:

18 W and 7 E on Rock
30 SW 14 N Tree
7 by 8 by 4

The island in the Wilkins book was not named and there was no latitude or longitude marked. The water surrounding the island was identified only by the words "Mar Del."

Wilkins claimed that the map and three similar to it had been in the secret compartments of a desk that had belonged to William Kidd. Such maps, Hedden would learn, really did exist, and the story of how they had come to the attention of Harold Wilkins enchanted him.

The principal players in this drama were a pair of "bachelor brothers" (as they were described in the British newspapers at the time) named Guy and Hubert Palmer. The Palmers were the curators of a well-regarded private museum of pirate and nautical history. Hubert Palmer was considered to be perhaps the planet's leading authority on the epoch of high seas piracy, and he maintained a particular interest in anything associated with the life and times of Captain William Kidd. In the better publications of his period, Hubert Palmer was regularly described as remarkably discerning, known to subject any items offered to him to the best available experts for authentication.

In the early 1930s, Hubert had acquired a desk he believed had been used by Captain Kidd aboard the *Adventure Galley*. During his inspection of the desk, Hubert found four hidden compartments, two made by false bottoms in drawers, one behind a mirror and the other—and presumably most significant—in a small hole that had been drilled in a side runner of the desk and fitted with a small brass cylinder. Each of the compartments contained a hand-drawn map.

These maps would become known as Captain Kidd's treasure charts after Hubert Palmer submitted them to the British Museum for authentication. The work was performed by a team under the supervision of R. A. Skelton, the superintendent of the museum's Map Room. In his report, Skelton wrote that the maps were so old and fragile they might be destroyed by "direct photographic reproduction," so he made hand-drawn copies of the originals with notes of what he could make out of the writing and markings on the maps.

Harold Wilkins had seen the treasure charts during a visit to the British Museum, where R. A. Skelton had permitted the author to examine but not to touch them. Apparently, Wilkins had used what he had seen as the basis for the maps that illustrated his book. Wilkins was an odd fellow to say the least, Hedden had been told. Once a Cambridge-educated journalist, he had become perhaps the most infamous "pseudohistorian" of his time, one who had first attracted attention with his claims about the *Mary Celeste*, an American merchant brigantine that on December 5, 1872, had been discovered deserted and adrift in the Atlantic Ocean near the Azores Islands. The mystery of what had happened to the captain and his crew was one that would fascinate the public for decades afterward, and Wilkins had fed that appetite with a largely unsupported claim that the men of the *Mary Celeste* had been lured aboard another ship and slaughtered. He also produced works that claimed a vanished white race had once populated South America, that the survivors of Atlantis were living deep underground in immense caverns, and that planet Earth was being watched by hostile aliens. In spite of all that, Hedden was riveted by what he found to be undeniable similarities between Wilkins's Mar Del map and Oak Island.

When Hedden wrote to Wilkins in the summer of 1937, however, pointing out those similarities and requesting additional information about how he had obtained his map, the author wrote back that there could be no connection to Oak Island because he knew the latitude and longitude of the island on the Mar Del map and it was in the Eastern Hemisphere. Furthermore, Wilkins added that William Kidd had never been anywhere near Nova Scotia, and he urged Hedden not to waste his time pursuing such a notion.

In spite of that, Hedden persisted. He was so convinced that there was a connection between Wilkins's map and Oak Island that in August 1937 he ordered his men to discontinue their excavation work in the Money Pit area and join him in a search of the island based on the distances and bearings from the Mar Del map.

Blair was not pleased, but he consulted with Hedden anyway, and for the first time informed his partner of some features that had been discovered by Captain John Welling back in 1897. One of these, Blair said, was a white granite boulder about 50 feet north of the Money Pit with a 1.25-inch hole through its center that had clearly been drilled by human hands. The other feature Blair described was the stone triangle, lost during the forty years since Welling first observed it.

On August 15, the curious Hedden ordered his crew to search for the triangle of stones Blair had described. A workman named Amos Nauss was "clawing around" with a hoe in the underbrush above Smith's Cove when, as he described it years later to the Canadian journalist D'Arcy O'Connor, "Suddenly I hit one rock, then another and another, all in line with each other."

When the rest of the crew helped Nauss clear away the underbrush, they found an equilateral triangle made out of round beach stones set in the grass just above the high-water mark on the south shore. Each side of the triangle was 10 feet in length. After further examination, Hedden noticed that from a point on the baseline 4 feet from the west corner of the triangle and 6 feet from the east corner, there was a medial line, also composed of round beach stones, which connected the base of the triangle with its apex. The triangle also featured a curved line of beach stones 3 feet below the base that connected both corners of the base, giving the entire design the outline of an enormous sextant.

What truly excited Hedden, though, was that when he followed the sight line from the stone triangle to the white granite boulder and then beyond, he discovered—just a bit more than 400 feet away—a second granite boulder that had also been drilled through and in exactly the same way as the other: with its hole in alignment with the hole in the first boulder. Hedden was at this point so convinced of the significance of his discoveries that he engaged the services of a land surveyor from Halifax named Charles Roper, who was boated to the island the next day, August 16, 1937, and immediately began making measurements between the drilled boulders and the stone triangle.

The distance between the drilled boulders was almost exactly 25 rods (about 415 feet) Roper reported to Hedden. Using the top numbers from the list of distances and bearings on the Mar Del map, Hedden instructed Roper to establish a point on the line between the drill holes that was 18 rods east of the drilled boulder near Smith's Cove and 7 rods west of the boulder nearer to the Money Pit. Roper did as instructed and found himself standing right next to the Cave-in Pit. Hedden was impressed enough to tell Roper he should lay in a course directly from this point toward the south shore. At a distance of 30 rods from the point next to the Cave-in Pit, Roper struck the medial line of the stone triangle just below the triangle's east-west base. It was then that Roper realized—stumbled on the realization, really—that the medial line of the stone triangle was pointing perfectly due north, directly at the pole-star. He and Hedden then followed that line toward the drumlin on the east end of the island and found that it led directly to the center of the Money Pit.

Hedden was flabbergasted and ecstatic. What convinced him he had made a monumental discovery, though, was when Roper determined that the sight lines of the drilled boulders not only ran through the medial line of the stone triangle, but also into the center of the Money Pit. There could be no doubt, Hedden told Blair, that the designer or designers of the original works on Oak Island had placed the drilled stones and created the stone triangle so the location of the Pit would never be lost to them.

Hedden was so excited that he dashed off a letter to President Roosevelt on September 1, 1937, detailing the discoveries he had made that summer. Hedden wrote that he had reached several solid conclusions:

> First, that a large amount of complicated and difficult engineering was done on the site for some purpose a long time ago, probably as early as 1640.
>
> Second, that Kidd [based on the Mar Del map, Hedden was at that point sticking with the story of the famous pirate's involvement] knew of the site and of the work and probably who did it, but was not aware of its exact location.
>
> Third, that the early legends of the discovery of the shaft, the tunnels, the peculiar fiber, the mysterious stone with the inscription . . . are to a large part true and can be, in large part, substantiated today.

FDR replied with a letter in which he thanked Hedden for the news, then added: "It vividly recalls to my mind our semi-serious, semi-pleasure efforts at Oak Island nearly thirty years ago. I can visualize the theories on which you are working. As I remember it, we also talked of sinking a new shaft on our main run out."

That autumn, Hedden decided he had to speak in person to Harold Wilkins. On November 10, 1937, not yet aware that the IRS was about to initiate the actions that would ruin him, Hedden boarded the Cunard ocean liner *Aquitania*, bound for London. Upon arrival, he found

Wilkins, but the meeting was not nearly so fulfilling as he had hoped. All we know of what transpired between the two men is in the letter Hedden wrote the next day to R. V. Harris: "Wilkins is a very peculiar character," Hedden told the attorney. "And it is difficult to describe him adequately. I would say that in appearance and manner of speech he is every bit as crazy as his book would seem to make him."

Wilkins had almost immediately admitted that the Mar Del map in his book was "a figment of his imagination," Hedden went on, "and apologized sincerely for not being able to tell me before that it was." To his astonishment, Wilkins had found himself under siege after the publication of *Captain Kidd and His Skeleton Island* and on the receiving end of letters from all over the world written by men who believed they knew exactly where the island on the Mar Del map was. And yet, Hedden wrote, "He admitted my claims to identify far surpass any others he had received and agreed that his drawing was according to the evidence undoubtedly of Oak Island." He had concocted the map for no other reason than that his publisher had demanded one for the frontispiece of the book, and "therefore drew the chart as shown, using symbols and marks shown on contemporary charts on file in the British Museum. Somehow, he had "unconsciously" drawn what he had seen when he looked at Hubert Palmer's Captain Kidd treasure charts.

Hedden was baffled. There was no satisfying or even entirely rational way to explain the similarities between Wilkins's Mar Del map and Oak Island, and the fact that Hedden's attempt to follow the measurements and bearings on the Mar Del map had led him to connections between the stone triangle, the drilled stones, and the Money Pit was perplexing to say the least.

Hedden returned home to New Jersey just in time to learn that the IRS was suing him. The court battles that ensued would bankrupt him, yet Hedden refused for another dozen years to surrender his ownership of the lots in Nova Scotia that included the Money Pit to pay off his debts. When the IRS attempted to put his Oak Island property up for sale, Hedden fought them off fiercely. And while he may not have done further exploration *on* the island, his search for answers about what had happened there continued to be a driving force in an unfolding narrative.

THE FIRST TIME I WAS ASKED publicly what I thought of the pirate treasure theory of Oak Island, I scoffed. It was difficult to imagine a band of pirates burying treasure in a hole more than 10 feet deep and the idea that buccaneers would create a complexly engineered shaft that went down more than 100 feet into the earth was ridiculous. Oak Island historian Charles Barkhouse readily agreed with me, which was something of a balm to my embarrassment when I learned months later about what pirates had done on the islands of Tortuga and Jamaica.

The labyrinths of tunnels and underground chambers on both Caribbean islands, created both to store booty and as avenues of escape, rivaled in complexity what had been done on Oak Island and surpassed it in scope. And it was pirates who had designed and dug the underground works on Tortuga and at Jamaica's famous pirate haven Port Royal. So there had been pirate engineers after all, and there were pirates either willing to do the hard labor of excavation on a tremendous scale or to make slaves do it. And they had done it mainly for the purpose of protecting their booty, I realized, a fact that disagreed with my belief that Oak Island must be about something more than gold or silver.

I learned of what had been done on the two Caribbean islands while preparing (I imagined) to skewer yet another of the alternative theories of Oak Island that had proliferated in recent years. This one involved the idea that what had been created on Oak Island was a sort of "pirate bank" where buccaneers from different bands could keep their loot in a secure repository. I found the idea absurd. Not only was the notion that pirates would have joined together in such an organized and trusting fashion far-fetched, but it was also incomprehensible to me that they would have left their booty untouched. And if they had come back for their gold and silver, they would certainly not have sealed things up so neatly before departing. After learning about the works that had been created on Tortuga and at Port Royal, however, I wasn't prepared to be quite so absolute in my opinion. This was what Oak Island did to people: gradually, it became impossible to completely dismiss any theory of what the works on the island were about.

I had been talking this over with the Lagina brothers and the producers of *The Curse of Oak Island* when one of them (I honestly don't remember who) brought up Harold Wilkins's Mar Del map, which had been featured on an earlier episode of the show. This led me to the discovery of the story of Hubert Palmer's Captain Kidd treasure charts, a subject with which the producers and the Laginas weren't familiar. The producers became interested, urging me to see if I could locate Palmer's original charts. Kevin Burns, who had created the show, seemed particularly excited. I learned that Hubert Palmer had held on to the charts up to the time of his death in 1949 at the age of eighty-five. Palmer had never suggested any connection between the charts and Oak Island, and in fact before taking ill had devoted more than a decade to attempts to organize an expedition to the South China Sea, where he believed Captain Kidd had buried his treasure on a deserted island. In his will, Palmer had specified that the charts and all of his other pirate artifacts should go Mrs. Elizabeth Dick, the "nurse-companion" who had cared for him during the last eleven years of his life and who had shared his belief that the Captain Kidd treasure charts were the genuine article. Mrs. Dick had lived on until 1965, when she died at the age of seventy-seven, but by then the woman had sold the treasure charts for what at the time was the considerable sum of $50,000. The auction house that brokered the sale in 1957 had identified the purchaser only as the agent of "a North American/Canadian syndicate." The charts were never seen again and I could obtain no more information about who had purchased them, I told the producers, unless I was sent to Eastbourne, England, where Hubert Palmer had maintained his home and where the maps had been sold.

Excited as they were about the maps, the producers weren't willing to spend what it would cost to send me (with a camera crew, of course) to England, especially after Rick and Marty Lagina insisted they would be coming along if the trip happened. "Find out what you can about the copies of the maps that were made," one of the producers suggested. "Maybe we can get a look at those."

I assumed the copies of the charts that R. A. Skelton had made back in the 1930s were still somewhere in the archives of the British Museum, but I got absolutely no help at all from the museum in locating them. Eventually, I was able to obtain copies of the copies that Skelton had made. When they arrived in Nova Scotia, I was terribly disappointed.

The famous treasure charts were four crudely hand-drawn maps of what appeared to be the same vaguely boomerang-shaped island. The island wrapped around what was marked as "Lagoon" on three of the four maps, with a simple directional chart that was identical on all four of them. There were some variations; an area on the opposite side of the island from the lagoon was marked "Sand and Coral" on two of the maps, but it had a notation that read "Wood—20 Turtles" above markings for twin "Reefs" on another. One map did note two hills on the island, but they were right next to one another rather than at opposite ends of the island. The most detailed map identified the body of water beyond the lagoon as "China Sea." There were a list of directions and bearings on two of the treasure charts, but they were quite different from those on Harold Wilkins's Mar Del map.

Chagrined, I took some comfort from the discovery that many before me had been led into some fruitless pursuit by stories of an Oak Island map. Back in 1894, Frederick Blair had been excited by a story that was published the day after Christmas in the *Boston Traveller* about some unnamed individual who nearly fifty years earlier had found a "plan" of an island on Nova Scotia's southeast coast that had once been a pirate rendezvous. A large ship's block hung from a branch of a large oak tree on the island where the block and its tackle had been used in the sinking of a deep shaft, the story went on, a shaft that was filled with seawater by a tunnel deep underground. For reasons unknown to the writer and his anonymous source, however, the pirate treasure had never been placed in the shaft, but instead it was buried only 20 feet belowground at a certain distance from the oak tree. The shaft was merely a "blind" intended to distract those who might stumble on the spot. Blair spent months trying to obtain a copy of the "plan" mentioned in the *Traveller* article, but was unsuccessful and eventually decided that the story had been invented by some joker who had read the prospectus of the Oak Island Treasure Company.

Blair was also captivated for a time by another story of an Oak Island map that had originated in Boston. This one repeated the story of pirates who had spent months excavating a deep pit and digging tunnels that would fill the shaft with seawater. In this iteration, the pirates and their ship were captured by two British frigates whose officers hanged the pirate leaders and sent most of the rest of the crew to an English prison. One slow-witted fellow, though, was spared punishment and made his way to Bristol, England, where he sketched a chart of the spot where the treasure pit had been dug and gave it to a young sailor who was about to set sail on his first voyage. When his ship docked in Nova Scotia, the sailor gave the chart to a Halifax harbor pilot who held on to it until he was an elderly retiree and showed it to his grandson. It was the grandson who realized that the chart was of Oak Island. He made his way from his home in Roxbury, Massachusetts, to Nova Scotia, only to learn that an insurance man living back in Boston by the name of Frederick Blair held the legal rights to search for treasure on Oak Island. When Blair heard this story, he assigned R. V. Harris to interview the grandson and his father and to obtain signed affidavits from each man. The affidavit of the younger man, one James H. Smith, read:

> When I was a boy living at home in Greenfield, Colchester County, Nova Scotia, I frequently heard my father, John J. Smith, speak of a chart, then in possession of his father, Amos Smith, who lived in Shaw's Cove, County of Halifax, Nova Scotia.
>
> According to my father, John J. Smith, the chart had reference to the burial of a quantity of gold on an island in Chester

Basin, Nova Scotia, and that my grandfather, Amos Smith, who
had been a pilot working in and out of Halifax Harbour, claimed
that the longitude and latitude given him of the said chart was in
the vicinity to the entrance to Chester Bay and that this island
was Oak Island.

His grandfather had described an island "about one mile in length
and about one-half mile in width, shaped like a bottle, two coves at the
northeast end forming the bottleneck; and the island was wooded with
oak trees." According to Amos Smith, pirates had dug a pit "to a depth
of 165 feet, near a large oak tree, from a limb of which they hung a block
and tackle, and that a vault was constructed at the bottom of the pit, and
the vault was lined with granite stone, eighteen inches thick and that
the inside was lined with gold bars, each four feet long and four inches
square, and it was then covered with granite slabs. Two tunnels were
dug forty-five feet below sea-level, at low tide, leading from the pit to
the shore, in opposite directions, and there was placed in each tunnel an
iron gate arranged so as to stop the flow of water, but these gates were
left open to permit the water to flow through."

Blair was tremendously excited until he discovered that Amos
Smith had never been a pilot for Halifax Harbour, but rather for St.
Margaret's Bay, the next major inlet to the west. Blair and Harris eventually concluded that Amos Smith had made up the entire story based
on things he had heard about the searches conducted on Oak Island
between 1804 and 1864.

A character known as Captain Allen actually did have an old chart
with him when he showed up in Chester during the summer of 1885.
The man had been careful about the questions he asked, the local people
told Harris, but suspicions arose anyway, because Captain Allen was
not the usual sort of fellow one met in these parts. He was a handsome
man with an accent suggestive of the American South who dressed in
expensive clothes and wore the same white broad-brimmed hat day
after day. The man also had a reputation for spending his money rather

freely, especially after paying the exorbitant price of US $1,200 for the little sloop he bought from a fisherman named Ganter at Shad Bay. Captain Allen then hired a pair of brothers named Zinck to work as his crew, paying them well to mind their business and do what they were told. The Zincks talked anyway, when they had a few drinks in them, and claimed that Captain Allen had no interest in fishing and instead spent all of his time aboard studying an old chart with writing on it in a foreign language that one brother said was Swedish and the other said was Spanish. Early every morning, according to the brothers, Captain Allen would have them sail out of Mahone Bay to a position thirty miles offshore where he took the altitude of the sun, then began to consult his chart, directing them back toward shore on a northwest compass bearing that would have taken him to Oak Island if he had continued on the same course, but for some reason he never did. Two full summers Captain Allen did this, then disappeared from Mahone Bay and was never seen again. The fellow who bought his sloop, though, a man from Halifax named Pickels, began doing pretty much the same thing Captain Allen had with the boat, the locals said. Pickels was less careful about what he said than Allen, and he confided to several local people that the captain had provided him with the latitude and longitude of his starting point and the compass directions he should follow. The captain said he had been searching for an island where there was "a huge cache of treasure, so huge that it was beyond imagination." Allen had said he was a wealthy man and didn't need the money, Pickels claimed, but he wanted to recover the treasure for the benefit of mankind. Pickels lasted three summers aboard the sloop, then gave up the search and went back to Halifax, leaving the mystery of Captain Allen's chart behind him.

In his 1899 book *A Search for Pirate Gold*, James Clarence Hyde claimed that Daniel McGinnis had been in possession of a "treasure map" at some point either immediately before or after the discovery of the Money Pit. Strangely, it seemed to me, there was no further published mention of this map until the early twenty-first century, when a descendant named George McInnes told a local investigator that his grandfather, who was born in 1886, had been in possession of this fabled map as a young man, but that it had been lost in a house fire in the 1920s or 1930s. What lent the claims of George McInnes some credibility, at least in my mind, was that he made no attempt to profit from any knowledge of the map that might have been handed down by his family, explaining that because "everything changed" on the island over the years and most of the landmarks on the map had disappeared, it would likely be useless even if it still existed.

Perhaps the most famous story of an Oak Island map appeared in a booklet titled *The Lure of Pirate Gold* written in 1917 by author Josephine Freda for the Chester Board of Trade. A dozen years earlier, in 1905, Freda had written an article for *Collier's* that was considerably more enthusiastic than the piece by Colonel Bowdoin the same magazine would publish in 1912. During the intervening years, she wrote, she had learned of at least one compelling new development in the Oak Island story that suggested the fabled pirate treasure really had been deposited by some among that "horde of lawless and adventurous spirits . . . sailing under the black flag":

> The last will and testament of one of these men has recently been discovered by a gentleman prominent in English literary circles. This gentleman, whose name I am not at liberty to disclose, recently purchased an old manor-house located near a certain seaport in England. Rambling over his new property he one day visited a long-unused room, where the dust lay thick on floor and furniture. His attention was attracted to an old oaken chest covered with quaint carvings. This he opened and discovered within clothing, nautical instruments and a casket containing a considerable sum of money, several old maps or charts and other documents, as well as the last will and testament of their owner.

> The will left all the testator's possessions to his only son, but the young man had been killed in action aboard a British naval ship in 1780,

the first year of the Fourth Anglo-Dutch War, Freda went on. After "care-ful and exhaustive inquiry," she wrote, "the present owner came to the conclusion that the information [contained in the maps, charts, and docu-ments] was of great value and was about to embark on a search for the hidden property when he chanced to read the story of Oak Island [written by Freda] in *Collier's* magazine. He was immediately struck by its remark-able similarity to a certain island indicated on the chart in his possession."

The documents found with the chart "showed that a removal and subsequent deposit of seven separate packages took place on certain dates" after the treasure vault was first created on this "certain island," Freda explained further, "each package bearing separate symbols and initials."

The gentleman currently in possession of both the chart and the documents had been forced to suspend his planned search because of the outbreak of World War I, Freda explained, and she had sworn to protect his identity. But she could reveal that in the casket within the chest in the unused room in his seacoast manor house in England, he had found "a diagram of the Cove on Oak Island . . . which has not been easy to decipher":

> Members of different companies engaged in excavation work
> on Oak Island always believed that documents were in existence
> which would make plain the mystery of the Island, and the dis-
> covery of the old sea-chest shows that their opinion was correct.
>
> I am not at liberty to go more fully into a description of these
> documents, for reasons which must be at once apparent to you,
> but when peace has at last been concluded and men once more
> take up the prosaic routine of daily life, some adventurous spirit
> will no doubt resume the search on Oak Island and finally solve
> for us its fascinating mystery.

Frederick Blair was among those who beseeched Freda to reveal more about the "gentleman" who had found the Oak Island chart, but she adamantly refused, and Blair would admit he could never be sure whether Freda had made the story up or actually interviewed this individual. In any event, the chart itself never surfaced, nor did the man who claimed to possess it.

In 1934, Blair had been offered what became known as the Doyle map. A Saskatchewan man named W. J. Doyle had written to Blair that December after reading an article about Oak Island in Canada's most widely circulated magazine, *MacLean's*, that purported to be a full account of the findings of the Oak Island Treasure Company's Captain John Welling. He had immediately recognized a map that was included in the article as an illustration, Doyle wrote:

> It was about fifty years ago, I was a small boy just starting to school. My father was a teamster and he hired a very old man by the name of Jim Thompson. He worked for my father for a long time and he took a great liking to me, and when he got sick I used to do all his little errands and before he died he gave my father a map of a buried treasure and told him it was for me.

He was in his midtwenties before he came into possession of the map and received the description of the treasure on Oak Island and how to recover it that had been given to his father by Jim Thompson, Doyle wrote: "I used to often take it out and study it, but I knew it would take more money than I had to recover it . . . then, about twenty-nine years ago, I had my place of business burned and I lost the map."

Only when he read the *MacLean's* article did he realize that the "Oak Island" that loomed so large in his imagination was real. Doyle went on:

> Just as soon as I saw the map [in the magazine] I recognized it, but the map I had was drawn with pen and ink; it was very clear; it showed how the water got in, how to shut it off and a few more details which I can still remember.
>
> With the knowledge I have, and if it can be applied, the water can be shut off inside of two or three days and maybe not that

length of time. If it cannot be used, I know of another way that might take two or three weeks, or maybe a little longer.

Despite having been burned before by claims of a lost and/or recovered Oak Island treasure map, Blair corresponded at length with Doyle and in 1935 invited him to Amherst for a visit. He naturally grew suspicious when Doyle, in his retelling of his story, now described Jim Thompson as "an old sailor" who had given his father the map sometime between 1884 and 1888. Nevertheless, Blair wrote a voluminous memorandum on his interview with Doyle for his attorney, Harris, and was particularly descriptive of the diagram the man had prepared for him: "The plan was marked 'Oak Island' and showed three pits, one at the shore about 80 or 90 feet deep, one on the hill about 470 or 480 feet distant and 176 feet deep, the third between the first two mentioned and about 270 to 280 feet from the shore and 125 feet deep."

Blair went on to describe just as meticulously the various tunnels and the other works that Doyle described. He seemed particularly captivated by the description of the "clapper" gate in the main flood tunnel that Doyle had offered: "It was arranged with two hooks, an iron bar, links of chain and a ball, or weight, so that when dropped by the pull of the chain, the hooks would catch under the bar of iron and keep the gate closed."

Only at the end of a memo that went on for pages did Blair write: "I put little credence in the story. Note how well the known facts compare with his map, and then consider his details after a space of thirty years, without seeing the map. It is simply too much for me to believe without better evidence."

Harris had no doubt Doyle was a fraud after interviewing the man himself and hearing that the map was "dated 1821," that it had "just come into his possession," and that it "had belonged to his grandfather, who received it from his brother, a sailor."

"Those who have pirate maps to sell should be careful to tell the same story on all occasions!" Harris observed, advising Blair to have nothing more to do with this W. J. Doyle.

At least Gilbert Hedden was not taken in for long by the man named Doyle who wrote to him in 1945. This Doyle (who may or may not have been the same one who wrote to Blair in 1934) had enclosed what he described as "a tracing or copy from an old pirate map that is the same as Oak Island, only a little larger." The difference in size, this Doyle explained, was due to the fact that the island had lost more than 20 feet of coastline in the past two centuries. The letter told an elaborate story of Kidd's visits to Nova Scotia—"I have proof of this," he declared—then suggested that the pirate had buried not one but two treasures on Oak Island, only one of which would be found in the Money Pit. The map he enclosed had been sent to him by "a highly educated gentleman," wrote Doyle, who requested that "when you are done studying it, please return it to me by registered mail."

Hedden did study the map—long enough to recognize that it was almost an exact copy of the Mar Del map in Harold Wilkins's *Captain Kidd and His Skeleton Island*, with a few slight alterations. While he did not respond to Doyle, Hedden once again puzzled over the map Wilkins had drawn, which showed no less than "fourteen resemblances" to Oak Island. Most perplexing to Hedden, though, was that the compass directions on the Mar Del map were an *exact* reversal of the compass directions to Oak Island. How could this possibly be a coincidence?

Perhaps this conundrum was why Hedden continued to correspond with Wilkins long after visiting the man in England in the autumn of 1937. Even after Wilkins began to claim that he was "channeling the ghost of Captain Kidd," Hedden kept in contact with him. And while there's no evidence that Hedden ever subscribed to such a claim, it's not clear either that he rejected it. The mystery of Oak Island had both baffled and consumed him so completely that he was afraid to rule out any possibility. Blair had long since become the same way, and by the time I'd spent a month on Oak Island in the summer of 2016 I felt I understood not only Blair and Hedden but also those who had decided that it couldn't hurt to listen to any idea, no matter how ridiculous it might seem.

CHAPTER ELEVEN

It was Blair who had sent his manager of operations, A. S. Lowden, to Boston in the late summer of 1895 to sit in on a series of séances that called up the ghost of Captain Kidd. In the report he submitted to Blair from a stopover in Concord on September 12, Lowden admitted, "I went to these sittings not exactly skeptic [*sic*], but with considerable doubt." That doubt wasn't terribly evident in what he wrote next:

> The mediums are a farmer and his wife and sittings are free. Their manifestations have been examined by professors from Harvard College and pronounced genuine. As I told you before, the "control" is the notorious William Kidd. The manifestations are made by raps as neither of the mediums are trance mediums although they can be if they wish. They materialize to the sense of touch and pretty severe touches in some cases. Writing on a slate is another accomplishment. During these séances, many of the answers were rapped out on my knees, not only to my feeling but could be heard as well. He (Kidd) tried to draw the course of the drain down my leg but I could not understand it.
>
> Now I will tell you some of the information he gave me, using the alphabet to spell out sentences:
>
> "I came about money."
>
> "The money is in Nova Scotia—Oak Island—was put there in 1782 by James (sic) Morgan."

He first stated the depth was 90 feet, but thought that it might have been 100 feet. We can get it if we can keep out the damned water. It is not where Morgan put it—sunk eight feet—is in the tunnel to 118 feet—money not all at bottom of Pit. Mate's money 29 feet south east of Money Pit—about thirty-five feet down—was put there by tunnel from Money Pit. Entrance to tunnel twenty-five to thirty feet down—will get this money in two weeks.

You will find the drain as sure as hell—you are under the drain—the dam water they have found comes down from the drain entrance to drain to south of the Halifax dam near the big stone. It flows between No. 15 and No. 4 and No. 12—It falls between No. 5 and air shaft—the gate is there—There is money in the air shaft—2nd Mate's, between one and $200,000—Mate's share between five and six hundred thousand—Morgan's share between seven and eight hundred thousand.

Lowden had attached a diagram to illustrate what he described. Blair apparently studied it closely, but as his attorney, Harris, would dryly observe in *The Oak Island Mystery*: "As Kidd died in 1701 and Henry Morgan, the pirate, flourished between 1670 and 1688, Blair's reply expressed considerable doubt as to the correctness of Lowden's theory."

Not to mention that the idea of people digging the Money Pit and constructing the flood tunnels without being noticed in 1782, when there were people living on Oak Island and all along the shoreline, was plainly impossible.

Almost forty years later, though, Blair was deeply interested in the claims of a man R. V. Harris would identify only as "Wilson" who said he had verified that it was the Incan treasure of Tumbes buried on Oak Island by means of automatic writing. Alternately described as either a psychic process or as a spiritual one—or as both—automatic writing essentially produces words on paper without the conscious intent of the person holding the pen. Scientific materialists describe it as an "ideomotor effect" that results from a person entering a dissociative state; persons under hypnosis can readily perform automatic writing they note. What Wilson claimed when he wrote to Blair in 1931 was that he produced his automatic writing by surrendering himself to the spirit minds of a group of men from a bygone age—"A. R." and "Circle" were two of their names—who had created the Money Pit and buried the great treasure of the Incas on Oak Island. There is no doubt that Wilson impressed Blair with the level of accurate detail he provided about Oak Island without ever having visited the place. In particular Blair was struck by the fact that Wilson said the Chappell shaft over-lapped part of the Money Pit, something that was only later proven to be true. Blair was also impressed that Wilson was prepared to invest his own money—between $25,000 and $30,000—into a new search of the Money Pit based on what he had learned from A. R. and the others. While Blair was never able to reach a deal with Wilson—there were negotiations—he clearly gave serious and continuing consideration to the information the man had provided about the construction of the Money Pit and what it meant. Much of what Daniel McGinnis and the others had discovered back in 1795—the sawed-off oak limb, the tackle block, the remains of a road or path between the Pit and the shore—was not left by the original depositors in the sixteenth century, Wilson told Blair, but by an early eighteenth-century search effort that had preceded the putative "discovery" of the Money Pit by more than fifty years. The treasure itself was in multiple locations inside the Pit, according to Wilson, who told Blair that part of it was at a depth of 126 feet about 20 feet behind the west wall of the original shaft. There was also treasure at a depth of 153 feet Wilson said, and more in a "Gothic chamber" that had been constructed at a depth of 175 feet.

Blair kept the plans and sketches of the Money Pit that Wilson had drawn in his files for the remainder of his life, and he referred to them regularly when planning or discussing some new approach to the problems the Pit posed. Somehow, the man *knew* things, Blair told Harris, who would observe that "the whole affair was most uncanny.

Mr. Blair was undoubtedly greatly impressed by the answers he received [from Wilson]."

Gilbert Hedden was even more inclined to lend an ear—or a dollar—to persons who approached him with ideas or inventions that would have furrowed the brows of more cynical men. One example of this was the correspondence Hedden carried on for months with J. P. Nolan, a longtime prospector from the mining town of Montague, Nova Scotia, who had introduced himself by writing: "After twenty-five years of study and labour, I have invented a small machine called a 'gold finder.' They will not find any mineral but gold and can pick gold veins to a depth of 600 feet and survey them. . . . Should you care to see a demonstration of my gold finder, I would kindly ask you to come here and see me."

After an exchange of several more letters between Nolan and Hedden, the old miner was invited to make a demonstration at the office of R. V. Harris. The gold finder was a mechanism made of four short rods suspended from strings that Nolan held in his hands. "I placed a bag of gold quartz about three feet east of the rods," the attorney recounted, "and immediately the rods swung in that direction. Then I placed the bag on the floor beneath and the rods turned quickly and definitely towards the floor. The bag was then placed west of the rods and the rods swung that way." It was all "very uncanny," Harris conceded wryly, given that "there was not enough gold in the quartz to gild a pinhead, and all this time I had in my vest pocket a rather large gold pocket watch." No matter where he moved in the room, Harris noted, the rods were not affected. Of course, Nolan and the associate he had brought with him didn't know about the watch in Harris's pocket.

The attorney advised his client, Hedden, to have nothing further to do with gold finders. His lawyer's advice, though, didn't prevent Hedden from signing a "no cure, no pay" agreement (meaning money would not be exchanged unless valuables were recovered) in February 1938 with an inventor who claimed to have developed a camera capable of locating the treasure in the Money Pit by taking a photograph from aboveground. The inventor had offered to demonstrate this unique camera to Harris in the offices of another Nova Scotia attorney who represented the inventor. Recalled Harris:

> Fifty two-dollar bills (not coin) were placed in a book on one of the shelves in his law office, their location unknown to the inventor who later entered the room and took a photograph of one side of the room. . . . The inventor then left the room to change his plate, or film, and the money was placed in the bottom of a briefcase lying on a chair. A second photograph was then taken of the other side of the room, including the chair. When the photographs were developed, copies were sent to the lawyer, marked with rings around the law book on the shelf and around the lower left hand corner of the brief case! The other attorney professed himself converted to a belief in the efficacy of his client's invention!

In his report to Hedden, Harris could not help observing that the other attorney's self-interest might well be served by such a conversion. Nevertheless, after the inventor pestered him for months, Hedden agreed to let the man take a series of treasure-seeking photographs on Oak Island. The man left shortly after arriving, however, claiming he had to make "adjustments" to his camera's internal circuitry. Hedden, flustered and infuriated, declared the whole thing a hoax and told the inventor never to come back.

Hedden, however, remained willing to hear out almost anyone who claimed to possess a solution to the problem of Oak Island. Over the years, he listened to many stories, but none was so fascinating as the one told by a professor of chemical engineering at Iowa State University named Burrell Ruth. In October 1939, Professor Ruth had read a story about Oak Island published in the *Saturday Evening Post*. He immediately fired off a thirty-page letter laying out the theory that at the bottom of the Money Pit was a vault containing the original manuscripts of the plays and poems that were attributed to William Shakespeare.

Just as I would when I first heard it suggested in the autumn of 2003, sixty-four years after Ruth's letter was written, Hedden found the idea preposterous. He was flabbergasted, though, by what the professor had written about the manner in which he believed the Shakespeare manuscripts had been protected against the ravages of time—by immersion in hundreds of gallons of mercury.

"Your prediction that the Money Pit contains mercury is one of the most amazing coincidences I have ever encountered," Hedden wrote back to Professor Ruth:

> You can be certain that before sinking nearly a hundred thousand in this venture I explored it from every angle. One of these angles was the folklore, superstitions and legends that have surrounded the Pit since 1800. One of the most widespread and persistent of these legends, and one for which I was never able to find the least basis, was the curious belief that the Money Pit contained mercury. I never gave it any serious thought; it seemed too fantastic. But one point in favor of your theory is that there does exist an old dump on the island in which are the remains of thousands of broken pottery flasks. That this dump is very old is supported by the fact that we found nearby an old coin and ivory boatswain's whistle which experts tell us date back to the Elizabethan period.

The "old dump" Hedden described had been found by members of his crew on the shoreline of Joudrey's Cove during the summer of 1937, while they were searching for markers that might be connected to the drilled boulders and the stone triangle. According to Amos Nauss, the liquid residue found inside the flasks was mercury.

Hedden kept up a correspondence with Ruth for years, drawing out the professor's conviction that the man behind the Money Pit and the rest of the works on Oak Island was Sir Francis Bacon, the Lord Chancellor in early seventeenth-century England who was also, according to

Ruth, the true author of the Shakespeare plays. This part of the theory, along with the claim that the Shakespeare manuscripts were hidden in a secret vault, was not original to Ruth. The professor himself had first heard it laid out in 1920 as a student at Michigan State University, when he listened awestruck to a presentation by one of the most colorful characters in modern American history, Dr. Orville Ward Owen.

A physician from Detroit by day, Dr. Owen had devoted his nights for more than three decades to the study of Elizabethan manuscripts. The culmination of this labor had been a multivolume work published under the title *Sir Francis Bacon's Cipher Story* that described how Owen had reached the conclusion that Bacon was the author not only of the works attributed to William Shakespeare, but also the author of volumes that had been published under the names of Edmund Spenser, Robert Burton, and George Peele, among others. Owen's claims were even more remarkable than that, though, because at the center of his theory was the contention that Bacon had used these works to encode teachings for which he believed the world was not yet prepared. He had decrypted these teachings, Dr. Owen maintained, by the application of his great invention, the "cipher wheel," which was actually a set of wheels, through which Owen had run a 1,000-foot-long strip of canvas onto which were pasted the complete works of Shakespeare, as well as samples of the works of Spenser, Burton, Peele, and the others, including Christopher Marlowe. This invention was inspired, it seemed, by a passage from one of the works that Bacon had written under his own name:

> *Take your knife and cut all our great books asunder*
> *And set the leaves on a great firm wheel*
> *Which rolls and rolls, and turning the*
> *Fickle rolling wheel, throw your eyes upon FORTUNE*
> *That goddess blind, that stands upon*
> *A spherical stone, that turning and inconsistent rolls*
> *In restless variations. Mark her the prime mover,*
> *She is our first guide.*

Owen explained that when he spun his cipher wheel he discovered that certain words were highlighted and messages were revealed.

By this process, he had uncovered a secret history of the Elizabethan period, one in which Queen Elizabeth had been secretly married to Robert Dudley, 1st Earl of Leicester, who had fathered two sons by her, one being Bacon, the other Robert Devereux, 2nd Earl of Essex. After the Queen had Bacon's brother, Devereux, executed for perceived disloyalty, Bacon had begun encoding his secret history of the realm in works ostensibly written by others, Owen explained, communicating them in the form of questions and answers composed in blank verse. But then Elizabeth discovered that her surviving son had authored the play *Hamlet*, forcing Bacon to become even more secretive, "circumscribing the scope of that mighty intellect, and forcing the hiding of its best work under masks and cipher, only to be revealed three hundred years later." The doctor also revealed that *Romeo and Juliet* was the story of Bacon's romance with the queen of France, Margaret of Valois, and that Queen Elizabeth had confessed Bacon was her son on her deathbed, only to be strangled by Robert Cecil to prevent her from proclaiming Bacon as her successor.

It was all quite fantastic and a considerable sensation when *Sir Francis Bacon's Cipher Story* was published over a three-year period in the last decade of the nineteenth century. Many critics savaged the massive work, among them the famous cryptologists William and Elizebeth Friedman, who scoffed at the notion that Owen's cipher wheel produced anything more than random variations. Even Owen's good friend Dr. Frederick Mann denounced him, writing that "we are asked to believe that such peerless creations as *Hamlet*, *The Tempest* and *Romeo and Juliet* were not prime productions of the transcendent genius who wrote them, but were subsidiary devices which Bacon designed for the purpose of concealing the cipher within."

Dr. Owen found supporters, however. The idea that the Shakespeare works had actually been written by Bacon had been around long before the doctor's invention of his cipher wheel. In fact, some of the

great minds in Anglo-American history had subscribed to it, among
them Samuel Taylor Coleridge, Oliver Wendell Holmes, Ralph Waldo
Emerson, Benjamin Disraeli, and Walt Whitman. Owen's contemporary
Mark Twain had written that he was "inclined" to believe that Bacon
had written the Shakespeare plays.

In the early years of the twentieth century, Owen announced that
he believed the original Shakespeare manuscripts, written in Bacon's
hand, were hidden in a vault containing sixty-six lead-lined iron boxes
of papers buried either beneath or beside the bed of the River Wye
where it divided England from Wales at Chepstow Castle. The expedition Owen undertook to search for these iron boxes in the late summer
of 1909 was widely observed. The *New York Times*, in fact, devoted two
full pages to a massive article that chronicled Dr. Owen's adventure,
datelined "London—May 3 [1910]":

At the time of Dr. Owen's arrival in Chepstow, he was accompanied by his friend, Dr. William H. Prescott of Boston, a
well-known physician and alienist, who had been interested in
the Baconian theory for years. Neither had been in Chepstow
before, and knew nothing about its history beyond what had
been revealed through the medium of the cipher. Yet to-day Dr.
Owen positively asserts he has found every landmark mentioned
in the cipher—many of which are known by new names, and
only remembered by the older names mentioned in the cipher,
by the oldest inhabitants of Chepstow, and, more wonderful
indeed, has succeeded in uncovering a strange oaken structure,
beneath which Dr. Owen is confident of finding the cache which,
he maintains, holds the missing relics.

"HID UNDER WYE" was the first message he had decoded with
his cipher wheel, as Owen explained to the *Times*. The next sentences he
found read: "Buried boxes found under famed Roman Ford" and "Bed

or braced beams under Roman Ford," then "At point off Wasphill." He even found sentences that described the exact dimensions of the vault, Owen told the *Times*. The ensuing expedition that was the subject of the *Times* article sounded so incredible that I was amazed the newspaper's correspondent (who was not identified by name, despite the fact that the article was enormously long) could report it in such a straightforward manner. The story made me gasp exactly once, when Owen told the *Times* correspondent that the cipher wheel had identified a "blue clay" in which the vault containing the Bacon manuscripts was surrounded. By then I had read literally dozens of descriptions of the belt of "strange blue clay" that had been found in the Money Pit and in which the Oak Island treasure was presumed to be embedded. Could this possibly be a coincidence?

After months of negotiations with the British government to get permission to explore the River Wye, Owen had also been required to make an arrangement with the Duke of Beaufort, who held certain rights to "flotsam and jetsam" recovered from that section of the river's banks, and as well to obtain the cooperation of Henry Clay, the eighty-seven-year-old Squire of Chepstow. Finally, on October 5, 1909, Owen was permitted to begin his excavation. The photographs accompanying the *Times* article depicted an extensive operation involving steam engines, pumps, massive wooden platforms, and more than a dozen workmen. Owen and his crew bored thirteen holes along the east bank of the Wye without finding anything before they reached bedrock, the *Times* correspondent reported, but the fourteenth hole had gone deeper than any of the others and Owens was ecstatic when his drill brought up blue clay. Two days later, the crew uncovered a "strange oaken structure, hectagonal in shape," according to the *Times* correspondent, who, based on his firsthand observations, described it in detail: 41 feet long by 10 feet wide, with a triangle at each end "pointed like the bows of a boat." There were five bars of oak across the width of the structure from side to side "and the space between these bars is filled up with rock and a *peculiar blue clay*" [italics mine].

Owen was convinced he had found what he was looking for. The *Times* correspondent noted that others doubted this claim, among them a "local historian" who said it was perfectly obvious that what Owen had found was the remains of the landing stage of an old bridge. Whatever it was, the structure did not contain even one box of manuscripts, let alone sixty-six. What he had been afraid of, Owen told the *Times*, was that Bacon had moved the manuscripts to another location.

There are numerous accounts that describe Owen as having uncovered a Baconian vault exactly where he was looking for it, only to find it empty. In other accounts, all Owen found was the remains of a Roman bridge and a medieval cistern. What he did not find, in any account, was Shakespearean manuscripts. At the end of his life, Owen was described in an article published in London's *Times Literary Supplement* as a "bedridden, almost penniless invalid" who was filled with regret over the years he had given to the "Baconian controversy" and warned others not to follow in his footsteps.

Burrell Ruth had ignored that advice and in the summer of 2016 so would I. But that part of the story comes later.

CHAPTER TWELVE

In the last years before World War II, and in the early stages of the global conflict, operations on Oak Island were directed by Edwin H. Hamilton, a professor of engineering at New York University. Hamilton had approached Gilbert Hedden in the spring of 1938 with an offer to take over the treasure hunt on Oak Island and to bear all the costs of the expedition. Frederick Blair had been glad to hear it at first, but he began to back off when Hedden suggested an even three-way split of any recovery. Every previous deal Blair made had guaranteed him half of whatever valuables were brought up from belowground, and he expected the same again. The subsequent negotiation consumed more than two months, but by the end of June the three men had agreed that Hedden and Hamilton would each receive 30 percent of the take, with the remaining 40 percent going to Blair.

Hamilton moved forward immediately, beginning in mid-July 1938, when he arrived on the island with a drilling crew from the same company Hedden had used, Sprague and Henwood. For the professor, step one was to locate the original shaft and to define it as precisely as possible. He and his crew began in the Chappell shaft (no. 21), where two sections of the cribbing were beginning to buckle. The crew spent five weeks working downward to reinforce the timbers between depths of 145 feet and 170 feet, then upward between 90 feet and 62 feet. Once that was done, they used a diamond bit to bore fifty-eight holes in the Pit down to the bedrock, which they struck at depths of between 168 and 171 feet. The lateral drilling began in August, and within a day or two the drill bit brought back splinters of what was described as "very old oak." Hedden believed they were from the remains of the timbers installed in 1850 that had sunk toward the bottom of the Money Pit during the 1861 collapse. Blair concurred, and both men felt certain that they were either in or right next to the original Pit.

In late August, Hamilton moved his crew to the northeast corner of the Hedden shaft (no. 22), where the drill went down to 117 feet but struck nothing of real interest. So the professor moved the crew to the shaft nearest to the shore of Smith's Cove, where their excavation unearthed a horizontal tunnel at a depth of 35 feet that was filled with broken timbers, running straight for a distance of about 15 feet toward the Cave-in Pit, then gradually curving around and coming to an end just below it. Deeper, at 45 feet, Hamilton's crew found another tunnel running south from the shaft for about 25 feet. It was filled with beach gravel and cribbing made of hemlock timbers that had been cut with an up-and-down handsaw and were badly deteriorated. This tunnel led to a sand streak (a bleed of fine aggregate) about 3.5 feet wide. Two posts were still in place in this part of the tunnel, just a few feet from where it extended for about 5 feet into hard blue clay. Hamilton made careful measurements in both of these tunnels showing that the sand streaks in them were in a perfect line between the Money Pit, the Cave-in Pit, and the stakes at the south shore marking what was believed to be the beginning of the water course.

Convinced he had found connections to the flood tunnel system, Hamilton ordered a new shaft sunk from the floor of the lowest tunnel to a farther depth of 11 feet, where the men were met with sand, beach gravel, small stones, and blue clay but no evidence of water. About 6 feet down in this shaft, they recovered a large flat stone that was "not native to this level," as R. V. Harris described it, lying next to several pieces of "chewing tobacco of the old fashioned type, in good condition." The tobacco—and the stone, too, most likely—had been left by earlier searchers, Hamilton decided, rather than by those who did the original work on the island.

The crew returned to the Hedden shaft, where at the 82-foot level they discovered a trench that had been dug downward to flood the Money Pit and made Hamilton even more certain of where the original shaft was located.

Amos Nauss, who was working for Hamilton now, recalled that "when we were down there [in the Hedden shaft], there was always saltwater coming in. But we couldn't find where it was coming from. We never saw the flood tunnels."

Hamilton decided to conduct his own dye test, similar to the one Blair had done in 1898, to try to trace the source of the flooding. As Nauss recalled it, the dye was dropped into both the Hedden and Chappell shafts "and it came out on the southeast side of the island, about one hundred yards out from the high tide. We took my boat out to it, and we could see the dye coming up from the bottom of the sea. So we knew there was a connection there with a waterway going through the Money Pit area." They also knew that the starting point of that connection was now completely underwater, even at low tide, due to the rising ocean and the eroding shore.

On November 4, 1938, Hamilton sent a summary of the work his crews had done that summer and what they had found to President Roosevelt. FDR seemed especially interested in Hamilton's report that he had measured water pouring into the Hedden shaft at the rate of "approximately 800 gallons per minute," indicating that it could not possibly be from the sort of "percolation" that Roosevelt's old boss Captain Bowdoin had described. The president, now in the middle of his second term, made plans to visit Oak Island the summer of 1939 during the Halifax stopover of his US Navy cruiser. Hamilton was so excited that he ordered the construction of a custom sedan chair to carry the polio-disabled president from the dock at Smith's Cove directly to the Money Pit area. The professor was crushed when at the last minute Roosevelt sent word through a friend that the imminent war in Europe "made it impossible."

The outbreak of World War II—which Canada entered alongside England when Germany invaded Poland in September 1939—made it difficult for Professor Hamilton to find workers in Nova Scotia. Eventually, by offering the exorbitant pay of forty cents per hour, Hamilton assembled a crew of eleven in the summer of 1940. During this same period, Hamilton also had to fend off a move on his flank by the film star Errol Flynn, who was attempting to assemble his own team of treasure hunters.

Flynn was considerably more than some celluloid swashbuckler. He was in fact an adventurer of remarkable nerve and determination, which he exhibited in spectacular fashion back in the autumn of 1927, when he sailed into Salamaua, a village on the northeast coast of New Guinea, then hiked the Black Cat Track to the fabled gold-mining village of Wau. This was one of the most treacherous treks on the planet, through a tropical forest infested with typhoid and blackwater fever, leeches and killer snakes, razorback boars and cassowaries—not to mention native tribes who were headhunters and cannibals. Most of the white men who attempted it never came back. Eleven years later, in 1938, Flynn sailed to Jamaica, where he attempted to recover the treasures lost when Port Royal fell into the sea, using deep-sea diving equipment that was absurdly primitive by today's standards. The movie star could never get deep enough to reach the pirate booty at the bottom of the ocean, but he did bring back various museum-quality architectural items. He seems to have been quite serious about his wish two years later to take over the Oak Island treasure hunt but found himself stymied by an inability to break through the agreement Hamilton had made with Hedden and Blair, and he eventually withdrew.

So in June 1940 it was Hamilton who directed the crew that tunneled from the Hedden shaft around the Chappell shaft in a search for the Halifax Company tunnel, which the men found just to the southeast of the Hedden shaft. The crew followed it to the top of the east-end drumlin, found a tunnel running toward the Cave-in Pit that divided just before it reached the (presumed) air shaft, then traveled around it on both sides. Original wooden tracks for the carts that had been used in its excavation were found on the bottom of this tunnel and convinced Hamilton absolutely that this was part of the Halifax tunnel, which he knew had terminated in the center of the Money Pit.

The net takeaway of this extended search, for Hamilton, was to confirm that the Money Pit and the Chappell shaft were close enough to be connected, but that the center of the Money Pit was at least a few feet—perhaps as many as five—to the south, in the direction of the Hedden shaft. In other words, the professor was fairly certain he had recovered the location of the original shaft. Buoyed, Hamilton returned to Oak Island in the summer of 1941 determined to explore the bottom of the Money Pit itself, but labor was now even scarcer. Once he finally had a few men, Hamilton was stopped by the failure of electricity on the island. His pump stopped, and so did his effort to drain the Hedden shaft. Despite this, Hamilton was back on Oak Island in the summer of 1942 and managed to sink a shaft 8 feet square between the Hedden and Chappell shafts, using the remains of two earlier tunnels to connect the two shafts at a depth of 155 feet. His crew's lateral drilling, though, produced no results.

During this work, the crew did intercept a watercourse 8 inches high by 10 inches wide that was cut through limestone. Hamilton sent a sample of the water running through this apparently man-made tunnel for analysis and was puzzled by a report that it had a slightly higher specific gravity than the water drawn from Smith's Cove, suggesting that it might contain minerals that gave it greater density.

Hamilton separated from his two partners when he asserted that the so-called coconut fiber that had been found both in the Money Pit and along the shore of Smith's Cove was really hemlock bark. Blair and Hedden found that ridiculous. The two pointed out that hemlock bark deteriorates far more rapidly than coconut fiber and would have been nothing more than goo had it been buried for years beneath the artificial beach at the cove. They noted the interview just five years earlier in which Captain Anthony Vaughan II (who was almost ninety-nine at the time) recalled being present as a boy of ten on the beach at Smith's Cove when the five finger drains were discovered after an enormous amount of what was clearly coconut fiber was removed from on top of them. A sample of this fiber had been submitted in 1916 to the Smithsonian Institution in Washington, DC, whose scientists reported: "The specimen of fibre submitted is undoubtedly from the fibrous husks surrounding a coconut. This fibre is especially resistant to the effects of seawater and under the conditions in which it was found may have been there for several hundred years."

A 1937 analysis by the Bureau of Plant Industry in Washington, DC, had confirmed the Smithsonian Institution report, but that same year a scientist at the Botanical Museum of Harvard University had reported that the fiber submitted to him was "readily distinguishable as manilla hemp." But while some small measure of uncertainty about the fiber existed, no scientist had ever said it was hemlock bark.

Whether the dispute among the partners about the composition of the fiber was a cause of Hamilton's decision to discontinue his operations on Oak Island is not clear from the record, but the timing certainly suggests this. At the same time, it's clear that the ongoing war was making it more and more difficult to continue. Furthermore, by the summer of 1943 Hamilton had sunk USD $60,000 (equivalent to slightly more than $1 million in 2018 value) into the Oak Island treasure hunt; he was quite possibly tapped out. Whatever the case, he concluded his work on the island in admirable fashion, constructing two stout platforms just above the waterline in both the Chappell and Hedden shafts, decked with heavy timbers that sealed them more effectively than had ever been done before on Oak Island. Another year passed before Hamilton admitted he had given up the search, but by then Mahone Bay had captured him for good. The professor retired from NYU to settle in Chester, where he and Amos Nauss became partners and founded a boatbuilding business—keeping front-row seats from which to observe the continuing drama on Oak Island.

In the mind of Frederick Blair, and therefore in the annals of the island, Edwin Hamilton's principal accomplishment had been to prove that neither the Hedden nor the Chappell shafts were directly over the Money Pit, but rather that the Pit was somewhere between them. The professor had come very close to pinpointing the exact location of the original shaft.

The other main thing Hamilton had proved was what a mess a century and a half of treasure hunting had made of Oak Island. Reading through the records of the professor's operations between 1938 and 1943, I could visualize more clearly than ever before the underground chaos created by the dozens of shafts and tunnels that had been driven into and under the ground on the east end of Oak Island. Each effort to reach the Money Pit—or to drain or divert or block the water flowing into it—had resulted in some form of contact with a flood system that still wasn't well understood, and as a result nearly all of the shafts and most of the tunnels were now filled with seawater that was endlessly replenished by the Atlantic Ocean. There was now enough water down there to fill a hundred Olympic-size swimming pools, I estimated. Its constant churning was steadily eroding the walls of the shafts and the floors and ceilings of the tunnels. The entire subterranean structure of the island was in danger of slowly collapsing into a kind of underground sea filled with detritus of human folly. The original engineering problem had been perplexing enough, but what existed now was a quandary of staggering proportions. Even if there was a treasure down there, the likelihood of getting to it had diminished year by year. Yet no matter how many tried and failed, there always seemed to be someone who believed that a bolder plan or some new and improved technology would deliver the success that had eluded all those who came before.

So the Oak Island treasure hunt would go on.

IN THE SPRING OF 1944, Frederick Blair renewed his treasure trove license with the Nova Scotia provincial government. At almost the same time, Gilbert Hedden moved to protect his property on the island from IRS seizure by transferring it to a trust managed by his attorney. Together, the two men began searching for someone to replace Edwin Hamilton. They swiftly entered into negotiations with a Toronto engineer named Anthony Belfiglio, who claimed to have backers willing to put up $50,000 to continue the treasure hunt. Offers and counteroffers went back and forth all through 1945 and into 1946; at one point Belfiglio offered to buy Hedden's Oak Island properties for $15,000, but no deal was ever consummated.

In late 1946, the Broadway stage singer Edward Reichert approached Hedden with an offer to lease the east end of Oak Island. Reichert claimed to have more than $150,000 from unnamed "backers" to finance his search. Hedden made a tentative agreement with the singer, and Reichert came to Nova Scotia in May 1947 to meet with Blair. In a foreshadowing of what was to come during later decades, Reichert explained that his plan was to use steam shovels to dig a hole 80 feet in diameter and more than 200 feet deep in the Money Pit area. He had made arrangements in Halifax to lease the necessary equipment for $4,500 a month and had budgeted the work to last ten months. During the next few weeks the singer gave numerous newspaper interviews that stirred public interest, then simply disappeared. Hedden spent several months searching for the man, before writing him off as "just another crackpot."

In spite of this exasperation, Hedden listened attentively when he was approached by Colonel H. A. Gardener, a retired US Army officer from Arlington, Virginia. Colonel Gardener had made a survey of Oak Island on his own during the summer of 1947, Hedden explained later, before bringing him a proposal unlike any he had heard before. He believed he could locate the treasure, Gardener said, with a portable radar scanner that had been developed by the army during WWII. He would place the device in various shafts that had been dug by searchers on the island and use it to locate the original tunnels and chambers on the island's east end. Hedden was so impressed by Gardener's description of the process that he agreed to lease the land and to take only 10

THE CURSE OF OAK ISLAND 159

percent of whatever Gardener found. The colonel's enthusiasm began to wane, however, when he learned that he'd also have to make a deal with Blair, who could be a much tougher customer and was almost certain to demand half of whatever was recovered on Oak Island.

In late 1947 Hedden wrote to a friend: "The present status seems to be a stalemate situation. I own property rights and Blair owns the treasure trove rights. Neither can proceed without the other, and Blair sticks to his 50 percent [demand], thereby scaring away all ventures of any kind."

Blair, though, continued to maintain at age seventy-nine that the Oak Island puzzle could and would be solved within his lifetime, if the effort to do so were properly funded. "Scientific engineering and modern equipment will do the work if properly financed," he wrote. "Previous failures, and there have been many, were due to lack of knowledge of conditions. In other words they knew nothing of the original work and in addition they lacked engineering skill and were short on the financial end. Today, it is the financial backing we need, not a method of recovery. The latter will come with the former."

Blair seemed not to recognize that the financial backing Hedden needed at this point was for his survival. In early 1948, Hedden agreed to sell his Oak Island property to Gardener for a small down payment, with the balance to be paid over ten years. The colonel arrived on the island in July of that year with the radar scanner he had obtained from the army, but after several weeks of belowground tests decided his equipment wasn't working as it should. He returned to Virginia to adjust it, promising to come back the next summer. Blair was furious when he discovered that Hedden had allowed someone to conduct a search in the Money Pit area without his permission. He contacted Gardener directly and became even angrier when the colonel told him that he had a deal to purchase Hedden's Oak Island lots. Blair threatened litigation, but what appeared to be an explosive situation fizzled into nothing when Gardener died suddenly in January 1949 and his widow canceled the agreement to purchase Hedden's land.

In late 1949, Hedden was approached by yet another potential
buyer, a New York mining and petroleum engineer named John Whitney Lewis. Hedden, increasingly desperate for cash, agreed to sell all
of his Oak Island lots to Lewis for just $6,000, plus a small percentage
of any treasure recovered. The deal was concluded on May 12, 1950,
and Lewis immediately flew to Nova Scotia to prepare for a summer
of operations in the Money Pit area. Only upon arrival did Lewis learn
that Blair intended to block him. Lewis accused Hedden of deceiving
him with the claim that Blair's treasure trove license had expired on June
30, 1949, but Hedden had told the truth. What Hedden didn't know
was that Blair, with the assistance of R. V. Harris, had surreptitiously
renewed the license for another five years.

Harris, acting as Blair's attorney, delivered the bad news to Lewis on
May 27, 1950, exactly two weeks after the New York man had completed
his purchase of Hedden's Oak Island lots. Mr. Blair, Harris explained, had
made a deal with William Chappell's now sixty-three-year-old son, Melbourne, to resume the treasure hunt in the Money Pit area. It appeared
there was a new stalemate, one in which Lewis was blocked by Blair's
deal with Chappell and Chappell was blocked by Hedden's sale to Lewis.
What Lewis didn't know, however, was that Blair and R. V. Harris had
been lobbying the Nova Scotia legislature for months to rewrite the
Treasure Trove Act so that treasure hunters had the same rights that
mineral prospectors had under the Mines Act.

Lewis appealed to the provincial secretary, claiming "misrepresen-
tations" by Blair and Harris. What really infuriated the New York man,
though, was his dawning realization that he was being stymied by an
old boys' network, all of them Freemasons and most of whom belonged
to the Grand Lodge of Nova Scotia. Blair was a high-ranking Mason
and his attorney, Harris, had actually risen to the top Masonic position
in Nova Scotia, provincial grand master, a position that was later held
by Melbourne Chappell. Gilbert Hedden was among the most prominent Freemasons in New Jersey, and Edwin Hamilton had served as
grand master of the Grand Lodge of Massachusetts. Many—some said

most—of high office holders in Nova Scotia's provincial government were also Masons.

THE MASONIC CONNECTIONS to Oak Island had always struck me as curious but not really an interesting avenue of investigation. At least a dozen Canadian writers, bloggers, and amateur historians had explored and tortured the subject, and more than a few of those had both explored *and* tortured it. Sure, there'd been a lot of Freemasons involved in the treasure hunt over the years (along with a lot of treasure hunters who weren't Masons), but that seemed to have to do with the fact that Masonic membership was so widespread, especially in Nova Scotia. Though it has antecedents that some claim predate the time of Christ, Freemasonry formally came into existence in 1717 with the establishment of the Grand Lodge of London and began to establish itself in North America around 1730. The Grand Lodge of Nova Scotia was established in Halifax in 1766, less than twenty years after the city's founding, and put down deep roots in the province. While Freemasonry appeared to be dwindling in the United States, it continued to thrive internationally, with as many as 6 million members worldwide, and it was particularly strong on the south shore of Nova Scotia. Within a week of arriving in Canada to work on *The Curse of Oak Island* I'd been told by two of the regular cast members, historian Charles Barkhouse and Tony Sampson, a diver whose company I had enjoyed over breakfast, that they were Masons and that membership was widespread among the men of the local community.

Charles and Tony both readily agreed that what could be regarded as Masonic symbols had cropped up again and again as the Oak Island story unfolded, and that this was probably significant. "The triangles, obviously," Charles said. The triangle was not just the Masonic symbol for the sacred number three but was also understood as a geometric representation of God.

"The stone triangle, the triangle of oak trees outlining the Money Pit that were described in McCully's *Colonist* article," I prompted.

"The triangular swamp," Charles added. I wasn't entirely comfortable with the inclusion of the swamp in the list of Oak Island triangles.
Admittedly, one could see the outline of an equilateral triangle if one
looked at the swamp from the air, but that involved filling in sections
of the three sides with the mind's eye. I had been told that there were
triangular swamps along the shorelines of other islands in Mahone Bay,
and my impression was that these had been created gradually by the
combination of erosion and rising water that surged forward to a point.
Maybe the Oak Island Swamp was man-made, as many believed, but I
needed more evidence. I filed the subject away as something to consider
in the future.

Still, there was a case to be made for Masonic fingerprints being
all over Oak Island. Interestingly, the most exhaustive claims of Masonic
involvement were made by those skeptical of the treasure story. Joe
Nickell had observed that "secret vault symbolism" was central in a
number of Masonic rituals, and he described certain inscribed stones
on the island as "explicitly Masonic." Nickell pointed in particular to a
stone discovered by Gilbert Hedden at Joudrey's Cove in 1936 that featured a cross next to the letter H, which he described as "a modification
of the Hebraic letter for Jehovah," and another carving of the Masonic
symbol known as the point within a circle that represented mankind
within the compass of God's creation. It was an intriguing possibility,
though this carving hadn't been dated, and it could have been made by
people involved in the treasure hunt rather than by those who had dug
the Money Pit and made the flood tunnels.

Nickell had stretched his argument further than that, however. His
list of Masons "associated" with the treasure hunt on Oak Island included
not only Franklin Roosevelt but also the polar explorer Richard Byrd
and the actor John Wayne. Wayne's closest connection to the treasure
had been some correspondence between a mining company in which
he was an investor and an Oak Island search company about renting a
piece of equipment. Admiral Byrd was a passive investor in a company
that proposed an expedition to Oak Island and had some conversations

with FDR about what might be buried there, but he was never directly involved in any of the operations on the island. Nickell went further out on a limb when he attempted to make something of an "old metal set-square" that had been found at Smith's Cove. "Indeed, the square is one of the major symbols of Freemasonry," Nickell had observed. It's also a common tool that's used by virtually everyone involved in mechanical engineering and technical drawing and was almost certainly left on Oak Island by a member of one of the early search companies.

At the end of his *Skeptical Inquirer* article, Nickell had equivocated, conceding that he couldn't be sure "whether the Masonic elements were opportunistically added to an existing treasure quest or whether the entire affair was a Masonic creation from the outset. " Still, he insisted the mystery of Oak Island had been "solved."

A far more thorough and compelling exploration of the Masonic symbolism on Oak Island—along with a more definitive conclusion—was provided by another skeptic, Dennis King, who had authored an Internet article entitled "The Oak Island Legend: The Masonic Angle." Though I found the arguments King made to be even weaker than Nickell's, the research on which he based those claims was admirably detailed and quite fascinating. I was especially impressed by the connections King (a Freemason himself) had made between the works on Oak Island and a pair of Masonic rituals practiced in the eighteenth century by those who attained the Thirteenth Degree in Freemasonry's so-called Scottish Rite:

> Prior to the flood, the biblical patriarch Enoch constructed an underground temple consisting of nine chambers descending vertically into the earth, and in the ninth or lowest chamber he deposited a treasure which included the secret name of God engraved on a triangular plate of gold. The temple was inundated by Noah's flood and was lost, until it was accidentally rediscovered by three searchers ("Grand Master Architects" in the Masonic description) during the building of King Solomon's

Temple, with the three searchers recovering the treasure and the
secret name of God from the lowest or ninth chamber.

The parallels to the Money Pit, with its nine tiers of log platforms and
the flood system that had rendered it impenetrable for the past 220
years, were obvious.

King had taken his material mainly from an exposé of Masonry
published in the 1850s by William Morgan under the title "The Mysteries of Freemasonry," but focused his attention mainly on the 1864
Colonist articles (which he definitely attributed to Jothan McCully, a
Mason, according to King), noting a number of claims made in it about
the discovery and exploration of the Money Pit that corresponded to
elements of Masonic rituals. In addition to the nine levels in the Pit and
the flood system, the triangle of oak trees that surrounded the Money
Pit in McCully's telling could conceivably be linked to the triangular
plate of gold on which the secret name of God was engraved according to the Masonic rituals described in Morgan's book. It was possible
also, I conceded, that the inscribed stone found at either 80 or 90 feet
in the Money Pit was analogous to the "cubic stone" with an iron ring
handle that covered the entrance to Enoch's temple, according to Morgan's description of the ritual of the Knights of the Ninth Arch, even
though the cubic stone was on the surface in the Masonic ritual and the
inscribed stone was buried deep belowground in the Money Pit. King
contended that the letters and symbols McCully had said were carved
into the trunks of the three oak trees could be compared to the inscription on the cubic stone, according to Morgan's account of the Masonic
rituals. He began to lose me, though, when he suggested that the story
of how McGinnis, Smith, and Vaughan had discovered the Money Pit
was an invention meant to echo the legend of the three grand master
architects in the Enochean ritual. McGinnis, Smith, and Vaughan were
real people and the story of the Money Pit's discovery had come from
them and those close to them, not from McCully.

I had to be impressed by how thoroughly King had researched the early accounts of the three small chain links that had been brought to the surface by the auger boring of 1849. In the three *Colonist* articles published in January 1864, there was no mention at all of any chain links or gold links being brought to the surface by the auger. They *had* been mentioned, though, in an article published eleven months earlier, in the *Yarmouth Herald*'s February 19, 1863, edition, which described "three links of a chain, of a copper colour, which, however, upon being tested proved to be gold." Yet the same newspaper on March 12 of that year had referred to "gold wire" rather than chain links as being what the auger brought to the surface. But in his 1867 diary, King noted, James McNutt had referred not to chain links brought up by the auger, but to three pieces of copper wire. And two articles published in September 1866 in the *New York Herald* and the *Scotsman* that were otherwise fairly complete accounts of the Oak Island treasure hunt so far made no mention of either chain links or wire being brought to the surface by the pot auger borings of 1849. That was all pretty interesting, though I found it difficult to draw any conclusions. For King, though, these variances were evidence of an attempt to introduce another Masonic element into the Oak Island story. "The aprons and other regalia worn by Freemasons are often adorned with metal epaulettes," he noted, "comprising chains of small links, and which were and still are frequently of gold or a metal resembling gold."

Again, King brought this back to McCully, drawing this time on a biographical sketch of the man that had been produced by Oak Island researcher Paul Wroclawski. McCully had lived most of his life in Truro, Nova Scotia, and had fathered ten children who were raised there. He had worked as an engineer, which was why he had been appointed manager of operations for the Truro Company in 1845. I wasn't sure about that; there were records that said he'd worked in a train station. Whatever his regular job, McCully had remained active in the treasure hunt on Oak Island for more than twenty years, working, among other things, as the secretary of the Oak Island Association and as a director of the Halifax Company.

"What Were McCully's Motives?" read the concluding section of King's article.

There were two possibilities, he wrote. First, "the more speculative and sinister possibility," was that "the Oak Island Treasure Hunt in the 19th century was a deliberate fraud, and McCully inserted the Masonic elements as a coded warning to his fellow Scottish Rite Masons that Oak Island was fraudulent and they shouldn't waste their money by investigating it." King did not explain why McCully would choose not to simply announce that the treasure hunt was a fraud or why he would invest the next several years of his life and a considerable portion of his fortune in that treasure hunt. At least King had been judicious enough to describe it as "speculative."

The second, and "more likely" motive for McCully's account of the treasure hunt, King went on, was that he had been "perpetrating a Masonic prank, or a kind of in-joke with his fellow Masons." At a cost of tens of thousands of hours and a commensurate amount of dollars over a period of almost a century, McCully and his mates must have been dedicated comedians.

I was beginning to think that the problem with the Oak Island skeptics—apart from the highly selective manner in which they sorted the evidence—was that they inevitably proposed explanations for the treasure hunt that were far more fantastic than what they called the Oak Island legend.

Still, there was something to this whole claim of a Masonic connection to Oak Island. I didn't think it had to do with who the treasure hunters had been, though I didn't rule that out completely. What interested me was the possibility of a Masonic connection to the original work on Oak Island. That didn't mean that Freemasons, per se, had done that work, but their precursors went back deep into history. It has been often claimed that the traditions underlying the creation of Freemasonry go back at least as far as the ancient Greek mathematician and philosopher Pythagoras (570–495 BC), who learned geometry from the Egyptians, arithmetic from the Phoenicians, astronomy from the Chaldeans, and philosophy and theology in Babylon. He's best remembered today for the theorem that bears his name, stating that the square of the hypotenuse of a right triangle is equal to the sum of the squares of the other two sides. What's not as well-known is the cult of devotion that grew up around Pythagoras after he moved to the Italian city of Crotone and began preaching his religious and ascetic doctrines, urging his followers to abandon material-ism to pursue spiritual development. This movement came to a climax when its adherents were attacked by a mob that set their meeting place on fire. The organized brotherhood of Pythagoreans disappeared from the face of the Earth, but a remnant carried on as a sect and it is claimed that they formed the earliest European mystery school.

Many of the mystery schools—associations that offered esoteric instruction—that arose on the Continent, though, declared as their founder not Pythagoras, but a master who had preceded him, known as Hermes Trismegistus. Hermes "Thrice-Great" was said to have mani-fested at three different times in three different places, first in Egypt where he was equated with the god Thoth, who had introduced civiliz-ing knowledge to men by carving the first teaching of sacred science in hieroglyphs (the American mystic Edgar Cayce claimed in his "trance readings" that Hermes/Thoth was an engineer from the sunken city of Atlantis who had designed and directed the construction of the Pyra-mids). Hermes's second incarnation was as the teacher of Pythagoras in Babylon, according to this tradition, and his third was as the first teacher of alchemy on the European continent, the one who introduced the rituals that eventually became Freemasonry.

There is another claim, either competing or complementary, depend-ing on who is making it, that Freemasonry arose from the surviving tra-ditions of the Knights Templar, the order of monk-warriors that arose during the Crusades and grew to become perhaps the wealthiest and most powerful organization on Earth before it was destroyed by a jealous French king in the early fourteenth century. According to this version of Masonry's origins, the knights who survived went underground in Europe until the eighteenth century, when they reemerged as the modern Freemasons.

It was true, Charles Barkhouse told me, that there was a Masonic order known as the Knights Templar, but that group didn't claim any direct descent from the original knights. That said, there were many Freemasons who believed that the origins of the group went back to the time of the Crusades. That claim had been extant since 1737, when Chevalier Ramsay, the famous Scottish Jacobite, declared that European Freemasonry had been born of a marriage between the Templars and another order of crusader knights, the Order of St. John, also known as the Knights Hospitaller.

There was also, of course, a claim that invoked Francis Bacon as the interface between the ancient mystery schools out of Egypt and Asia and European-based alchemy, and as the foundational figure in the rise of Freemasonry. What's certain is that Bacon did regularly assemble the leading men of Elizabethan England at Gray's Inn to discuss politics, science, philosophy, literature, and religion. Whatever the truth is about Bacon's centrality in the founding of Freemasonry, it is known that Bacon's sixtieth birthday was celebrated in the year 1622 with what was called a Masonic banquet at which the poet Ben Jonson read a "Masonic ode."

What all that meant, I had no idea, but I was resigned to the fact that I would be required to investigate further. There was some kind of connection between Oak Island and what became Freemasonry, I tentatively believed. It was tempting to try to weave the loose threads into a whole cloth.

I wasn't buying the idea that Oak Island was an inside joke—or even an inside job—among the Freemasons of Nova Scotia, however. The leaders of the various expeditions to Oak Island who had been identified as Masonic bigwigs—Blair, Hedden, Hamilton, among others—all had dedicated a huge portion of their lives and fortunes to the treasure hunt on the island. They had been believers in a big way, every one of them. And the mystery of the place had been a large part of what captivated them.

Blair alone offered an overwhelming refutation of the "Masonic prank" theory. The man had invested more than half a century—nearly

THE CURSE OF OAK ISLAND 169

three-quarters of his life—along with the bulk of his fortune and a huge part of his energies in the Oak Island treasure hunt. His commitment had been as close to absolute as seemed humanly possible, and in early 1951, as the twentieth century rolled into its second half, he was approaching the end of his life still holding on tightly to the treasure trove license to the Money Pit. He might have grown cantankerous in the eyes of some, and he was certainly stubborn, but it was impossible not to admire the man for his perseverance in the face of failure after failure.

Blair's death in March 1951 at the age of eighty-three marked the end of an epoch and the breaking of the last living link between the nineteenth and the twentieth centuries on Oak Island. The legacy he left behind included not only the vast collection of documents, letters, and records that still serve as the foundation of any attempt to tell the Oak Island story, but also any number of enduring quotes from various newspaper interviews he gave, including the one that among archeological accomplishments, arriving at the solution to Oak Island would be "equaled only by the discovery of King Tutankhamun's tomb."

R. V. Harris, who had been Blair's attorney, friend, and colleague for almost a quarter century, offered this posthumous tribute to the man:

> Mr. Blair was a good community man and actively interested in the First Baptist Church, Alexandra Masonic Lodge No. 87 and other organizations, and his excellent memory made him an interesting conversationalist. His tall spare figure was very familiar to many citizens of Amherst. . . . Mr. Blair had, in the course of sixty-five years, gathered a vast amount of information respecting the efforts to find the Oak Island Treasure; he believed implicitly in its existence and in its ultimate recovery. . . . Mr. Blair received thousands of letters from eccentric as well as sane people who had suggestions to make for the sure and certain recovery of the treasure. In answering them, he was invariably courteous as well as lucid.

Though he died before I was born, researching this book made me feel compelled to pay my own respects to Frederick Blair, and that included a consideration of the theory of Oak Island on which he had become fixated in his last years. As did a number of others, this theory originated in seventeenth-century England. The execution of King Charles I had been the climax of a nearly a decade of upheaval, a good deal of it owing to the monarch's refusal to submit to the British Parliament's demands for a constitutional monarchy. Under a claim of divine right, Charles levied enormous taxes and spent as he saw fit. This included amassing what was arguably the finest personal collection of art that has ever existed, an estimated 1,760 paintings by, among many others, Rembrandt, Raphael, Rubens, Titian, Correggio, Brueghel, Velázquez, Caravaggio, and Da Vinci. Charles's gold and silver alone, most of it in the form of royal and church plate, was worth what would be billions in today's dollars. And that's what disappeared, along with a trove of historical artifacts, after the king was beheaded in 1649 under the protectorate of Oliver Cromwell. Although he was never very specific— at least in his journals and letters—about who precisely was responsible, Blair became convinced that the missing treasure of Charles I had been transported around 1650 to Nova Scotia, where "very probably it now lies buried on Oak Island."

I could find no particular reason to believe this was so, but as was the case with several dozen other Oak Island theories, it hadn't been disproved. If nothing else, there was a thrill in learning that yet another great treasure had gone missing and remained unaccounted for. Among the most seductive aspects of Oak Island was the way the place nourished one's sense of possibility.

Frederick Blair had never achieved what he set out to do, but what he had gotten done was enough to inspire new generations to follow in his footsteps. The difference between those who thought he should be praised for that and those who believed he ought to be blamed was for me as close to the crux of the Oak Island mystery as any test that could be devised.

CHAPTER THIRTEEN

Shortly after Frederick Blair's death, Mel Chappell, who had bought out the fed-up John Whitney Lewis, acquired Blair's treasure trove license. This meant that for the first time ever, both the license and the land belonged to a single person. Chappell would hold on to both and maintain control of the treasure hunt for nearly thirty years.

Towering, long-jawed, and bespectacled, Chappell had been present as a boy on Oak Island in 1897 when his father, William, brought up that fabled scrap of parchment from the Money Pit, and he had followed events on the island closely since his young adulthood. He was a former grand master Mason of all Nova Scotia whose engineering background and proclivity for technical language made him seem to some the epitome of pragmatism. Even Chappell, though—a man who had looked askance as Gilbert Hedden indulged the inventors of the gold finder and the money-finding camera—would demonstrate how tempting the difficulties of the Oak Island problem made it to take a flier on the wackiest proposals. Months before Blair's passing, in late 1950, Chappell had become intrigued by reports of successful metal detection being achieved by the photographic technology of the Parker Contract Company based in Belleville, Ontario. In December 1950, Chappell invited the inventor Parker to bring his Mineral Wave Ray machine to Oak Island. The fellow showed up with a black box about 2 feet long that was filled with radio tubes, wires, batteries, and resistors, with a lens attached to the front of it. A sample of the treasure being sought after (a gold coin, in this case) was placed inside the box, then the lens was

scanned across much of the east end of the island. About 150 feet from
the Money Pit, Parker declared he had located a deposit of gold that
lay 20 feet below the surface. Chappell was so excited that he barged a
steam shovel out to the island that dug a hole 30 feet wide and 50 feet
deep. Nothing was found. Still, Chappell drilled in four locations located
by the Mineral Wave Ray, but found no sign of treasure in any of them.
By that point he had invested $35,000, a loss that seems to have injured
him far more deeply than the humiliation.

As a result, Chappell decided that moving forward he would invest
only other people's money in the Oak Island treasure hunt, which would
require partners. Chappell's refusal to personally finance any operations on the island seems to have been the main basis for his refusal to
consider teaming up with perhaps the best-known treasure hunter in
the Western Hemisphere, Edward Rowe Snow.

Snow was a Harvard College graduate who had served with the
air force's XII Bomber Command during World War II, then returned
to Massachusetts to work as a columnist for the *Quincy Patriot Ledger*.
While holding down his newspaper job, Snow wrote dozens of books
and articles about New England maritime history, with a special empha-
sis on the age of piracy. He also began to host a radio show for youth
called *Six Bells* that each week chronicled the adventures of some buccaneer and was perhaps best known as the "Flying Santa" each year at
Christmastime, hiring a small plane to drop wrapped gifts for each of
the lighthouse keepers along the New England Coast.

Snow's 1951 book *True Tales of Buried Treasure* had spread the legend
of Oak Island across the United States. He had first visited the island two
years before that, and immediately afterward issued a pronouncement
that startled many, given his reputation as a chronicler of buccaneers:
"Although there have been many theories and explanations regarding
the Oak Island treasure, I personally like to think that it is an immense
hoard brought to Oak Island from a South American country at the time
the Spaniards threatened that part of the world. The average pirate or

freebooter had neither the inclination, the patience, nor the engineering ability to bury a treasure by such elaborate methods."

Though neither Blair nor Chappell seemed ready to welcome Snow to join their efforts on Oak Island, the man had made big news in Nova Scotia and beyond in the summer of 1952, when he announced that based on a map he had obtained in 1947—one that he believed had belonged to the pirate Edward Low—he intended to search for a cache of buried treasure on Isle Haute, just off the mainland in the Bay of Fundy. Snow had already garnered headlines as a treasure hunter, beginning in 1945, when, based on documents containing "secret codes," he recovered a copper chest in Chatham, Massachusetts, filled with gold and silver coins that had been minted in eight different countries between 1694 and 1854. As a result, his trip to Isle Haute "armed with a metal detector and a mysterious old map" as one reporter put it, was considered newsworthy—especially after Snow unearthed not only a stash of eighteenth-century Spanish and Portuguese doubloons, but also a skeleton that was "clutching the coins" as one breathless newspaper account had it.

In spite of Snow's renown, though, Mel Chappell was not interested in going into business with him—unless Snow was ready to sink his own money into the enterprise. Another three years would pass before Chappell finally found a partner who was well funded enough to be considered "suitable." That man was George Greene of Corpus Christi, Texas, a petroleum engineer who claimed the backing of five large oil companies willing to spend "any amount of money," as Greene put it, to solve the mystery of Oak Island.

Greene came on like a caricature of Texan bravado, invariably described in contemporaneous accounts as a blustering, burly, cigar-chomping character perpetually outfitted in a wide-brimmed Stetson hat and hand-tooled cowboy boots. He'd made international headlines a few years earlier when, conducting a geological survey in Turkey, he claimed to have photographed the remnants of Noah's Ark during a flyover of Mount Ararat. It was enough to launch an expedition to the site, but nothing was found and some who had joined the effort later accused Greene of hoaxing them.

Loud and flamboyant as he may have been, the Texan's personal interest in Oak Island actually could be traced back to that paragon of northeastern gentility, Franklin Delano Roosevelt. Greene's uncle, John Shields, had worked with FDR on Oak Island in the summer of 1909, and as a boy Greene had marveled at his uncle John's stories of that great adventure.

"My principals have sent me up here to prove or disprove the legend, and if there's anything there we are going to find it," Greene told the first Nova Scotia newspaper reporter who interviewed him. His plan, basically, was to apply oil-finding methods to the search for gold by doing core drilling all over the Money Pit site. "If we don't hit a concrete vault with this drilling, we'll pack up and I'll head for South America." Even if his operation failed, Greene added, he believed he could recoup his investors' money by selling the movie rights.

Chappell and Greene signed their agreement in September 1955, under which Greene would receive a free lease on Chappell's Oak Island properties in exchange for the promise to pay for all operations out of his own pocket and to split the take equally. The two began with a review of drilling records on the island that went back to 1897, in an attempt to locate the Money Pit. Greene and his crew then used a 4-inch core drill to bore four holes on a line 2, 6, 10, and 14 feet on the north side of the Chappell Shaft. In the first three holes, layers of oak timber were struck at 10-foot intervals, and voids were encountered below that. In the fourth hole, oak timber 8 inches thick was struck at 100 feet. Below was a void 10 feet deep. The drill then bored through another 8 inches of oak before entering a large cavity that was 45 feet deep, after which it reentered clay at 190 feet. Greene and his men poured 100,000 gallons of water into the void the fourth borehole had passed through, but it all ran out through a tunnel Greene could never locate.

Greene told Chappell he needed bigger equipment and would return in the spring of 1956 with 30-inch drills. In early 1956, though,

Greene wrote that he had important business elsewhere and his return to Oak Island would be delayed. He never made it back to the island and was murdered during a 1962 expedition in the jungles of British Guiana not far from where cult leader Jim Jones would set up the Jonestown colony a few years later. Nevertheless, the Texan did enter the annals of Oak Island as the first to prove conclusively that there was a cavern beneath the Money Pit.

After Greene's departure, Canada's national engineering journal ran an editorial in which it described the failure to solve the problem of Oak Island as "a national embarrassment." It's unclear whether this assessment spurred two Ontario brothers, William and Victor Harman, to join the fray, but in April 1958 the Harmans entered into a one-year agreement with Mel Chappell to fund a new round of operations on Oak Island and to split what they believed to be $200 million in Spanish gold that was buried at the bottom of the Money Pit.

The Harman brothers hired professional drillers who in May 1958 began a probe of the Money Pit area that brought up fragments of oak and spruce, along with bits of coconut fiber and ships' caulking from depths below 150 feet. Within two months, though, their private funds were exhausted. The Harmans attempted to raise more money by forming Oak Island Exploration Co. Ltd. and offering 1 million shares at twenty-five cents apiece. The Ontario Securities Commission refused to license their company, however, before the brothers had secured a five-year lease on Oak Island. Unconvinced that they would be able to raise the capital needed, Chappell refused to renew the Harmans' lease and, like so many before them, the brothers quit the island without having produced anything more than those tantalizing but minor discoveries.

MY FAVORITE OF ALBERT EINSTEIN'S MANY APHORISMS is the one about how there are really only two ways of looking at existence: either everything's a coincidence or nothing is. I like to think of myself as standing on the "nothing is" side of that argument, but even if it was merely a fortuitous coincidence, my encounter with Lee Lamb and Rick Restall during my first visit to Oak Island in 2003 was the most moving part of that trip. It was probably the most memorable, too, even if I was at moments tempted to try to forget about it.

Lee and Rick were the oldest and youngest children of Robert and Mildred Restall, the couple who had been the leading players in Oak Island's great tragedy, a calamity that seems to haunt the island even now, more than fifty years later. It certainly haunted Rick. A small dark-haired man in his early fifties when I met him, Rick looked younger but for his eyes, which were filled with so much pain that it hurt to hold his gaze. He was just eight years old when his parents brought him to Mahone Bay in 1959 and so could claim literally to have grown up on the island. Almost forty years after leaving, he still knew nearly every inch of it. Not that this did him much good, because Rick hated the place. Rick paid his first visit to Oak Island since the 1960s the day before our interview and the experience had stirred up memories of what the island had taken from him all those years earlier. I'd like to think he was happier on other occasions.

Even though it was a September afternoon at the tail end of summer, the weather was as dank and gloomy as it had been from the moment I arrived in Nova Scotia about a week earlier. When I think of the two hours I spent with the surviving children of Robert and Mildred Restall, at a table in a restaurant that had bad food but a good view of Oak Island, the first image that comes to mind is the way Lee sat between her younger brother and me, as if even at this stage of life she felt obliged to protect him. Lee was in her early sixties, wore thick glasses, and had gray hair that she wore shorter than mine. She had long since raised her children and seemed to have achieved some sort of contentment as she settled in for the transit to old age. She also seemed much cheerier than her brother, perhaps because she had paid only a couple of brief previous visits to Oak Island and never lived there. I directed most of my questions to her, both because it made me feel vaguely guilty to interrogate Rick and because Lee was

a marvelous source of information about the people her parents had
been before they came to Oak Island.

Mildred was a seventeen-year-old British ballerina in 1931 when
she met Bob, who was twenty-five, from Toronto, and working as a
daredevil motorcyclist with a circus that was touring Europe that summer. Within a year the two were not only married, but partners in one
of the most famous and heart-stopping carnival acts on the planet. The
Restalls' Globe of Death was a steel mesh sphere 20 feet in diameter
within which Rob and Mildred rode a pair of motorcycles at sixty-five
miles an hour—she horizontally, he vertically. "It was all about split-
second timing and perfect trust," Lee Lamb told me. The couple did it
for years and suffered only one serious accident, in Germany, in which
Mildred broke her jaw and Bob broke an arm.

By the 1950s, though, the advent of television had decimated the
carnival circuit. Bob brought Mildred and their three young children
back to Canada, where they settled in Hamilton, Ontario. Bob was soon
working as a pipe fitter but he never got comfortable with domestic life.
In 1954 he read an article about Oak Island and one year later arranged
a trip to Mahone Bay. "Dad came home from his first visit to the island
absolutely enchanted," Lee recalled. "It was all he could talk about. He
thought it was the most fascinating puzzle on Earth." Four years passed,
though, before he could persuade Mildred to join the adventure. When
the Harman brothers quit Oak Island in late 1958, Bob saw his chance
and began to hector Mel Chappell to give him a chance to take over the
treasure hunt. With no better offer on hand at that moment, Chappell
in the spring of 1959 signed a one-year agreement with Restall, who
agreed to pay the government its 5 percent of any treasure recovered,
then to split what was left equally.

Bob and his eighteen-year-old son, Robert Restall Jr.—Bobbie—
arrived in October of that year to set up their camp on Oak Island. Mildred and nine-year-old Rick (Ricky back then) followed in the summer
of 1960. Lee had just married and was living in Oakville, Ontario. "So
I was spared," she told me.

The family's life savings of $8,500 was mostly gone within months of Mildred's arrival on Oak Island. Lacking the money to hire men or lease heavy machinery, the Restalls worked the ground on Oak Island with picks and shovels, the same way it had been done back in the eighteenth century. Bob had come to Nova Scotia determined to make up for what he lacked in resources with energy and applied knowledge. For most of the previous three years he had not only pored over the records of every Oak Island expedition between 1850 and 1900, but he also studied dozens of charts of Mahone Bay, looking for whatever might have been overlooked by previous treasure hunters. By the time he arrived on Oak Island, Bob knew the details of the 1937 Roper survey commissioned by Gilbert Hedden backward and forward, and he had made exhaustive comparisons of notes and journals that had been created not only by Hedden, Blair, and Hamilton, but also by McCully, McNutt, and Adams Tupper, among other searchers from the nineteenth century.

Based on what he had learned, Bob announced that he would devote his energies first to exploring the drains at Smith's Cove in an attempt to solve the riddle of the flood system. With Bobbie working alongside him, Bob concentrated his efforts on the span of the shore-line between the old cofferdam and the high tide mark. According to the journals they both kept, the two dug sixty-five holes, all between 2 and 6 feet deep, and uncovered multiple sections of the five finger drains, along with thick mats of eel grass and coconut fiber under the man-made beach. In the progress report he submitted to Mel Chappell in 1961, Bob Restall wrote: "We now have a complete picture of the beach work, and it is incredible." Though a good bit of it had been torn up by the Truro Company crews that first found it in 1850, this work stretched for 243 feet along the inner edge of the cofferdam, according to Bob's report, composed entirely of "paving stones" overlaid with eel grass, coconut fiber, sand, and rocks. While he had determined that the five finger drains all converged at one point just above the low tide mark, he had not been able to locate the main channel, Bob wrote to Chappell. There were two possibilities: either the drains were no longer connected to that channel, or it was much deeper underground than he could reach by hand digging.

He had enjoyed that first summer on Oak Island, Rick Restall remembered. His parents let him explore the island from end to end, accompanied by the family's Belgian sheepdog, Carnie, who was utterly devoted to the nine-year-old. He fished, swam, and hiked through the woods. In the evenings the family entertained one another by dreaming out loud about how they would spend their future wealth—$30 million by Bob's estimate. Bob wanted a yacht and talked about sailing around the world. Older brother Bobbie wanted a sports car, a new make and model each week. His mom just wanted a snug home on the mainland with flowers in the yard and neighbors nearby.

Then winter came. They were living in two 16-by-10-foot shacks without plumbing, running water, or electricity. One doubled as Bob and Mildred's sleeping quarters and as the kitchen where Mildred cooked their meals on a propane stove. The other was a combination tool-shed and bedroom for the boys. The interiors grew colder, darker, and danker as the rain that fell day after day turned gradually to sleet and snow. There was a tiny oil heater in the main cabin that put out a small amount of heat, but the boys' bedroom—"if you could call it that," Rick said—was always freezing. He and Bobbie slept in socks and knit caps, but still shivered in their sleeping bags some nights. "I guess the only blessing for me was that I was so young and didn't have much to compare it to," Rick told me.

Mildred, though, *could* remember what her life had been like before Oak Island. She became increasingly miserable, exhausted by the continual talk of the search that was the only conversation that Bob and Bobbie seemed interested in. For entertainment, they had not even a radio, only a kerosene lamp to read by and a chessboard. Mildred spent hours every day helping Ricky with his homeschooling courses, but her evenings were becoming long and empty. Bob regularly regaled the family with his theory that Oak Island had been used as a "sort of Ft. Knox" built by forced labor over a period of twenty years under the supervision of the privateers headquartered at LaHave, who needed a place to store the booty they seized in raids on Spanish ships and settlements. Bob thought some of it was the loot that Henry Morgan had carried away from his sacking of Panama City back in 1671. He pointed to the tunnel systems that had been created by pirates in the West Indies, "which could be flooded at will by sea-water" as he put it to a reporter for the *Hamilton (Ontario) Spectator*. Mildred became convinced that the work on the island had been done by the Acadians shortly before their expulsion from Nova Scotia in 1755, and that they had long since come back to retrieve it, meaning there was no longer any treasure to recover.

"We were poor and lonely," Rick told me. "And my mom suffered for it the worst."

"I remember watching my mom cut out the rips and tears in one of Dad's old shirts to make a shirt for herself," said his sister, Lee, recalling the trip she made to see her family while the rest of them were living on Oak Island. "And I thought, 'This is insane!'"

Rick didn't realize the effects of their deprivation on him until he was much older. "I have splayed feet because rubber boots were the only shoes I owned," he said.

By the end of their second winter on Oak Island, Rick said, "My mom went from being a pretty sunny person to a very unhappy one. She became bitter."

"Bitter because she couldn't understand Dad's obsession," Lee added. "The mystery of Oak Island was all that mattered to him."

Bob was tireless. You had to give him that. And he had drawn his oldest son almost as deeply into the adventure as he was willing to go. The two of them worked seven days a week, literally from dawn to dusk, and then spent hours each evening writing in their journals and discussing what they had learned. Mostly the two of them dug, but they also explored the island and made discoveries that have become part of Oak Island's lore. There were the three huge piles of stones that formed a triangle on the slope of the east-end drumlin, just below the Money Pit on the northwest side, also. Bob described them as "the ruins of early sentry stations." He and Bobbie also measured the key distances in what would have been the standard unit of measure for seventeenth-century Englishmen, rods, determining that the distance between the base of the stone triangle and the center of the Money Pit was precisely 18 rods, that it was 2 rods exactly on a true northeast course from the Money Pit to the nearest drilled rocks, and 25 rods from the other drilled stone. Restall was also the first to decide that the Oak Island swamp might be the key to solving the mystery of place. His son Bobbie's journal is filled with descriptions of their search for the metal "mystery box" that Edwin Hamilton's caretaker Jack Adams had claimed was buried in a corner of the swamp.

Bob believed his family's most important discovery was what became known as the "1704 stone." Some would later accuse Restall of planting the stone, but when I asked Rick Restall about that he was indignant. "My dad and brother were digging up one of the areas that covered the five finger drains, dumping the stones off to one side with a bucket and trolley line. My mother and I were wandering on the beach through the stones when one of us turned over a stone by stepping on it, and we saw the date carved into its center: 1704."

The stone may have been—probably was, R. V. Harris thought—one found by Edwin Hamilton in 1939, the practical joke of a workman who later admitted to carving the stone. Bob Restall thought the stone was critically important, though, because the date—1704—was when Jacques de Broullain, the French governor at LaHave, had welcomed the pirates of the North Atlantic to rid him of the raiders from Massachusetts.

Be that as it may, it was on the basis of his discovery of the 1704 stone, along with the 1961 report that he had submitted to Chappell, that Bob Restall was able to raise $11,000 from an assortment of Ontario friends and investors who had been promised half of his share of the treasure. Restall spent most of that money to purchase the very same 1,000-gallon-per-minute electric pump that both Hedden and Hamilton had used to drain the shafts surrounding the Money Pit. Bob set the pump up over the Hedden shaft, recribbing sections of it down to 155 feet, then went to work on the Chappell shaft, using both of these pits to explore the old searcher tunnels that had been dug by the Oak Island Association back in the 1860s. Connected to the surface only by a rope that extended between him and his teenage son, Bob found that many of these tunnels were still in good shape and drove several new stubs off in various directions, but still couldn't locate the main flood tunnel.

Restall's enthusiasm for the search seems never to have waned, even slightly, but by 1964 he was beginning to feel the pressure, not only because of the unhappiness his wife was finding it more and more difficult to conceal, but also because of the fear that Mel Chappell was going snatch his dream from him. Chappell refused to sign more than a one-year agreement with Restall, so each spring Bob endured a period of nearly unbearable tension as the previous year's contract came up for renewal. Chappell made no secret of the fact that he was looking for a "big fish" with the wherewithal to conduct the treasure hunt on the scale he believed was required, and he brought a steady stream of potential partners to the island, all of them introduced to the Restalls and encouraged to describe their grand schemes. In the summer months, Bob constantly worried about whether this or that group of campers were tourists or potential rivals.

The worst part for Restall was that the stress of his situation was being aggravated by one of his own investors, a petroleum engineer from California named Robert Dunfield. Restall had invited Dunfield to Oak Island to take a look at his operation, but shortly after the California man arrived Chappell met him and decided that Dunfield might very well be the big fish he had been trolling for. Dunfield's Beverly Hills business address impressed Chappell mightily, as did the engineer's analysis of the situation. Oak Island was "a problem in open-pit mining," Dunfield had declared, one that could only be solved with a combination of high explosives and heavy machinery "on a scale never before tried." Dunfield admitted it would be expensive, but the California man claimed to have backers who were willing to foot the bill. By the summer of 1965, Dunfield was negotiating his own deal with Chappell, one that would cut out Robert Restall.

Restall found his way to a wealthy Montreal businessman named David Tobias, who gave him $20,000 for a percentage of the treasure, if one was ever recovered. A mineralogist and marina operator from Massapequa, Long Island, named Karl Graeser also invested in Restall. Bob approached Chappell with an offer to purchase his Oak Island property but was shocked to learn that the price was now $100,000. He had no choice, Bob told his family, but to deliver results to his investors before his latest agreement with Chappell expired in the spring of 1966.

In June, Restall used some of the money he had received from Tobias and Graeser to hire three men from the mainland to work with him and Bobbie. They were a Mi'kmaq Indian from Robinsons Corner named Jim Kaizer, who was hired as his foreman, and two teenagers from Martin's Point, seventeen-year-old Andy DeMont and sixteen-year-old Cyril Hiltz. They would concentrate entirely on locating and stopping the flood trap, Bob told his crew of four, concentrating their efforts on the Hedden shaft, but also working in a shaft he and Bobbie had dug previously, 10 feet by 6 feet wide and 26 feet deep, on the line between the finger drains at Smith's Cove and the Cave-in Pit.

Bob, Bobbie, DeMont, and Hiltz were working in the Hedden shaft for the first half of the day on August 17, 1965. Jim Kaizer was not present. The air was sticky that day, heavy and still, without even the faintest breath of a breeze, Rick Restall would remember: "The kind of day when the only place you wanted to be was the water."

Bob and Bobbie and the two teenagers had gone to work at six that morning, just as they did every other day, though. Bob was excited by what he described as a "corkscrew tunnel" he had found near the Money Pit, and in his journal the night before had written that he believed he was "within a few feet" of discovering the treasure and that only four or five more days of work would be required. At 2 p.m. he came up out of the Hedden shaft to remind Mildred he had a meeting in town later that afternoon and would be at the cabin in about an hour to wash up and change his clothes.

It was about 2:45 p.m. when Bob walked down toward Smith's Cove to check on the other shaft, where the pump had been running all day. No one actually saw him fall. He was perhaps climbing into the shaft or simply leaning over to look into it when he went in. He must have made some sort of sound, though, because Bobbie told DeMont and Hiltz something was wrong, then ran from the Hedden shaft toward the cove. When he reached the shaft where the pump was running, Bobbie saw his father lying in the black water at the bottom of the shaft, shouted for help, then climbed onto the ladder to go after his father.

The Restall investor Karl Graeser, visiting from Long Island, made it to the shaft just seconds before DeMont and Hiltz did. The three of them stood on the lip and looked down to see the Restalls, father and son, lying side by side in the stagnant water, unconscious. They shouted for help also, attracting a crowd of tourists and some teenagers who were camping on the island. All three climbed onto the ladder to go down after the Restalls, with Graeser in the lead. Not one of them made it to the bottom before they fell from the ladder and lay in what was now a pile of unconscious people at the bottom of the shaft. DeMont, the only one to make it out alive, said the last thing he remembered was seeing Bobbie in the water, his hand on his father's shoulder.

It was fortunate for DeMont, if no one else, that one of the tourists on Oak Island that day was fire captain Edward White from Buffalo, New York, who had been camping near the shore with his family. Recognizing that there must be some sort of deadly gas in the shaft, White tied a rope around both thighs and his waist, then had the other tourists lower him into the shaft. Captain White had managed to lash a second line around the body of the unconscious DeMont before he, too, passed out. Moments later, he and DeMont were pulled out of the shaft by tourists tugging on the ropes and then revived by two men named Richard Barber and Peter Beamish. Robert Restall, Robert Restall Jr., Karl Graeser, and Cyril Hiltz, however, were all dead. Beamish, a teacher at Phillips Academy in Andover, Massachusetts, had talked to Bob just the night before, listening with fascination as Restall described how he had found the key to the network of tunnels between Smith's Cove and the Money Pit. "He was really excited," Beamish told the *Ogdensburg (NY) Journal*, two days later. "He was sure he had it this time."

It had to have been a ghastly scene on Smith's Cove that day, but all I know about it is what I heard from Faron and Tim Kaizer, the son and grandson of Jim Kaizer, whom I interviewed one afternoon fifty-one years later at the Fo'c'sle Pub in Chester. According to Faron (who was ten years old back then), by August 1965, Jim had been working with the Restalls for months and had become close to Bob. "He and Mr. Restall were two peas in a pod, both tough and hardworking," Faron said. "They were the type of men who didn't have a lot of education, but just knew how to do things." Jim was a short, stocky, swarthy man with a broad forehead and a heavily muscled physique. He had inherited those characteristics from his four-feet, seven-inch mother, a full-blooded Mi'kmaq, and he got her ferocity as well. "Dad was a hard man," recalled Faron. "We didn't cross his words, put it that way." But his father seemed to have become "calmer" since he started working with the Restalls on Oak Island, Faron said. "Dad really enjoyed goin' over there. He rarely missed a day, because it was exciting for him." On August 17, though, Jim had stayed home. Their water pump was busted and Jim's wife, Beulah, demanded that he repair it; the couple had eight children, all sons, and the laundry was piled to her shoulders. "I remember every time Dad would think he was done, he'd start to go out to his truck and Mom would come out after him and say, 'It's not fixed yet,'" Faron told me. "So he'd have to go back inside. Then when he came out the third time, his truck wouldn't start." It would haunt Jim later that all these delays had probably saved his life. "Dad was outside workin' on his truck when my Uncle Maynard drove up with Melbourne Chappell. And Maynard said, 'Jim, somethin' happened over at the island.'"

When he arrived at the shaft near Smith's Cove that he had helped the Restalls dig, Kaizer saw a crowd gathered around it. Those closest to the edge were the young volunteers of the Chester Fire Department, red faced and sweaty in their black coats, helmets, and rubber boots, all wearing frightened expressions. They had agreed among themselves by then that the people at the bottom of the shaft were dead, and all that was left to be done was retrieve the bodies. None of the firemen was willing to be lowered into the shaft; they had decided that the only feasible plan was to lower a three-pronged gaff called a treble hook into the pit and pull the bodies up one at a time with that. The firemen were saying to themselves and to onlookers that it would be a bloody mess, but what else could they do. "My dad said, 'No way, you're not doing that,'" Faron remembered. "He said, 'I'll go down.'"

One of the firemen had an old World War II gas mask and Jim put that on, along with a pair of coveralls, then soaked some rags in water and wrapped them around the mask to help keep it sealed. He tied a rope around both thighs and his waist and told the firemen to lower him into the shaft. He went down four separate times, bringing up the bodies one at a time.

"After that, Dad wasn't the same," Faron told me.

"My grandmother said it changed him," Tim agreed, "but that it might have been more what happened after. It was hard to know, because Jim wasn't one to talk about his feelings."

RICK RESTALL AND HIS MOTHER were too numbed by shock to say much to each other or anyone else in the days that followed. "We could barely function and my mother had no idea what to do or where to go," Rick said. Robert Dunfield, the petroleum engineer from California, and Mel Chappell moved in quickly, ostensibly to offer their help and support. "Dunfield had this aura that was very charming, especially to women," recalled Lee Lamb. "He seemed like some sort of movie star and people trusted him." It was Chappell, though, who "before my husband and son were even buried," as Mildred Restall would put it, urged her to come with him to Halifax to sign a legal transfer of the search rights to Dunfield.

Within a week of Bob and Bobbie's deaths, Dunfield had persuaded Mildred to move with Ricky off the island to a house on the mainland, promising to pay the rent for the rest of her life. He kept that promise for a few months, Ricky remembered bitterly, then "just stopped paying." His mother was most devastated, though, by the disappearance of every chart, map, and document she and her husband had collected before and during their six years on Oak Island, her surviving son said. "Dunfield and Chappell even took our photo albums," Rick remembered. "My mother never got over it."

Bob and Bobbie were buried in the Western Shore Cemetery, where Mildred herself would eventually be interred. The grave of Cyril Hiltz was nearby. Though just sixteen, Cyril was supporting himself by his labor and taking care of his pregnant girlfriend. Before being employed by the Restalls, he had worked as a scallop dragger on a boat based out of Lunenburg. It was lucrative work, but it was also dangerous. Cyril had given it up after a few months because, as he confided to his girlfriend, he was afraid of drowning at sea. Drowning was the official cause of his death on Oak Island just a few months later. The coroner's verdict was that all four of those who died in the shaft at Smith's Cove on August 17, 1965, had drowned in the water at the bottom after being overcome by "toxic marsh gas." Methane, though, is colorless and odorless, and all of the witnesses at the scene had described a rotten egg smell coming from the shaft that day. "My grandmother told me that when my grandfather came home that day she hung his overalls out back," Tim Kaizer remembered. "But she said they stank even after a week." And his grandmother agreed it had been a rotten egg smell. "Eventually the overalls got hung up in our mudroom," Faron recalled. "But my dad never wore them again. He said he could still smell the gas on them."

Carbon dioxide, the kind of gas that would have been produced by the fumes of the pump running that day in the shaft at Smith's Cove, is notable for the rotten egg smell it produces when it collects in an enclosed space.

"I say Oak Island killed my parents," Lee Lamb would declare when I interviewed her in 2003 (Mildred Restall, who had never recovered from her heartbreak, had died just a few years earlier). While Rick listened somberly, nodding once or twice, she and I talked about the eerie feel of the island. A gloom created by fog and drizzle had shrouded the island since my arrival in Mahone Bay, but the chills I had experienced on the one visit I made to the island after dark were accompanied by a distinct sense that it was more than the weather that made Oak Island such a spooky place. "There's a darkness to the place, even when the sun shines," Lee said. Ten years later, in an appearance on *The Curse of Oak Island*, she would repeat the sentiment to the Lagina brothers in even stronger language: "I certainly believe there's a malevolent spirit of some kind on Oak Island."

The Kaizer family—Jim Kaizer in particular—would live with that belief. About two weeks after that terrible day, Robert Dunfield offered Jim a job as his night watchman on Oak Island. It was good money for not doing a whole lot, so Kaizer accepted. He didn't hold it for long, however. Early that autumn, Jim came home in the middle of the night badly shaken. "What I remember most is the way my dad swore," Faron recalled. "He was just swearing up and down, not like he was angry, but like it was just comin' out of him. It really scared us. Because we seen him when he would get mad. But he wasn't violent this time. I realize now he was scared. But he was a man who never got scared so he didn't know how to express it except by swearing. It went on for about a week and then he sort of settled down. And I remember Mom sayin', 'Thank God it's over.' Because even she was scared. But Dad still wouldn't go back to Oak Island. He never went back on the island again, not once after that night."

Gradually Jim revealed to his family what had happened, telling Beulah first, letting her tell their sons whatever she saw fit, then eventually confiding in the boys himself. "He told me I wouldn't believe him, but he was tellin' me anyway," Faron remembered. He was in the

Restall's old cabin, Jim said, where he had spent most of his nights on Oak Island. "Dad said it was about eleven or twelve o'clock. He said, 'I had a little fire goin'. I put some wood on the fire and then I lay down on the cot and closed my eyes.' And apparently he fell asleep. And he said, 'I woke up and I couldn't breathe.' And he said there was two of the biggest red eyes you would ever want to see looking right into his. And the whole body was covered with hair, tight and curly black hair. He said that was all he could see, because the . . . whatever it was, was holdin' him down by his arms and had him pinned so tight that he couldn't move. But then it smiled at him and said, 'Don't ever come back.' My dad said when it let him go and disappeared the whole building shook. He said it was just unreal. There was no wind, nothin'. And he got in his truck and drove back across the causeway. And he wouldn't ever go back on the island again after that. He told me, 'It was the only thing that's ever scared me.'"

Even after Jim Kaizer "settled down," as his son put it, he was different. He drank more heavily and was silent for days at a time, but also erupted regularly into frightening rages. "My brothers and me, when we saw him comin' back home, we'd all scatter from the house," Faron remembered. Jim still worked on and off for a local cement contractor and had his own beer bottle recycling business, but he became an increasingly sporadic earner and was in trouble often with the Royal Canadian Mounted Police.

His anguish only increased when he tried to confide in others. "People would ask him if he was drinking that night or maybe was overtired," Tim Kaizer said. "When he realized people didn't believe him, he stopped talking and just bottled it up inside."

"I remember Dad tellin' Mom certain things," Faron recalled. "And she would just shake her head and walk away. But he wanted to tell somebody that it was on his mind."

He should have seen what was coming, Faron said, when "my dad took me aside to apologize for the way he had treated me and my mother."

That was 1976. Just a few weeks later, not long before he would turn fifty, Jim Kaizer shot himself in the head with a rifle outside a bar in Western Shore.

"What I pick up is that there was a group of people and one of them had a gun," Faron said. "Dad took it, but it had no bullets. But there was a woman, and she gave him a bullet. And he walked away, and he told everybody to stay away from him. And then he done it."

When I asked him about it, Dave Blankenship, son of the old Oak Island hand Dan Blankenship and now part of the Lagina brothers' treasure hunt, said that Jim was remembered more locally for "playin' Russian Roulette with a single shot twenty-two" than for going down into the shaft at Smith's Cove on that August day in 1965 to bring up four bodies. The fireman from Buffalo, Edward White, had been honored with Canada's Medal of Bravery for going down once into that poison gas, Jim had reflected on more than one occasion. But the four times he had gone down were completely forgotten.

Beulah's own pain increased considerably after the company that issued Jim's life insurance policy refused to pay out because the cause of death had been suicide. "Mom had no money, so she went to work in the fish plant," Faron said. "Her life had been hard and it got a lot harder." Beulah and Mildred Restall would become close friends. They had both lost their men in tragic circumstances, they both felt cheated and betrayed by people and institutions they had trusted, and they both were forced to work menial jobs to make ends meet.

Tim Kaizer had grown up hearing about what had happened to Grampa Jim on Oak Island, he told me. "I thought it was a cool story, because when you're a kid, it's mythical. But as I've understood more about who Jim was, it's made it seem more and more real. Because for someone like him who was so fearless to be so scared by something that he would never go back to the island, you know it had to be something remarkable."

Tim admitted that he had never set foot on Oak Island. A short, thick power lifter who looked like he could have been carved out of a boulder, Tim worked as a paramedic aboard a medevac helicopter and was conditioned to remain calm in traumatic and often frightening situations. "But Oak Island scares me," he said. "I believe there's a bad spirit on the island. I believe my grandfather encountered it."

Some of that may have to do with what Beulah Kaizer told him when he asked her about that night, Tim said, whether or not she had believed Jim's story. "My grandmother looked at me, and then she told me that when he came home that night Jim had showed her his arms. And they had huge bruises on them that had been made by handprints."

CHAPTER FOURTEEN

Robert Dunfield became the great malefactor of the Oak Island story not for how he treated Mildred Restall, but for how he treated the island itself. Dunfield's motives may not have been as petty as Colonel Henry Bowdoin's, but the blunt instrument methods the man employed have delivered him to infamy. Whether that is *entirely* fair can be argued. That it is just in general is beyond dispute.

The most generous assessment is that Melbourne Chappell and Robert Dunfield decided that since everything else had been tried they might as well declare war on Oak Island and get this thing over with once and for all. Only later would Chappell realize that Dunfield was not everything he appeared to be when he first arrived in Nova Scotia. He was not, for instance, from Beverly Hills but rather from the modest San Fernando Valley suburb of Canoga Park. In 1965, Dunfield was a thirty-nine-year-old UCLA graduate who had made some money drilling oil wells, but not so much that he could personally finance a major operation on Oak Island. To proceed, he had needed investors and found three. There were two other Californians who had made money from oil wells, G. R. Perle of Bakersfield and Jack Nethercutt, whose Beverly Hills home address Dunfield had used on some business documents, giving rise to the wealthy image. The third investor was Dan Blankenship, a successful building contractor from Miami, Florida, whose name would eventually become as closely associated with Oak Island as any in history.

With the backing of his investors, Dunfield had begun work on Oak Island less than a month after Robert Restall and his son were buried.

He started by barging two bulldozers out to the island and with them made clear immediately that he was going to leave his mark on the place. The dozers skimmed 12 feet of soil off the drumlin where the Money Pit was located and dumped it by the tons onto the man-made beach at Smith's Cove. He succeeded in exposing what all agreed was some of the cribbing of the original Pit, but he had no success at all in stopping the inflow of water. So Dunfield went large.

In ten days in early October, he built the causeway that has made it possible for countless people (me among them) to drive across a narrow stretch of Mahone Bay from the mainland. Boats and barges had been the only way to reach Oak Island since the beginning of time, and the 15,000 cubic yards of fill that Dunfield used to construct the causeway created a transformation that was dramatic, but not entirely appreciated. The first enemies Dunfield made in Nova Scotia, in fact, were the fishermen who for two centuries had been using the narrow protected passage between Crandall's Point and Oak Island to access the deeper waters of the bay. Going that way not only shortened the trip for fishing boats, but allowed for a much gentler transition to the sea. I understood how jarred Mahone Bay's fishing fleet must have been by the change Dunfield wrought one day when I rented a kayak at my hotel in Western Shore and set out to paddle around Oak Island. The gentle waves created by the combination of the island and the breakwaters offshore let me cross the inward bay with surprising ease; my greatest difficulties were negotiating the rocks and massive yellow-brown kelp beds when I got too close to shore. When I paddled around the eastern tip of the island though—the elephant's nose, Rick Lagina called it—the change was shockingly sudden. The waves here were abruptly two, three, four times as high as they had been just a couple of minutes earlier, and they fell with choppy gray violence all around. It dawned on me very quickly that I was paddling in the Atlantic Ocean. My tiny kayak took on water at an alarming rate, becoming increasingly unstable. I spun it around finally and paddled hard back the way I came, making for a landing spot where I could tip the kayak and empty it before it dumped me into the sea. Gasping from the exertion and momentary panic, I understood how infuriating it must have been to the captains and crews of the fishing boats who found themselves not only adding twenty minutes to their outbound commute but also being forced to deal with the ocean from almost the moment they left the mainland shore. On bad weather days—and there are a lot of them in Nova Scotia—they must have been truly pissed off. And they let Dunfield know it.

If that bothered him, Dunfield didn't show it. The first thing he did with his new causeway, the day after its completion on October 17, 1965, was haul out a 70-foot-tall crane that was equipped with a 3-yard link belt "clam-digger" bucket capable of removing 800 cubic yards per hour. Right behind the crane and clam digger was a truck loaded with pumping equipment that could remove 111,000 tons of water per hour.

Dunfield headed his heavy equipment straight for the south shore, where he ran two shifts of crews numbering up to a dozen men in an all-out effort to block the flow of seawater into the Money Pit. The work began with the excavation of a huge trench 22 feet deep and 200 feet long, parallel to shoreline. Dunfield claimed to have found a previously undiscovered shaft at a depth of 60 feet where "water rushed in, giving us the evidence of a new flood system leading into the Money Pit." He had confirmed the dye tests made by William Chappell in 1898, when the red dye had come out at three points on the south shore, Dunfield said, and this was one of the places the dye had leaked into the bay.

The clam digger had been scraping against rock-hard clay up to that point, when suddenly the bucket dropped 3 feet in soft ground. They had entered an 8-foot-square pocket of refill—beach rock, beach sand, eel grass, and other vegetation—that was clearly the work of human hands. He and his crew were on the brink of uncovering the main sources of the flood trap, Dunfield said, but a week of probing in all directions with the clam digger at a depth of 60 feet revealed no branch that led to the Money Pit and in the end all Dunfield had accomplished was to wreak even more havoc on the south shore than his bulldozers had done on the beach at Smith's Cove.

In early November Dunfield directed his men and equipment back to the Money Pit. Within two weeks the clam digger had opened a shaft 50 feet wide and 98 feet deep that encompassed both the Money Pit and the Hedden and the Chappell shafts and erased much of what had been left behind on the east-end drumlin. Ten days later the massive hole was 148 feet deep. Dunfield estimated that he had another 48 feet to go, and he told reporters that either he would reach the treasure or "call it quits." The owner of the crane, however, chose that moment to remind Dunfield that he had a contract to use it elsewhere. Dunfield had foreseen this eventuality and swiftly brought in a replacement with a 90-foot boom. Almost immediately, though, the machine was beset by a series of mechanical problems that included a blown gasket and a cracked engine block. Many of the crane's "broken" cables had actually been cut with hacksaws, said Mel Chappell, who accused local fishermen bent on punishing Dunfield for the causeway of being the saboteurs.

When his workmen demanded a holiday over Christmas, Dunfield busied himself by making a complete examination of debris from the Money Pit, all of which had been run through an enormous sluice with a water-filtration system. The only things of note he found in the debris were shards of porcelain dishware and old drill casings that he assumed were from previous expeditions, Dunfield said. When he examined the pit his clam digger had created, though, he found exposed old timbers and hard clay walls with pick marks in them, the last remaining evidence of the original excavation and proof of where exactly the Money Pit was located.

Persistent rain had begun to fall in early December and by the time his crews returned to Oak Island, Dunfield was faced with a pit where daily slides had filled it nearly to the top with sand and soil. He ordered a "reexcavation," but the slides continued and progress was slow. He would deal with the weather by widening the diameter of the hole to 100 feet so that the sides would be gently sloped, then go down to a depth of 184 feet, Dunfield said. He was essentially proposing to turn the top of Oak Island's east drumlin into an enormous crater. The

rain continued, though, and so did the slides. The work was now cost-
ing Dunfield USD $2,000 a day and on January 2, 1966, he ordered his
crew to halt the excavation, refill the pit with soft soil, and prepare to
begin again the following summer.

Dunfield wasn't done, though. He had a huge oil-drilling rig hauled
out to the island and used it to bore four 6-inch holes down to a depth
of 140 feet. At 139 feet the drill dropped into a chamber with a 2-foot
wooden roof that went all the way down to 184 feet.

The half ton of material the drill brought up was sent to the University of Southern California for spectrographic analysis. Other than
saying that the drill had struck cast iron on the floor of the "chamber,"
Dunfield refused to reveal what the USC lab had found. But he did
announce that he would proceed with his plan to dig out the Money
Pit on a huge scale when the weather was drier.

In an interview with local reporters, Dunfield said he was certain
that "somewhere on the surface of the island there is an entrance to the
treasure chamber." It would be on higher ground, according to Dunfield,
who said he had been convinced of this by the pockets of "dry, stale air"
his drill had found. In the same interview, though, Dunfield revealed that
he had already spent $120,000, nearly three times what he had estimated,
and that if he did not recover the treasure by the end of the summer of
1966, he would go back to drilling oil wells until he made up his losses.

Dunfield never really mounted a major operation in the summer
of 1966, though. The problem, he said, was that his lease with Chappell
was going to expire soon, and he had come to the conclusion that he
needed to own the island to justify the level of commitment required.
He issued a press release that "several friends in the oil business have
stated that they were willing to buy the treasure island area and are
interested in the negotiations." The main effect of the press release was
a loud howl of outrage from the Municipal Council of Chester, which
was soon joined by a number of other Lunenburg County organiza-
tions in entreating the Nova Scotia provincial government to declare
Oak Island a national historic park and keep it out of Dunfield's hands.

By then, word of the destruction Dunfield had wrought on Oak Island was spreading throughout Mahone Bay and beyond. The east end and south shore of the island were devastated, those who visited reported. The few days of excavating Dunfield had done at the Cave-in Pit had left it a shapeless hole filled with water. The finger drains at Smith's Cove were broken apart and buried, and the drilled boulder nearest to the cove was gone, never to be recovered. Worse, Dunfield's trench on the south shore had opened so wide during the rainy season that it swallowed the stone triangle whole, and a feature that many thought was key to solving the Oak Island mystery was lost forever.

In the end the provincial government had elected to acquire Grave's Island rather than Oak Island as its new historic park, but by then Robert Dunfield had fled Nova Scotia and would never return. "Nuking the island" was how Dunfield's work was described by Nova Scotia surveyor and historian William Crooker, who claimed that because of the California man "a vast amount of 'visual history' was lost."

Not everyone agreed. Canadian journalist D'Arcy O'Connor wrote that Dunfield deserved credit for rediscovering the site of the original Money Pit and for helping stem the flow of water to the Pit from the south shore flood tunnel." Reacting to my 2004 observation in *Rolling Stone* that Dunfield was "widely regarded as the greatest villain in the Oak Island story," his son Robert Dunfield Jr. (a stakeholder in a subsequent search operation on the island) complained this was unfair. His father's "approach may have been heavy-handed," Dunfield Jr. conceded. "But very little credit is given to the positive aspects of his work" or to the toll that it took on the man. "My father aged ten years in only two years. He put his heart and soul into the effort."

One day in July 2016, as I stood with Rick and Marty Lagina on what was left of Oak Island's east-end drumlin, I asked the brothers if they thought I had been in any way unfair to Dunfield. I told them I had been heavily influenced by what I had heard from Rick Restall in 2003 about his first return trip to Oak Island after he and his mother had moved to the mainland. "When I went back, I was shocked by how the island had changed," Rick had said. "The hilltops had been hacked off, the Money Pit looked like a giant bomb crater, the beach at Smith's Cove had been buried—even the shoreline had changed. I felt sick."

My description of Dunfield as a villain had been fair in his view, Marty Lagina said. Rick didn't disagree, but the older brother, who I would come to know as a man who looked for the good in everyone, said this: "What people need to remember is that Dunfield truly believed he was going to find the treasure. And if he had, no one would have cared what he had done to the island."

"But he *didn't* find the treasure," Marty said.

"That's right. He didn't," Rick agreed. "So he's paid the price of failure. Lots of people have done that on Oak Island."

FOR A FULL HALF CENTURY after Robert Dunfield quit the island, right up to the time that the Lagina brothers showed up in 2006, the treasure hunt was dominated by two men whose heroic efforts and remarkable discoveries were constantly overshadowed by the bitter rivalry between them. One was Dan Blankenship. The other was Fred Nolan.

Blankenship was the one I met first when I came to Oak Island in 2003 and also the one who provided me with the greatest assistance in researching and writing the *Rolling Stone* article. That assistance, though, was not obtained easily. He'd "had it up to here" with reporters, Blankenship told me the first time I got him on the phone, and he hadn't let one on the island in years. "You're all looking to stir up trouble," he said in a voice that made his words sound as if he were chewing them up before he spat them out. Not me, I replied with as much self-assurance as I could muster. All I wanted to do was bring the story of Oak Island up to date for readers who had mostly never heard of the place. I'd already learned that being a writer for the *Rolling Stone* was not the advantage in Mahone Bay that it was in most other places I'd visited in the twenty-plus years I'd been writing for the magazine, but Dan Blankenship drove the point home. "I guess

I've heard of your publication," he said. "But I've never looked at it. Was started by a bunch of hippies for kids who wanted to read about rock music, wasn't it?" I told him it was just one hippie, who now wore an expensive haircut and $5,000 suits. "I just don't see what good it would do me to talk to you," Blankenship said. The best I could do was get him to agree to think it over, which gave me a reason to call back the next day and convince him to come over to the Oak Island Inn, where I was staying, to let me buy him a drink and see what he thought when he met me in person.

He stalked into the hotel bar that evening like a man who didn't want to be bothered by any damn tourists and made me start the conversation with the two of us standing pretty much toe-to-toe next to the table I had been saving for our meeting. He was imperious and irascible and, to me, impressive. Just a few months shy of his eightieth birthday, Blankenship was still a lantern-jawed, big-shouldered bull of a man who had no trouble convincing me that he had cleared out more than a few bars with his fists when he was younger. Still, there was a twinkle in his eyes and a smile he barely suppressed when he tried to provoke me. As it happened, he was a lot like my father, and Blankenship started to soften up when I told him my dad had been a longshore foreman who more or less ran the docks in Portland, Oregon. He even seemed to start liking me a little about a half hour later, because I not only knew what a come-along was, but I had also used one to move some boulders on a piece of property in Woodstock, New York. By then we were sitting down over one apiece of Dan's favorite beverage, a gin martini, dry with olives. When the old man finished his drink, he told me to meet him at the chained-off entrance to the causeway the next morning and he'd bring me up to his house to continue the conversation "and see how much of my time I think you're worth." Given that we spent most of the next forty-eight hours in each other's company, I think it would be fair to say the meeting at the house went well.

At least part of the reason we hit it off was that I didn't hear braggadocio as much as a simple statement of fact when Dan told me,

"I made the decision to come up here in the first place because I had never met an obstacle I couldn't overcome." Blankenship was a highly successful forty-two-year-old building contractor who had just finished the construction of a hospital in Palm Beach, Florida, in 1965, when he picked up a copy of *Reader's Digest* that contained an article about Oak Island condensed and reprinted from the *Rotarian* magazine under the title "Oak Island's Mysterious 'Money Pit.'"

"As soon as I learned about this place, I knew it was the greatest unsolved mystery in the world, and I believed I was the man to solve it." A little later, when I met his wife, Jane, she told me wistfully how different her life might have been if she'd "never let Dan see that damn magazine." Once Dan *had* seen that damn magazine, though, there was no stopping him from making a trip to Nova Scotia to take a look.

Robert Restall was running the treasure hunt at that time, though, and Restall was wary of strangers who showed up there, especially if they were being shown around by Mel Chappell—M. R., as Blankenship was already calling him. Even among those potential interlopers, however, Blankenship was standing in line behind Robert Dunfield, who had taken over the treasure hunt within days of the Restall tragedy. So he invested $21,000 in Dunfield's operation, Dan explained, becoming one of the California man's several limited partners: "Dunfield was going at it the wrong way, but he was my only way in."

Dunfield was gone within a year and Blankenship needed no more than a day or two to persuade Chappell that he was every bit the man he thought he was. Becoming M. R.'s designated treasure hunter was no easy task, though, when Blankenship also had a construction business to run and three children to support back in Miami. For seven years or so he split his life in two, Dan told me, spending his winters in Florida with Jane and their three children, working long days on his company's building projects and spending his summers in Nova Scotia, focused on solving the mystery of Oak Island. "That's how committed I was to figuring this thing out," he said. He stayed for weeks on end in Halifax, poring over the records in the Public Archives of Nova Scotia, the bulk of them collected by Frederick Blair and R. V. Harris. The rest of the time he lived and worked out of a motel in Western Shore, interviewing everyone he could find who had been part of previous expeditions, including not only Mel Chappell, but also Gilbert Hedden and Edwin Hamilton.

One of the earliest conclusions he drew, Dan explained, was that the log platforms that had been found in the Money Pit by the Onslow Company were intended by the people who had done the original work to reduce the compaction of the soil over the years, so that it would subside into only a slight dent in the ground rather than a deep crater and help conceal the Pit. "Clearly they weren't planning on tearing out those platforms to gain access to the treasure when they came back," he told me. "That meant they must have another way to reach it." The key to finding that other way in, Blankenship decided, was to do what so many before had tried and failed to do—stop the flow of water into the Money Pit area. "I thought I was just a little smarter than the other guys," Dan admitted.

He hired botanists and geologists to confirm the construction of the artificial beach at Smith's Cove and to study whatever was left of the five-fingered drainage system there. After mapping out his rough diagram of the flood system, Blankenship laid out plans for an elaborate drilling program and for a series of excavations that would be based on what he found with the drill.

The one thing he hadn't really worked out, however, was how he was going to pay for his elaborate operations. "I was becoming so focused on Oak Island that my construction business was suffering, and so were my finances," Dan told me, lowering his voice slightly, so that Jane, who was in the next room, wouldn't hear him. The truth was that despite a business that was still netting six figures annually, by early 1967 he was "starting to feel the strain, financially." It was at that moment that David Tobias entered his life.

Tobias had first visited Oak Island in 1943, back when Edwin Hamilton was still running the treasure hunt. Tobias had been a young Royal

Canadian Air Force officer training as a combat pilot at the Maitland, Nova Scotia, base when he heard about the island and its history. He made the long drive south on a free day to take a look and left unimpressed. Why they didn't just dig up whatever was down there escaped him completely, he would admit with a laugh sixty years later. It was only in 1963, when he read a newspaper article about Robert Restall's search operation, that he became fascinated enough to invest $20,000 in the project. Tobias had the money to spare; apart from a share of his family's considerable investment portfolio, he was the owner of a very successful Montreal company called Jongerin Inc. that manufactured labels and packaging. Not only was that $20,000 gone after Restall's death in 1965, but also Tobias found himself on the outside looking in as Robert Dunfield tore the island apart during the next year.

In early 1967, though, after Dunfield headed back to California, Tobias approached Mel Chappell and told him about a Toronto company called Becker Drilling Ltd. that was working with a new type of drill, one that operated inside a pipe that was pounded into the ground with a pile-driving hammer. Once the drill bit was sent to the bottom of the pipe, a constant stream of high-velocity air pressure sent the cuttings back up through the pipe. It offered a tremendous advantage over any other piece of equipment so far invented for the recovery of artifacts from underground. A compact man with bright eyes who spoke with remarkable self-assurance, Tobias impressed Chappell enormously, especially when the Montreal man offered to pay for the Becker drilling program on Oak Island personally (at a cost of $130,000) in exchange for two-thirds of whatever treasure was recovered.

Dan Blankenship was even more excited than Chappell about the Becker program Tobias had proposed, but he was not exactly thrilled that Tobias was going to claim two-thirds of the Oak Island treasure if it succeeded. During the previous year, working on a limited budget, Blankenship had made what followers of the Oak Island story considered to be a series of spectacular discoveries after deepening the Dunfield shaft on the island's south shore. At a depth of 60 feet, Dan had uncovered a handwrought nail that was at least three hundred years old and another artifact that was described as either "a nut or washer" formed out of the same primitive low-carbon steel. At 90 feet down the shaft, Blankenship found a layer of round granite stones, each about the size of a man's head, lying in a pool of stagnant black water. He was positive he'd discovered a branch of the south shore flood system, and Chappell was inclined to agree. Blankenship spent months trying to crib and deepen the Dunfield shaft, but he lacked the funds to do it properly and was forced to abandon the effort when earth began to collapse the sides of the pit. Exhausted and tapped out, he was receptive when Tobias approached to explain that he was too busy running his company in Montreal to take charge of the Becker program on Oak Island and needed a "field operation director." Blankenship agreed to take the job for a small salary and a cut of the treasure if the Becker drill located it.

The Becker program began on Oak Island in January 1967 and continued for eight months. His preliminary goal, Tobias told Blankenship, was to prove beyond doubt that there were "man-made underground workings" on Oak Island. And these could only be identified as such at 150 feet or more underground, he said, because only when one went deeper than previous searchers could one be certain that what was found was connected to the original work. Only if he saw the evidence with his own eyes, Tobias said, would he keep the project going.

As far as both Blankenship and Tobias were concerned, that evidence came quickly. The Becker drill would sink 49 six-inch diameter holes in and around the Money Pit area during the eight months it was operating on the island, and only about a dozen of those holes had been bored before Tobias was convinced that they had found the proof they were looking for. Exploration using the Becker drill had established that the bedrock in the Money Pit area began at a depth of about 160 feet, with variances of up to 10 feet in either direction. That was bearing in mind that Dunfield had scraped away enough of the "overburden soil" from the island's east-end drumlin to lower the ground level by about 12 feet from where it had originally been. The bedrock was mostly anhydrite (crystallized calcium sulfate), with some seams of gypsum and limestone in the upper layers. The Becker drill found its first cavity at about 40 feet down in the bedrock, covered on top by two layers of wood that were each several inches thick and separated by a thin layer of blue clay. After passing through the wood, the drill had dropped through a void that was 6 to 8 feet deep before again striking bedrock.

The materials that came out of the drill's tube were fragments of china, cement, wood, charcoal, and metal, including brass that was shown by spectrographic analysis to possess high levels of impurities, meaning the brass was "smelted early," though putting a specific date on its age was not possible. Most exciting, though, were the oak buds found in the blue clay. Geologists said the seeds of oak trees could not possibly have been deposited by the glacial movements that had formed Oak Island, which could only mean they had been placed in the clay by human activity—170 feet belowground. Samples of a "bricklike" material had also been brought to the surface by the Becker drill. Testing by mineralogists confirmed that this material had been exposed to intense heat at some former time. The speculation was that a primitive kiln had operated far below the surface of the island to make and repair iron tools. The charcoal mostly had been used to fire the kiln. The cement was submitted for analysis by experts at Canada Cement LaFarge who identified it as a primitive type that had been common during the sixteenth and seventeenth centuries. The Steel Company of Canada (Stelco) examined the metal pieces brought up from the bedrock and reported that they were at least several hundred years old. The wood that had come back from the deepest levels penetrated by the Becker drill was originally carbon-dated to 1585, but that estimate was plus or minus eighty-five years. A more thorough carbon-14 analysis was performed by Harold Krueger of Geochron Laboratories in Cambridge, Massachusetts. In his report, Krueger cautioned that since it was impossible to know how old the tree had been when it was cut, he could only say that he had found a 67 percent probability that the wood's age fell between 1490 and 1660. To calculate the tree's age with 95 percent accuracy, Krueger wrote, he would have to expand the possible date range to between 1405 and 1745.

For Blankenship, the interesting moment during the Becker drilling had come when the drill was at a depth of 198 feet, only to be absolutely stopped by hitting hard metal. He and the drill operator agreed that it must be metal because of the high keening noise that came up through the tube. "It took us close to half an hour just to bore through a half inch of it," he recalled. "I was tremendously excited to see what it was, but when we tried to bring up the core sample we lost it. I ask you, what would metal hard enough to stop a drill be doing almost two hundred feet belowground? People had to have put it there."

He had done a good deal of searching on his own away from the Money Pit during the months of the Becker drilling program, Dan told me, mostly at Smith's Cove. Dunfield had destroyed most of the old five-fingered feeder drain system, but there were some sections left and he had spent weeks probing them with a shovel. One of the things he had turned up was a heart-shaped stone that had been chiseled. Another was an old set square that metallurgists dated to before 1780. His most amazing discovery had been a pair of handwrought iron scissors that he had pulled from beneath one of the drains. Mendel Peterson, the former curator of the Smithsonian Institution's Historical Archeology division, examined the scissors and said they were of a type made and used by the Spaniards in Mexico during the mid- and late 1600s, though he had added that they might have been made more recently than that.

"The stone and the set square might have been left by early searchers," Blankenship told me. "Probably were. But those scissors, it's almost certain that they were used by the people who did the original work on Oak Island to cut up the coconut fiber and the manila grass that was used as a screen under the artificial beach." I remarked it was hard to know the difference between what was almost certain and what was a distinct possibility. This raised one of Dan's shaggy eyebrows, but he let it pass.

For David Tobias, the most compelling discovery during the Becker program was made when the drill entered a previously undiscovered chamber about 30 feet in diameter, extending from depths between 160 and 190 feet, almost directly beneath the Hedden shaft. It was riddled with holes that were filled with a heavy, puttylike blue clay in which layers of small stones were found at semiregular 18-inch intervals. Colin Campbell, a former army general and mining engineer who was considered Canada's leading historian of underground workings, wrote a report in which he stated that the clay almost certainly had been puddled on the surface, then poured into the holes in layers. Small stones in the clay would sink to the bottom of each layer and produce the sort of stratification found in the drill cores. Before the development of cement, Campbell noted, clay had been commonly used as a water seal in underground workings.

Tobias was heartened by Campbell's conclusion that an enormous amount of human effort had gone into the creation of the Money Pit and the flood system, sometime before the middle of the eighteenth century. "A large number of men were engaged for a few years driving various shafts, inclined and lateral headings, some of which were apparently prepared for flooding in order to discourage any inquisitive searchers," Campbell had written. A little later he added, "In my opinion the early operations by the 'pirates' or other parties were too elaborate and well planned to be for any minor venture and therefore it is reasonable to assume that the operations were for the purpose of hiding treasure which must be of great value to warrant the effort."

The Becker drillings, combined with the conclusions Campbell drew from them, were more than enough to convince both Tobias and Blankenship that they had proved the existence of man-made tunnels with ceilings of wooden planks shored with logs that had been dug at depths of up to 200 feet or more below the island's surface. He was now all in with the treasure hunt, Tobias said, and ready to start reaching out to other people of means who could help him finance it on the scale it merited.

This took a bit longer than expected, but by April 1969 Tobias had put together Triton Alliance, a limited partnership in which he and

Blankenship were joined by "a largely unidentified group of some of Canada's wealthiest and best known businessmen," as Toronto's *Financial Post* would put it. The investors did not remain unidentified for long. They included the past president of the Toronto Stock Exchange, the chairman of the board for one of Canada's two largest supermarket chains, and a former Nova Scotia attorney general, along with a handful of Americans, among them the wealthy Boston land developer Charles Brown. Together, they were prepared to put $500,000 into the operation, according to Tobias, who told the *Financial Post*: "We are the first people to know what to expect and what we are after."

Dan Blankenship had been at it long enough to know that nobody *ever* knew what to expect on Oak Island. "Even I, though, didn't imagine all the trouble Fred Nolan could make for us," he admitted.

CHAPTER FIFTEEN

When I thought about it later, I was fascinated by how determined the partners in Triton Alliance were to portray Fred Nolan as an interloper, given that Fred had been involved in the Oak Island treasure hunt longer than any of them had.

Nolan was a surveyor living in Bedford, Nova Scotia, and working out of an office in Halifax in 1957 when he first visited Oak Island, just as George Greene's operations were winding down. R. V. Harris's *The Oak Island Mystery* was published one year later, and he had read it "forward and backward, at least a half dozen times," Nolan told me when I spoke to him in 2003. He had been thrilled to discover that Harris's office was just a few blocks from his own and began paying visits to the attorney, who seemed to welcome him, even when the surveyor peppered the lawyer with questions about the history of the treasure hunt. Harris would tell people later that he had been impressed with the originality of Nolan's thinking process.

Nolan said he went back to Oak Island to "poke around," only to be informed by Mel Chappell that the Harman brothers were about to take over the treasure hunt and that Robert Restall was waiting in the wings behind them. Nolan, who had become fascinated by the survey Charles Roper conducted for Gilbert Hedden in 1937—in particular by the links Roper had found between the stone triangle, the Cave-in Pit, and the drilled boulders—asked if Chappell would mind if he conducted a survey of the complete island, so long as he did it on his own time and paid for it with his own money. Reasoning that he was getting an expensive service for free, Chappell agreed.

What Nolan didn't tell Chappell was that he had been horrified by the damage to the surface of Oak Island the other man was doing by operating a drag line—essentially a tractor pulling a digging bucket behind it—that tore up everything in its path. Nolan feared that valuable landmarks were being obliterated, which was why he had pressed to conduct a survey immediately.

During 1961 and 1962, Nolan spent thousands of dollars on labor and equipment (and devoted hundreds of hours that his family wished he were putting into his business) to lay out a grid that covered every inch of Oak Island and reference every object that might be considered a "marker." It would have been much more expensive if not for the fact that he did most of the work himself, Nolan told me, crisscrossing the island with dozens of lines cut through the trees and brush. In total, these stretched for tens of thousands of yards, Nolan said, and laying them out had been "backbreaking work."

Fred was seventy-six years old in 2003, a short man with wispy white hair and a physique that might generously be described as spare. He was more sturdy-looking in photographs from the 1960s and 1970s. A flinty-featured fellow who squinted suspiciously beneath the brim of the tweedy porkpie hat he favored, he was never caught on camera smiling. In fact, he smiled exactly once during our conversation, when I told him that Dan Blankenship had, grudgingly it seemed, acknowledged the "significant discoveries" his island neighbor and mortal enemy had made. I was pretty sure Fred had only agreed to speak to me because he knew I had already interviewed Dan. He was curious to know what Blankenship had said about him and wanted the opportunity to defend himself against any accusations that might have been made.

I can't say I found him to be the least bit warm, unlike Dan, who had become almost avuncular after I had spent a couple of hours in his company. But one winning quality possessed by Fred Nolan that nobody—not even Blankenship—could deny was perseverance. The man was also meticulous, as he had demonstrated while conducting that free survey for Chappell back in the early sixties, installing twenty-three concrete survey markers, each crowned with a numbered bronze disk on which a transit or theodolite could be mounted. Nolan had also been the first person to photograph the stone triangle, which he surveyed as well, actions that would be much admired years later, when it began to dawn on people the havoc Dunfield had wreaked when he destroyed the triangle.

Another idea that originated with Fred Nolan was that the flood tunnels on the island were not dug in straight paths. The clay down there was "unbelievably hard," Nolan said, and he was convinced that the original diggers had followed the line of least resistance, which is to say the tunnels meandered. "If they came to a boulder, they dug around it," he said in 2003.

In late 1962, convinced that he had accomplished something important—and that Mel Chappell would surely recognize it—he arranged a meeting with the man who now owned all of Oak Island and proposed that he be allowed to lease the search rights. Chappell, though, already had Robert Restall and his family installed on the island and planned to keep them there until he found the individual or group that was willing to spend the serious money he believed was required to retrieve the treasure. Whether it was because Nolan was pushy or Chappell was testy, or both, the surveyor's attempted negotiation blew up in his face, and the conversation ended with M. R. telling him to "get off my damn island and go to hell," as Fred recalled it.

Instead, Nolan went to the Registry of Deeds in Chester. "I was playing a hunch," Fred told me. That hunch would pay big dividends. Nolan traced the Oak Island records back to 1935, when Gilbert Hedden bought lots 5 and 9–20 from Sophia Sellers's heirs (three grown children and nine grandchildren). The deed office's records, though, stated that Hedden had purchased only lots 15–20. The issue was muddled further by a survey plan dated September 9, 1935, stating that Hedden had

purchased "52 acres" on Oak Island, which would have included lots
5 and 9–14. So Nolan jumped forward to 1950, when John Whitney
Lewis had purchased the same property from Hedden. Again he found
that the sale had not technically included seven of the lots: 5 and 9–14.
Thus, neither had the sale made by Lewis to Chappell later that same
year. What he suddenly realized was that because lots 5 and 9–14 had
not been properly conveyed to Hedden by the Sellers heirs in 1935 or
to Lewis by Hedden in 1950 or to Chappell by Lewis after that, that
property still belonged legally to the last remaining Sellers heirs, two
elderly ladies living on the mainland. Nolan immediately paid separate
visits to the sisters and arranged to purchase the seven lots—one-quarter
of Oak Island—for $2,500.

In April 1963 Nolan went to Chappell without first making arrange-
ments for a meeting, showed him the deeds to lots 5 and 9–14, then
offered to trade the seven lots for a lease on the Money Pit. Chappell
reacted with fury, calling Nolan a sneak and again ordering him the hell
off his property. The man who had believed he owned Oak Island in its
entirety hired R. V. Harris to investigate the matter and was outraged
when Harris reported back that it appeared Nolan could indeed claim
ownership of the seven lots in question.

He was "set back and disappointed," Nolan admitted to me in
2003, that Chappell had rejected his offer. He soon began to cheer
up, though, when he realized that he now owned a swath of land that
extended across most of the east end of Oak Island, permitting him to
block anyone coming from the west if he chose to. He also had his survey
notes and an immense collection of maps and documents. Rather than
worry about Chappell and the operations at the Money Pit, he would
hunker down and study all the materials in his possession to see if he
could make connections.

Nolan directed his attention first to the three piles of stones at the
top of the hill just beyond the eastern boundary of his property, each rising from a 12-foot base to a point 5 feet aboveground. It had long been
presumed these were the remnants of an observation point—a "sentry

post," as Robert Restall had called it. When he studied the survey grid he had laid out on that part of the island, though, Nolan recognized that the piles of stones formed a perfect isosceles triangle, with sides 150 feet long and a base about 100 feet wide. He looked at that triangle again and again, Nolan recalled, until he realized that it could be seen as an arrowhead pointed directly at the center of the swamp. He was already convinced, just as Robert Restall had been, that the swamp was a meaningful feature of Oak Island, probably man-made, possibly to conceal something buried beneath it.

He filed that thought away and concentrated for a time on two granite boulders on which ringbolts had been fitted into drilled holes and fixed with a primitive cement. During 1963, he drew lines between the stone piles and the boulders with the ringbolts and decided to excavate where the lines intersected. Nolan demonstrated just how driven a man he was the following year in 1964, when he hired a six-man crew to dig two 30-foot-deep shafts at those locations. He was disappointed—but not at all discouraged—that the only object found was an old brass belt buckle buried more than 20 feet underground.

Whether or not it was because he had no access to the Money Pit I was never sure, but during his time on Oak Island in the 1960s Nolan came to believe that the original shaft was not nearly as significant a feature of the island as people imagined. I never could get out of him exactly why, but Nolan was convinced that the treasure everyone sought was in a watertight vault at the end of a tunnel that ran off from the Money Pit. Or maybe, he seemed to be saying at one point, this tunnel was not even connected to the Money Pit. Fred's reluctance to reveal anything more than he absolutely had to created a haze around his work that no one would ever entirely penetrate.

He had spent hours, days, and weeks over a period of years searching for that tunnel and the vault at the end of it on his own property, Nolan said. Along the way he found more rocks with round holes bored or chiseled into them; some had pieces of metal inserted. He also excavated pieces of old hand-cut wood that he believed were from an ancient treasure chest. One of the pieces had old iron hinges attached. He also discovered a number of rocks that he believed had been used as survey markers many years earlier. One in particular fascinated him. It was a piece of sandstone that had been cut to leave two smooth sides and the other two rough. How Nolan found it says a good deal about the man. He had been crawling along on the ground on his hands and knees, following a survey line with a hand compass that had bumped into the rock. Nolan said that when he saw that the sandstone was standing on end, he immediately recognized it as significant. He actually paid to have it examined by a geologist who wrote a report confirming that "this is not a natural stable resting position for a rock of this shape." The geologist also agreed that the burn marks on the rock indicated that heat had been used to cut it. Nolan found any number of other sandstone rocks that he described as having "marks and figures" on them. All of the granite stones he had noted as potential markers were positioned naturally, but the sandstones had been placed by human hands. Eventually Nolan decided that the sandstones were not native to Oak Island, but instead had been brought there to use as survey markers.

Nothing Fred did during the 1960s, though, was as impressive as his decision at the end of the decade to drain the Oak Island swamp. He wouldn't tell me what it had cost, other than "a lot," but there had to be a considerable amount of labor and equipment involved. He did not find a tunnel entrance or a treasure chest under the swamp, Fred admitted, but he did discover numerous markers, most notably a number of spruce stakes driven into the ground that clearly were intended for some purpose of identification. He also found what he believed to be a gold-branding bar and part of a wooden ship's gunwale. He was convinced that the swamp had once been low-lying ground, used possibly as either a docking or boat-repair yard.

By 1969, the year he drained the swamp, though, the biggest news Fred Nolan was making involved his battles with Dan Blankenship and Triton Alliance. The conflict actually went all the way back to 1965, when Robert Dunfield—who had absorbed the animosity toward Nolan from his then-partner Mel Chappell—had built the causeway and posted an armed guard at the entrance to prevent Nolan from using it. Dunfield himself used to sit out there with a rifle, Fred said, "and threaten to shoot me if I tried to drive onto the island." Dunfield and Chappell managed to force Nolan to use a boat to reach his land on the island and to barge out his equipment, but they also learned the hard way that Fred was not about to lay down for anyone. In 1966, he spent $3,000 to purchase the quarter acre of land on Crandall's Point that butted up against the entrance to the causeway, then barricaded it, making it impossible to move any sort of oversized load between the mainland and the island. When Dunfield left Nova Scotia, Nolan negotiated a deal with Dan Blankenship, who paid him $1,000 to remove the barricade, at the same time giving Fred permission to use the causeway. Eventually that morphed into a deal that gave Nolan a small share of Triton's Money Pit operation in exchange for doing some surveying work for Tobias and giving Blankenship a right of way through his property.

The situation seems to have been reasonably amicable during 1967, Canada's centennial year, when Fred built a museum at Crandall's Point, where he exhibited the artifacts he had collected on Oak Island. He even managed to negotiate a deal with Canada's Department of Tourism to collect a percentage of the revenue from public tours of Oak Island, in exchange for the right to cross his Crandall's Point property.

All of those agreements were annulled in 1969, though, when Triton Alliance was formed. After each side accused the other of breach of contract, Nolan again blocked off the entrance to the causeway, which forced Triton to build a bypass road. Triton retaliated by chaining off the causeway where it touched the island, on Chappell's property, preventing Nolan from crossing and again forcing him to boat and barge out to his island property. Fred answered back by chaining off the trail to the eastern end of Oak Island that ran through his property, blocking Triton from road access to the Money Pit. To say that the conflict grew hot at this point would be an understatement. Nolan and Blankenship had a number of what were described as "nose-to-nose shouting matches," although technically those would have been Fred's nose to Dan's chin. One afternoon in 1970 Blankenship became so incensed that he confronted Nolan at the chain armed with a hunting rifle. Fred called the Royal Canadian Mounted Police, who arrived in time to seem Dan still manning the chain with the rifle in his hands. He was protecting his property, Dan told the Mounties, who confiscated his rifle anyway.

"OF ALL THE THINGS FRED HAS DONE, nothing has ever infuriated or outraged me as much as his systematic removal and destruction of the markers and artifacts he's found—a lot of which weren't even on his property," Dan Blankenship told me back in 2003. Nolan admitted nothing when I asked him about this. "I have recorded the precise location of every single marker or other significant object I've found on Oak Island," Fred told me. "If I choose not to share that information with Dan, well, that's my right."

Nolan's obstruction of the existing path to the Money Pit compelled Triton to build a new road around his property in 1970. Fred had also forced his adversaries to spend some serious money creating bypasses at the causeway entrance and to reach the east end of Oak Island from the west, but he lost nearly all of his leverage against Triton in the process. He had just two advantages left—the proximity of the southeastern border of his property to the Money Pit and, as of early 1971, his own treasure trove license from the province of Nova Scotia. When Nolan began a major excavation about 650 feet northwest of the Money Pit, Tobias and Blankenship realized how serious their island neighbor was about his search and about his theory that the treasure was in a tunnel that had been driven downhill from the Money Pit. The partners could not completely dismiss the possibility that what they were after might lie on Nolan's property, not theirs. This was the basis for the negotiation of a new deal struck in late 1971. It guaranteed Triton at least 40 percent of any treasure found on Nolan's land in exchange for giving Fred the right to drive to the island on the causeway, plus a promise that Triton would not challenge Nolan's acquisition of his seven lots.

Triton had convinced Nolan that its operation on Oak Island was a formidable one. In summer 1970 the Alliance had built a 400-foot-long cofferdam around the perimeter of Smith's Cove, 50 yards farther out to sea than the previous dams built by searchers. Blankenship had done much of the work (mostly with bulldozers) and supervised all of it. Triton's was an impressive structure, but like previous dams, it would ultimately be battered, beaten down and broken by the Atlantic Ocean's winter storms.

The construction of the cofferdam, though, had unearthed what might have been the most significant find of the twentieth century on Oak Island: a large U-shaped wooden structure buried beneath the sand and gravel just below the low tide line. It was made of logs 2 feet in diameter ranging in length from 30 to 65 feet, all of them notched at 4-foot intervals, each hand bored, and several still fitted with dowels that must have once secured cross pieces joining the logs. (Almost certainly this was the rest of what Gilbert Hedden had discovered when he spotted those two logs with hand-carved notches at Smith's Cove back in 1938.) A different Roman numeral was carved into each log. Triton called in archeological consultants who concluded that the structure was the remains of an ancient wharf or slipway or of workings used in the construction of the original cofferdam that had held back the sea while the Money Pit was dug and the flood tunnel system constructed. Dan Blankenship maintained that the structure was a wharf, though he considered it possible that it had been both a wharf and a dam and was of the opinion that it had been destroyed purposely after the completion of the Money Pit and the flood system. Carbon dating at Ontario's Brock University established only that the wood was at least 250 years old, which meant that the structure had been built sometime prior to 1720.

Blankenship had also discovered two smaller and more crudely constructed wooden structures beneath the beach on Oak Island's west end. He believed they were skidways that had been used to haul boats out of the water. A number of handwrought iron nails and metal strips were recovered in the vicinity of these two structures, and lab analysis found they had been forged prior to 1790. The Blankenship find that made the most news, though, was a large granite stone that had been uncovered by accident as bulldozers were backfilling the Cave-in Pit that summer. Dan had caught sight of some "cutting" on the stone as it was being pushed out of the ground toward the Pit and rushed in to retrieve it before it was buried. The cutting was a hand-carved G inside a rect- angle. In Freemasonry, the letter G inside an "oblong square" denoted the "Grand Architect" of the universe—God, by another name. Formac Publishing author Mark Finnan had asserted that "the presence of this symbol on Oak Island and its location in the east, seen as the source of light in Masonic teachings, is further indication that individuals with a fundamental knowledge of Freemasonry were likely involved [in the original works on Oak Island]." That was certainly possible, though it was equally likely that the G had been carved by someone involved in a previous treasure-hunting expedition.

In his constant poking around the island, Blankenship had made a number of other notable discoveries in the late sixties and early seventies. One was a pair of old leather shoes buried 9 feet below the surface of the island's western beach. Dan also found three more drilled boulders not far north of the Money Pit, similar to the two found in 1937 by Gilbert Hedden. Blankenship discovered several rock piles that he knew were man-made as well. When he dismantled them, he found mounds of ash beneath. Lab analysis later revealed this to be the remains of burned bones, though whether they were human or animal was not possible to say.

Later in the summer of 1970, after the cofferdam's construction, Triton had hired Golder Associates of Toronto, a geotechnical engineer- ing firm, to conduct the most complete study ever performed of what lay beneath the surface of Oak Island. The company bored a series of deep holes across the island's east end, removing core samples to be analyzed at their laboratories. Golder also ran seismic and other tests intended to determine the precise nature and porosity of the soil and the underlying bedrock of the east-end drumlin. Among other things, these tests determined that the seawater was pouring into the Money Pit and surrounding shafts at a constant rate of 600 to 650 gallons per minute, which laid Captain Henry Bowdoin's "percolation" to rest.

All told, the Golder project cost Triton more than $100,000, for which the Alliance received a trove of charts and cross-sectional drawings of the island's underground, with both natural and man-made formations mapped out. Golder's engineers also estimated that given the tools and technologies of the sixteenth and seventeenth centuries, it would have required approximately 100,000 man-hours to create the original works on Oak Island, meaning that forty men could have done it in one year.

In terms of future events on the island, the most significant moment of the Golder project came when the company's engineers were conducting a piezometer test (to determine the flow and pressure of the water beneath the surface) at what was designated as Borehole 10X. The borehole had been made in 1976 by a company called Bowmaster Drilling with a 6-inch rotary drill. At a depth of 140 feet in the hard-packed glacial till the drill had dropped into a 5-foot cavity. It hit a similar cavity 20 feet farther down, then reached the bedrock at a depth of 180 feet and continued boring deeper all the way to 230 feet, where it found yet another 5-foot cavity. At that point the drill was removed and a steel casing was inserted all the way to the bottom of the borehole. High-pressure air was injected to blow out loose material, and from a depth of 165 feet came enough "thin metal" to fill both of a man's hands. The metal began oxidizing within minutes of exposure to the outside air and turned so brittle it would crumble if touched. What this meant, the geologists said, was that it had been starved of oxygen for a very, very long time. The metal was sent to Stelco, which reported back that it was a primitive form of smelted steel, extremely low carbon, possibly of Swedish origin that "in all probability was produced prior to 1750."

Dan Blankenship was at least as impressed when 10X filled with water that brought pieces of bird bones, seashells, and glass to the surface.

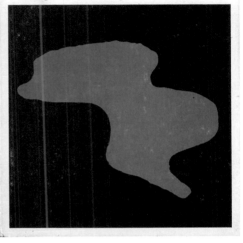

The Oak Island Mystery
R.V. Harris

The Oak Island Mystery fulfills all that the most romantic seeker of buried treasure has ever dreamed.

R.V. Harris, attorney and advisor to Oak Island treasure hunters for decades during the mid-twentieth century, wrote the book that first made the story well known outside Nova Scotia.

CAUSEWAY
(BUILT IN 1966)

MONEY PIT
DISCOVERED IN 1795

27 INCH BOREHOLE
(METAL, CHAIN LINKS
AND CAVITIES)

PRESUMED PATH
OF FLOOD TUNNEL

NOTCHED LOGS
BURIED BELOW
SEA-BED

1970
COFFER DAM

OAK ISLAND
NOVA SCOTIA

SMITH'S
COVE

Oak Island's east drumlin, where the Money Pit was found and the treasure hunt has been focused for more than 220 years.

Captain William Kidd, whose pirate treasure generations of people digging in the money pit believed they would find.

Henry Morgan, legendary seventeenth century pirate whose Treasure of Panama, worth well over $100 million at current value, has never been found. Some believe it could be buried on Oak Island.

William Phipps, seventeenth century privateer turned politician who captured the treasure-laden Spanish ship *Concepcion*. Some believe he may have stashed part of the haul taken from the *Concepcion* on Oak Island.

Samuel de Champlain, who in 1608 established "New France" in what is now Canada. Some speculate that the Oak Island treasure vaults were dug during the struggle between France and England for control of Nova Scotia.

Samuel Ball, freed from slavery to serve on the royalist side during the Revolutionary War. He settled on Oak Island and grew wealthy there. Some believe the source of that wealth was his share of a treasure found on the island.

and editor. But the two positions can no longer be united in one man. Where are the owners and financiers that dare to gather to their employ the men of powerful minds and trained pens and give them right of way? "Now do your best; you are free, only do your best; keep close to the facts and seek to see only the right, and then do your best. If we lose, we lose; but do your best, and we shall never complain. Differ from us if you must; differ among yourselves if you must; but speak your own convictions, and do your best." I would go without food or clothing if need were, but I would have that paper to read and ponder and learn from. O. W. WILLITS.

❡ *This is another expression of the same thought:*

LOS ANGELES is a town of one newspaper, the "Times."

There are four other dailies printed and circulated here in a more or less general way, but when one thinks of the town in a newspaper way, he thinks of the "Times."

Every one reads the "Times" and nearly every one despises it.

I read the "Times" every day just as I would go to see the devil if he were on exhibition, once at least, and as many times afterward as I could do so safely and he continued to be interesting. I have read the "Times" seven years and it continues interesting.

The "Times" has the Associated Press news service. What I read under their heading I consider news. It sustains a private news service in addition, which makes a specialty of items of a labor-baiting nature, no matter where they originate.

If there is a strike of any kind in any part of the world, if the jinrikisha carriers of Tokyo or the window-cleaners of Cape Colony ask for more pay the "Times" plays it for a front-page story.

If a robbery or an assault is committed in New South Wales by a former member of the Archangel Amalgamated Plumbers' Union, it matters not how long since he abandoned his union affiliations, the old familiar scare-head, "Union Thug Commits Another Atrocity!" finds its way to the fore.

I doubt if the "Times" has a dozen readers who consider its special news items as *news*. Aside from its non-union attitude, and no one who has ever read a copy needs to be told how virulent that is, the "Times" carries on a consistent procorporation fight.

There are no bad corporations in the category of the "Times."

Is the local gas company threatened with a reduction of rates or a coerced improvement of service, is the Southern Pacific Railroad, the colossus of California corporation corruption, in need of comfort or support, they ask not twice of the "Times" for succor.

When the San Francisco United Railways could find no local daily to champion their cause the "Times" turned over its columns, both news and editorial, to the corporation five hundred miles distant and deluged San Francisco with tens of thousands of copies.

Los Angeles is a peculiar town, full of retired merchants and farmers and health and pleasure seekers. If it were a manufacturing town the "Times" would never have gained its preeminence. As for actual influence, it has but little and has lost every big fight it has made for years, whether against school bonds or local probity or State honesty. We read it, but when election time comes we vote the other way. Experience has taught us that it is the safer way.

And so, while we detest the "Times," we continue to read it, because of its typographical perfection, *(Concluded on page 22)*

Solving the Mystery of Oak Island

The Hundred-Year Search for the $10,000,000 Supposed to Have Been Buried by Pirates

❡ *In* COLLIER'S *of September 23, 1905, appeared an account, written by Josephine Freeda, of the hundred-year search for the pirate gold supposed to have been buried on Oak Island. A year later, in the issue of September 29, 1906, the same author wrote another article containing further details of the explorations. Mr. Bowdoin's article, below, is the final chapter of the romantic story of the treasure of Oak Island.*

By H. L. BOWDOIN

OAK ISLAND, one of the three hundred-odd islands in Mahone Bay, Nova Scotia, has been a spot of peculiar interest for a hundred years or more, owing to the legend of vast treasure buried by pirates in a pit over one hundred feet deep, said to be flooded by water let in from the bay through an underground tunnel. According to the legend, they dug the tunnel from the Money Pit to Smith's Cove, over six hundred feet distant.

Further, the legend is that in 1795 three young men—Smith, McGinnis, and Vaughan—landed and began strolling about on the then uninhabited island, among the great oak-trees which gave the island its name. They came across a small clearing, in the center of which was a large oak-tree. From one of the lower limbs hung a block and tackle. Directly beneath this was a circular depression in the ground about twelve feet in diameter. It looked as though something had been buried—treasure, of course—so they decided to dig it up. When they returned with shovels, the tide was unusually low, and they discovered a great iron ring-bolt imbedded in a rock; a boatswain's stone whistle was picked up, and, later, a copper coin bearing the date 1713 was found. After digging a few feet they found they were in a well-defined shaft, the walls being hard, while the center was soft. At every ten feet they found a layer of planking. At a depth of thirty feet, the work being too heavy for them, they gave up.

Six or seven years later Dr. Lynds of Truro visited the island; talked with Smith, McGinnis, and Vaughan; returned to Truro, and formed a company and resumed the digging. Marks were found every ten feet, and at ninety feet a large flat stone was found, upon which was a curious inscription. The stone was taken to Halifax, and one expert declared the characters read as follows:

"Ten feet below two million pounds lie buried."

Too Much Water

NINETY-FIVE feet was reached on a Saturday night, and on Monday morning the shaft was found to be full of water. They tried to bail out the water, but, finding this impossible, decided to sink a new and deeper shaft near the old pit, so that by tunneling beneath the treasure it could be taken out from below. The shaft was dug, but the water

Here in Smith's Cove the machinery and stores were landed

flooded them out at one hundred and ten feet, and ended the operations of the company.

In 1849 another company began digging in the Money Pit, but was flooded out. Next, men were sent to the island with a boring apparatus that was used in those days in prospecting for coal. At ninety-eight feet a layer of planking five inches thick was struck; the auger dropped twelve inches, and then it went through four inches of oak; then it went through twenty-two inches of metal in pieces; it then went through eight inches of oak, the bottom of one box and top of another; then through twenty-two inches of metal in pieces, as before; then through four inches of oak and six inches of spruce; then seven feet into clay without striking anything. In withdrawing the auger three links resembling an ancient watch-chain were brought up. The next boring struck the platform at ninety-eight feet; passing through this, the auger fell eighteen inches and came in contact with, as supposed, the side of a cask. The flat chisel revolving close to the side of the cask gave it a jerky, irregular motion. On withdrawing the auger several splinters of oak were found. The distance be-

A map of Oak Island, showing the line of the supposed tunnel

tween the upper and lower platforms was six feet. In 1850 another shaft was put down near the Money Pit, and flooded out; then, with horse-power gins, they bailed night and day for a week. They discovered that the water was salt, and that it rose and fell in the shafts with the tides.

Acting on the theory that if the water had come through a natural channel the pirates would not have been able to bury their treasure so deep without being flooded out, it was figured that the pirates themselves had dug an underground tunnel from the shore to protect their treasure. A search was made to discover the inlet.

A well-constructed drain was found at Smith's Cove between low and high water mark, and in order to keep the water out while digging in the drain a coffer-dam was built, enclosing this part of the beach. The coffer-dam did not stand, however, and was abandoned. More shafts were sunk, but they caved in, or were flooded, and work was suspended.

Nearly forty years later, in 1896, another company was organized, and started work with powerful steam pumps and other apparatus. Several shafts were sunk, but the pumps could not keep the water out. Boring apparatus was then installed. Oak was struck at one hundred and twenty-five feet; at one hundred and fifty-three feet they struck cement six inches thick; directly under this cement they found five inches of oak wood; when through the wood the auger dropped one and one-half inches, and rested on soft metal. They carefully withdrew the auger and kept the borings brought up with it. Among these borings was found a very small piece of sheepskin parchment, upon which was written, or printed, two letters—"vi."

Several other borings were made, and boxes filled with metal in pieces were struck, but no samples of the metal could be secured. The company being out of funds, work was abandoned.

Another Attempt

SO RAN the legend of Oak Island when it was brought to my attention early in the year 1909. It was represented that the treasure was surely there; that there were two tunnels leading from the shore to the Money Pit, and that their exact locations were known, but that no one could stop them up so that the water could not reach the Money Pit.

Having hunted treasure in the South, with more or less success, enjoying an adventure of any kind, and feeling that my engineering ability was equal to the occasion, I took hold of the project.

I saw the piece of sheepskin parchment, the holder of which has paid a yearly lease on the property since it was found. The man who did the boring was with me at Oak Island and believes absolutely in the legend. I have seen the rock found in the Money Pit, which is now in Creighton's bookbindery in Halifax.

With a few more adventurous spirits I formed a company; I secured a permit from the Canadian Government, and left New York August 18, 1909, arriving in Halifax, Nova Scotia, August 20. Some machinery was sent from New York and more purchased in Halifax. We landed on Oak Island August 27.

While in Halifax we examined the stone found in the Money Pit, the characters on which were supposed to mean: "Ten feet below two million pounds lie buried." The rock is of a basalt type, hard and fine-grained.

Exploring the Island

OUR machinery and stores were landed at Smith's Cove, and we made an examination of the island, guided by the man who had charge of the last expedition, who brought up the piece of sheepskin parchment, and who had located the two tunnels leading to the Money Pit. We saw the remains

The mouth of the money pit

The diver entering the pit

of the coffer-dam built in 1850 around the drain and entrance to one tunnel. We found no evidence whatever of a drain or entrance to a tunnel; the beach is of the same character all along. The coffer-dam itself is dry at low water, and the ring-bolt in the rock has disappeared.

Locating the Pits

THE man showed us a depression a few feet back from the beach where he had put down a five-inch pipe and struck the tunnel at seventy-five feet, and his belief was that the tunnel ended in a shaft somewhere off the beach in deep water. How such a shaft could be built and kept open for a hundred years he could not explain.

Not being able to locate the tunnel, we hauled our machinery to the Money Pit; erected derricks and built our camp.

There are two pits side by side, the Money Pit, five feet by seven feet, heavily cribbed to one hundred and ten feet, and another pit, seven feet by seven feet, built by the last expedition. We found the Money Pit floored over at the water's edge, thirty feet below the surface, and partly filled with rocks and dirt. This accumulation was cleaned out, the cribbing strengthened in places, and the flooring removed.

In sounding, we found an obstruction ten feet under water. A pump was set at work and the water lowered thirty feet, disclosing a cross-beam in the center of the pit with a platform every ten feet and ladders from platform to platform. The pump was removed, and with our orange-peel bucket and other gear we broke out the cross-beams, platforms, and ladders to one hundred and seven feet. Our diver was sent down to make an examination. He reported the cribbing in bad shape and the bottom covered with plank and timber sticking up in all directions.

The bucket was again put to work, clearing the pit to one hundred and thirteen feet. As the pit was not cribbed below this point, we decided to locate the treasure with our core-drill and then sink a caisson down to it. The man showed us the spot where he had bored and brought up the sheepskin parchment, after passing through cement at one hundred and fifty feet. He had bored with a chisel in a pipe and with an auger on a long rod.

Boring for the Box

A CORE-DRILL brings up a core or continuous piece of the material through which it goes, one and a half, or more, inches in diameter. The bit will cut through metal or rock, so that in boring through a box containing gold or treasure a fine sample would be brought up.

We bored in the spot indicated: through seventeen feet of coarse gravel and sand; then sixteen feet of blue clay, small stones, and sand, and struck the cement at one hundred and forty-nine feet, as predicted.

We cut through six inches, and withdrew the core so as to start clean on the box of gold. The core showed a solid piece of cement about six inches long. Our hopes ran high. The drill was again placed in position and started; down it went through eighteen feet of yellow clay and stones to a bed-rock of hard white clay, or gypsum and quartz, one hundred and sixty feet from the surface. We had missed the box of gold that time; but try again.

We did. We put down holes vertically, and with as wide angles as possible, so that a larger space than the area of the pit was perforated with holes to depths of from one hundred and fifty-five feet to one hundred and seventy-one feet, and so placed that anything over two feet square must have been struck. We struck cement six inches to ten inches thick at depths of one hundred and forty-six feet to one hundred and forty-nine feet, but no traces of boxes, treasure, or anything of that kind.

Side and End Sections of the Money Pit

Showing the different strata and the core drill holes: (A), The cribbing in the pit; (B), Water; (C), Porous strata of coarse gravel and sand; (D), Blue clay, small stones and sand; (E), Limestone; (F), Yellow clay and stones; (G), White clay or gypsum and quartz

The cement was analyzed by Professor Chandler of Columbia University, and found to be *natural limestone pitted by the action of water.* This was also the opinion of Professor Kemp, Professor of Geology at Columbia University, and of Dr. Woolson, an expert on building materials and cement, of Columbia University.

We housed the machinery and gear, and left Oak Island November 4, 1909.

My experience proved to me that there is not, and never was, a buried treasure on Oak Island. The mystery is solved.

Conclusions

FIRST—*There never was a pirate, or other, treasure buried in the Money Pit at Oak Island.*
Because:

(a) There was no need to bury it so deep.

(b) Below the cribbed part of the pit is natural formation, which would not be the case if filled in.

(c) Our borings prove it.

SECOND—*There is no tunnel from the Money Pit to Smith's Cove.*
Because:

(a) It is over six hundred feet to Smith's Cove, while but one hundred and fifty feet to the nearest shore on that side of the island.

(b) It would have been a long and tremendous operation to dig such a tunnel by hand over one hundred feet underground.

(c) The opening, or drain, could not have been kept open on a sea beach.

A view of Camp Kidd, the scene of operations

THIRD—*Water did not reach the Money Pit through a tunnel.*
Because:

(a) Water was always struck at the level of the seventeen-foot strata of coarse gravel and sand.

(b) It was salt water and percolated through from the bay, one hundred and fifty feet away.

(c) The more it was pumped the easier it came; the sand settling to the bottom of the strata; the clay above remaining intact.

FOURTH—*There never was a ring-bolt on the beach.*
Because:

(a) It was easier to tie a line to an oak-tree than to drill a hole in a rock and set in a ring-bolt.

(b) There are still a number of large oak-trees at Smith's Cove.

FIFTH—*No borings ever brought up links of chain or anything valuable.*
Because:

(a) Such things do not stick to a flat chisel, or auger, through one hundred and twenty feet of water.

(b) Different operators found the treasure at different depths, from one hundred and ten feet to one hundred and fifty feet, all in a five-by-seven hole. The treasure must have dropped forty feet.

(c) The sheepskin parchment was not found by the man who did the boring. The borings were sent to the home office of the company, and the first examination showed nothing. A later examination was made, and the sheepskin parchment discovered. (I understand that more stock was then sold and more work done, without result.)

SIXTH—*There never were any characters on the rock found in the Money Pit.*
Because:

(a) The rock, being hard, they could not wear off.

(b) There are a few scratches, made by Creighton's employees, as they acknowledged, but there is not, and never was, a system of characters carved on the stone.

In 1909 Captain Henry Bowdoin mounted the most publicized treasure hunt thus far on Oak Island. He brought in a young Franklin D. Roosevelt as both an investor and crewmember. When he was denied access to the island, Bowdoin retaliated with a malicious article for *Collier's* magazine that debunked the Money Pit "myth."

Frederick Blair, who devoted more than a half-century to the treasure hunt. Along the way compiling maps, charts and documents that make up the bulk of the Oak Island files in the Nova Scotia Archives.

William Chappell, who was manning the drill when the fabled parchment scrap was lifted out of the Money Pit in 1897. His son Melbourne would later control the treasure hunt on Oak Island for decades.

Melbourne "M.R." Chappell with his family. Chappell controlled the treasure hunt on Oak Island for most of the 1950s and 1960s.

The young Franklin Delano Roosevelt was an enthusiastic member of the Bowdoin expedition and followed the Oak Island treasure hunt for the remainder of his life, even while serving more than twelve years as U.S. president.

the logs had been embedded in the sides of the pit to prevent a sinking at the surface, causing a depression which might be detected and eventually cause whatever was buried in the pit to be discovered. Dr. Lynds climbed down into the hole and scraped away at the final tier of logs, thirty feet below the surface, where the boys had ceased their labors. Later he examined a strange ringbolt attached to one of the beach boulders.

Dr. Lynds then traveled to Halifax, where he interested several prominent men in forming a company. Before long equipment began arriving on the island.

Down, down and down the diggers went. At forty feet, fifty feet and sixty feet platforms were reached and passed. At seventy and eighty feet there were platforms containing a strange, fiberlike material placed next to charcoal. A substance resembling putty was found at another tier. The mystery grew stranger and stranger, but when the ninety-foot mark was reached, the greatest mystery of all awaited the diggers. It was a round, flat stone, about three feet high and sixteen inches wide. On the face of the stone curious characters had been cut:

$$\nabla \times \emptyset \triangle \swarrow \triangledown :: \triangle \; \dagger : \complement \times \square \; \triangle \square \times$$
$$\swarrow \therefore \complement \complement \therefore \times \times \; \ominus \times + \swarrow \amalg \odot \; \cdot \emptyset : \; \dagger \dagger \emptyset \therefore : \amalg$$

Reverend A. T. Kempton of Cambridge, Massachusetts, believes that an old Irish schoolmaster worked out the code and translated the inscription to read, letter for letter, as follows:

FORTY FEET BELOW TWO
MILLION POUNDS ARE BURIED

What symbols were carved on the "Inscribed Stone" has been debated for nearly a century and is not truly known. The translation "Forty Feet Below Two Million Pounds Are Buried" was first produced by "a very bright Irish teacher" in 1909, and has been repeated with variations numerous times since.

Gilbert Hedden directed the treasure hunt on Oak Island for only a couple of years in the 1930s, but made an astonishing array of discoveries and connections during that time. He remained involved with Oak Island for decades afterward.

The theory that William Shakespeare's works were actually written by Francis Bacon emerged during the nineteenth century and has maintained currency ever since. The idea that the original Shakespeare manuscripts are cached on Oak Island was first proposed by Prof. Burrell Ruth in the 1940s.

Francis Bacon's *Novum Organum Scientiarum* is widely credited with establishing the modern scientific method.

Bacon served as Lord Chancellor of England. His achievements in science, law, philosophy, and literature made him "one of the three greatest men who ever lived" in the opinion of Thomas Jefferson. Generations of devotees have made him into a religious figure as well. Many of those believe the works he intended for "future generations" were buried on Oak Island.

David Tobias (r) with his partner and rival Dan Blankenship. Tobias poured hundreds of thousands of dollars into the Oak Island treasure hunt between the 1960s and his death in 2012, and never stopped believing something of great value was buried on the island.

Robert Dunfield (r) shaking hands with Mel Chappell. Dunfield's attempt to bring heavy equipment and open pit mining methods to the treasure hunt devastated Oak Island physically and made him, for many, the greatest villain in the island's history.

Fred Nolan conducted hundreds of surveys on Oak Island and in the process made as many discoveries as anyone who has ever hunted for treasure on the island. His acquisition of a considerable portion of Oak Island property embroiled him in a nearly ruinous legal dispute.

Of all the surveyor's discoveries, "Nolan's Cross" is the most famous and, for many, the most significant.

Dan Blankenship became the central character in the Oak Island treasure hunt back in the late 1960s and is still living on the island. His labors and discoveries, along with his outsized personality, have made him an epic character in the Oak Island story.

Blankenship's discovery of the "G Stone" led to many theories about the involvement of freemasons in the original work on Oak Island.

Once a world-famous carnival daredevil, Robert Restall settled with his family on Oak Island in 1959. Convinced that the Panama Treasure of Henry Morgan was buried on Oak Island, Restall attempted to compensate for what he lacked in financial resources with intensive research and relentless physical labor during the six years he devoted to the treasure hunt.

Four Perish Seeking Pirate Treasure

OAK ISLAND, N.S. (AP) — A six-year, $200,000-hunt for a legendary pirate treasure has ended in death for Robert Restall, his son and two others.

The four men died Tuesday on tiny Oak Island, off Nova Scotia's south coast. They were overcome by gas in a shaft 27 feet deep, one of about 200 bored by treasure seekers in the past 170 years.

Two treasure hunters who escaped from the shaft thought the men were overcome by "swamp gas." Others theorized that a gasoline pump engine over the mouth of the pit had filled the hole with carbon monoxide.

A fifth man was pulled unconscious from the pit. Two others climbed to safety before they were overcome.

The dead were Restall, 59, of Hamilton, Ont., his son, Robert Jr., 24, Cyril Hiltz, 22, Martin's Point, N.S., and Karl Graeser, about 40, a mineralogist from Massapequa, N.Y.

Restall was convinced he had found the key to the network of tunnels and shafts where legend says Captain Kidd and other pirates hid treasure worth between $30 million and $200 million.

"I talked to him last night," said Peter Beamish, a teacher from Andover, Mass., who was treasure hunting himself. "He was really excited. He was sure he had it this time."

The legend had fascinated Restall since he was a schoolboy, friends said. He moved onto the island in 1959, obtaining search rights from the island's owner, M.R. Chappell of Sydney, N.S. He had spent almost $200,000 on the search, much of it his own.

Restall's plan was to drive a shaft 100 feet down and another horizontally to the spot where he believed the treasure was.

Rescuers said Restall apparently entered the shaft first and was overcome by pump fumes. His son, attempting to rescue him, also was overcome. Graeser, Hiltz and Andrew DeMont, Gold River, N.S., followed, then revived DeMont.

After police, firemen and a doctor arrived the pit was pumped out. Jim Keizer, Gold River, was lowered into the pit and recovered the bodies.

According to legend, the pirates in 1704 constructed an underground "money pit" that was flooded from the sea to protect their treasure.

The treasure hunt began in 1795, when three boys discovered a depression in the ground and dug down 10 feet to an oak platform. Hundreds have searched in the years since. One was President Franklin D. Roosevelt, who came to the half-square-mile island in 1909 with John W. Shields of Oklahoma City. They found nothing.

Chappell said he doubts there is a treasure although "there have been stories about finding gold coins and links of gold chains."

"But I never saw them, and I don't think I talked to anyone who did,".Chappell said.

but climbed out when they became dizzy.

Edward White, a vacationing fireman from Clarence, N.Y., was lowered into the shaft by students from Phillips Exeter Academy who were camping on the island. White put a rope around DeMont, and the boys and Beamish pulled them out.

House May Approve Reapportionment Bill by Next Week

HARRISBURG (AP)—A Democratic leader said today there is enough advance agreement on a House reapportionment bill to assure passage, possibly by next week.

Chairman Harry R. J. Comer of the House Committee on Elections and Apportionment made the prediction prior to the scheduled unveiling of the commit-section of the 1965 law which made contractural obligations made by a community college's board of directors binding on sponsoring districts.

University of Pittsburgh—The House passed a bill to provide an additional $2.5 million in emergency aid to the University of Pittsburgh, along with its regular appropriation of $5.8 million

Congress May End in September

WASHINGTON (AP) — Now that the long deadlock over foreign aid has been broken, congressional leaders are talking more confidently of going home some time in September.

Senate Democratic Leader Mike Mansfield says he is shooting for adjournment around Labor Day of the session that has seen enactment of more legisla-

Mississippi Plan Favored by Voters

JACKSON, Miss. (AP) — Mississippi lowered its requirements it might get fewer registrars under the new federal act.

Over 30,000 Negroes were eligible to vote in the election. Under state law, 4,524 Negroes registered in the past week by federal registrars in two counties were not eligible to vote because they had not been on the books the required four months.

Gov. Paul B. Johnson's plan to ease constitutional requirements for voter registration was approved Tuesday by Mississippi voters.

The 2-1 vote was an endorsement of Johnson's course of moderation in dealing with the federal government.

With 1,530 of 1,899 precincts reported, the vote was 113,072 to 44,084.

Only two of the larger counties — Adams (Natchez) and

The August 17, 1965, deaths of Robert Restall, his son Bobbie, his worker Cyril Hiltz and his investor Karl Graeser were the greatest tragedies in the long history of the Oak Island treasure hunt.

Robert Restall (center) with his wife Mildred and their sons Bobbie (l) and Ricky.

Dan Henskee's participation in the Oak Island treasure hunt began in the mid-1960s and continues to this day. He may know the island as well as anyone alive. Henskee's experiences have also fed the narrative of Oak Island as a cursed place.

Michigan brothers Rick and Marty Lagina have held the main control of Oak Island since 2007. As the stars of the immensely popular cable television show *The Curse of Oak Island*, they have drawn millions into the treasure hunt.

Randall Sullivan visits the set of the History Channel's
television series *The Curse of Oak Island*.

To him, that meant 10X had found a connection to the flood system. Because of this, combined with the discovery of the cavities and the recovery of the old steel, it was decided to make 10X into an actual shaft, the twenty-ninth excavated on Oak Island, one large enough for divers to be lowered into it.

One of Triton's consultants suggested that an Aspen, Colorado, company named Statesman Mining owned a perfect piece of equipment for this job, a hybrid drill/clamshell digger capable of scooping out a 25-inch diameter hole to a considerable depth. Statesman Mining was best known for the fact that the movie star John Wayne was one its owners. During the negotiations for the lease of the company's machine it was suggested that Wayne might narrate a documentary about Oak Island. The actor's representatives eventually insisted his schedule wouldn't permit this and that deal fell apart, though it did leave behind the legend of John Wayne's "involvement" with Oak Island.

Triton may not have gotten John Wayne, but it did obtain Statesman's machine, which arrived on Oak Island in October 1970 and was immediately put to work reboring 10X. At first it looked to be the right piece of equipment, bringing up more of the thin metal from a depth of 45 feet. The Statesman machine couldn't deal with the boulders that began to block its progress below that point, though, and by Christmas had reached a depth of only 85 feet. After Triton sent the Statesman rig back to Colorado, Dan Blankenship insisted on bringing Parker Kennedy of Halifax—"the best damn driller I've ever had on the island"—out to finish the job. Kennedy's big churn drill opened a hole 27 inches wide in 10X right down through the bedrock to a depth of 235 feet. A quarter-inch-thick steel casing was driven down against the walls of the shaft to 180 feet, leaving the last 55 feet of the borehole with natural anhydrite walls.

Kennedy's drill had brought up more of the thin metal, along with several links of steel chain and a significant number of spruce borings. When the spruce was submitted for carbon-14 testing, the results were at first glance the most astonishing in the history of Oak Island. The wood was dated to the year 3005 AD—more than one thousand years in the future. It was eventually discovered that the reason for this bizarre result was that the wood was coated with pitchblende, a radioactive uranium ore that is today known as uraninite. Pitchblende, Triton was advised, had been used between the fifteenth and eighteenth centuries as a preserving agent on Britain's wooden ships, and also on mineshaft supports.

The churning action of Kennedy's drill had also extracted chunks of cement from 10X at the 165-foot level. These were analyzed by W. S. Weaver of Canada Cement LaFarge, who reported: "It is likely that these materials reflect human activity involving crude lime. . . . Furthermore, the presence of rust [on some of the samples] indicates contact with man-made iron."

The nature of the debris recovered from 10X, along with the fact that it continued to fill to sea level with saltwater, convinced Triton that it would be worth the cost of sending a remote-controlled television camera into the shaft, all the way to the bottom. In August 1971, the camera was slowly lowered to the 235-foot level while Blankenship watched on a closed-circuit monitor that had been set up (with the assistance of the Canadian Broadcasting Corporation station in Halifax) in a nearby shack. As Blankenship was describing the scene to me in his basement office in September 2003, he produced an envelope filled with still photographs that had been made from the videotape recorded that day. He pulled the photos out of the envelope and lay them facedown on the table between us, clearly relishing the suspense he was building.

"For the longest time all I saw was the snow of static," he recalled. "Then all of a sudden I saw these." Dan turned one of the photos over and showed me what he said were the outlines of three chests. "See that right there," he said, pointing at one of the supposed chests. "There's the curved top, and there just below it is the handle." Well, they could be chests, I thought. They seemed perfectly rectangular anyway, except on top. And that *might* have been a handle. Dan then turned over another photo and showed me what he said was a pickaxe that lay on the floor of the chamber at the bottom of 10X next to three logs. Again, the most I could concede was that it *might* have been a pickaxe. And I had to strain to imagine that the silt-covered bumps on the floor of the chamber could have been the body lying on its side that Dan traced with a fingertip.

There were no photographs, only Blankenship's memory, to verify what was perhaps the most compelling piece of apocrypha in the entire Oak Island story. "Out of nowhere, right in front of the camera, I saw a human hand floating past," Dan said. The hand had been severed at the wrist and hung suspended, half clenched, in front of the camera for several seconds. He had called over Parker Kennedy, who was in the shack with him, and Parker had seen the hand, too. Unfortunately, Kennedy hadn't known to advise Blankenship against trying to take a photograph of the floating hand with a camera that had a flash attachment; the reflection of the flash off the glass of the monitor had resulted in what was nothing more than a picture of the glare.

The emotion in Dan Blankenship's voice in 2003 when he spoke of 10X was unfathomable to me at the time. Sitting with Dan in his basement office on that first sodden day I felt myself leaning toward him as I listened. It was almost as if he had placed me in a hypnotic trance and was willing me to be seduced by the mystery of that hole in the ground, one that had gone unsolved because of his partner's lack of faith. "David just never believed in 10X," he said. "He didn't get it."

It seemed to me that Tobias had actually been pretty forbearing, especially considering the method by which Blankenship had selected the spot where 10X was dug in the first place. Dan had done it by dowsing, or water witching as it's sometimes called. The forked witch hazel branch that the Romans Cicero and Tacitus suggested for dowsing had been replaced by two metal rods in Blankenship's hands. More than forty years later he vividly conveyed the "force" with which those rods had pointed him to the spot where 10X had been dug and was not the least bit embarrassed to be telling me about it. Gilbert Hedden had located two tunnels between the Money Pit and Smith's Cove with a twig from an apple tree, Dan pointed out. Back in 1897, Frederick Blair had been highly impressed by a Massachusetts man named Chapman who had used a divining rod to correctly trace the Halifax Company's main tunnel, then staked off what he said was the pirate tunnel and predicted that its entrance into the Money Pit could be found at a depth of 110 feet.

Science pretty much puts water witching in the same category as automatic writing, but that hasn't prevented the mining and energy businesses from employing it with regularity over the years. Marty Lagina would tell me in the summer of 2016: "Dowsing is still used by a lot of people in the oil business. They say they don't believe in it. I say I don't believe in it. But I've seen it work and so have they. Which is why people keep resorting to it."

Tobias only occasionally mocked the way Blankenship had "found" 10X, and while he was openly skeptical about what Dan had claimed to see when the camera was sent down 10X, David readily agreed to spend the money to expand the borehole to a diameter of 8 feet in order to search for a tunnel to the Money Pit. A team of divers led by Phil Irwin of Brooklyn, Nova Scotia, was to be sent down wearing helmets that fed air through a tube connected to a compressor on the surface. Irwin, who made the first dive alone, radioed up from a depth of 170 feet that the water was becoming murky. At 180 feet, where the metal casing ended, Irwin had reported a current of water so powerful it was about to tear the helmet off his head. Irwin descended farther anyway, but by then the turbidity of the water was so dense that he couldn't see his hand in front of his face.

After Irwin's solo dive, Dan Blankenship led those aboveground to Smith's Cove, where the water along the shore was muddied. They had done this with the pumps in 10X, he said, which proved that 10X was connected to the flood system. Triton paid to have a bulldozer hauled to the island in order to pile tons of clay on the spot at Smith's Cove where Dan believed he had found a tunnel entrance, hoping that might block the flow of water into 10X. A week later Irwin made a second descent into 10X accompanied by two other divers. This time there was no rush of water at 180 feet, indicating that what Blankenship had done was succeeding. The divers went all the way to the bottom of the borehole, 235 feet, where they found themselves floating in a large cavity about 7 feet high. Even with the strongest underwater lights in Nova Scotia, though, the divers couldn't see the width of the cavity. Their shoulders rubbing against the anhydrite walls of the shaft had clouded the water, they realized later; it was like swimming in a vast tub of skim milk. The divers groped around the bottom directly beneath the shaft, afraid to venture any distance away, and found only loose stones.

Blankenship went down the hole in a wetsuit himself a few months later. Nothing the man had done impressed me more than that. Almost fifty years old at the time, Dan had squeezed through the 27-inch opening that extended for the last 55 feet below the metal casing and emerged into a chamber where he was "hanging from a cable like a pendulum in this big void," as he put it. Because of the powerful pressure of the water flowing into 10X from the sea, the constant suck of the pumps on the surface, and the solubility of the anhydrite bedrock, he had been in considerable danger. Even though he was describing something he'd done more than thirty years earlier, I felt actual physical relief when Dan told me he not only realized it would be suicide to venture too far from the bottom of the shaft but also that the lack of visibility made exploration impossible. So he went back up. He went down 10X a second time in 1972, and on this occasion he found the bottom of the cavern covered with rubble. The pumps working around the clock above him were wearing away the bedrock walls of the bottom part of the shaft, Dan explained to me in 2003, and he knew it would be "ridiculously dangerous" to go back down a third time.

"There was nothing to do but move away from 10X for a time," Blankenship said. "And it was what David was pushing me to do, anyway." During 1973, Blankenship, on behalf of Triton, sank three drill holes on the north side of the Money Pit. A borehole 660 feet away from the Pit was turned into a 12-by-6-foot shaft (no. 30) after a piece of wire and metal plate were found just below the 100-foot level. Stelco analyzed the wire as "a corroded low carbon material which has been drawn by cold workings, probably in the 1500s to 1800s." No. 30, like so many shafts before, was abandoned when every effort to staunch the flow of water into it failed.

It was not until August 1976, after the borings that Tobias wanted in the Money Pit area proved fruitless, that Blankenship was able to persuade the Triton partners to return to 10X. One of the things that persuaded Tobias to support this was Dan's discovery that 10X was on the exact line between the two drilled rocks found by Gilbert Hedden in 1937, a fact that neither Blankenship nor any of the others had been aware of when the borehole was drilled.

This time Dan went at 10X armed with a special piece of equipment that had been created by Triton partner Bill Parkin, a military weapons systems designer from Massachusetts. It was a highly sensitive ground-penetrating sonar sensor that detected a number of previously unknown cavities in the bedrock connected to or near 10X. Blankenship installed a pair of pumps capable of drawing up 2 million gallons of water a day and ran them continuously for a week to get the water level below 160 feet, until the drive on the larger of the two pumps snapped. Within two days the water level was back to nearly the surface.

Not until September was Blankenship to get inside 10X and explore the cavities that had been detected with Parkin's sonar device. All of them turned out to be shallow natural voids, probably created by the initial drilling of the borehole.

BY THE TIME HE WAS EXPLORING 10X, Dan had persuaded Jane to leave Florida and live with him full time in Nova Scotia. The couple rented a house in Mahone Bay for two years, then in 1975 Dan acquired lot 23 on Oak Island's west end, close to the spot where the causeway ended, and built the two-bedroom bungalow where he and his wife planned to spend the rest of their lives.

Jane's situation on the island was far more tolerable than Mildred Restall's had been. She was living in a modern home with electricity and indoor plumbing; even the TV reception was pretty decent. It took the Blankenships less than five minutes to drive across the causeway to the mainland, where they could sit down for drinks or eat a restaurant meal. Dan was popular among the locals, especially by comparison to Robert Dunfield and George Greene, and the Blankenships made friends in the community. Still, it was lonely out on the island a lot of the time, especially in winter when visitors were infrequent. Less than a year after they'd moved into the house, though, Oak Island added one more full-time resident with the arrival of Dan and Jane's son David, then in his midtwenties, who wanted to join his father's treasure hunt. A few months later, Dan would be awfully glad that Dave had shown up.

It was November 26, 1976. Dan was deep inside 10X, hanging by a cable at a depth of 145 feet, while Dave manned the winch on the surface. Father and son communicated by the headsets each wore. He heard "a bad sound," Dan recalled, then chunks of clay began to rain down on his head. In a fraction of a second, he realized that the metal casing was giving way above him. "Bring me up! Bring me up! Out, out, out, out!" Dan had shouted into his microphone. We know his exact words because the conversation was recorded on a tape, which would be played to great effect on *The Curse of Oak Island* almost forty years later. Dave turned the winch up to full speed as he tried to lift his father out of the borehole. It felt like slow motion to him, Dan said; the sound of tearing metal and falling rocks scraping against the sides of the casing was deafening, and he knew that if the metal collapsed completely, 10X would become his tomb. "Keep bringing me up!" he shouted to David. "Don't stop! Bring me up! It's still over my head! Bring me up! Bring me up!"

Dave had just raised Dan to above the 90-foot level, so that his father was looking down on the twisted metal and falling debris, when the casing crumpled completely and the rocks and clay poured into the shaft. "The sound was godawful," Dan would tell me years later. "But it sounded a lot better when I was above it."

It had taken thirty-five seconds to raise Dan from 145 feet to 95 feet, where the casing was collapsing. Dave had handled the situation about as well as humanly possible that day, but even in that moment seemed overshadowed by his father's big personality. When Dan got to the surface, he told his son: "For God's sake, don't tell your mother, David."

Dan, being Dan, went back into 10X the next day. Dave had lowered his father only 73 feet into the shaft before Dan found himself standing on solid ground; that much material had fallen into the borehole. Dan would drill 22 feet down through the rubble, until his bit caught on the twisted, shredded steel where the casing had collapsed. After studying the damage, Dan concluded that a man-made flood tunnel was passing very close to 10X at a depth of about 90 feet and the continuous pumping had created a fault between the shaft and the tunnel that caused tons of soil and rock to push against the metal casing, gradually crushing it.

Describing this in 2003, Dan admitted that he moved away from 10X for a couple of years after his near-death experience, but he said he was still determined to get back into the borehole. And by 1978 he was taking 10X on again. The plan this time was to create a much more solid casing by using railroad tank cars. After cutting off the ends of the cars with an acetylene torch, Dan was left with a collection of three solid steel cylinders, each 34 feet long and 8 feet in diameter, with half-inch walls twice the thickness of the original casing. Getting them into 10X was a monumental job. The interior of the borehole had to be broken up with a jackhammer. Men working with picks and shovels loaded the broken rocks and boulders to the bucket that brought the debris to the surface, where a dump truck removed it. The noise, the dust, and the darkness had to have made working in 10X absolutely hellish, and Dan Blankenship at that point was more than sixty years old. Dave Blankenship had left Oak Island by then, married, and gotten a job as a construction steelworker on the mainland. Dan did have help, though, in the person of his future minority partner: Dan Henskee.

Henskee had grown up on a farm near the town of Alden in upstate New York. Like Blankenship, he had first learned of Oak Island from the 1965 article reprinted in *Reader's Digest*. He was still a teenager at the time, and during college he spent his summers on Oak Island working with and for Blankenship. Even when he finished school, Henskee came back to the island, summer after summer. Despite his lanky frame and perpetually underfed appearance, "Dan was a hard worker," Blankenship said, and a "real asset when it came to repairing equipment." Henskee's mechanical skills were so remarkable that he would modify some machines to the point that they could practically be called new inventions. It would not be until 1982, after Henskee's mother died and the family farm was sold to pay the debts racked up during her illness, that he began to live in Nova Scotia year-round. Blankenship helped him negotiate a deal whereby he would get 4 percent of any treasure recovered, then installed Henskee in a shack that doubled as an equipment shed, where he lived with his cat, Hoser. He was by any standard a quirky character and a sometimes eccentric thinker, but his quiet intelligence combined with his considerable kindness and generosity won Henskee the appreciation of just about everyone who got to know him. As Rick Lagina would remark to me during the summer of 2016, "This world would be a better place if everyone was like Dan Henskee."

Henskee was still just a Triton employee in 1978 and worth a lot more than he was being paid. It was Henskee who did the majority of the work deep in 10X that summer, including most of the jackhammering. I remarked that the noise, the dust, and the darkness had to have been nightmarish. But Henskee's reply made the experience sound almost cheerful. "I felt like I was part of really making something happen," he would tell me in 2003. "And to be honest, I didn't believe that I had anything better to do." He had made numerous observations while underground that convinced him the legend of Oak Island was rooted in actual events, Henskee said. He was especially impressed by how hard the ground was down there; they had been forced to use a pneumatic pavement breaker to excavate, and the bedrock was so solid that it didn't cave in even in places where no shoring was used. "There was no way a water channel would form down there naturally," Henskee said. "It had to be man-made."

After 10X was cleared, the tank car cylinders were tipped into it, then driven one on top of the other until an impermeable 90-foot shaft had been created.

It took two full summers (but only $35,000 in cash) to finish 10X to a depth of 126 feet, and he was convinced he could finish the job by the end of the summer of 1981, Blankenship said. "But then out of nowhere Triton pulled the plug on me."

It was Mel Chappell who had convinced Tobias they should return to the Money Pit. Chappell had sold all of his Oak Island property to Tobias in 1977 for $125,000 but remained a Triton director. And with 18 percent of the stock, Chappell was still the Alliance's third-largest shareholder behind the Tobias family (31 percent) and Dan Blankenship (19 percent). M. R. was ninety years old by then but still sharp, everyone agreed, still able to recall the details of previous expeditions to Oak Island clearly and in detail. Dan had even less success convincing M. R. of the importance of 10X than he'd had with David Tobias. During his appearance in a 1978 documentary for Canadian television, Chappell had stood next to the Money Pit smacking the ground with his cane as he declared, "*This* is where father brought up the wood and parchment, and *this* is where the treasure is." When David sided with Chappell against him and announced that Triton intended to focus its entire operation on the Money Pit, Dan said, "It was never the same between us." Even after Mel Chappell died in December 1980 at age ninety-three, Tobias continued to insist that Triton's main objective was to make the Money Pit into a much deeper and wider shaft. They would need $2 million to do that right, and Tobias was committed to raising the money, according to the newspapers in Nova Scotia.

It was a bitter time for Dan Blankenship. During the previous several years he'd been making do with a Triton operation so scaled down it barely existed. Triton's budget for Oak Island was just $30,000 per year at that point, which included Blankenship's annual subsistence salary of $12,000. Even with such limited resources, Dan had continued to explore Oak Island. In early 1979, in fact, he had made one of the most significant discoveries in the history of the treasure hunt.

That winter was severe, so cold in early February that the sheltered waters of Mahone Bay had frozen all the way from Chester to Lunenburg. "Using our derrick for an observation vantage point, it appeared that the ice extended all the way to [Big] Tancook Island," Blankenship had written in the "activity report" in which he described his discovery. Even without Triton's support, Dan continued to try to get deeper into 10X, which meant running the big pump there each day for about ten hours. He had been on the derrick when he "noticed an area to the south that wasn't frozen," Blankenship wrote; it was hard to really make out any distinct shape at first: "The colder it got, though," Dan added, "the more the ice froze, the more distinct the shapes became." The "shapes" were four large holes in the ice, about 200 feet from the shoreline, evenly spaced about 150 feet apart. The only conceivable explanation for the holes was that warmer water from underground was being pushed up from the seabed by the pump running in 10X.

This was confirmed, Dan wrote in his activity report, when the pump broke down. From the derrick, "We noticed a thin film of ice forming after the second day we were shut down." By the time the pump was repaired, four days after it had stopped running, "the ice covering those spots was about one to one-and-a-half inches thick." From the derrick, sight lines to the four holes were spotted and steel pipes driven into the frozen ground so that he would be able to inspect those locations when the cold weather broke, Blankenship explained in his report to Triton. By the beginning of March, the ice had melted, and he rowed out to the four locations in a "view boat" he had made himself. Dan continued: "The whole area was riled up and you couldn't see the bottom. However you could see air bubbles rising in the water on our sight lines."

He had interviewed several people from the Nova Scotia Department of Fisheries who "do a lot of flying and asked them if they have ever seen any holes like this in the bay, and they said 'NO.'" He was therefore confident, Blankenship wrote, that these anomalies had been caused by the action of the pump in 10X, which meant he had discovered the locations of the starting points of the south shore flood system.

In his report to Triton, Blankenship included a suggestion for how to stop the flow of water from the south shore to the Money Pit area. Since the four holes he had discovered were so deep underwater they couldn't be plugged by simply dumping dirt on them as he had done at Smith's Cove, he was proposing to bring in "concrete pumpers" that would use a 3-inch hose to fill each of the holes "maybe to as much as twenty stories high."

David Tobias was willing to go as far as bringing in a team of geologists, who concluded there had to be a connection between the Money Pit and the ice holes and that this was almost certainly not a natural connection. But the cost of bringing in the concrete pumpers, as Dan suggested, would be prohibitive without a major financing plan in place. Tobias and Blankenship went back and forth about it. Dan was so dogged that David made plans for a summer dive in the areas where the ice holes had supposedly been spotted. In water that varied in depth from 14 to 22 feet, Tobias probed the bottom in each of the four locations, but reported seeing only kelp-covered rocks and the shapeshifting bottom of the seabed. Without stating it explicitly, Tobias seemed to be saying that he doubted Blankenship's report about discovering the ice holes. He already said he'd doubted Dan's claims about what he had seen when the camera was sent down 10X. The two old friends soon weren't anymore. It was becoming the sort of situation in which the only sure way to prevent a complete fracturing of the relationship was to find a common enemy. And for that they had Fred Nolan.

CHAPTER SIXTEEN

From Triton's point of view, the problem posed by Fred Nolan had never gone away. Animosities were revived in 1974, when the province built a wider bypass road to the causeway at the request of the Department of Tourism, which had been operating tours on Oak Island for the past decade. Nolan insisted that part of the new road was on his property and responded by again lengthening his museum in order to block it. Rather than push back, the Department of Tourism chose to walk away, announcing that it was getting out of the Oak Island business. By 1976, Blankenship and Tobias had formed their own company, Oak Island Tours Inc., equally shared by each of them, to replace the government operation. For the next twenty years, tours of Oak Island would be run by this new private corporation. Most of the work, though, was done by Jane Blankenship, who managed the Oak Island Museum near the home she and Dan had built on the island's west end and hired the locals who worked as guides when summer tourists began to arrive. It was fun for a while, Jane said. You never knew who might show up on Oak Island, a point that was driven home one summer afternoon in 1979 when the island's tourists had included former Canadian prime minister Pierre Trudeau and his three sons (one of whom, Justin, would become Canada's PM himself a little more than thirty-five years later). It became exhausting after a time, however, and there was never any really significant amount of money to be made from tourism. For Dan and Jane, and to a lesser degree David Tobias, this increasingly burdensome situation was one more that had been created by Fred Nolan's obstinacy.

At the same time, Blankenship was becoming increasingly curious about what Nolan was up to. Fred was still conducting his never-ending survey of Oak Island, which produced an increasingly detailed and elaborate grid system, covered by the crisscrossing lines he had drawn between markers. What looked to others like an absurdly complex maze was filled with meaning, Nolan said—even if he himself still didn't fully grasp what it was. He told a local reporter he was on to "something big" but refused to reveal what that might be. In 1982, Nolan confided to a handful of people that he had verified his great discovery, but he wasn't yet ready to reveal it. He was still studying his grid, searching for new levels of meaning. That work was continuing in March 1983 when he had been "blindsided," as Fred put it to me twenty years later, by the lawsuit filed against him on behalf of Triton Alliance.

Tobias said he had no choice because Nova Scotia's twenty-year statute of limitations on civil action was about to expire, meaning that any attempt to recover the seven lots on Oak Island that Nolan had acquired by "sneaky and surreptitious means" would have to be made now or never made at all. Also, Triton needed a resolution of the situation with Nolan if it was going to attract the financial backing required to mount a major operation in the Money Pit area, Tobias added.

"David's position was: 'Let's get this taken care of, once and for all,'" Dan would tell me in 2003.

The resulting litigation would consume more than two years of their lives and tens of thousands of dollars. The court battle would prove nearly ruinous for Nolan, but Fred never retreated, not even in the face of upward of a thousand documents that Triton's attorneys submitted to the court and the countless hours of discovery his own lawyers subsequently billed him for. By December 1985, when the case finally went to trial, Nolan estimated that the more than $50,000 he'd paid so far in legal costs was small potatoes compared to the couple of hundred thousand dollars in losses from his survey business. He was especially injured by how successfully Triton had portrayed him in the press as a kook. Fred confided that the companies that hired him to testify for them in court were leery of putting a man publicly identified as a "treasure hunter" on the witness stand and that part of his business had evaporated almost completely. He made up his mind that he was going to fight these guys to the bitter end.

Dan Blankenship would later describe December 17, 1985, as "the worst day of my life," because that was the day supreme court judge A. M. MacIntosh upheld Fred Nolan's claims to the seven disputed lots and dismissed entirely the claim of damage to their property caused by Nolan's "trespassing." The judge did require Nolan to pay Triton $15,000 for interfering in its tourism business and ordered him to move his museum off the causeway path, but the court's ruling was on the whole a big victory for the surveyor. However, it didn't last long. Within weeks, Tobias instructed his lawyers to file an appeal, despite being warned by his son, Norman, a Toronto attorney, that Triton's chances of victory were slim and that the additional legal fees would be at least $20,000.

Part of what motivated Tobias to continue the fight was his wish to control every inch of Oak Island. In 1977, David had acquired all of Mel Chappell's holdings on Oak Island for $125,000. Nearly all of that land—lots 1–4, 6–8, 15–22, 24, and 26–32, 78 percent of Oak Island—was assigned to Oak Island Tours Inc. Except for the lot where the Blankenships had built their house, all of the other land on the island that did not belong to Tobias was the property of Fred Nolan. Tobias hoped his appeal of Judge MacIntosh's ruling would serve as leverage to persuade Nolan to sell his seven lots for $125,000, the same price David had paid to Mel Chappell just a few years earlier for nearly four times as much land. Nolan not only refused to sell—"for any price," he said—but he also filed his own cross complaint against Triton with the appeals court and continued to pay the legal fees that were threatening to bankrupt him.

The ruling on the Triton appeal and the Nolan cross complaint was issued on April 15, 1987. Fred had won again, and this time the $15,000 he had been ordered to pay Triton for interfering with tourism was reduced to $500. By then, he had spent $75,000 on lawyers and the loss from his survey business exceeded a quarter million dollars, Nolan said. I could still hear the bitterness in his voice in 2003: "I was forced to spend another eighty thousand dollars to construct a dock on my property because the only access I have to the island is by boat. On top of that, I have to barge all my equipment out to the island, which is very expensive."

It took me by surprise that Nolan's rancor was much more intensely directed at Blankenship than at Tobias, given that David was the one who had launched and driven the legal action against him. In the end, Tobias had taken the position that it was just business, nothing personal, Nolan said, congratulating him on his victory after the appeals court ruling in 1987, even handing over one of his expensive Cuban cigars. "Dan, though, wanted to destroy me. And he was willing to do anything, no matter how dirty, to do it."

Blankenship said pretty much the same thing about Nolan, telling me: "Fred did some terrible things to win the court case." Dan didn't say what those terrible things were, and Fred wasn't specific about Blankenship's supposed dirty tricks, but the depth to which the two despised one another was striking. Other people told me that Dan's grudge against Fred might have softened a bit over the years, perhaps because David Tobias had become a bigger enemy in his mind than Nolan was.

Tobias had sold Jongerin Inc. in 1985, saying at the time that he intended to devote more time to managing his family's investment company, Ilex Capital Corp., to piloting his Beechcraft airplane, and to the Oak Island project. Tobias was taken aback, however, by the results of a 1986 "feasibility study" of Triton's plans for the Money Pit, which estimated that it would cost as much as $8 million to seal off the inflow of seawater to the Money Pit area and explore it below bedrock. By then Triton's partners had poured $1.25 million into the Oak Island project and had made it clear they weren't going any deeper into their own pockets without the level of fund-raising that could probably only be accomplished by a public stock offering. The Triton partners voted almost unanimously to put 10X aside and to offer shares in a plan to conquer the Money Pit once and for all.

The one dissenting vote was Dan Blankenship's. In March 1986, Dan sent a letter to all of Triton's shareholders urging them to make "one final effort" to complete 10X, arguing that the borehole might be a "backdoor" to the treasure that would be far less expensive than the complete excavation of the Money Pit and avoid a stock offering in which "all of our shares will be greatly diluted proportionately."

In the short term, that letter paid off. Part of the reason was that January 1987 had brought another spell of bitterly cold weather to Nova Scotia's south shore, and again Mahone Bay had frozen over. Blankenship decided to once more run the big pump in 10X for as long as twelve hours a day during this cold spell, and again the four holes appeared in the ice in exactly the same places as they did in 1979. This time Tobias conceded that the intake/outlet openings of the south shore flood system might be down there, hidden beneath the debris that covered the seabed. By the following spring, Triton had given Blankenship $70,000 (half of which was from Tobias personally) to continue with the completion of 10X, which had been left at a depth of 126 feet for the past six years.

For the next eighteen months, the two Dans, Blankenship and Henskee (with only occasional help from laborers, brought to the island from the mainland) had replaced the tank cars in 10X with a ten-inch-thick casing of reinforced concrete. The work had been both difficult and dangerous. Several times Dan Blankenship had nearly suffocated at the bottom of the borehole when the compressor on the surface that supplied his fresh air cut out. Inside the shaft, the electrical generator, combined with the air compressor, the drum-winch hoist, and the turbine pump it powered, produced a sound that was deafening even to people who stood above looking down. It must have been positively bone rattling inside, where string bean Dan Henskee was using a jackhammer to break up the boulders that got in the way. After a pair of supposedly man-made cavities that had been detected at depths of 140 and 160 feet were revealed to be only pockets of loose sand blown away by the original churn drilling back in 1970, though, Tobias had had enough.

No more "frigging around," David told D'Arcy O'Connor. They were going back to the Money Pit.

Triton's "big dig" was being planned on a scale that overwhelmed all previous operations on Oak Island. The Ottawa engineer Triton had hired as its primary consultant on the project, Bill Cox, liked to tell people that in the previous two hundred years of treasure hunting on Oak Island, there had been a total removal of 300,000 cubic feet of earth; the big dig was going to take away nearly a million cubic feet in six months. Still, to anyone who knew the history of the search operations on the island, the big dig sounded like more of the same, only on a much larger scale. The plan was to excavate a shaft 80 feet in diameter to a depth of 215 feet, then seal its perimeter with interlocking steel plates reinforced by concrete. A $300,000 cofferdam would be built at Smith's Cove, a $700,000 dam at the south shore. Any remaining flood tunnels or water fissures found would be sealed with cement grouting. And now Bill Cox, who wrote the phone book–size document titled "Engineering and Operational Plans Including Cost Estimates" that was to be the central piece in Triton's stock offering, was pegging the cost at about $10 million.

The Triton prospectus was sent to twenty separate Canadian and US underwriters in the winter of 1988, with the stated purpose of beginning the big dig the following June. The response from the investment community was underwhelming. Tobias hadn't taken into account how traumatized many major investors had been by the Black Monday crash in October 1987. Triton waited until 1990 to make the actual public offering, putting 1 million shares of Oak Island Exploration Company Ltd. on the NASDAQ market. They couldn't sell a tenth of them.

Blankenship had objected to the stock offering just as vehemently in 1990 as when it was first proposed four years earlier. Dan was so incensed when Tobias pushed forward anyway that he resigned from the Triton board of directors. He was derisive when Tobias and Triton approached the Canadian government one year later, applying for a $12 million loan guarantee in exchange for the promise to create fifty jobs and the biggest tourist attraction in Nova Scotia. After the Atlantic Canada Opportunities Agency rejected the loan guarantee request because it "falls outside our guidelines," Tobias turned to the Department of Tourism. But Minister Greg Kerr told reporters: "The Triton Alliance is a treasure hunt and the Department of Tourism and Culture does not fund that kind of thing."

Blankenship continued to push for a return to 10X, where completing his exploration would cost a tiny percentage of what Triton was proposing to spend on its big dig. Tobias, though, had only hardened his position. Speaking to reporters, David mocked Dan for having "wasted time, credibility, and hundreds of thousands of dollars on a worthless hole that he found by dowsing, for God's sake." Blankenship answered that "10X is the only place where any real evidence has come up. But David doesn't want to hear about it, because he's got his nose stuck in the Money Pit. And where's that got him? Absolutely nowhere."

Perhaps the worst part for both Blankenship and Tobias was that their longtime archrival Fred Nolan was about to steal the spotlight with the announcement of a discovery that was the biggest on Oak Island in decades.

IT STARTED WITH FIVE LARGE GRANITE STONES that were spread in different directions in the vicinity of the house Nolan had built on Joudrey's Cove. The one right at the water's edge had caught Fred's eye first. It was about 8 feet wide and 6 feet high, set into the ground on a flat bottom. Nolan was pretty sure the top of the stone had been carved into its cone shape. Because it was so different from any other rock on the shoreline along Joudrey's Cove, Fred also had a sense that it might have been moved to the spot where he found it. That would have been a considerable task, given that he estimated the weight of the stone to be about ten tons.

Nolan found a second cone-shaped stone that was almost identical about 400 feet southeast of the first one, then the third conical rock, a near perfect match for the first two, another 400 feet or so southwest of the second. Eventually he found two more of these cone-shaped boulders on a line directly southwest of the second stone.

As he always did, Nolan marked the exact locations of the stones and added them to his grid of the island. He was fairly certain that these five stones were the only ones of their kind on Oak Island, which suggested they might be significant. It was only in the course of the many hours that he spent studying his grid, however, looking for connections or meaning in the places where various lines intersected with the stones or with the lines between the stones, that it occurred to Nolan to try looking at the five "cone stones" independently, without reference to any other marker. When he did this, Fred told me, he was "literally stunned" by the realization that the cone stones formed a geometrical shape and that this shape was a Christian cross, one with two 360-foot arms and a center post that stretched 867 feet from tip to tip.

Nolan did a second survey of the cone stones and their relationships to one another, then a third. The result was the same each time: the cross formed by the cone stones was almost perfectly symmetrical. Fred told me in 2003 that for years on Oak Island he had been exploring places where his survey lines crossed. And after discovering the cone stones and the cross they formed, he decided to see what he might find at the point where the line of the two arms and the line of the post intersected. He did find another rock but this one was a craggy piece of limestone, not granite, and had no discernible cone shape.

Nolan told me he had discovered the cross and confirmed its dimensions by the end of 1982. So why had he waited until 1992 to reveal its existence, I asked. As I found Fred inclined to do, he avoided giving me a direct answer. I had only inferred that he enjoyed keeping the secret to himself and felt sharing it with other people might diminish his pleasure in some way. The next day I learned that it was not until 1991 that Nolan had finally decided to take a closer look at the limestone rock he found at the intersection of the two lines that formed the cross.

He used his backhoe to tip the rock, Nolan told me, and immediately recognized that it had been hand carved to resemble a human head.

I have to admit that when I first saw the famous "headstone" of what was by then known as Nolan's Cross, I found it very difficult to make out any human features. Only when I stood at exactly the right spot could I see the outlines of the headstone's eyes, nose, and chin.

And had they really been carved, I wondered. It was possible, but it also looked to me as if the stone might have been shaped by natural forces. Joe Coleman, one of the executive producers of *The Curse of Oak Island* during the summer of 2016, told me a couple of geologists had been brought over from the mainland to examine the headstone. "What they told us, basically, was that it might have been carved, or it might not have been carved."

Whether it was carved or not, the headstone seemed certainly to have been placed in the spot where Fred Nolan found it. When the producers of *The Curse of Oak Island* brought a pair of stonemasons out to the island in the summer of 2016, they also had refused to say whether the headstone was carved, because it was so weatherworn. When they looked at the cone stones that formed the bottom of Nolan's Cross, however, both the stonemasons agreed that the smoothness of the undersides was not natural, but rather it was evidence the boulders had been dragged a good distance.

In 1991, Fred prevailed on his friend and fellow Nova Scotia surveyor William Crooker to verify his measurements of the cross. Crooker had done so. He had also, with Nolan's permission as I understood it (though Fred himself wouldn't confirm it), announced the discovery of the cross to the world in a 1992 book titled *Oak Island Gold*.

Why reveal the cross then? I asked Nolan in 2003. In a tone that was surprisingly frank, Fred answered that he was motivated by worry that "if something happened to me" (the clear implication was that he feared Dan Blankenship might make it "happen") what he had discovered might be lost forever.

For those who followed the Oak Island story, Nolan's Cross was the biggest news in decades. The dimensions and measurements were clearly laid out, checked, and rechecked. The symmetry and exactitude were simply too remarkable to explain the cross away as a coincidence of nature. And if the cross had been made by men, this meant that the stones that formed it not only had been carved with hammers and chisels, but they also had been moved into their current positions by people who had to rely on the machinery of the sixteenth, seventeenth, or early eighteenth centuries. The amount of labor and planning it would have required to move and align five ten-ton stones was comparable to what it must have taken to construct the artificial beach and drainage system at Smith's Cove. Once more, the sheer enormity of what had happened on Oak Island, combined with the mystery of it, captivated public imagination.

Even Dan Blankenship, who initially scoffed at news of Nolan's Cross, came around fairly quickly to accept that his mortal enemy had made a major discovery. By 2003, when I first interviewed him, Blankenship's own elaborate survey grid of Oak Island featured the cross in red highlights. "My problems with Fred are well known," Dan told me as he explained his grid that afternoon. "But I sincerely admire the excellent work, extraordinary work, he's done."

Nolan chose the moment when the evidence of the cross was revealed in Crooker's book to make a public display of some other items he had discovered during the past three decades of exploring Oak Island. Perhaps the most intriguing was a lock with a cross-shaped keyhole that, when turned, opened to reveal a second, smaller keyhole inside. Fred refused to say where on the island he had found it. When I asked him, he simply smiled with sealed lips and gave a slight shake of his head. Nolan had also produced a pair of hand-forged scissors similar to the ones Blankenship found at Smith's Cove, though again he wouldn't say where exactly they had come from. Fred was willing, though, to tell me and the world where he made what might have been his most remarkable find. This was an old railway trolley with wheels still attached that had run on a track. He had found it buried beneath the mud when he drained the swamp and hauled it out with a timberjack.

All of a sudden Fred Nolan, the troublemaking outsider, seemed to have become the central figure in the Oak Island treasure hunt. That was acceptable to neither Blankenship nor Tobias, but by then the two partners were so estranged that they either would not or could not work together, even against their common enemy. In 1993 and 1994, what Blankenship described as a "pitifully underfunded" Triton program aimed at tracing the island's underground tunnels through magnetometer detection had produced no useful results. In 1995, Tobias attempted to raise more money by bringing in two new partners, wealthy Bostonians David Mugar and Daniel Glazer, who proposed to spend at least $200,000 on an "aggressive exploration" of the Money Pit area. Blankenship, though, was incensed when he learned that what the Boston partners would be getting in return was "exclusive worldwide [media] rights to the entire Oak Island saga." Dan accused David of plotting to "sell away our media rights, which are worth millions, and dilute our shareholdings as well."

Blankenship also refused to support Triton's decision to spend $80,000 on a series of scientific tests to be conducted on Oak Island by a team of scientists from Massachusetts's Woods Hole Oceanographic Institution. In July 1995, twenty of the institution's scientists were preparing to create complete tomography (X-ray and ultrasound exploration) and bathymetry (sea-depth measurement) maps of the island, along with a chart of the island's groundwater. Woods Hole would also run seismic, side-scan sonar, and piezometer tests in 10X, at Smith's Cove, and across the entire Money Pit area, and to perform new carbon-dating of the coconut fiber and wood fragment samples collected by Triton over the years. Tobias, thrilled by the prospect of what might be learned from an exploration of Oak Island conducted by what he considered to be the leading marine sciences organization on the planet, was startled by the fax he received from Blankenship just as the Woods Hole team was arriving in Nova Scotia: "I wish to inform you that I will not be participating in this venture nor cooperating with it."

Tobias and the rest of the Triton board chose to deal with Blankenship's objections by ignoring them—and him. Dan couldn't help gloating a little in 2003 when he showed me the 150-page report Triton had gotten for its $80,000 investment in Woods Hole. What the report said, in a nutshell, was that the evidence that supported the existence of man-made tunnels and chambers on Oak Island was "inconclusive." The report also stated that it still considered Oak Island to be a valid unsolved mystery, then proposed a "preliminary" two-year plan that would involve drilling and analyzing core samples from new test holes, performing camera and sonar investigations, combined with the reexcavation of Smith's Cove, new dye and radiocarbon tests, plus morphological and geographical studies. A rough estimate of the anticipated cost was between $700,000 and $1 million. "So, in other words, what Woods Hole told us was, 'Hey, give us another million bucks and we might be able to tell you something,'" Blankenship said.

Tobias and Blankenship would briefly reconcile in early 1996. Again the catalyst was old friends rallying against a common foe. In this case the enemy was David Mugar, who had been trying, Tobias now agreed, to snag the Oak Island media rights for a song. By the spring of 1996, Triton and Mugar had ended their relationship. Perhaps this was why Dan had been amenable when David proposed bringing in Canada's counterpart to Woods Hole, the Bedford Institute, based in Dartmouth, Nova Scotia, to conduct a "multibeam bathymetry study" of the waters surrounding Oak Island.

During the summer of 1996, Bedford scientists aboard the research vessel *Puffin* circumnavigated the island while bouncing sonar signals off the bottom of Mahone Bay that produced color-coded images of the seabed, including any notable features. Bedford reported that while most of the features this study had found were of natural origin, a significant number were believed to be "anthropogenic," as the report put it. In other words, they were man-made. The Bedford scientists had been particularly struck by what they described as "two parallel linear slight depressions" found off the island's southeast shore, speculating that

THE CURSE OF OAK ISLAND 243

these might be "large linear scours in the mud attributed to unknown anthropogenic processes."

On the basis of that, the Bedford Institute was invited back to Oak Island in October 1997. Scientists Gordon Fader and Bob Courtney, now aboard the research vessel *Plover*, scanned the south shore in waters that were between 15 and 30 feet deep. A video of the complete mission was shot, but most of the attention would focus later on a single twenty-second snippet of conversation, when Fader and Courtney had relocated the "linear scours."

> FADER: Gee, that feature sure is unusual. . . . Doesn't look natural. Too linear . . . I've never seen anything quite like that.
>
> COURTNEY: Almost looks like it has been dredged.
>
> FADER: If I look at the image, there are some features on there that look unusual: the circular depression, the circular mounds, the long linear feature extending to the east off the island. . . . It looks like it may be man-made . . . as if maybe someone constructed a rock wall or dug an excavation of some sort.

Blankenship was thrilled by Bedford's conclusions, because they fitted nicely with what he had inferred from the appearance of the ice holes during the winters of 1979 and 1987. On November 3, 1997, Blankenship wrote to Tobias to remind David that for some time he had "strongly suspected" that the main flooding of the Money Pit was coming from the island's south shore, adding that he was convinced the Bedford scientists had found clear evidence of this. Tobias was intrigued enough to approach the governments of both Canada and the province of Nova Scotia to fund a more elaborate search of the waters off Oak Island, using the best side-scan radar and seismic reflection instruments available. The cost would be $1,000 a day. Both the national and provincial governments said no, again because a treasure hunt was not a public project.

So Triton would close the twentieth century on a sour note of continuing failure to secure the funding it had been after for most of the previous twenty years. Tobias, who had by this time sunk almost $750,000 of his own money into the Oak Island treasure hunt, decided to scale back. Triton's corporate offices were relocated to a corner in the basement of David's Montreal mansion. Yet Tobias, now in his late seventies, continued to insist he was an Oak Island believer. If they ever got to the bottom of the Money Pit and found nothing, Tobias told D'Arcy O'Connor, "it would mean that what I have seen or thought I saw with my own eyes doesn't exist. I would be like something out of *The Twilight Zone*, and I would have wasted all of these years." This he refused to accept. Tobias added: "We'll find it."

But time was running out.

CHAPTER SEVENTEEN

During my interviews with Dan Blankenship and Fred Nolan in 2003, I had to make an effort not to show my disappointment with their answers when I was able to steer either man toward the questions that arose from the Oak Island mystery. The revelation of Nolan's Cross had only increased my inclination to believe that the original works on Oak Island weren't created for the purpose of concealing a treasure of gold and silver. The scope of those works—from the excavation of the Money Pit, to the building and demolition of an enormous cofferdam and wharf, to the arduously, elaborately constructed artificial beach and the drainage system at Smith's Cove, to the flood traps that poured water into the Money Pit from a source that was hundreds of feet away—was far beyond what anyone would have found necessary or been willing to do to hide a cache of monetary treasure, no matter how enormous, in my opinion.

There had to be a *greater* reason than concealing wealth for what had been done on Oak Island, and the discovery of the cross strongly suggested what I already suspected, which was that the Money Pit and all the rest had been created by people whose motivations were spiritual or religious. Though neither Dan nor Fred said as much to me, I got the distinct feeling from each of them that they thought I believed what I did because it made the mystery of Oak Island deeper and richer; that it was, in short, a better story.

Nolan said he believed the cross was "one aspect" of a geometric code constructed by military engineers to pinpoint the location of an enormous cache of gold and silver that had been created after the sacking of Havana, Cuba, by the British military in 1762. "Look at the evidence," Fred advised me. "You'll see that it adds up." I did as he suggested, and was forced to admit that the evidence was indeed quite compelling.

The expedition to capture Havana had launched from England in March 1762 under the command of Lieutenant-General George Keppel, 3rd Earl of Albemarle. Sir George Pocock commanded the British naval forces, with George Keppel's brother Augustus serving as his second in command. The English fleet reached the Caribbean around April 22 and spent two weeks gathering six hundred black slaves from the islands of the Lesser Antilles, then arrived in Havana Harbor on June 6 with an enormous force of two hundred ships and more than eleven thousand troops. Among their many advantages was that the British had taken the Spanish by surprise. Havana's fortifications, however, were so stout that the Spanish were able to keep the English outside the city's walls until early August, when an additional three thousand British soldiers arrived from New York. Just days later, on August 12, 1762, the Spanish surrendered Havana. The amount of wealth the British plundered during the next six months can only be guessed at, but it was certainly enormous. In today's value, tens of billions of dollars of gold and silver had been either mined by or seized from the native peoples of South and Central America during the previous 250 years of Spanish rule, and nearly all of it had passed through Havana. The Catholic Church's share of the take was considerable and there is evidence that the church had chosen to keep most of that gold and silver in Havana rather than putting it at risk in sea voyages.

The main evidence of how the Spanish treasure was divided among the British conquerors is contained in a letter sent by the Admiralty on behalf of King George III to Sir Pocock on February 18, 1762, about two weeks before the fleet set sail for Havana. The letter directed Lord Albemarle and Sir Pocock to distribute any booty recovered during their expedition among the land and sea forces under their command in such "manner and proportion" as they saw fit. Albemarle and Pocock, naturally, intended to take care of themselves first and foremost. Their agreement stipulated that a full one-third of whatever was seized from Cuba would be divided equally between the two of them. Then one-fifteenth of the total would be split between their two seconds in command, with the remainder to be divided among the officers and men in descending order of rank.

Fred Nolan's theory of what actually happened was laid out in his collaborator William Crooker's *Oak Island Gold*. How much of this was Nolan and how much was Crooker I was never able to fully distinguish, but the essence of the theory is that Albemarle and Pocock decided to first conceal and then divert a shipload or two of the Havana treasure to a hiding place that became Oak Island. The primary evidence in support of such a theory is the apparent discrepancy between what the British seized in Havana and what was reported to the Crown. According to Albemarle and Pocock, the forces under their command had seized a total of 737,000 British pounds in treasure from the Spanish. Crooker (although Fred Nolan seemed to suggest it was really him speaking through Crooker) would point to a search of Spanish archives in 1977 that placed the value of the plunder seized in Havana at more than 10 million British pounds. Nolan and Crooker each pointed also to a biography of Augustus Keppel that placed the value of the treasure seized in Cuba at more than 3 million pounds. The two further noted records showing that after Havana fell, a number of Spanish galleons sailed unawares into the harbor and were taken by the British, who then seized large cargos of silver and gold that were never accounted for by Albemarle and Pocock.

Albemarle was "accused of being a greedy man" by more than one of his fellow British officers, Crooker would note, but he and Nolan suggested the conspiracy might have gone all the way to the top—King George himself. The evidence they pointed to was the very fact that Albemarle had been put in charge of the Havana expedition. Albemarle "had never held an important command and his military career had been without distinction," Crooker wrote. "Furthermore he was not imaginative or particularly quick-witted." Albemarle's main social and political advantage seems to have been the patronage of the Duke of Cumberland, King George's uncle, who was implicated in the plot, according to Nolan and Crooker.

The most solid piece of evidence for the theory as presented by Nolan and Crooker might be the letter written by Lord Pocock to John Cleveland, first secretary to the Board of Admiralty, on October 19, 1762, a little more than two months after Havana was surrendered by the Spanish. After describing how and to where he would dispatch the ships under his command by the first of November, Pocock threw in a mention of the fact that he had already sent three ships to Halifax, Nova Scotia, in response to the French invasion of Newfoundland. Nolan and Crooker would maintain that at least one of those three ships made its way to Mahone Bay, where a military engineer and his crew, along with a contingent of British soldiers, constructed a subterranean complex of chambers and vaults in which the largest part of the Havana treasure was concealed.

Nolan and Crooker supported their theory with evidence that suggested the clearing where the Money Pit was found "would unlikely have been more than 50 years old and probably had been there in the vicinity of 30 years when it was discovered," as Crooker put it. The main basis of this claim are the descriptions in the early accounts of younger oak trees growing among the stumps of larger trees that had been cut down. Crooker relied heavily on a senior forester for the Canadian government who said he had seen farm fields turn into forests within thirty years. He also cited an estimate from the Nova Scotia Department of Natural Resources that a Nova Scotia red oak with a diameter of between 6 and 8 inches (the description of the younger trees in the Money Pit clearing) would probably be between forty and fifty years old. I didn't point out to Fred Nolan that a number of sources said those trees weren't red oaks. I wasn't sure it mattered, anyway.

And I was impressed by what Crooker had found in a 1948 history of Nova Scotia's capital city titled *Halifax, Warden of the North*, written by Thomas H. Raddall. In late 1762, Raddall had written, members of the British fleet and army that had captured Havana earlier that year arrived in Halifax with "enormous loot" and partied lavishly on the mainland while their ships were moored in the harbor for the winter. "There followed a saturnalia as this rabble of gaunt, sunburned adventurers . . . flung their pistareens, pieces of eight, and doubloons over the tavern bars and into the laps of prostitutes." The level of dissipation "was something beyond belief," according to Raddall. "The prize money they distributed among so many soldiers and sailors was worth 400,000 pounds sterling, which they almost threw away. The birds of prey drawn here from all quarters by the hope of plunder made Halifax more like a pirates' rendezvous than a modest British settlement."

If the common soldiers and sailors had 400,000 pounds to spend in Halifax, Nolan and Crooker contended, how much more must Albemarle and Pocock have taken?

They asked a good question and offered a substantial theory, except for one glaring problem. In 1762, the township that would become Chester (it was still called Shoreham then) had already existed for three years. While the population was small, there were enough people on the shore of Mahone Bay to make it highly unlikely that work on the scale of Oak Island's could have been done without anyone noticing. Crooker (speaking for Nolan) acknowledged this more as a possibility than as a near certainty: 'Although the subject island is hidden from Shoreham by other islands, someone might see the project from an elevated position and come to investigate or a fisherman might suddenly appear." Absurdly understated, in my opinion: there were already dozens of people fishing in Mahone Bay by 1762 and there is no way they would not have noticed the work that, for example, created the drainage system at Smith's Cove.

Except this explained the early stories of "strange lights" out on Oak Island. So, once again, I found myself conceding a sliver of potential to a theory that I considered to be fundamentally flawed. I was coming to accept that the best I could ever do was arrange the various propositions in a descending order of plausibility. On that scale, I found Blankenship's theory a bit more believable than Nolan's.

WHILE FRED NOLAN WAS INSISTING that it was the British who had done the work on Oak Island, Dan Blankenship was growing increasingly adamant that it was the Spanish. When I first sat with him in the early autumn of 2003, Blankenship was obsessed with a book that was published in 1556, *De Re Metallica* by Georgius Agricola. "My bible," Dan called the book the first time he showed me his copy. A standard text in mining engineering courses into the late twentieth century, *De Re Metallica* had actually been a lost work for several centuries. The medieval Latin text was "discovered" around 1910 by future US president Herbert Hoover, who was working at the time as a freelance mining engineer. Hoover and his wife, Lou, translated the work to English and published it in book form in 1913, creating a considerable stir in academia and in the engineering world. For many people, Hoover among them, the most remarkable thing about *De Re Metallica* was how convincingly it proved the sophistication of mining techniques that existed long before the machine age. "You read this book and you understand there's no question that the technology existed, well before the sixteenth century, to have created the underground works on Oak Island," Dan Blankenship told me as we flipped through the illustrated volume. "What Agricola describes and what we've seen belowground here match up perfectly." Reading *De Re Metallica* had helped convince him of a theory he was already inclined to embrace, Dan said. Sometime between the late 1500s and 1700, Oak Island had become the repository of a huge cache of gold purloined by Spanish ship captains who used Incan slaves to excavate their hiding place, then slaughtered those who had done the work.

There is certainly no question that enormous wealth was taken from South and Central America in the 200 years after Christopher Columbus made his first voyage to the New World. Until about the middle of the sixteenth century, this wealth had consisted mainly of booty seized from the native peoples: gold and silver artifacts, plus pearls and emeralds. The gold and silver pieces were melted down and re-formed into bullion for shipment back to Spain. By the time *De Re Metallica* was published, though, the Spanish had realized that they could recover far greater wealth by seizing the natives' gold and silver mines, then using the enslaved men of those tribes (Incan mainly) to perform the labor. By this means, the conquistadors collected tens of billions of dollars of ore that was smelted into coins and ingots before being shipped back to Spain aboard galleons that sailed in convoys from the Caribbean ports of Colombia, Panama, and Mexico. The Gulf Stream route carried the Spanish ships much farther north than one might imagine, to within three hundred miles or so of Nova Scotia.

The scale of the Spanish operations in the New World was made stunningly clear in 1985 when the sunken six-hundred-ton galleon *Nuestra Señora de Atocha* was discovered off the Florida Keys by the treasure hunter Mel Fisher and his team. Laden with gold, silver, emeralds, and other valuables collected from Cartagena, Colombia, and Porto Bello, Panama, the convoy to which the *Atocha* belonged had been struck by a powerful hurricane about thirty-five miles off the coast of what is today Key West on the morning of September 6, 1622. The *Atocha* was stripped of its masts by the fierce winds, then lifted by a huge wave and slammed against a reef that ripped open its hull. It sank within minutes along with a cargo that included forty tons of silver and gold and seventy pounds of emeralds. The gold and silver alone would be worth nearly $500 million today. Bearing in mind that the *Atocha* was just one of twenty-eight ships in the Spanish convoy and that this was just one of the many convoys launched from Latin America to Spain during the late sixteenth and seventeenth centuries, the scale of the transfer of wealth that took place during those years is staggering.

The Spanish convoys of that period were frequently hit by storms that scattered them, Blankenship would point out. Some ships straggled home days or weeks behind the others, while some were never seen again and presumed to have been sunk. But what if one or two or three of those stragglers had been captained and crewed by men who saw an opportunity in a near disaster? What if those captains had decided to steer their ships north in search of a spot so isolated that a treasure of hundreds of millions or even billions of dollars could be safely hidden until an opportunity to return and retrieve it became available? Wouldn't that serve as an explanation for what had been done on Oak Island? Look at the carbon-dating results Triton had received over the years, Dan told me. They consistently occurred on or around the year 1575 and generally encompassed a range between 1525 and 1625, the pinnacle of the Spanish conquest of Latin America. "The Spanish theory makes sense on so many levels," Dan said. "No other theory is as comprehensive."

People, of course, had been suggesting it was the Spanish who engineered the works on Oak Island long before Blankenship made that argument to me in 2003. A professor of economics at the University of Michigan named Ross Wilhelm had in 1970 presented the theory that Spain used Oak Island as a depot for repairing storm-damaged ships during the reign of King Philip II (who reigned from 1556 to 1598). The works on Oak Island had been created, Wilhelm argued, as a place to store the bullion from those ships so that they could sail back to Spain unencumbered. Other, undamaged ships would pick up the gold and silver and carry it across the Atlantic. The Spanish surely had devised a system that permitted them access to the treasure vault at the bottom of the Money Pit without springing the flood trap, contended Wilhelm, who pointed to the inscribed stone that was found 90 feet deep in the Pit by the Onslow Company in 1803. The symbols carved into that stone were nearly identical to the ones used by Giovanni Battista, a sixteenth-century Italian cryptologist whose cipher disks had been constructed of two metal rings, the one on the inside displaying various symbols and the one on the outside bearing letters of the alphabet.

Wilhelm had used one of Battista's disks to translate the symbols carved into the Money Pit's inscribed stone, then translated them into English to reveal the following message: "At eighty guide maize or millet

[into] estuary or drain. F." What it meant, Wilhelm said, was that the Money Pit's flood trap could be stopped up by pouring maize or millet into the drainage system, then waiting for it to expand and plug the flow of water. Once that was accomplished, the wooden platform on which the stone had been found—a cleverly designed air lock, Wilhelm said—could be removed, the shaft bailed out, and the treasure vault entered. The grain would gradually rot after the Pit was resealed, and the flood trap would once again be set. The "eighty" in the inscribed stone's message, according to Wilhelm, was the depth at which the air lock had been built, and the F stood for Felipe, as Philip II would have been known to his own people.

Wilhelm's theory sounded quite compelling when I first heard about it in 2003. I quickly realized there was considerable reason to doubt it, though, because neither the professor nor anyone else could say with certainty what had been carved into the inscribed stone. No photograph or rubbing of the stone or its inscription existed, which seems astonishing in retrospect, though not nearly so surprising as how the stone was treated by those who possessed it in the last decades of the nineteenth century and the first decades of the twentieth.

According to most accounts, the stone that had been lifted out of the Money Pit in 1803 remained in the fireplace jamb of John Smith's house on Oak Island until 1863 or 1864, when it was removed to Jothan McCully's home in Truro and displayed there to hundreds of curious visitors. In 1865, the stone was conveyed to Halifax by A. O. Creighton, treasurer of the Oak Island Association, to be displayed in the window of A. and H. Creighton, the bookbinding business on Upper Water Street that A. O. owned with his younger brother Herbert, for the purpose of attracting investors to the treasure hunt. When A. O. retired in 1879, Herbert formed a new bookbinding firm with Edward Marshall that was called Creighton and Marshall. One of the few who left any record of what happened to the stone was Edward Marshall's son Harry, who went to work at the bookbinding company in 1890. In a sworn statement made in 1935 to Frederick Blair and R. V. Harris, Harry Marshall said:

I well remember seeing [the stone] as a boy and until the business was merged in 1919 with the present firm of Phillips and Marshall.

The stone was about two feet long, fifteen inches wide and ten inches thick, and weighed about 175 pounds. It had *two smooth surfaces* [italics mine], with rough sides and traces of cement attached to them. Tradition said that it had been part of two fireplaces. The corners were not squared but somewhat rounded. The block resembled dark Swedish granite, or fine-grained porphyry, very hard, and with an olive tinge, and did not resemble any local Nova Scotia stone. While in Creighton's possession, someone had cut his initials "J. M." on one corner, but apart from this there was no evidence of any inscription either cut or painted on the stone. It had completely faded out. We used the stone for a beating stone and weight.

When the business was closed in 1919, Thomas Forhan, since deceased, asked for the stone, the history of which seems to have been generally known. When we left the premises in 1919 the stone was left behind, but Forhan does not seem to have taken it. Search at Forhan's business premises and residence two years ago (1933) disclosed no stone.

Thorough searches of the old premises in 1935 and of the stone yards of Brookfield Construction Company on Smith and Mitchell Streets, Halifax, have failed to discover the stone.

The most remarkable thing about Harry Marshall's statement is that the stone had no inscription when he first saw it during the last years of the nineteenth century: "It had completely faded out." Colonel Henry Bowdoin would write in his notorious *Collier's* article that he had seen the stone in 1909 and that there was no inscription on it then. Bowdoin, who implied that there never was any inscription, can be substantially discounted as a source but not entirely dismissed. Others who worked at the bookbinding company would say that the inscription on the slab had been worn away over the decades it was used as a "beating stone" to prepare leather hides as book covers. If this is true, given how hard the stone was said to be, the inscription must have been more scratched than carved into it. None of that information, though, or anything else that's known about the stone, explains how a supposed copy of what has been widely accepted as the original inscription on it surfaced in the middle of the twentieth century.

That inscription might actually have surfaced in the early twentieth century, when James Liechti, a professor of languages at what was then Dalhousie College in Halifax wrote that he had seen the inscribed stone and decoded the message, which read, according to the professor, "Ten feet below two million pounds lie buried." That Liechti was being employed by a prospective treasure-hunting company to help sell stock makes his claims suspect. But the "two million pounds lies buried" version of the stone's inscription became more or less official in 1951, when Edward Rowe Snow's book *True Tales of Buried Treasure* was first published and included not only a drawing of the inscription on the famous Money Pit stone but also a translation of that inscription by "an old Irish schoolmaster" that was identical to the one produced by Liechti, only with "ten feet below" replaced by "forty feet below."

Snow claimed he had obtained his copy of the inscription and the translation from Reverend A. T. Kempton of Cambridge, Massachusetts. Not a lot is known about Kempton, though the amateur local scholars at Blockhouse Investigations, a group who had been researching Oak Island for years, were able to trace him back to his 1891 birth and upbringing in Nova Scotia's Annapolis Valley, then through his education at Arcadia University in Wolfville to his appointment as the minister at a Baptist church in Massachusetts. In New England, Kempton was an enthusiastic amateur historian who gave lectures throughout the region on his two favorite topics, the Acadians and the Mi'kmaq tribe.

From the papers of R. V. Harris, we know that in 1909 Kempton asked a clergyman working in Nova Scotia to find someone to help him write an Oak Island book. This information comes from one of the

several letters Kempton wrote to Frederick Blair, with whom the reverend began a correspondence in 1949, the same year that Rowe claimed
to have received the inscription on the Money Pit stone from Kempton.
What Harris kept of that correspondence mainly concerns Reverend
Kempton's theory that the works on Oak Island had been created by
the Acadians. In one letter, though, Kempton tells the story of how in
1909 he contacted a fellow clergyman based in Mahone Bay to ask "if
he knew of someone who would write me a good account of Oak Isl."
The minister had referred him to "a school teacher," Kempton went
on, who eventually sent him a manuscript. "I paid him for it," Kempton
wrote to Blair, but he never turned this manuscript into a published
book. "The teacher who wrote my MSS. did not give me any proofs of
his statements," Kempton explained to Blair, but had maintained that
"characters" were cut into the so-called inscribed stone and that "a very
bright Irish Teacher had worked out this statement as printed in Snow's
book." A number of years later, Kempton traveled to Mahone Bay to
find the teacher, but the man had died. On that trip, "I learned that the
stone was in the Historical Society in Halifax. I went there several times
but never found anyone who could tell me about the stone. So I let the
matter drop until I showed it to Ed. Snow and he set it in his book."

In other words, we have only the word of a long-dead and unnamed
teacher on which to base the assumption that the cipher reprinted hundreds of times since it was published in Snow's book is actually what had
been carved into (or scratched onto) the inscribed stone. At least half a
dozen authorities have agreed that this inscription can be decoded by
a very simple cipher substitution code to read: "Forty feet down, two
million pounds are buried." But that doesn't mean such an inscription
ever actually existed.

This leaves the question of why anyone would have felt it necessary
to place a message 90 feet deep in the Money Pit stating that another
40 feet down there were 2 million pounds. To keep them digging? The
only theory of Oak Island with which this comports is the claim that
the entire thing was an elaborate ruse. And that theory is preposterous.

Professor Wilhelm, of course, came up with a translation of the message on the inscribed stone that was quite different and considerably more interesting than the one originally printed in *True Tales of Buried Treasure*. Wilhelm was only able to do this, however, by making a number of changes in the supposed inscription to make it read as he claimed. And on what basis the professor made those changes, we have no idea.

Still, the theory that the Spanish buried a purloined Incan treasure on Oak Island holds up to inspection better than any other theory involving a treasure of gold and silver. D Arcy O'Connor refuted those who have claimed that the island's original works couldn't date back to the sixteenth century (because the large oak tree with the cut-off limb that grew over the Money Pit in 1795 wouldn't have lived that long) by consulting with botanists at Harvard who "informed me that Nova Scotia red oaks commonly live for 300 years." The coconut fiber, the traces of mercury, the parchment fragment, and the handwrought iron scissors that have been found at various locations on Oak Island also point to the Spanish, O'Connor maintained: coconut fiber was commonly used as packing material in the holds of Spanish ships; Spaniards used mercury to separate silver from its ore; their documents and charts were often written on sheepskin parchment, and the scissors found at Smith's Cove were, according to an archeologist associated with the Smithsonian Institution, of a design that matches the scissors used by the Spanish conquistadors in Mexico.

What O'Connor doesn't say, though, is that nearly all of the same items could be linked to the ships of Elizabethan England. Nor does he address the claims in early accounts of the Money Pit's 1795 discovery that it was the stumps of larger, older trees standing among younger trees that tipped off Daniel McGinnis and his friends that something had happened in this spot; such a contrast would almost certainly not have been visible if those trees were cut down in the 1500s, more than two hundred years earlier. Nevertheless, when I spoke to Dan Blankenship in 2003 he seemed quite taken with O'Connor's proposed scenario, which was this:

Sometime around 1600 a convoy sails from Cuba to Spain on the Gulf Stream route but is hit by a storm that separates one treasure-laden galleon from the rest. The captain of the damaged ship looks for a sheltered spot to make repairs and finds his way to Mahone Bay, where the vessel is run aground off the east end of Oak Island. The decision to bury the ship's valuable cargo on the island is motivated by the knowledge that the patched-up galleon stands a better chance of making it back to Spain if it isn't loaded down with gold and silver. So the crew of the ship (and possibly the slaves aboard it) dig the Money Pit, build the cofferdams just above the low tide line at Smith's Cove and on the South Shore, then construct the drain and flood trap system and bury their treasure, planning to return for it aboard a rebuilt ship. Riding a bit higher in the water, the galleon sets sail for Spain, but en route it is hit by a storm and the makeshift clay-and-fiber caulking with which the holes in the hull have been repaired begins to fall apart. The ship sinks with its captain and crew to the bottom of the North Atlantic and is assumed by the Spanish to have been lost at sea still carrying its cargo of gold and silver.

"Not impossible," I conceded to Dan Blankenship when he laid the theory out for me, and I was relieved that he accepted this without pushing me to be more enthusiastic.

DAVID TOBIAS HAD FOR A NUMBER OF YEARS favored the Robert Restall theory that Oak Island had been a "communal bank" created by a number of pirate captains and their crews. This proposition was based on the idea that each set of buccaneers had dug a tunnel leading away from the Money Pit where they placed a watertight vault to hold their booty, each one protected by the same system of flood traps. The theory was that only the pirate group that had done the digging would know the precise location of its tunnel and the vault at the end of that tunnel, so only that group would be able to return to the island and retrieve its loot by shoveling straight down through virgin ground to the spot they had previously measured and recorded. Most people who heard this theory rejected it out of hand, believing that separate pirate groups would never have worked cooperatively in such a way. In the late 1960s, Tobias had been swayed to the theory by what he heard about Albert Lochard, the Haitian engineer who claimed to have discovered just such a communal bank at Kavanach Hill in southern Haiti. Tobias actually convinced Dan Blankenship to make a trip to Haiti in 1970 to look into Lochard's story, but Dan had been unable either to locate Kavanach Hill or to find anyone who knew about the supposed discovery of a pirate bank there. Blankenship eventually tracked Lochard to New York City, where he was living under an assumed name as a political refugee. Dan had been at least a little impressed when Lochard told his story without asking anything for it. He had found the remains of the communal bank in 1947 and spent the next three years exploring them, collecting about $50,000 in eighteenth-century coins in the process. He was not nearly finished with his excavation of the site in 1951, when he was forced to flee Haiti under "government pressure," Lochard told Blankenship. The engineer eventually gave Tobias a diagram of the Haitian site that described a 40-foot-tall, 35-foot-wide underground chamber with a domed roof that was connected to five large tunnels and a number of smaller tunnels that would channel water into the vault when the clay plugs inside were removed. Just like the treasure hunters on Oak Island, he had been forced to constantly fight an inflow of water to gain entrance to the chamber. The main problem with Lochard's story was that he could offer no witnesses to verify it. He had found the Kavanach Hill site on his own, the Haitian said, and had told no one about it.

Tobias eventually came around to a new belief that involved both the English *and* the Spanish. Tobias had indicated the direction in which his thoughts were turning as early as 1987, when Triton Alliance had issued its prospectus for the big dig project. Within that document, Tobias had observed that the carbon-dating of artifacts recovered from underground on Oak Island indicated that the creation of the original works on the island had taken place during the period of the second or third voyage of Francis Drake.

Drake was not only the greatest explorer in British history, but he was also, and by far, England's most successful privateer. Beginning in 1572, Drake captained vessels that made a series of attacks on Spanish ships and forts all along the Atlantic coast of the Americas, in the process introducing piracy to the Western Hemisphere. He took some enormous prizes during this period, the largest coming when he joined the French buccaneer Guillaume Le Testu in an attack on a Spanish mule train making a huge transport of silver and gold. Le Testu was wounded in the battle and captured by the Spanish, who eventually beheaded him. Drake and his men, however, escaped with more than twenty tons of silver and gold. It was more than they could carry, so the English buried much of it, then dragged the rest through eighteen miles of mountainous jungle to the cove where they had left their raiding boats. The boats were gone when Drake and his men reached the coast, with the Spanish on their heels. Drake ordered his men to bury the treasure on the beach, then built the raft on which he and two volunteers would sail ten miles south to the bay where the flagship was anchored. Drake eventually recovered both of the treasures he had buried (all subsequent stories of buried treasure arise from these events) and returned with them to England, now a wealthy man.

Drake's greatest voyage, the one that made him the second man (after Magellan) to circumnavigate the Earth, took place between 1577 and 1580. Drake's *Golden Hind* took any number of Spanish vessels along the way, the richest being the galleon loaded with twenty-six tons of silver and gold, plus chests stuffed with emeralds and pearls, which Drake and his men captured off the northwest coast of Ecuador.

Tobias's theory was that during one of his earlier expeditions Drake had sent one or more of his ships north to Nova Scotia to establish a small secret colony on what would become Oak Island. There were two purposes, Tobias would explain: Drake's early raids on the Spanish were not officially sanctioned by Queen Elizabeth I, because the British were bound by a peace treaty with Spain. Transporting the booty Drake and his men had taken back to England would have been politically risky during this period; a secret depository for this treasure in the New World would have been necessary for a period of years. The second purpose was to establish a safe base on the North American continent, Tobias added, one where Drake could repair, refurbish, and reprovision his ships. In the 1570s, the only claim to land in the Western Hemisphere the British could make was in Newfoundland and Nova Scotia, where John Cabot had planted the flag of England in 1490.

A great deal of what Tobias was saying made sense in the abstract. His was yet another of those theories to which one had to concede plausibility. What makes it difficult to believe is that not one of the thousands of historians who have pored over Francis Drake's life and career during the past four-plus centuries has found even the slightest evidence to support it.

CHAPTER EIGHTEEN

By the first time I visited Oak Island in 2003, Tobias and Blankenship were diverging about a lot more than their theories of who had buried what. It was almost five years since Dan and David had first filed suits and countersuits against one another, and neither man showed the least sign of backing off. Tobias accused Blankenship of misappropriating operating funds from Oak Island Tours for his personal use and damaging the company's reputation. Dan not only denied those allegations, but made a counterclaim stating that he had kept the company going with his own personal money and was owed $45,000 in back wages.

The dispute between the two men had been hot ever since April 1998, when Tobias, writing as president of Oak Island Tours, announced that "on behalf of Oak Island Tours Inc., the owner of all lots on Oak Island, exclusive of 23, 5 and 9 through 14, I hereby confirm that Oak Island Exploration Company is entitled to access to those lands for the purpose of exploration and exploitation of the Treasure on Oak Island." Blankenship, who owned half of Oak Island Tours but had resigned his positions on the boards of Triton Alliance and Oak Island Exploration Company, found himself hemmed in. He had no power at all within the latter two companies and was subject to Tobias's veto power over Oak Island Tours. To try to get around David, Dan had applied for a treasure trove license that allowed him to conduct his search not only on lot 23, the only one on the island he owned independently of Tobias, but also on lots 19 and 20 in the Money Pit area. Tobias responded by filing for his own license to search privately for treasure on lots 19 and 20. Both men's personal applications were refused by the Canadian government, which meant that Triton's license to explore the Money Pit area was the only one in effect. Because David maintained effective control of Triton, he could use the company to block Dan from searching anywhere on Oak Island beyond lot 23. And for the next five years, he did. Blankenship's frustration and fury grew month by month.

In January 2003, the rumor that Oak Island Tours intended to sell its Oak Island property for $7 million was reported in the local press. Dan and David each accused the other of planting the story. I found Dan a bit more convincing when I asked about it nine months later, but I honestly didn't know which of them to believe.

Meanwhile, Triton's treasure trove license was set to expire in July 2003. The renewal application Tobias filed was swiftly followed by one from Blankenship, who again demanded the right to search for treasure on all lands owned by Oak Island Tours. David hadn't "done shit" with Triton's treasure trove license during the past five years, Dan said, and if he was allowed to proceed on his own he would demonstrate just how little Tobias had gotten done without him. David accused Dan of being delusional, devious, and determined to stop Triton at any cost. When I arrived in Mahone Bay in September 2003 to research the *Rolling Stone* article, the treasure trove applications of both Blankenship and Tobias were still "under consideration" by Nova Scotia's Department of Natural Resources, which explained that "conflicting" claims had complicated the process. The province also had not yet ruled on the application of Fred Nolan, who complained publicly that the enmity between Blankenship and Tobias was stalling the renewal of his own treasure trove license. Not surprisingly, Nolan blamed Blankenship most, accusing Dan of "doing his best to scuttle the ship before he goes down."

Fred had not produced another major revelation since the announcement of Nolan's Cross in 1992. He had kept busy, though, moving his portable drilling rig to various places on his property where survey lines intersected. Fred's most compelling discovery came when he began aligning various rock markers he discovered and using them to trace a survey line that he would probe at 2-inch intervals with a steel rod. Very quickly, he had discovered a spruce stake, driven so deep into the ground that only the round top showed. Following the same line, Nolan found fifty-eight more spruce stakes, all similarly concealed from view. Those stakes were carbon-dated to the 1600s, Fred said.

Fred seemed to take little satisfaction from the fact that Dan had gradually conceded not only the existence of Nolan's Cross but also its importance to solving the mystery of Oak Island. For more than a decade, Fred had been publicly declaring that the Money Pit was a "decoy" and that the Oak Island treasure was in tunnels that ran off in different directions. Naturally he was startled to read in the *Halifax Chronicle Herald* that Dan Blankenship was now declaring the Money Pit to be an "elaborate decoy," that the treasure was in tunnels running deep beneath the opposite end of the island, and that the cross was the key to finding those tunnels. "The man actually thinks my ideas are his ideas," Fred told me in 2003.

There were other players in the game by then. One was Robert Young, a wood-carver who in 1999 had purchased lot 5, on the northwest end of Oak Island, from Fred Nolan for $100,000. In the sales agreement, Fred had retained the right to search for treasure on lot 5, but now Young was applying for his own license. Also in the mix was the Oak Island Tourism Society, a nonprofit of Mahone Bay residents headed by a man named Danny Hennigar, who had worked as a tour guide on the island in the 1980s and whose grandfather had been part of Gilbert Hedden's search crew in the 1930s. After the story about Oak Island being up for sale at a price of $7 million was published in January 2003, Hennigar had tried to prevent what he regarded as "an absolute disaster" by attempting to mediate the conflicts between Blankenship, Tobias, and Nolan and convince the three men they could work together. This had begun shortly before I arrived in Mahone Bay in 2003, but by the time I first set foot on Oak Island, paranoid accusations were already flying back and forth between the parties. Tobias was sending faxes and making phone calls to Nolan about how they might partner up, but at the same time Nolan was making identical overtures to Blankenship. In no time, each of the three men was accusing the other two of trying to stab him in the back.

On the last day of 2003 Blankenship startled everyone, including me, with an announcement in the *Halifax Chronicle Herald* that he had at last solved the mystery of Oak Island. In the past six weeks, "I've been able to confirm all my suspicions and I can say definitively who did it, how they did it, and where they did it. But until I get down there, I can't say exactly what it is," Dan told the *Chronicle Herald*. He found the evidence he had been looking for of tunnels on the west end of Oak Island, Blankenship said: ten-foot-wide holes that he was convinced had served as air shafts for the tunnels during their construction.

My *Rolling Stone* article was just hitting newsstands, and I was more than a little annoyed that Dan had never showed me these supposed air shafts, or advised me that he believed they marked the path of the tunnels that contained the Oak Island treasure. Fred Nolan must have been infuriated when he read Dan's claim that he had located these air shafts by using measurements made from the coordinates of the cone stones of the cross. David Tobias could not have been very happy about the *Herald* article, either, especially after reading that Blankenship had just met with the minister of the Department of Natural Resources to "lay out his findings" and make the case that he, rather than Triton Alliance, was in the best position to recover the Oak Island treasure. If he received his treasure trove license, Dan declared, he could bring up the treasure in seven months. "I turned eighty in May and won't get another chance," he told the *Herald*. "If they give Tobias a license for property he's never been interested in, it will be a very sad day." David, who was just about to turn eighty himself, had to have fumed when he read that.

Part of what made the *Herald* article so discouraging to me was that I had half convinced myself that I'd orchestrated the rapprochement between Dan and David that so many others had tried and failed to achieve. This imagined accomplishment was admittedly inadvertent: As my *Rolling Stone* story was being prepared for publication, the magazine's photo editor and I had convinced Blankenship and Tobias to pose together for a photograph that would accompany the article. The two old men were all smiles in the photo proofs I was shown and the photographer told me that Dan and David had seemed like dear friends the day he got them together, cracking jokes and sharing memories. That conviviality was short-lived. Hostilities between the two men were revived in 2004, when the treasure trove license applications of Triton Alliance and Fred Nolan were approved by the Department of Natural Resources and Dan Blankenship's was again refused. Tobias pushed the blade a little deeper in Dan by announcing plans to raise $15 million for an excavation of the Money Pit.

Nothing came of either David's plans for raising funds or for renewing Triton's operations on Oak Island's east end. A frosty stalemate had once again settled over the island and no one was doing much of anything. I was saddened but not really surprised in July 2005 when I read a *Chronicle Herald* article that ran under the headline: FOR SALE: ONE "MONEY PIT." The subhead was: PARTNERS GIVE UP TREASURE HUNT, PUT OAK ISLAND TOURS ON MARKET.

Blankenship was the only one of the two partners quoted in the article. "I've been in litigation with my partner for quite some time and we've agreed to disagree on just about everything," Dan had told the *Herald*. "We couldn't work together. It's been too long, the better part of fifteen years since we really worked as a team." He and Tobias had agreed to abandon their court claims against one another, to liquidate Oak Island Tours, and to put their 78 percent of the island on the market for $7 million, Blankenship confirmed to the newspaper, but then he added that any sale "would depend on the buyer and their reasons." I was a bit heartened, if not entirely convinced, when I read that Dan had said he would not agree to any transaction that involved a developer who planned to break the island up into lots and build condominiums on it: That "won't happen in my lifetime," Dan had declared. "Money's not my god. It never has been, and it isn't now."

It was clear to me when I sat with Dan three years earlier that advancing age was wearing the old lion down, no matter how he tried to deny it. I heard the evidence, though, when Blankenship had contrasted himself with Fred Nolan. He told me that "the difference between us is that Fred thinks he's going to live to be two hundred years old, and I realize I won't."

Afterward, I'd flown home from Nova Scotia convinced that the long story of Oak Island might be winding down toward bleak endings of these three elderly men who had dominated the treasure hunt for the last half century. I thought of my *Rolling Stone* article as an opportunity to prevent that from happening. Millions of people would read that article, I imagined, and perhaps at least one of them would have the combination of youthful enthusiasm and financial wherewithal to join the narrative and turn it in a new direction.

New blood, that was what Oak Island needed. Unbeknownst to me, a great infusion of just that stuff was on the way.

CHAPTER NINETEEN

Rick and Marty Lagina each told pretty much the same story about how they'd gotten involved with the island. As viewers of *The Curse of Oak Island* know, it all began back in 1965, when Rick (who was thirteen at the time, not eleven, as Rick mistakenly once said during an interview) read that same *Reader's Digest* article that had prompted Dan Blankenship's first trip to Nova Scotia. Rick was so entranced that he insisted on reading the article to his ten-year-old brother, Marty, and "I just sort of absorbed his enthusiasm by osmosis," as the younger Lagina put it to me.

The most remarkable thing about Rick's "enthusiasm" was that it hadn't waned at all during the succeeding decades. He'd read everything in print about Oak Island and in the early 1990s, not long after he turned forty, Rick, joined by brother Marty, had traveled to Nova Scotia to introduce himself to his hero Dan Blankenship.

The official account, which Rick and Marty each repeated to me in pretty much the same way, is that the two brothers got as far as the entrance to the causeway at Crandall's Point and stopped, afraid to drive any farther. The only person living on the island to whom either brother had spoken was Jane Blankenship, who hadn't extended an invitation, but rather told Rick over the phone that if he wanted to drive the nearly fourteen hundred miles from his home in Iron Mountain, Michigan, to Oak Island, she couldn't stop him. As Rick would later describe it to *Traverse* magazine, they eventually worked up the nerve to drive across the causeway "and who's there but Mr. Blankenship. This very imposing man that we've read about is actually standing there at the other end of the causeway clearing trees. And we got out of the car, and he looked up, and he didn't say a word." Rick's story was that he broke the ice by silently going to work alongside Dan, pushing over the trees that the older man was whipping with a chainsaw. In Marty's telling, it was the bottle of whiskey he had brought that got them invited back to the house. Both brothers agreed that they were barely past some opening small talk and pouring three glasses of whiskey before Dan got a phone call and said he had to go. "We basically got the bum's rush off the island," as Rick recalled it, before even getting to the point of asking how they might join the treasure hunt.

Rick went back to Michigan's Upper Peninsula, where the Laginas had grown up, to put in the last of his thirty-five-plus years working for the US Postal Service. Marty, meanwhile, had spent that time running an energy business that made and managed natural gas and coal investments. As a consequence, he was loaded. In 2004 he'd sold his company, Terra Energy—which had been extracting natural gas from shale since the mid-1990s—for $58 million.

THEN IN 2007 an ad listing for sale all of David Tobias's Oak Island holdings appeared in *Islands* magazine. Marty, who at the time was flush from the sale of Terra Energy three years earlier, told me he was vacationing in Florida when he spotted the ad and immediately called Rick to let him know a big piece of Oak Island was for sale. Rick's recollection was that *he* had seen the ad and made the call to Marty. Either way, the *Islands* ad turned out to be both quite misleading and the Lagina brothers' point of entry to Oak Island. The real estate agent who was supposedly handling the sale had overstated his position, Tobias told the Laginas. All he was offering for sale was one small parcel of what he owned on Oak Island, lot 25. The brothers went in together to buy the lot, "to get a foothold on the island," as Rick put it, and eventually were able to persuade Tobias, who was now eighty-three years old and on his last legs, to sell them all of his property on Oak Island as well as any rights he had acquired through Triton Alliance. Marty put together the consortium that made the purchase, making the Laginas and their partners Craig Tester and Alan Kostrzewa fifty percent partners in Oak Island Tours with Dan Blankenship.

It was during my first one-on-one conversation with Rick that he asked about my trip to Oak Island in 2003. I remarked that I had spent the majority of my time on the island sitting with Dan Blankenship in his basement office. "Lucky you," Rick told me. "I've never been there." You've never been in Dan's office? I asked. Rick shook his head. "I've never been invited." I had simply assumed that Rick and Dan were tight and that the old man had welcomed not only the enthusiasm but also the financial backing the Lagina brothers had brought to Oak Island. Rick said no, that Dan believed he and Marty had "backdoored" their way into the treasure hunt, and he had never forgiven them for it.

I wasn't sure what to make of that. Back when the Laginas were trying to buy the Tobias holdings on Oak Island, Blankenship, who had the right of first refusal on his longtime partner's shares of Oak Island Tours, had chosen the offer by "the Italians from Michigan" over a higher one offered by a Swiss property-development company. I never saw any sign of friction between Dan and Rick during the weeks I spent on the island in the summer of 2016, and in fact about a month after I left Nova Scotia in late August, Rick *was* invited into Dan's basement, where a scene was shot for the show in which Dan was displaying various artifacts.

I had spent enough time around Rick by then to be certain that he mostly meant anything he said and that the man he appeared to be on television stuck very close to the person he was. Marty thoroughly enjoyed the performance aspect of the show as well as the celebrity it had brought him. Rick generally did his best to ignore being famous. When I ran into him around the hotel where we were both staying, Marty would regularly steer our conversations toward some subject other than Oak Island. His older brother's fascination—obsession might not have been too strong a word—with Oak Island was just as ardent off camera as on. He could talk about Oak Island for hours on end and I rarely heard him speak about anything else.

Marty was a complicated character, a very bright fellow and a polymath of sorts, an engineer who liked to quote poetry and had a repertoire suitable for just about any occasion. He was fanatic about exercising and kept in splendid shape, often highly competitive, and a good deal more sensitive than he let on. When I asked him about being in the energy business Marty told me: "It's made me hated my whole life. People think we're the worst, the exploiters, the polluters." He told me a story about a meeting in northern Michigan in the middle of winter at which the people who had shown up "to call me names" all left their gas-guzzling SUVs running in the parking lot, so they would stay warm inside. "You get really familiar with people's hypocrisy in the energy business," Marty said. He had recently switched to wind-driven turbines, starting (along with Craig Tester) a company called Heritage Sustainable Energy that was poised to become the largest producer of wind energy in the state of Michigan. "And yet people still hate us," he said. "People think we're killing birds, we're giving the people who live nearby headaches. You better learn to live without love if you want to be in the energy business."

THE LAGINAS AND THEIR PARTNERS had accomplished almost nothing on Oak Island during the next several years after buying out Tobias. They were blocked by the fact that Canada's Treasure Trove Act had been revoked by parliament, which meant that nobody anywhere had a right to search for treasure within the national boundaries. Both brothers told me it had been a long and boring process—and a very expensive one too, Marty said—to sort through this obstacle, but in 2011, three years before *The Curse of Oak Island* began shooting, Canada had replaced the Treasure Trove Act with what it called the Oak Island Treasure Act, meaning that Oak Island had been singled out as the only place in Canada where one could be licensed to search for buried treasure. The deal was that the partners in Oak Island Tours would get 90 percent of any findings, with 10 percent going to the Canadian government. Canada also would keep any artifacts. The problem being, Marty told me, no one had ever defined what "artifacts" meant.

Marty claimed that neither he nor Rick had been interested in the television show when Kevin Burns first approached them. Burns was up to that point best known for a number of Emmy-winning documentaries and reality shows, most notably *Ancient Aliens* and *The Girls Next Door*, about Hugh Hefner's relationships with his three much younger live-in girlfriends. Rick and Marty each told me they had turned Burns down flat when he first approached, and each then explained changing their minds with exactly the same words: "Kevin Burns is very persuasive." Burns had apparently tailored his appeals to the brothers' individual motivations for investing in Oak Island. The show would spread the legend of Oak Island worldwide, Burns told Marty. Then he pointed out to Rick that the production would attract not only investigators and theorists from all over the planet, but also the best people from the applied sciences. By the summer of 2013 the brothers and Burns had a deal with one another and with the History Channel, which had agreed to finance a five-episode first-season tryout. Those episodes started running on television in January 2014 and were so successful that the network promptly ordered another ten that were produced and edited in time to start running during November of the same year. A third season of thirteen episodes began running in November 2015. From the start, the participants in the new Oak Island treasure hunt had included Blankenship and his son Dave; Charles Barkhouse, whose family had been in Mahone Bay for generations; Dan Henskee, whose story had been a significant section of my *Rolling Stone* article; Marty's business partner, Craig Tester; and various younger members of the Lagina and Tester families. When Kevin Burns called me in the spring of 2016, he said he wanted me to join the group for "four or five episodes" of the fifteen the History Channel had ordered for the show's fourth season. It sounded like a sweet deal: I would be getting paid while doing research for a book, all expenses covered, during a summer month when Nova Scotia's south shore offered some of the loveliest and most dramatic scenery on the planet.

BECAUSE THE EXACT LOCATION of the Money Pit had been lost for decades and the area around it was riddled with other shafts and connecting tunnels, many of them collapsed, Dan Blankenship had urged the Laginas and the show's producers to approach the problem through 10X. He pointed out the obvious connection to the Money Pit; when air was pumped down one shaft, bubbles rose on the surface of the water in the other. Additionally, they were the only two holes on the island where freshwater floated on top of saltwater. The Laginas and their partners had agreed to send a robotic high-definition camera down 10X to see what might be found. The camera they used, the Spectrum 90, was built to withstand an underwater depth of as much as 1,000 feet and had the capacity to pan, tilt, zoom, and enlarge images by as much as forty times their actual size. Afterward, Dan joined the rest of the team in what I recognized as the shack that once housed the offices of Oak Island Tours but was now known for the purposes of television as the War Room. Dan was ninety years old when the scene was shot and I could sense the depth of the old man's emotions as he looked into 10X for the first time in more than thirty years. When Dan began to tell the others he believed he might be seeing the top of a tunnel and then an anchor, though, I felt myself grimace, reminded of all the things that Dan had told me he saw in the still pictures from the video that had been shot in 10X in 1971: the chests, the old tools, the body lying on its side. I hadn't been sure I was seeing any of those things back then and I felt more than a little doubt that Dan was seeing a tunnel or the anchor onscreen now. I wondered if he was being set up for a crushing disappointment, but I knew he'd risk that to satisfy his curiosity.

Marty supervised an operation at 10X that relied on a technique he had seen employed in drilling oil wells; it involved using compressed air to bring up whatever was down there. Mostly, that appeared to be a great deal of water. Jane Blankenship had died in 2011, and I saw her surviving husband's vulnerability for the first time ever when Dan showed up at 10X wearing his deceased wife's old straw hat, with the bright blue-and-white ribbon still attached. This was a proud man who for most of his life had been better at controlling fear and concealing pain than just about anyone I had ever met. Now, as I listened to him admit his "obsession" with Oak Island, I could hear someone desperate to see a solution to the mystery in the short time the ninety-three-year-old had left.

Straining the sediment from the muddy water pumped out of 10X had produced only a single tiny scrap of metal. A decision was made then to send a diver down the shaft, and from that point forward nearly all the drama connected to 10X involved finding someone who could get to the bottom of it.

The first to try was a former military policeman named Dan Misiaszek, better known as Frog. He and his wife, Kathy, had dived as a team in search-and-rescue missions all over the planet. Together they had decided to try 10X wearing rebreathers that would provide an ideal blend of nitrogen and oxygen. Before the two dove, geophysicist and sonar imaging expert Brian Abbott arrived to explore the path of the dive and the obstacles it would present. Of the latter, by far the most difficult would be the bar of a bit that had slipped off one of the many drills claimed by Oak Island, now wedged crosswise in the lower, 27-inch-diameter pipe at the bottom of 10X. Negotiating it would be, at best, a tight squeeze. A backup diver and an EMT team would need to be present in case an emergency situation developed.

Frog went down alone first. Kathy followed in a bucket lowered by crane, riding with Rick Lagina, who was wearing nothing but jeans and a work shirt as he was submerged to the chin in water that was forty-one degrees Fahrenheit.

Kathy Misiaszek never really joined the dive because her husband had gotten stuck in the lower pipe, wedged between the wall and the drill bar. The man sounded sincerely frightened for a few moments before he worked himself loose and began the climb back to the surface, aborting the dive.

After the Misiaszeks called it quits, Brian Abbott came back to 10X to do a more thorough sonar exploration of the shaft's floor. As he studied the resulting images on a screen where they all appeared in red and black, Abbott was struck by what he described as objects with edges cut at 90-degree angles. "Mother Nature doesn't make rectangular things," he said, speculating that what he was seeing might be a chest, probably the same one Dan Blankenship had described seeing himself more than thirty years earlier. He had also found a stand-alone column, made of wood he believed, Abbott said, and an opening in the wall of the chamber at the bottom of 10X, 7 feet tall and 5 feet wide, which he suspected might be the entrance to a tunnel.

The scanning sonar was again sent down the shaft. The technician operating it, Nick Burchill, confirmed Abbott's observations, adding that there were two posts, not one, and that he also thought they were wood. He saw the rectangular structure Abbott had found as well, Burchill said, describing it as 2 feet by 2.5 feet with a curved top. He too thought it was a chest. "Ninety percent certainty," Burchill said. He had also seen an object that looked to him like human remains, Burchill told the Laginas. It was all tremendously exciting, especially for Dan Blankenship, who said he was convinced that there was the preserved corpse of a man lying on his side who had been chained to a post down there.

It was what they heard from Abbott and Burchill that sent the Laginas and their partners in search of someone who could get down there. Eventually they were led to John Chatterton, whom Marty described as "the most qualified diver we could possibly find." Chatterton, who had dived shipwrecks that included the *Lusitania*, the *Andrea Doria*, and the *Titanic*, listened to the litany of other failed attempts to get down 10X, described it as "a very challenging and interesting dive," then assured the Laginas that he would make it successfully if that were "humanly possible." Chatterton was lanky and handsome with graying sandy hair, and he never seemed to blink. "To describe someone as oozing confidence is a cliché," Marty would tell me over breakfast one morning in July 2016, "but Chatterton oozes confidence. I mean it actually comes out through his pores."

The day of Chatterton's dive Mahone Bay was about to be struck by the biggest wind and rainstorm it had seen in years. Marty Lagina and Craig Tester were going to have to follow the dive by video conference from their offices in Traverse City, Michigan, where their flight to Nova Scotia had been grounded by the impending storm. Chatterton himself, though, was unfazed. "I like that," he said when advised of what weather on the ground would be that day. "It makes me feel like I'm getting away with something."

He had decided to go down 10X in a water suit (through which warm water would be pumped) and steel-toed boots, Chatterton said, wearing a Kirby Morgan helmet through which umbilicals would feed his trimix, with just one very small "bailout" tank attached to his waist. His partner, Mike Huntley, would go down into 10X as well, but would stop at the bottom of the wider section of the shaft, and remain floating in the water there unless Chatterton got himself into trouble and needed help. Shortly after Chatterton reached the drill bar at a depth of 204 feet, it sounded as if Huntley might have to rescue his partner. Chatterton still sounded cool when he reported that "I'm having a little trouble turning around here," but there seemed to be some agitation in his voice when he added a few moments later that his breathing and communication apparatus was caught on the bar. Something that approached actual strain entered his tone when he said, "My hose is hung up." Chatterton's nerves were as steely as advertised, though, and within a minute or so he had maneuvered past the drill bar and continued his descent. Only another minute passed before those listening on the surface and in Michigan heard Chatterton say, "I'm standing on the bottom." He was the first person to reach the chamber since Dan Blankenship's last dive in the 1970s, and the first in a position to actually explore it.

Chatterton's first report was discouraging to those listening: The "post" that Blankenship had first seen more than thirty years earlier, and that had been confirmed by both Abbott and Burchill, was metal, not wood. It was stuck in the clay of the chamber's floor, Chatterton said, and standing next to it he could feel that the water in the chamber was moving, not still. The increasingly glum listeners perked up when Chatterton suddenly announced, "I'm in the tunnel." Then a moment later he said that the opening he had stepped into "appears very much rectangular." The walls were clay and rock and the ceiling was crumbly and irregular, the diver reported. It narrowed ahead and he would have to crawl to continue.

Chatterton began his climb back to the surface soon after this, and the next time his voice was heard the diver was sitting in the Oak Island War Room in his hoodie sweatshirt, providing what was described as a "debriefing" to the Laginas and other members of the cast. The cavern was somewhere between 10 and 12 feet tall, Chatterton said, and the pipe—not post—was the only vertical object in it. What had been described to him as a "chest" was, he believed, a rock, and where he had been told the body might be he had found instead a sinkhole. He was all but certain that the chamber at the bottom of 10X was a natural formation, not a man-made one.

After hearing all of this, Marty Lagina said he was ready "to put an X in 10X," but his brother Rick resisted, and so, of course, did Dan Blankenship. Chatterton's search of the chamber had been too brief and too limited to make a final determination about what was down there, Rick argued. The ensuing back and forth established the dynamic between the brothers that would play out repeatedly during the first three seasons of *The Curse of Oak Island*: Rick led with his heart, while Marty stayed in his head, the romantic versus the rationalist, the man of faith vying with the man of science.

CHAPTER TWENTY

After the exploration of 10X, of the second-largest block of screen time during the first three seasons of *The Curse of Oak Island* had been devoted to the theory that the original work there had been done by the Knights Templar. I'd found the Templar theory thrilling back in 2003, when I'd worked it into my *Rolling Stone* article. The claims that this ancient order of warrior-monks had conveyed a treasure that might include the Holy Grail or the Ark of the Covenant, or both, from Jerusalem to Scotland to Nova Scotia and buried it on Oak Island added such a rich layer of possibility to the island's legend that I found it nearly irresistible, even admitting its unlikeliness.

Looking back on what I wrote then, I'm glad I included the disavowals of Dan Blankenship and Fred Nolan. "I can't entirely dismiss the Templar theory, but I don't accept it," Dan had told me. "The Templars were bankers, not miners. And there's no record of them using slaves. The Spanish, though, were miners, and they had no compunction about using native peoples as slave labor." I had been prompted to ask Nolan about the Templar theory after Robert Restall's daughter, Lee Lamb, told me Fred had confided to her that he believed the knights had buried the Holy Grail, along with other treasures, on Oak Island. Nolan would only tell me that "there's a lot of evidence to support that theory," but like Dan he was more inclined to believe the Spanish were responsible for the original works on the island. "So many ideas have been put forward that have at least a little plausibility," Fred had said. "But you have to go with what's most likely."

The Templar theory had been introduced early in *The Curse of Oak Island*'s first season with a question about how the oak trees had gotten there. It had been "long speculated," the narrator told the audience, that the fourteenth-century Scottish nobleman Henry Sinclair, "whose family took over the mantle of the Knights Templar," had come to Oak Island in 1398 to hide the Templar treasure and planted the oak trees for the Templars who would come centuries later. Sparating what was true from what was possibly true, likely untrue and definitely false would be a thorny task, however. I started with what was actually known about the order of the Knights Templar.

The knights had been a product of the First Crusade, launched by Pope Urban II in 1095 in Clermont, France. The Crusade had initially been directed at the Seljuk Turks, the ferocious horseback warriors whose attacks on Byzantine Christians were threatening Constantinople itself, but it quickly morphed into a mission to liberate Jerusalem from Muslim rule. Armies led by European nobles marched toward the Holy Land at the urging of a reformist pope who roused Christianity to make a valiant stand against the various Muslim kingdoms that had conquered Syria, Egypt, and most of North Africa, then taken southern Spain and Catalonia and were, the pope said, preparing to capture the entire Mediterranean Basin. While religious fervor was the primary driver of the Crusade, plundering, pillaging, and simple bloodlust played their parts as well. After laying siege to Nicaea and Antioch, the Crusaders marched on Jerusalem in June 1099 and by the middle of July had conquered the city. The scale of the massacre that followed has been debated among historians but it was certainly considerable. Even the Muslim soldiers who retreated to the Al-Aqsa Mosque were slaughtered, and most of the city's Jews were killed when the Jerusalem synagogue was burned to the ground.

The Christian Kingdom of Jerusalem was created by a council held in the Church of the Holy Sepulchre, built on the spot where according to legend Jesus Christ had been crucified. During the next several decades, various orders of knights arose to lay claim to assorted

powers and jurisdictions. The Knights Templar was one such order. They were the Poor Knights of Christ and the Temple of Solomon at their founding in 1118, a mystical order of warrior-monks who wore white capes decorated with red crosses and proclaimed their dedication to the protection of civilians traveling to the Holy Land. They were famously abstemious, unshaved celibates who were said to dine in silence while listening to prayers.

The earliest legends that grew up around these knights derived from their base of operations in the Al-Aqsa Mosque, where, according to tradition, the Temple of Solomon had once stood. Rumors that there were secret chambers beneath the mosque where the greatest and holiest of treasures had been stored in the time of Solomon were the original basis of these legends, for which there is no solid historical evidence. It is a fact, though, that the Knights Templar grew not only wealthy but also powerful. Their power resulted from the admiration they commanded, which grew in part from Templars' insistence that they were obedient only to the pope himself and would not serve any earthly king, prince, or prelate. Their most illustrious sponsor, the Catholic Saint Bernard of Clairvaux, said of them: "They are milder than lambs, and fiercer than lions. They combine the meekness of monks with the courage of knights so completely that I do not know whether to call them knights or contemplatives." Paradoxically, the Templars' wealth was initially produced by the vows of poverty the knights took. Their pledges to sign over all possessions upon entering the order began to swell Templar coffers as the sons of noble families joined them by the dozens.

The Templars remained powerful even after they were forced out of Jerusalem in 1187 by Islamic reconquest of the city by the army of Saladin. The Christian retreat was gradual and the final defeat did not come until 1291, when the coastal stronghold of Acre fell amid a slaughter by the Muslims that was even more terrible than what had taken place in Jerusalem almost two hundred years earlier. The Templars then moved their headquarters to Cyprus, where they swiftly became the first international bank, financing, for a price to be paid in interest, the projects of kings, lords, and other nobles all over Europe. No one fell further in the order's debt than the profligate King Philip IV of France. In the year 1307 Philip decided to cancel those debts in the most lethal way imaginable. Templar leader Jacques de Molay and about sixty of his knights were invited to Paris for a conclave with the king. But it was to be a capture, not a conclave. On the morning of Friday, October 13 (this may or may not be the beginning of Friday the thirteenth representing bad luck), de Molay and nearly every one of his knights were arrested and imprisoned by Philip's soldiers. During the following months, they were subjected to gruesome tortures that extracted confessions that they had practiced such things as sodomy, idol worship, and spitting or urinating on crucifixes. Then, despite a commission dispatched to Paris by Pope Clement V that reported there was very little if any evidence to back up the accusations against the Templars, Philip ordered de Molay and fifty-four other knights burned at the stake as heretics. Witnesses later testified that de Molay had gone to his death most bravely, warning King Philip that he would one day pay to God for what he was doing. At least six and perhaps as many as twelve Templar knights had escaped France after the arrest of de Molay and the others. Where they went and what they did is not truly known, but claims about it are what have fueled the Templar legend for the seven centuries since.

The first story to surface—when is difficult to say, since it did not appear in print until the nineteenth century—was that the surviving knights had loaded the "Templar treasure" on eighteen ships that sailed from the port of La Rochelle in northern France for parts unknown. The Templars certainly were wealthy, but whether they possessed any treasure is no more than speculation based on rumor. Claims have been made that while excavating beneath what was once the Temple of Solomon they had discovered a buried room where the Ark of the Covenant or the Menorah of Moses or the Holy Grail, or all three, were kept. There is, again, absolutely no historical record to support these claims, but they have not only endured but also expanded. What history does tell us is that the Templars kept copious records of their transactions and treaties, and that all of them disappeared in 1307 and have never been found.

The story of the so-called Templar fleet carrying a treasure out of La Rochelle rests entirely on the protocol of the interrogation by Dominican inquisitors of one Jean Chalons, a French count who told it while under the threat of torture. There is no other source. Chalon's claim was that he had heard (secondhand) that the preceptor of the French Templars, Gérard de Villiers, was warned in advance of his impending arrest and escaped France with fifty horses and eighteen galleys. That tale is undercut by what is actually known about the Templar fleet. The Templars did have ships, but the majority of these were lightweight craft suitable only for skirting the Mediterranean shoreline to carry pilgrims and supplies between Marseilles and Acre and could not have been used to make an ocean voyage. There are references to four larger "galleys" that could presumably have navigated the Atlantic, but the evidence of even that is sketchy. And none of the ships that existed in the early fourteenth century could have crossed the English Channel in October.

Nevertheless, from the tiny, fragile seed planted by Jean Chalon, an entire industry reaching into publishing, film, and television has arisen and from the late twentieth century to the present actually flourished.

The story of how that happened turns on the addition of two additional written records that were first introduced into the narrative in the mid-sixteenth century by a Venetian nobleman named Nicolò Zeno. He was the descendant of a family that had helped build Venice in the eighth century and that in the centuries afterward had become the owners of one of the greatest fleets on the planet. The Zenos remained wealthy and powerful but by the 1500s were in decline.

In 1558, Nicolò Zeno published a book he hoped might not only restore his family to its full status but also possibly support a claim that Venice had discovered the New World a hundred years before Christopher Columbus. Its primary contents were a map and a series of letters that Nicolò claimed to have discovered hidden away in the Zenos' family home. These had been created, Nicolò wrote, sometime between

1390 and 1404, by two of his ancestors, a previous Nicolò Zeno and his brother, Antonio, and they described the fantastic voyages the two had made across the North Atlantic.

The book produced by the Nicolò Zeno of 1558 employed an unusual style. It was a first-person narrative written by the author that was freely interspersed with quotations from the letters supposedly written by his relatives more than a century and a half earlier. The letters to his brother, Antonio, written by the previous Nicolò Zeno were the main source the author claimed to have relied on. Nicolò began his tale with a description of being shipwrecked on an island he called Frislandia, "much larger than Ireland," as his letter described it. "By chance, a Prince with an armed following happened to be in the neighborhood," he continued. The name of that prince was Zichmni, according to Nicolò's letters. Zichmni was preparing to seize the island of Frislandia from the king of Norway, and he offered to employ Nicolò as a pilot, according to the Zeno narrative. When Nicolò served valiantly in the subsequent victory, Zichmni had made him a noble of the island nation he now ruled.

As the story continued, the fourteenth century Nicolò had written to his brother, Antonio, inviting him to visit Frislandia. Antonio not only came, Nicolò recounted, but he also stayed for fourteen years, becoming Zichmni's captain and leading his forces in an attack on Iceland. That great island nation was too well defended for his forces to so much as make landfall, let alone penetrate and conquer, so instead Zichmni turned his attention to seven small islands to the east, capturing them one after the other. On one of these islands, called Bres, Zichmni built a fort and placed Nicolò Zeno in charge of it. After Zichmni sailed off, however, the fourteenth-century Nicolò explained, he had set out on his own voyage of discovery, one that would last between four and five years. He returned to Frislandia seriously ill, with just time enough left before his death to send one last letter to Antonio.

Antonio was the source of the narrative as it continued from there, with a story of Zichmni learning that a group of fishermen were telling a tale of having visited island countries called Estotilanda and Drogeo in the far west. In Estotilanda, they had encountered a tribe of cannibals that were persuaded not to eat them by being taught how to catch fish, the fishermen claimed.

The final two sections of the Zeno narrative describe (through Antonio's letters) Zichmni's voyage west with Antonio to find Estotilanda and Drogeo, a voyage that would seem to have taken place in 1397 or 1398. Zichmni would never locate those two fabled island nations, according to Antonio's letters. What he did instead was land on a previously undiscovered promontory of land that he called the Cape of Trin, later giving the name Trin also to the "excellent harbor" it enclosed. Spotting plumes of smoke rising from someplace in the interior of the great island beyond Trin, Zichmni dispatched a company of his men to seek the source. Eight days later they returned exhausted and reported that they had found the cause of the smoke, a great natural fire that burned at the bottom of a hill where there was a spring that flowed with a black, pitch-like substance. The stream coursed all the way to the sea the men said. They had also encountered a large group of natives, the men told Zichmni, according to the Antonio letters, who were small in stature and so timid they hid in caves upon seeing white men for the first time.

Zichmni was delighted by the location, the climate, and the soil of Trin, the Antonio letters went on, and he announced that he would build a town there. Zichmni's men were not so enamored, however, and their grumbling turned from insistent to threatening. Finally, Zichmni sent them off with Antonio to return home but chose to remain in Trin himself and said he would explore the entire coast on foot, alone. And there the Zeno narrative ends.

The book produced by Nicolò Zeno in 1558 was an enormous sensation at the time of its publication, widely accepted as both historically and geographically accurate for the next three centuries. In the immediate aftermath of the book's appearance, at least three explorers mounted Arctic expeditions. Gerardus Mercator, in creating his 1569 world map, which would endure as *the* primary chart for more than a century, had relied on the Zeno map to place Trin as an outcropping of land on the southernmost point of Greenland. But no one proposed to have any real idea who the great prince Zichmni had been. That would not change until the latter part of the eighteenth century, when the famous naturalist Johann Reinhold Forster began to study the Zeno narrative.

Forster was best known as the naturalist who had accompanied Captain James Cook on his second Pacific voyage; his work in that capacity would become a significant basis of the development of anthropology and ethnology. So it is not surprising that Forster commanded attention and regard with his announcement that he had identified Prince Zichmni as one Henry Sinclair, a Scotsman who in the latter half of the fourteenth century had held the title of Earl of Orkney under the auspices of the Norwegian crown, which then held the island.

It was an astonishing claim, given that up to this time Henry Sinclair was not known for having done much of anything beyond managing his domain and collecting its rents. Henry had been the son and heir of William Sinclair, Lord of Roslin, and in 1358 had succeeded his father to that title. Twenty-one years later, on August 2, 1379, Haakon VI, the king of Norway, had invested Henry as the Earl of Orkney in exchange for a pledge by Sinclair that he would pay a fee of one thousand nobles, and, when called upon, serve the king militarily with one hundred armed men for no less than three months. Henry Sinclair was again in Norway in 1389 to hail the new king, Eric, and to pledge an oath of fealty. That, essentially, is the historical record of Henry Sinclair.

Johann Reinhold Forster's reputation was such, however, that the claim that Henry Sinclair had been the famous Prince Zichmni from the Zeno narrative immediately caught hold. This belief really took off in 1873, when Richard Henry Major produced a translation of the Zeno narrative that included not only the claim that Henry Sinclair had been Prince Zichmni, but also that he had been the leader of the Knights Templar after the order reconstituted itself in Scotland following the horrific events in Paris under King Philip.

Like Forster, Major was a man widely admired, an author and geographer who at the time was serving as curator of the British Museum's map collection. So the claim that Henry Sinclair was Prince Zichmni seemed to have been confirmed when Major said so. His translation of the Zeno narrative inspired a member of one branch of the Sinclair family, Thomas Sinclair, to interrupt the 1893 Chicago celebration of the four hundredth anniversary of Christopher Columbus's great voyage west to read aloud a paper in which he contended (and was apparently the first to do so) that the journey Zichmni/Henry Sinclair described in the Zeno narrative had not ended in Greenland as had been previously supposed but rather in North America. His illustrious ancestor, Thomas Sinclair proclaimed, was "the one and only discoverer of America."

IT WAS NOT UNTIL 1950 that all these threads were woven together by a college professor named Frederick J. Pohl, who that year began a life's work dedicated to connecting the Zeno narrative not only to Henry Sinclair but also to North America—and to Nova Scotia in particular. Pohl's starting point was the passage in the Zeno narrative about the discovery by Zichmni's men of the fire that burned in a stream at the base of a hill where the water ran black, filled with some sort of pitch-like substance.

Intrigued by the claim of an American geologist named William Hobbs that he had found such a natural feature in the mining region of Stellarton, just south of Pictou, Nova Scotia, where open seams of coal regularly caught fire and burned for days, Professor Pohl decided in the summer of 1950 to investigate for himself. The result was his 1959 booklet *A Nova Scotia Project* in which he placed the burning stream from the Zeno narrative at Stellarton. It would be the first of many future instances in which Pohl, over a twenty-year period, produced works where the omissions were more meaningful than the inclusions. In this case, what Pohl had failed to mention was that the "burning seam" was not a constant feature of the Stellarton landscape. More significantly,

Pohl left out the fact that while it had caught fire on and off since 1830 when mining began in the Stellarton region, there was not a shred of evidence to suggest it had ever burned before or that even a single coal fire had been caused by anything other than mining activity.

The main thrust of Pohl's work was his effort to prove that linguistic differences between the language spoken and written by fourteenth-century Scots and fourteenth-century Italians had resulted in the mistranslation of "Orkney" into "Zichmni." The Z in "Zichmni" could easily have resulted from a misreading of the *d'O* in "d'Orkney," Pohl contended. Also, since Italian does not use the letters *k* or *y*, they needed to be represented by other letters; for instance *ch* is a hard *k* sound in Italian, Pohl pointed out.

By the time Pohl was ready to deliver what he regarded as the capstone of his work, the book *Prince Henry Sinclair: His Expedition to the New World in 1398*, he was arguing that Sinclair had been Glooskap, the mythical, magical being who had taught the native Mi'kmaq people of Nova Scotia how to hunt and fish with nets and how to gather plants and herbs for food and medicine. Pohl made much use of the work of Silas Tertius Rand, a nineteenth-century missionary and linguist who had lived among the Mi'kmaq and who had been first to put the legend of Glooskap in writing. Rand also made recordings of tribal songs. Those songs, Pohl wrote, sounded eerily similar to Scottish sea shanties.

The most remarkable thing about Pohl's claims is how widely they spread. In 1996, at Chebucto Bay, in Guysborough County, Nova Scotia, the Prince Henry Sinclair Society erected a fifteen-ton monument bearing a black granite narrative plaque that described the erstwhile Zichmni's landing there in 1398 and his career as Glooskap. Twenty years after that, the Sinclair/Glooskap story had become a recurring meme on *The Curse of Oak Island*.

What makes this so confounding is that by the time Pohl was writing his books and booklets, the Zeno narrative on which the entire project was based had been almost totally discredited. That process had begun as early as 1898, when a geographer named Fred W. Lucas produced a work that meticulously linked various passages in the Zeno narrative to literary works that had been created well before Nicolò Zeno's book was published. In his deconstruction of the section in the narrative in which the Frislandia fishermen described their voyages to Estotilanda and Drogeo, Lucas was particularly devastating, showing how various passages corresponded closely to the letters of Columbus and Amerigo Vespucci, among various other works. Lucas was also able to show how the Zeno map had borrowed from various other maps created by sixteenth-century cartographers, the Carta marina map of the north by Olaus Magnus, the Caerte van oostland by Cornelis Anthonisz and the multiple maps of the north made by Claudius Clavus. He convincingly demonstrated as well how many of the islands on the Zeno map, including Frislandia, Estotilanda, and Drogeo, simply did not exist.

Then in 1933, an Italian genealogist named Andrea Da Mosto authored an article titled "The Voyage of Nicolò and Antonio Zeno" that was based on hundreds of previously unpublished records from the Venetian archives. Da Mosto was able to demonstrate beyond any doubt that the Nicolò Zeno who had purportedly visited Frislandia in the 1380s and 1390s was a real person, a prominent navigator and public official in Venice in the period between 1360 and 1400 whose career was well documented. In May 1389, Nicolò had taken command of a squadron of naval galleys in the Gulf of Venice. The following year, he had been elected military governor of the cities of Corone and Modone in southern Greece. By the end of 1392 he had returned to Venice and in August of that year he had set sail for Corfu, where he served as bailiff and captain. These four years were, according to the Zeno narrative, the period when Nicolò Zeno had been fighting battles alongside Zichmni in the North Sea.

It may have been fortunate for Frederick Pohl, and it certainly was for Richard Henry Major, that they were dead by the time Brian Smith put the nails in the coffin of the Zeno narrative. Smith, the archivist at the Shetland Museum and Archives, and a historian of Shetland and Orkney, began by declaring the once-admired Major as "the villain of this story," then presented a painstaking description of the myriad ways in which Major had altered—actually rewritten in numerous instances—the Zeno narrative in his translation. Major began by changing the dates of not only the Zeno narrative but of the documents he would claim supported it, Smith demonstrated. Major then proceeded to change the locations of islands that appeared on the Zeno map and were described in the narrative, moving Grislanda, for instance, from the south coast of Iceland to the North Sea just above Scotland, in the vicinity of Orkney. "Major's treatment of Shetland is even more outrageous," Smith charged. In the original narrative, Zichmni makes a failed assault on Estlanda (assumed to be Shetland) before retreating north to the seven mythical islands on the east side of Iceland. Major, though, has Zichmni attack Shetland, then retreat to Orkney, then return to Shetland, where he places Zichmni's fort at Bres, when the original Zeno narrative had placed Bres in Iceland. Major's work was a "shocking piece of deception," Smith wrote. "But it was very successful, because of the man's scholarly reputation," and "most readers swallowed his distortions whole." Major's falsified narrative was especially welcome among some members of the Sinclair family, one of whom would begin calling his largely undistinguished distant ancestor Henry the Holy.

Smith did not spare Pohl, noting that the professor most certainly was aware of Da Mosto's genealogical work, since he had listed it in his bibliography, but had omitted the overwhelming evidence it offered that the Zeno narrative was a fraud.

EXCELLENT AND AUTHORITATIVE as Smith's work was, it had been published in the rather obscure *New Orkney Antiquarian Journal* and made little impression on a public imagination that had been inflamed during the 1980s by a pair of works that became the pillars of an "alternative history" that reverberates through the culture to this day in manifestations that have ranged from Dan Brown's novel *The Da Vinci Code* to *The Curse of Oak Island*. The first, published in 1982, was

Holy Blood, Holy Grail, authored by Michael Baigent, Richard Leigh, and Henry Lincoln. The second, which appeared in print seven years later, was *The Temple and the Lodge*, authored by just Baigent and Leigh. The two books, the former in particular, conflated historical fragments, fraudulent documents, and "facts" drawn from poems and novels into a vitriolic condemnation of the Catholic Church, all of it imaginatively packaged into a thrilling narrative, but one that did not hold up to any scrutiny.

    Holy Blood, Holy Grail incorporated many of the Knights Templar myths and tales, including the "lost fleet" that sailed from La Rochelle to carry the Templar treasure "to the New World by following old Viking routes." The Sinclair legend was introduced with the alleged transport of the Holy Grail to the family's Scottish domain. *Holy Blood, Holy Grail*, however, began its story even before the Templar order was established early in the twelfth century, starting at the time of Christ. Both the daring and the transgression of the book were rooted in its claim of a deeper secret society, the so-called Priory of Sion, which, it was claimed, had created the Knights Templar as its military and financial operatives. This was one piece of a centuries-long plan to install the Merovingian dynasty (which did exist and had ruled the Franks from 457 to 751) on the throne of the entire European continent. It was further claimed that the Merovingians descended from Jesus of Nazareth and his bride, Mary Magdalene, and that the Catholic Church was dedicated to killing off the entire bloodline in order to preserve the claim of apostolic succession that had started with Peter.

    Holy Blood, Holy Grail had many antecedents beyond the ones I've described. The authors drew, for instance, on the 1835 claims of a French scientist named Claude Thory, who wrote that Robert the Bruce had created what he called the Order of St. Andrew in Scotland for Freemasons who had supported him at the Battle of Bannockburn; this had been taken up in 1837 by James Burnes, who asserted that it was the Templars themselves who had brought Freemasonry to Scotland. One of Burnes's sources was the 1820 novel *Ivanhoe* by Sir Walter Scott, in which the villain was a Templar Knight. The authors of *Holy Blood, Holy Grail* also borrowed from an obscure 1773 book called *The Jesus Scroll* that was the first to claim that Mary Magdalene had given birth to the child of her husband, Jesus.

Holy Blood, Holy Grail was a huge bestseller, in spite of its reliance on such spectacularly dubious sources as *The Protocols of the Elders of Zion*, a foundational text of modern anti-Semitism that emerged from Russia in the early years of the twentieth century. Despite the fact that *Protocols* was exposed as a forgery as early as 1921 and after that was published only to aid assorted fascist movements, the authors of *Holy Blood, Holy Grail* made use of it, claiming that what the *Protocols* actually described were the master plan of the Priory of Sion. The main source cited for the Priory of Sion story, though, was a work titled *Dossiers Secrets* that the authors of *Holy Blood, Holy Grail* had found at the National Library of France in Paris. Somehow it had escaped their attention that *Dossiers Secrets* was also a forgery, one created by the notorious con man/lunatic Pierre Plantard, who along with his partner had physically planted it in the National Library. Plantard was a former collaborator with the Vichy government of France in World War II, who following the war had recast himself and his group, the Alpha Galates, as a cell of the Resistance. After a series of bizarre scams and a career as a "clairvoyant" named Chyren, Plantard had in the 1960s become a public figure by teaming up with author Gérard de Sède to announce the existence of the Priory of Sion, its relationship to the Merovingians, and through them to the descendants of Jesus and Mary Magdalene. To this he added the claim that he himself was part of the bloodline, a direct descendant of the Merovingian king Dagobert II.

Plantard actually outed himself in 1982, in an apparent fit of pique at how successfully the authors of *Holy Blood, Holy Grail* had incorporated his hoax into their work; he went on French radio to reveal that the Priory of Sion documents on which the authors had relied were fakes—his fakes. Yet it was not until 1996 that the fallacies that were the foundation of *Holy Blood, Holy Grail* were truly publicly exposed in a documentary that aired on the British Broadcasting Company (which was in a way responsible for the book ever coming into existence, having in the 1970s broadcast the series of documentaries produced by Henry Lincoln that were based on Plantard's "work").

In spite of the fact that *Holy Blood, Holy Grail* was more fiction than fact, the book continued to sell and to spawn literally dozens of offshoots and spinoffs. Up until 2003, the most successful of all of these was Baigent and Leigh's *The Temple and the Lodge*, which more deeply "explored" how the Templar order came to Scotland, survived though Jacobite Freemasonry, and made its way to America. The first and most successful attempt to connect all of this to Oak Island had come in 1988, when Michael Bradley's *Holy Grail across the Atlantic* was published. Bradley's breathless book had the Templars concealing the Holy Grail at the Cathar fortress of Montségur until the castle was sacked by the forces of the Inquisition in 1244. The Templars had protected the Grail, Bradley suggested, by transporting it to Scotland, where Henry Sinclair (of course) eventually took possession and transported it to Nova Scotia, where the Money Pit on Oak Island was dug as a hiding place, before the Grail was eventually hidden in Montreal by a mysterious secret society.

The capstone of the whole Templar treasure/Henry Sinclair/Priory of Sion/Merovingian dynasty fantasy was, of course, *The Da Vinci Code*, which became an enormous international bestseller when it was published in 2003. In 2005, Baigent and Leigh sued author Dan Brown and his publisher for plagiarizing *Holy Blood, Holy Grail*. The result was a rare but delicious instance of true justice in which the High Court of Justice in London ruled that since Baigent and Leigh had attempted to pass off their fiction as history, they could not sue an author who had actually produced a work of fiction based on it. The court also noted that the success of *The Da Vinci Code* had only resulted in increased sales for *Holy Blood, Holy Grail*, which has continued to be a moneymaker for the authors and their publisher, despite the fact that imitators publish at least one new iteration of their false narrative every year.

One of these derivative authors, Kathleen McGowan, presented the Sinclair/Priory of Sion/Merovingian theory in season two of *The Curse of Oak Island*. A former public-relations copywriter, McGowan initially self-published her 1989 novel *The Expected One*, which became a million-copy bestseller when it was republished by Simon and Schuster immediately after the release of the movie *The Da Vinci Code*. The reissue was a blatant piggyback on Dan Brown's 2003 blockbuster, but McGowan offered a special wrinkle, declaring herself to be a direct descendant of Jesus Christ and Mary Magdalene. She had turned that success into a series of novels featuring her alter ego's investigation of historical events that didn't exist anywhere outside the pages of *Holy Blood, Holy Grail* or *Holy Grail across the Atlantic*, featuring, of course, a main character named Sinclair. She had also become the principal in a "Holy France" tour business that was itself quite successful.

Marty Lagina and his twenty-nine-year-old son Alex (also an engineer) had made the first leg of *The Curse of Oak Island*'s European excursion to meet McGowan in the south of France. They rendezvoused at Montségur, the citadel castle where the author began the tour by presenting an ostensible history of the Cathar heresy's rise and fall. "There is an idea that the Cathars had all the most sacred treasures in human history right here in this place," McGowan told the Laginas. Those treasures of course included the Holy Grail and the Ark of the Covenant. It had been for the purpose of stealing these holy objects that Pope Innocent VIII (who is also regularly credited with initiating the Inquisition) had launched his crusade against the Cathars, McGowan explained, a campaign of slaughter that came to a climax right here at the mountain fortress of Montségur. Only by negotiating a two-week truce were the Cathars able to send four of their number out under cover of darkness to lower the Grail, the Ark, and the rest of their treasure down the side of the mountain by a system of pulleys that delivered it to the waiting Knights Templar, who would carry it out of France to Scotland, and then, of course, to Oak Island.

As it happened, I knew a good deal about the Cathari (as they're properly called), because I had researched them for two prior books.

They were a final flowering of what had been since the first century the primary heresy of Judeo-Christian faith, gnosticism. The Persian sages Zoroaster and Mani were the early drivers of gnosticism, which made its way to Europe during the tenth century with the Bogomil movement in the Balkans. The great heresy of the Bogomils, as with the gnostic movements that preceded them, was a dualism that essentially elevated the Devil to the same stature as God, envisioning the world as a struggle between darkness and light that had been ongoing since men were created. The Council of Constantinople suppressed the Bogomils by sentencing all the heretics to be burned alive. Rome, on the other hand, insisted on an attempt to "reconvert" the Bogomils, killing only those who refused salvation. The urgency of the church's mission increased dramatically when the gnostic revival spread from the Balkans into Italy, then into the Swiss Alps, and finally into the Languedoc region of southern France, where the Cathari arose. The Cathari, disgusted with the corruption and indulgence of the Catholic clergy (more than three centuries before Martin Luther), recognized no priests, instead dividing themselves into two categories, the Believers and the Perfects. The Perfects were required to surrender all worldly goods to the larger community, to vest themselves in simple corded black or blue robes, and to serve as mendicant monks who devoted their lives to prayer, preaching, and charitable work. Even the Believers were expected to eat a vegetarian diet and refrain from procreation, which would only serve to increase the power of Rex Mundi, the name they had given to the devil. Escape from a realm of materiality where Rex Mundi ruled into a realm of pure spirit where the God of Light dwelled was the ultimate goal of all Cathari. The church, naturally, had a problem with the fact that the Cathari's dismissal of the visible world required them to spurn the symbol of the cross. The Cathari likewise rejected the concepts of salvation and damnation, embracing instead a belief in reincarnation that had been imported from the East.

Innocent VIII found this no less abhorrent than had his predecessors and after a failed attempt to corral Count Raymond VI (ruler of the Languedoc) in January 1208, immediately called for a Crusade against

them, strengthening the incentive by decreeing that all lands owned by
the Cathari and their supporters were to be confiscated. Charged with
devil worship, human sacrifice, cannibalism, and incest, among other
iniquities, the Cathari were slaughtered by the thousands. During an
early battle, Arnaud, the abbot-knight leading the Crusade, was asked
by his men who among the heretics should be put to the sword. He
answered with a line that is refrained among military men to this day:
"Kill them all. God will know His own."

The Cathari movement suffered its final defeat in March 1244, at
Montségur, in the foothills of the Pyrenees, where more than two hundred heretic priests were massacred. Based on my research, the suggestion that the Cathars had been an extension of the Merovingian dynasty,
dedicated to protecting the Jesus Christ–Mary Magdalene bloodline,
however, was likely false. What had most offended Innocent VIII was
that the Cathari, like the Docetists ten centuries earlier, insisted that
Jesus's body had been an illusion and that therefore His crucifixion and
resurrection were illusions also. Obviously, an illusion could never have
fathered a child with Mary Magdalene. Equally impossible was the story
of the Cathari passing their holy treasure to the Knights Templar. First,
there is no evidence the Cathari possessed any such treasure; the idea did
not even exist until *Holy Blood, Holy Grail*. McGowan's story conflated
the persecution of the Templars by King Philip with Innocent VIII's
campaign against the Cathari. But Philip's roundup of the Templars in
Paris took place in 1309, sixty-five years *after* the Cathar surrender at
Montségur. In 1244 the Templars were still headquartered at Acre. There
were a few Templars in France during the campaign against the Cathari,
but every one of them had fought with the Catholic army *against* the
heretics. The Templars were devout Catholics loyal to the pope.

FROM MONTSÉGUR, McGowan led Marty and his son Alex to
Rennes-le-Château. Rennes-le-Château was where the story that Jesus
had not died on the cross but instead fathered the child who founded the

Merovingian dynasty had actually begun. It all started with a priest who had presided over the village church dedicated to Saint Mary Magdalene during the late nineteenth and early twentieth centuries. Father Berenger Saunière had supervised a remarkable degree of construction in the poor parish, not only achieving the restoration of the church (including the presbytery and cemetery) but also building a spectacular personal library called the Tour Magdala on the edge of the village, featuring a circular turret connected to a tower with a promenade that led to his villa, perhaps the loveliest home in Rennes-le-Château. Questions about how all of this work had been financed eventually led to Saunière being convicted of trafficking in masses at an ecclesiastical trial and suspended from the priesthood.

The scandal came to the attention of a Belgian journalist who visited Rennes in 1948. He reported the sordid story of Saunière but also declared the church he had built was an architectural masterpiece, admiring even its most unusual feature, the stoup (basin for holy water) at the entrance to the chapel that was held by a horned devil with cloven hooves. A local named Corbu, who had opened a restaurant in Sauniere's former villa, read the article and began promoting Rennes as a place of mystery and enchantment. It was Corbu who first produced the story that Father Saunière had discovered "parchments" during the renovation of the church that led him to the treasure of Blanche of Castile, what remained of 28,500,500 gold pieces that the French crown had assembled to ransom Saint Louis from the infidels. Corbu's tale got picked up by an author named Charroux who wrote a book that captured the imagination of Pierre Plantard, who adapted it to the mythological story of the Priory of Sion, then collaborated with Gérard de Sède on the book *L'Or de Rennes*, the precursor to *Dossiers Secrets*. Henry Lincoln read *L'Or de Rennes*, which inspired him to produce the BBC documentaries that led to *Holy Blood, Holy Grail* and the presumed descent of the Merovingian fantasy to Kathleen McGowan.

What McGowan told Marty and Alex Lagina was that Rennes was where the Cathari-affiliated Templars had first taken the Grail and the

Ark and the rest of the holy treasures. For proof she led father and son to a cottage with an iron Templar cross hanging over the front door. It was the home of McGowan's Holy Tour associate Tobi Dobler, who now identified himself as a member of the Knights Templar of the New Order, whose members claimed to be descended from the original Templars.

The group soon headed off to Scotland, there to meet up with Rick Lagina, Charles Barkhouse, Dave Blankenship, and the rest of the team to hear the story of the Templars' eighteen-ship fleet that had escaped from La Rochelle to the protection of Robert the Bruce and the Sinclair family. In claiming the Templars were connected to the British Isles via an actual historical person, the English Lord Ralph de Sudeley, McGowan was most likely drawing on the work of Graham Phillips, an author whose histories verged even further into invention than *Holy Blood, Holy Grail*. In one of his works, Phillips described how de Sudeley, as a Crusader, found the Ark of the Covenant with the Maccabean treasure at Jebel al-Madhbah, then carried it back to Britain for safekeeping.

Various elisions helped McGowan connect the Knights Templar, the Cathari, and Henry Sinclair to the team's ultimate destination, Rosslyn Chapel, where the climactic scenes of *The Da Vinci Code* film had been shot. The chapel had been built and commissioned by William Sinclair more than half a century *after* Henry the Holy's death. Rosslyn is a small chapel that was never completed, but its interior is rich with stone carvings. Eight Nordic dragons ring the base of one particularly ornate pillar, while 110 carvings of the pagan sylvan deity known as the Green Man peer through the carved foliage that grows all around them, as well as through their ears, mouths, and noses. One arch is covered with a fantastically detailed danse macabre in which men and women dance with their future skeletons.

Queen Victoria had visited Rosslyn in 1862, more than four hundred years after its construction, to find it abandoned and in disrepair, yet she was so impressed by what she saw through the weeds and vines covering the building that she urged it be restored. It was, and it was rededicated in 1862. The strangeness of Rosslyn had sprouted legends even before the advent of *Holy Blood, Holy Grail* and *The Da Vinci Code*, especially about what was inside the stone crypt that had been sealed shut for centuries. Stories that the Holy Grail, sacred scrolls from the time of Christ, a large fragment of the cross, or even the actual mummified head of Jesus were entombed in the crypt had gained currency over the years, especially after *The Da Vinci Code*.

Because they encouraged such stories despite knowing how false they were, the Sinclair family had been accused by the historian Louise Yeoman, curator of manuscripts at the Museum of Scotland, among others in the country, of "cashing in" on the chapel's appearance in *The Da Vinci Code*. More than a hundred thousand tourists were showing up every year at the chapel, paying customers all, and the Sinclairs benefited while doing nothing to discourage belief in the legend of Henry the Holy, which at least a couple of Sinclairs (Andrew Sinclair, most notably) had promoted in books and articles.

"Christian, Jewish, Egyptian, Masonic, Pagan," the character played by Tom Hanks had ticked off the influences he saw in the carvings inside Rosslyn Chapel in the film version of *The Da Vinci Code*. The idea that the Sinclairs were the founders of Freemasonry (intent on creating a disguise for the Templar order after it was dissolved by the pope in 1312) had become part of what, in the popular imagination, was encoded in the chapel's carvings. This despite the fact that the Masons had not come into existence until more than a century after Rosslyn Chapel was built. The blending of history and myth so annoyed the curator of Scotland's Grand Lodge, Robert L. D. Cooper, that he had written a book called *Rosslyn Hoax?* to attack at length and in detail the claims that *The Da Vinci Code* drew on.

At Rosslyn, the chapel's "keeper" regaled the Laginas and company with the legend that Scottish knights went to the Americas long before Columbus and that their leader could have been Henry Sinclair. Nova Scotia was Latin for "New Scotland," the keeper noted, then pointed out carvings of plants that were "said to be" shucked corn and trillium blossoms and aloe cactus, all species native to North America, and recounted the legend that these had been drawn by Henry Sinclair in North America and brought back to Scotland. At least a few botanists, however, had argued that the carvings at Rosslyn were of plants native to the country. The "corn," for instance, was actually bundled wheat, they said.

Alan Butler also made his first appearance on the show in connection to the team's visit to Rosslyn Chapel. Butler and his podcast partner Janet Wolter based their work on goddess worship and gnosticism, especially the book of Enoch, an allegedly suppressed book of the Bible that told the story of the "Watcher" angels referenced briefly in the book of Daniel and, perhaps, in Genesis 6:2: "The sons of God saw how beautiful the daughters of man were, and so they took for their wives as many of them as they chose." In the book of Enoch version the Watchers, sent to Earth by God to watch over mankind, instead procreated among them, illicitly instructing humans in making weapons, cosmetics, and mirrors and practicing sorcery; the Great Flood had happened in order to cleanse the Earth of the Watchers' offspring, the Nephilim. Butler and Wolter transformed the Watchers and their offspring from the villains of the story to its protagonists and incorporated the Roman cult of Venus, the symbolism of Freemasonry, and of course the entire Merovingian meme in which the Jesus Christ–Mary Magdalene bloodline was destined to rise again to power in the Kingdom of God on Earth forecast by the book of Revelations. The two had also made much of what they called the Tariot Tomb Conspiracy that claimed the bones of Jesus had been hidden by the early Christians in Jerusalem, that the Templars had discovered this tomb, and that the skull and crossbones flag that most people associated with pirates was really a reference to Christ's rotting corpse.

Butler did not mention most of this, but he did explain on camera that the flagstones found in the mouth of the Money Pit were actually a "threshing floor" like the one the Templars and their gnostic compatriots (again, the Templars were not gnostic) had used to mark spiritually significant sites. From this Butler had transitioned to the book of Enoch, the Masonic Royal Arch of Enoch, and a calculation based on various obscure texts that there was a second treasure vault on Oak Island, 996 feet due west of the Money Pit. Some broad humor erupted when Marty Lagina discovered that this would put them right in the middle of the "stinky swamp" he so despised.

In the same *Newsweek* article from the Rosslyn Chapel visit, Rick Lagina asked, "Has there been a find on Oak Island that we can say is a definitive tie-in to the Templars? No, but are there curious facts and bits of discovery that indicate the possibility? Yes."

The main example Rick cited was the similarity between the flag of the Mi'kmaq and the Templar battle flag that supposedly had been flown from the ship Henry Sinclair steered to North America in 1397 or 1398. This claim had been presented in an earlier episode of the show, when viewers were shown the two flags, one atop the other, in order to see that they were virtually identical, both white with red markings, a horizontal cross with two symbols on opposite sides of the vertical post, one a star and one a crescent. The only difference was that the crescent was on the top of the Templar flag while it was on the bottom on the Mi'kmaq flag.

This discovery had been presented on *The Curse of Oak Island* through one J. Hutton Pulitzer—he preferred to be called Treasure Force Commander J. Hutton Pulitzer—a theorist who had appeared in a few episodes of the show during season two. Pulitzer (born Jovan Philyaw) was outfitted in a getup of khaki pants tucked into knee-high boots and a safari shirt worn with a shoulder holster like a villain in a campy remake of *King Solomon's Mines*. Pulitzer's earliest appearances had centered on some petroglyphs that were found on an outcropping of rock at Bedford Barrens, Nova Scotia, about fifty miles northeast of Oak Island. The eight-pointed star inside a circle was a link to the ancient Middle East and, ultimately, to the sacking of Solomon's Temple in Jerusalem by Nebuchadnezzar around 597 BC, as Pulitzer had it.

From this, the show had pivoted to the similarities between the Templar/ Sinclair and Mi'kmaq flags.

Historians who made the counter argument relied on a 1610 book by Marc Lescarbot titled *The Conversion of the Savages*, which described how the tribe was introduced to the symbol of the cross by a Catholic missionary named Jesse Fleche (more than two hundred years after the supposed voyage of Henry Sinclair) and had begun to use it to decorate various cloths and ornaments, resulting ultimately in the creation of the flag.

CHAPTER TWENTY-ONE

After the contribution of Kathleen McGowan, *The Curse of Oak Island* featured another theorist named Robert Markus, who would argue that the lost treasures of King Solomon's Temple *had* been buried on Oak Island, but not in the Money Pit. He was basing this claim on the Zeno map. Well, actually it was based on the map Harold Wilkins had drawn for *Captain Kidd and His Skeleton Island*, which was itself based on the Zeno map, as Markus had it. The Zeno map, Markus explained, had been created not just by the Venetian brothers, but also by Henry Sinclair, who had encoded a message on it with the numbers written in the margins. Wilkins unfortunately had misread one of those numbers. By correcting that mistake and applying the resulting code to a GPS triangulation of the Westford Stone, another stone in Overton, Nova Scotia, on which what was described as a Templar Cross had been carved and the Money Pit on Oak Island, Markus had helped the Laginas arrive at the spot where they would dig—and find nothing.

Yet another Oak Island theorist, Jeff Irving, had showed up at the end of season three of the show to declaim the proposition that while Henry Sinclair had come to the island in 1398, he was only working as an advance scout for Christopher Columbus, who had *actually* installed the Ark of the Covenant in the Money Pit vault. Henry the Navigator got worked into Irving's narrative, as did the Zeno brothers, who, as part of a secret Templar plan to bury the treasures of Solomon's Temple on Oak Island had come to Nova Scotia, married aboriginals, and disappeared into their tribe.

* * *

BY THE TIME I ARRIVED in Nova Scotia, I had become determined to find some middle ground. After all, these people were not only paying me for coming here, but they were also covering all of the costs of my research and personal expenses. They'd given me a decent room in a resort right on Mahone Bay and a brand-new Jeep to drive. In return, I owed them at least a good faith effort to serve the show.

That quite possibly had more than a little to do, I realize now, with my growing interest in the subject that had received the third-most screen time during *The Curse of Oak Island*'s first three seasons: the theory that Francis Bacon and his followers were behind the works on Oak Island.

This was a theory tethered—at some points, at least—to historical evidence. The people who had promulgated it may have veered off into esoteric, eccentric, or maybe even simply crazy tangents, but even those were connecting dots that actually existed. As with the Knights Templar, I began with what could be most reliably known about Bacon: the official history, so to speak. I was quite fascinated by how much struggle, suffering, intrigue, treachery, and pathos even this version of Bacon contained.

He was born in 1561, the son of Sir Nicholas Bacon, who would serve as Lord Keeper of the Great Seal under Queen Elizabeth. Bacon was twelve when he entered Trinity College at Cambridge, where he developed the convictions that formed the basis of what is most widely considered his greatest legacy, the modern scientific method. While he was a student in Cambridge he rejected the strictures imposed on scientific inquiry by preconceived notions; in particular he objected to any compulsion to fit one's observations into the limits of religious dogma.

At nineteen, Bacon declared that his goals were three: to uncover truth, to serve his country, and to serve his church. A year later he won election to Parliament and at twenty-five was made clerk of the Star Chamber, the collection of privy councilors that effectively operated as the supreme court of sixteenth-century England. By the time he turned thirty, Bacon was widely known for his opposition to feudal privileges and religious persecution and had acquired the reputation of a liberal reformer. He fell in and out of favor with Elizabeth, who denied him the positions of attorney general and master of the rolls, but was much favored by her successor James I, who made Bacon his solicitor general in 1607, his regent in 1617, and his lord chancellor in 1618.

From this great height, Bacon would fall hard and fast in a scandal orchestrated by his longtime archnemesis Sir Edward Coke, the leader of the opposition party in Parliament, who accused Sir Francis of twenty-three counts of corruption based on his negligent management of debt and his practice of accepting gifts from the litigants who came before him. Bacon was fined 40,000 pounds and committed to the Tower of London, but James let him remain in the tower only a few days and remitted the fine. Nevertheless Parliament declared Bacon ineligible to hold future office or to sit in their company. He narrowly avoided degradation, which would have stripped him of his titles of nobility. At the age of sixty, he withdrew from public life to devote himself to study and writing. Five years later, on April 9, 1626, Bacon died of pneumonia contracted while studying the effects of freezing on the preservation of meat.

THE OUTLINES OF BACON'S LIFE, of course, do not account for the enormous expansion of his posthumous reputation and the cult of devotion that would form and spread about his name and accomplishments. The process by which that happened seems all the more remarkable when one considers that in the early aftermath of his death, most of the historical revision was anything but flattering to Bacon's memory.

Much of this early writing focused on the question of Bacon's sexuality. One of the earliest and for many years the most influential portrait of Bacon to appear between hard covers was in John Aubrey's *Brief Lives*, written in the last decades of the seventeenth century. On the one hand, Aubrey portrayed Bacon as a martyr to science who had been journeying to Highgate with the King's physician in April 1626 when he was struck by the idea that snow might serve as a meat preservative. Bacon and the doctor "alighted out of the coach and went into a poor woman's house at the bottom of Highgate hill, and bought a fowl, and made the woman [disembowel] it," Aubrey wrote. It was immediately after stuffing the fowl with snow that Bacon had contracted his fatal case of pneumonia by Aubrey's account: 'I remember Mr. Hobbes told me, he died of Suffocation." This was the great philosopher Thomas Hobbes, a close Bacon friend.

The restoration of Bacon's reputation began with his literary executor, William Rawley, who declared Bacon's genius by editing and publishing his many works. Of these, *Novum Organum* was especially influential in the years after Bacon's death. Bacon's insistence on empirical evidence and the search for the essence of a thing by a process of reduction made him a hero of the Restoration. In 1733 Voltaire would introduce Bacon in France as the "father" of the modern scientific method, and during the French Enlightenment the Englishman Bacon became more influential than the former icon of French science René Descartes. By the early nineteenth century Bacon was being hailed not only as the founder of the scientific method, but as the "Father of Experimental Philosophy" for his advocacy of inductive reasoning.

Bacon was also becoming immensely admired for his writings on legal reform. As early as the seventeenth century Sir Matthew Hale had acknowledged Bacon as the inventor of the process of modern common law adjudication. By the nineteenth century, Bacon's *Verulamium* was being described as the basis of France's Napoleonic Code, while in England there were many who were saluting Bacon as the founder of modern jurisprudence. Thomas Jefferson declared that Bacon was one of "the three greatest men that have ever lived," along with John Locke and Isaac Newton. By 1861 historian and biographer William Hepworth Dixon was writing: "Bacon's influence in the modern world is so great that every man who rides a train, sends a telegram, follows a steam plough, sits in an easy chair, crosses the channel or the Atlantic, eats a good dinner, enjoys a beautiful garden, or undergoes a painless surgical operation, owes him something."

Bacon's greatness was by then a given among the educated, but among some admirers his legend was taking on dimensions that exceeded human scale. There was near-unanimous agreement that Bacon had been one of the authors of the King James Bible—some said the main author—but many of those who had studied him most closely contended that Bacon had also been, among many other things, the founder of the British Royal Society. That was a remarkable claim, given that the Royal Society had not been formally founded until 1660, thirty-four years after Bacon's death, but the claim that the Society had actually originated in the circle that gathered around Bacon at Gray's Inn was not without merit. Many extraordinary men had been part of that circle, including not only Ben Jonson and Thomas Hobbes, but the greatest physician of the period, Robert Fludd, and the greatest architect, Inigo Jones. It was among them and around Bacon that the idea of a group—the Invisible College—dedicated to "improving natural knowledge" had first arisen. The Elizabethan era was a time when men were contemplating the perfectibility of the human condition, to be brought about by full development of human faculties and a deeper understanding of the laws of nature. Bacon and his circle—among whom he does seem to have taken his seat as first among equals—were the planetary locus of these ideas more than a century and a half before they spread across the Atlantic Ocean and inspired the men who invented the United States of America.

Some of Bacon's nineteenth- and twentieth-century admirers, though, were beginning to describe him as more than a genius. For them, he was taking on the aspect of a religious teacher and spiritual master. Some called him the founder of the Rosicrucian order, although he almost certainly was not. The author of the two manifestos that first appeared in Germany during the early seventeenth century and declared the Order of the Rosy Cross is widely agreed to have been Johann Valenin Andreae. A case can be made, however, and has been by any number of historians and biographers, including the estimable Frances Yates, that Bacon was the leader of an English movement closely associated with the Rosicrucians of the European continent. The modern Rosicrucian order based in the United States, the Ancient Mystical Order Rosae Crucis, claims Bacon as the "imperator" (master) of the order in both England and on the European continent during his lifetime. Other evidence connects Bacon to the founding of Freemasonry.

There was no real dispute of Bacon's greatness during the first 250-plus years after his death, only about what the degree of that greatness might have been. It was not until people began to claim that he had written the plays of William Shakespeare that the real controversy took hold.

The contest over the authorship of the greatest body of literature in the history of the English language also did not exist during most of those first two and a half centuries. It may or may not have begun in 1785. Letters dated that year, supposedly written by the Reverend James Wilmot, described how in the course of researching a Shakespeare biography he had discovered that the bard had little if any education, owned no books, and did not mention the disposition of any literary works in his will. There was no convincing evidence that the actor from Stratford had ever written a word, the Wilmot letters asserted, not even a letter to the wife from whom he was apart much of the time. And he had not been eulogized as a playwright in Stratford at the time of his death. Francis Bacon had to have been the author of the Shakespeare plays, the Wilmot letters declared. It's entirely possible those letters were a fraud perpetrated by the reverend's sister, a notorious prevaricator. Anyway, they did not surface until the early twentieth century.

The claim that Bacon had authored the works attributed to Shakespeare only certainly arose in 1856, when American playwright and scholar Delia Bacon (no relation to Sir Francis) produced an article for *Putnam's Monthly* titled "William Shakespeare and His Plays: An Inquiry Concerning Them." Delia Bacon, who had performed ten years of research under the sponsorship of Ralph Waldo Emerson, delivered the first public announcement of the claim that Shakespeare's plays had been written by a "little clique of disappointed and defeated politicians who undertook to organize popular opposition against the government" through these works of imagination. This committee of writers had included Sir Walter Raleigh and Edmund Spenser, Ms. Bacon wrote, and was headed by Francis Bacon. One year later, Delia Bacon's book *The Philosophy of the Plays of Shakespeare Unfolded* was published and stunned the English-speaking world.

The author's credibility was enhanced by the fact that she had been assisted by the inventor of the telegraph himself, Samuel Morse, who had advised her about Francis Bacon's fascination with ciphers and the nature of encryption. Though there was a storm of criticism, the author received support from influential admirers, among them Harriet Beecher Stowe, Nathaniel Hawthorne, and Walt Whitman, along with Emerson, who would praise Ms. Bacon as "America's greatest literary producer of the last ten years" upon her death in 1859, two years after the Shakespeare book was published.

The Bacon-wrote-Shakespeare controversy was revived and expanded in 1888, when Minnesota congressman Ignatius Donnelly authored *The Great Cryptogram*, a book that generated an enormous cultural uproar with the claim that Francis Bacon alone had actually written Shakespeare's plays and had filled them with secret codes (that Donnelly never fully deciphered). Donnelly was already famous for his book about the lost continent of Atlantis, which had been destroyed, he claimed, by a comet that scorched the Earth in prehistoric times, and an 1891 novel *Doctor Huguet*, about a liberal white intellectual who wakes up one morning to discover he has become a Negro and gets to experience racism firsthand, a book that was more than a half-century ahead of its time.

During the decades that followed, the ranks of those who expressed public disbelief that Shakespeare had written Shakespeare's plays grew to include Sigmund Freud, Mark Twain, Benjamin Disraeli, Henry and William James, Charlie Chaplin, and Orson Welles. So it was hardly a void into which Orville Ward Owen had entered in 1909 when he embarked on his quest to find the vault where Francis Bacon had hidden the original Shakespeare manuscripts. And there was certainly a foundation for Professor Burrell Ruth to stand on in the 1940s when he became the first to connect the never-found original Shakespeare manuscripts to Oak Island, where he'd come to believe that Francis Bacon's followers had hidden them.

It seems clear from their correspondence that over time Ruth convinced Gilbert Hedden that the Baconian theory was the most likely explanation of the works on Oak Island. In a letter written in 1967, Hedden advised a fellow treasure hunter that "I date the original work [on Oak Island] as about 1630 and I am convinced that the engineer who made the original layout had no intention of making a recovery in his lifetime, but intended to leave it for future generations." Ten years later, after her husband's 1974 death, Hedden's widow, Marguerite, told an interviewer: "Gilbert was willing to believe the Bacon manuscripts might well have been in the Pit; he knew it had to be something precious because of the engineering job that was done there."

In the summer of 1952, when attorney Thomas Penn Leary from Omaha, Nebraska, visited Oak Island, Hedden briefly described the Bacon theory after the lawyer asked him what his favorite ideas were about the original works on the island. This was enough to inspire Leary to dedicate the next year to researching Bacon's life. During that time he corresponded regularly with Burrell Ruth and absorbed many of the professor's ideas. Leary seems to have been taken with Ruth's interpretations of various markers, the stone triangle in particular, which both men would agree was intended to point toward the "truth" or "knowledge" that lay within the Money Pit. It was Ruth who directed Leary toward the record R. V. Harris had made of a workman named Baker who in 1937 had reported bringing up specks of mercury on a drill at the Money Pit. Leary put it all together in a thirty-six-page booklet titled *The Oak Island Enigma: A History and Inquiry into the Origin of the Money Pit* that he paid to have published in 1953. Though it's become an especially obscure part of Oak Island's written record, it was the most detailed and compelling exposition up to that point of the theory that Francis Bacon was the man behind it all.

Reading Leary's booklet led to the first time I saw any basis for taking the whole thing seriously. The Omaha lawyer had drawn heavily on one of Bacon's lesser-known works, *Sylva Sylvarum: Or, a Natural History in Ten Centuries*. The detailed description of Bacon's ideas about preserving manuscripts in mercury did seem curious, especially since Bacon didn't really explain *why* one would want to preserve manuscripts in some underground vault for centuries. The directions in *Sylva Sylvarum* of how to create "an Artificiall Spring," though, gave me pause. Leary made a compelling case that what Bacon had described was a very close match to the actual construction of the flood system that flowed to the Money Pit from Smith's Cove: it should be made of a "Trough of Stone" with one end upon high ground and the other on low, that was covered with "Brakes" (which in Bacon's day would have meant thickets of fern) over which was laid sand. All that was missing was the coconut fiber.

It was enough to send me to *Sylva Sylvarum* to read this section of Bacon's work, and when I did I was stunned to find that the first line in the instruction for the creation of a perpetual spring read: "Dig a pit up on the seashore."

I STARTED TO BACK AWAY from Leary's argument because he had built the entire thing around his assertion that "the cumulative weight of the documentary verification that Shakespeare did not, and Bacon did, write the plays is . . . enormous." I doubted that, but decided to at least take a look at the "documentary verification."

I first became aware that there was a purported Bacon/Shakespeare connection to Oak Island back in 2003, when Dan Blankenship told me about a fellow from Norway who was going to be arriving just a week or two after my departure to try to find evidence of his belief that the original Shakespeare manuscripts—written in Bacon's hand, of course—were buried on Oak Island. In a later phone conversation I learned that the Norwegian—Petter Amundsen—had dug some holes on the island in locations that were connected to Nolan's Cross. Dan sounded pretty impressed Amundsen had found a rock buried in the exact spot where he had said it would be. I didn't have a lot of space for any of this in my *Rolling Stone* article, but what I heard from Dan was enough to persuade me to give some brief consideration to the Bacon-wrote-Shakespeare theory. I became quickly annoyed, however, by what I read. As near as I could tell, the main reason for saying that the William Shakespeare from Stratford-upon-Avon couldn't have written the plays bearing the Shakespeare name was that he didn't come from the right class background: this village bumpkin son of an illiterate glove maker was far too untutored and unrefined to have possibly produced such timeless works of literary art, various authorities had submitted. To me that sounded a lot like saying Bob Dylan couldn't have grown up in northern Minnesota as the son of an appliance dealer named Zimmerman. Genius, as I understood it, wasn't impressed by social barriers. So I cast the whole subject aside, gave Amundsen a brief mention in the article and forgot about the entire subject.

After reading Leary's booklet, though, I thought I should examine the "anti-Stratfordian" case, as it had become known, a bit more thoroughly. When I did, I had to admit these people made some compelling arguments; I could see why the likes of Twain and Whitman were impressed by them.

There was no evidence that Shakespeare had ever attended school. Neither his parents nor his two daughters were literate; not one of them could so much as write their own names. No letters or signed manuscripts written by Shakespeare have ever been found. There are six "authenticated" Shakespeare signatures, which the doubters describe as having been written in "an illiterate scrawl," and none of these signatures match the spelling of his name as it appears on most Shakespeare title pages, where his name was often hyphenated as "Shake-speare" or "Shak-spear," pseudonyms, the doubters say, for the true author. The surviving documents that bear his signature establish him as a business-man and real estate investor but not as a writer. The will Shakespeare left after his death on April 23, 1616, was utterly mundane, and it makes no mention at all of his plays, poems, or papers. The only slight reference to a theatrical career was in connection to the money he left to some fellow actors for the purchase of mourning rings, and it was a clause inserted into the will after it had been written. There is no record of public mourning at the time of Shakespeare's death, and no eulogies or poems memorializing him were published until seven years after his death, with the *First Folio* of his plays.

To these hard facts the anti-Stratfordians had added that the absence of biographical information about Shakespeare was suspicious on its face; some went as far as to suggest that it indicates an organized attempt to expunge all traces of his life from the historical record, so as to conceal the true author's identity. They contrast Shakespeare's back-ground to the familiarity in his plays with court politics, high culture, and sports that were only played by aristocrats: falconry, tennis, and lawn bowling. The Shakespeare plays mock the sort of social-climbing commoners that Shakespeare himself grew up among, say the doubters, who see upper-class snobbery in how often the common folk assembled into groups in those plays turn into mobs. There is more, but it grows increasingly tenuous. Still, there can be little doubt that those who say Shakespeare was not Shakespeare have made some telling points.

The Stratfordian side, though, has an even stronger case. They say he was largely self-educated but most likely did attend the free Kings New School of Stratford that was only a half mile from his home, where instructors who were all Oxford graduates would have taught him Latin, the classics, and rhetoric free of charge. Contemporaries Ben Jonson and Christopher Marlowe came from backgrounds every bit as humble as Shakespeare's, and no one doubts that they wrote the works that bear their names. And of course there is the funerary monument to Shakespeare in Stratford that depicts him with pen in hand, with an attached plaque saluting his talents as a writer. The anti-Stratfordians

have claimed the original monument was a different image. But a paint-
ing made in 1748, before the monument's first restoration, shows that
it looks pretty much the same as it looks today. And the monument
was specifically referred to in the *First Folio* on its publication in 1623.

If there was some sort of conspiracy to turn a hapless actor into the
front man for a committee of geniuses who actually wrote the Shakespeare plays, the Stratfordians have pointed out, it had to have been quite
enormous. Ben Jonson, who published the *First Folio*, obviously would
have had to be in on it; how else to explain his eulogy "to the memory
of my beloved, the Author William Shakespeare" in which Jonson hails
Shakespeare as a playwright, a poet, and an actor. William Camden,
the foremost antiquary of the time, would also have had to be among
the conspirators, because in 1605 he hailed Shakespeare as among the
"most pregnant witts of these ages our times, whom succeeding ages may
justly admire." There are any number of others who would have had to
be directly involved in the plot and countless others who would have
been required to turn a blind eye to it. The more names accumulate,
the more the whole thing strains credulity.

For me, the most convincing evidence is the plays themselves.
There is consistency to both thought and expression that make it obvious
the plays are not the work of a committee, but of a single transcendent
genius. That genius could have been Francis Bacon, or any one of the
dozen or so other candidates who had been proposed over the years,
but I saw no compelling reason to believe so.

Neither do the overwhelming majority of American college professors who teach Shakespeare classes. In 2007, the *New York Times*
published a survey of 265 of them who were asked if there was good
reason to question Shakespeare's authorship. Just 6 percent answered
yes, though an additional 11 percent answered possibly. The other 83
percent said there was no basis for doubt.

When I spoke to the people who have been most prominent among
those who believe that the Shakespeare manuscripts are buried on Oak
Island I heard repeatedly that academics have a vested interest in "the

Shakespeare industry," and so by shielding the bard's reputation were protecting their own livelihoods. This line of thought was a staple of Oak Island theorists, and I was as sympathetic to it as anyone with an Ivy League diploma could be. Still, when the pinheaded professors had facts and logic on their side, I had to give them credit for being scholars who might very well know more about the subject they had been studying for decades than I did after a few weeks of feverish research. I had found that that line of thinking was scorned as a sort of intellectual cowardice among all too many of the self-discovered authorities on Oak Island. Take J. Hutton Pulitzer, for example, who had rebranded himself as the "History Heretic" and expressed disdain for academic rivals who had spent $300,000 or $400,000 on their advanced degrees and "were still paying off student loans in their forties."

Anyway, I had come to the conclusion that I wasn't going to be able to fully embrace a theory that required me to believe that Francis Bacon or anyone else had written Shakespeare's plays. The best I could do was concede a remote possibility. But doubting Sir Francis had written the greatest theatrical works in the history of the English language didn't necessarily preclude consideration of a Baconian connection to Oak Island.

There was a line that Leary had pulled from Bacon's will that kept coming back to me, the one in which Sir Francis had declared, "For my name and memory, I leave it to men's charitable speeches, and to foreign lands, and the next ages." It certainly sounded as if Bacon had imagined he would be rediscovered by people from faraway places in future times. It was enough of a tease to prompt a series of contacts with the people who, nearly four hundred years after his death, were the dedicated members of the Francis Bacon Society. To a person, they insisted that I had to make contact with Peter Dawkins, who for more than forty years had been the director of the Francis Bacon Research Trust. That was not an especially easy thing to do, but eventually I was able to reach Dawkins by phone at his home in England. It was only during the series of conversations that resulted that I began to understand that the Baconians were members of a religious sect.

CHAPTER TWENTY-TWO

Weeks later, after returning home, I hired my college student daughter to transcribe my interviews with Peter Dawkins. When my proposed due date came and went, I called to check on her progress. "This is really hard," she told me. I was preparing to remind Grace that I'd paid her in advance and really needed this done when she added, "He sounds so cultured and intelligent, like a perfect English gentleman inviting you to tea. I'll be enjoying just listening to the sound of his voice when I realize that he is saying some really crazy stuff."

I was nowhere near calling Dawkins crazy, but I did know what she meant. Over the course of a couple of phone conversations and the on-camera Skype interview with the man that the producers of *The Curse of Oak Island* arranged, I found that he sounded exactly as I would have imagined a Cambridge-educated architect—which is what he had been as a young man. Things had begun to change, Dawkins told me, in 1973, shortly after he took a job in Edinburgh and married his wife, Sarah, when he met a woman associated with the Francis Bacon Society. It was about three weeks later that he had "an extraordinary dream" in which he encountered "the soul who is Francis Bacon, you might call him the master soul, and he literally told me, 'Right, so now we begin our work together.'"

There almost certainly were academics who would claim to know as much about the historical Francis Bacon as Dawkins did, but none who even approached the level of research he'd done into the esoteric Bacon. An astonishing amount of it was rooted in written records that had sat on dusty shelves for centuries, some of them Bacon's own unpublished writings, Dawkins told me. The story they told was of an Englishman who had been selected at a young age as the leader of a group that was known by many names, the best known being the Knights of the Golden Helmet. "It was only later on that they called themselves Rosicrucians, the fraternity of the golden rosy cross," Dawkins said.

They were men dedicated to the construction of a golden age, Dawkins went on, and their project had been ongoing since long before Bacon was born. "It was a whole line of wisdom traditions that had been carried by secret societies across Europe from the East for many years. They had kept it fairly quiet, something held among themselves, until the supernova of 1604, which they took to be a sign they should announce their existence publicly."

That 1604 event is better known today as Kepler's supernova, for the great astronomer who tracked it. This explosion of a giant star only twenty thousand light-years away from Earth was visible even in daylight for three weeks. At night it was far brighter than any other star in the sky, nearly as bright as the moon. There has not been a supernova in our galaxy since, so one can imagine the impact on the people of Earth as they observed it more than four hundred years ago.

It certainly had a great effect on the Invisibles, as the group called themselves, who began preparing to make themselves known with a series of letters that were posted and published under the authorship of one who was first known as Frater C. R. C. and later as Christian Rosenkreuz or Christian of the Rosy Cross. The letters first appeared in Germany but the real center of the group was in England, the home of the man who had been chosen years earlier to lead the Order of the Rosy Cross, Sir Francis Bacon. "They had selected him—found him, is more like it—around 1570," Dawkins said, which would have made Bacon nine years old at the time.

The men who would follow him at first mentored and instructed him, Dawkins said. Probably the most influential of these had been John Dee. Several of the Baconians I had spoken to or corresponded with previously had mentioned Dee, and I noticed that he was the subject of more articles published by the Francis Bacon Society than anyone other than Bacon himself. All I really knew about Dee was that he had been a famous mathematician of the Elizabethan era, but I was about to find out he was far more than that. Studying Dee's life, even more than Bacon's, drove home what a different place the world was in the sixteenth and seventeenth centuries and how differently people thought of knowledge.

Dee certainly had been a mathematician. At twenty he was lecturing on Euclid in Paris. He studied with and befriended the two greatest cartographers of his time, Mercator and Ortelius, and turned down a position as Reader at Oxford in his middle twenties to devote himself to his writing, which included the "Mathematical Preface" to the English translation of Euclid's *Elements* that would itself become an enduring work.

While Dee believed that numbers were the basis of all things, he placed that belief squarely within the nexus of religion, philosophy, and esoteric science known as the hermetic tradition and viewed math as a means of accessing divine power and ancient wisdom. While he served for years as Queen Elizabeth's main scientific adviser, the Queen seems to have valued him more as her astrologer; Elizabeth actually allowed Dee to select an auspicious date for her coronation. Astronomy and astrology were essentially one science in the post-Renaissance world Dee inhabited, and in fact he made no real distinction between his studies of mathematics, cartography, navigation, and philosophy on the one hand, and his deep interest in hermetic magic, divination, and spirit summoning on the other. All were the processes by which one arrived at the "pure verities" that underlay all of creation.

Even as Dee became Elizabeth's main adviser on England's voyages of discovery, personally trained and prepared navigation charts for many of England's greatest explorers, including Raleigh and Drake, designed the British navy, coined the phrase the "British Empire," and invented the term "Britannica" to describe it, he was at least as deeply invested in his practices of conjuring and alchemy. The latter he considered the

supreme science, aiming as it did for the creation of the so-called philosopher's stone that would heal mankind physically and spiritually and,
Dee hoped, bring forth the unified world religion that would recombine
not only the Protestant and Catholic churches, but the great wisdom
of the ancients.

This was a point of view that made sense to the people of the
era, among whom Dee's reputation as a magician rivaled his status as
a scholar. It was widely believed among the British populace that the
English defeat of the Spanish Armada in 1588 had been aided if not
accomplished by the hex Dee put on the enemy fleet. In the Baconian
version of Dee, much of which Peter Dawkins repeated to me, he was
eventually persecuted for his hermetic practices to the point of being
driven out of England. Dee was in fact brought before the Star Chamber in 1555 on a charge of "calculating" the horoscopes of both Queen
Mary and Queen Elizabeth, and this charge eventually expanded into
one of treason. He was acquitted, however.

It was his yearning for a deeper and more unified knowledge that
seems to have compelled Dee's departure from England and Elizabeth's
court. Discouraged by the Queen's refusal to adopt his heliocentric
calendar and the blame she seemed to cast his way for the failure of
North American explorations, he plunged ever more deeply into the
metaphysical and supernatural, attempting to communicate with angels
through a crystal ball he called a scryer. It was during this period that
Dee met a young man called Edward Talbot, whose real surname, Kelley, had been abandoned in order to distance himself from a conviction
for "coinage," the production of false coins, equivalent at the time to
forgery. Kelley was, to Dee's mind (and in the Baconian tradition), the
greatest alchemist of his age. The two men, almost thirty years apart in
age, together with their wives began a tour of the Continent that lasted
six years, along the way staging "spiritual conferences" for royal families
in much of eastern and central Europe.

I noticed that the Baconian articles about Dee always left out the
fact that Kelley had convinced him, on the instructions of the angel Uriel,

that the two of them should share all of their possessions, including their wives. The stress this produced eventually sent Dee back to England, where he discovered that his personal library, the largest in the entire country, had been ransacked, and that many books were stolen, along with his most prized instruments. The country he came back to was now looking askance at occult practices, which forced Dee to become more covert. Queen Elizabeth did make him warden of Christ's College in Manchester. It was a position he held to the end of his life in either 1608 or 1609, but in all historical records he is described as impoverished and miserable during these last years.

Peter Dawkins told me this was not entirely accurate; Dee had taken on the role of instructing those who were about to take the Rosicrucian movement public, including and especially the chosen leader: Francis Bacon. The goal was to "raise the consciousness of people by using the arts and sciences," Dawkins said, "so as to bring them to an understanding of what Bacon called 'the summary law,' which is the law of love, how to practice love in every single situation." But this had to be done under a veil of secrecy and with the aim of speaking ultimately to people of a more enlightened age. Bacon's junior associate Robert Fludd, for instance, was relatively forthright about his interest in the occult, publicly exchanging arguments with Johannes Kepler on the merits of the hermetic versus the strictly scientific approach to knowledge. Fludd even wrote a defense of the Rosicrucian movement, but he never admitted to being part of it for fear of the consequences, as Dawkins had it.

I admit I became a bit restive as Dawkins went on to describe how Bacon and "his good pens" (among them Ben Jonson) had created the Shakespeare plays as part of the great Rosicrucian project, but I was so fascinated by the overarching story that I simply kept silent until Dawkins had moved on to the subject of the sky and land zodiacs that Bacon and his circle had created in order to bring about the marriage of the heavens and the Earth they envisioned. This was what ultimately linked Bacon to Oak Island, as Dawkins had it.

The sky and land zodiacs had all been calculated in connection to the constellation that was most commonly known as the Northern Cross, which was itself only a part of the larger constellation known as Cygnus (the swan), Dawkins explained. The triangle formed by the bright star Deneb and two others was the key to this calculation and was referred to repeatedly in the alchemical texts of the Elizabethan era, as they were in the works from Egypt, India, and Sufi Islam from which those had emerged. Much of what he had learned about all of this came from a woman named Betty McKaig, Dawkins said. I was impressed immediately by the admiring, almost reverent, way Peter spoke of her.

"I've never heard of Betty McKaig," I admitted.

"You should have," Dawkins told me. "She's an important part of the Oak Island story."

McKaig was working as a freelance journalist in California in the early 1970s, when she was hired by a famous surgeon to ghostwrite his autobiography. She went to live in the physician's home while working on the book, and while there she became fascinated by the two enormous collections that filled much of his library. One was made up of works—many rare—by and about Francis Bacon. The other consisted of texts that chronicled the history and practice of alchemy and other hermetic arts. "When she started to look at what he knew, in order to write his biography, she got enthralled herself," Dawkins explained. "She became so absorbed that this was the total focus of her research, and then the doctor died." Before his death, however, the physician had bequeathed his Bacon and alchemy collections to McKaig, "who carried on [with] all the research and became convinced that many of the alchemical texts that were written under the name 'Philalethes' had actually been authored or inspired by Francis Bacon."

The history of alchemy, McKaig found, was far richer and stranger than she had imagined. The roots of the tree that had produced Philalethes stretched in three directions, into Taoist China, dharmic India, and a more complex network that was threaded over time from hermetic Egypt to Platonic Greece to Sufi Islam and ultimately into medieval Europe.

The sciences of medicine, chemistry, and metallurgy all had emerged either from or alongside alchemy. The first alchemist in recorded history, McKaig was pleased to discover, had been a woman, one known only as Mary the Jewess, who had lived in the great melting pot of the age, Alexandria, Egypt, during the late second and early third centuries. Modern science credits Mary with nearly all of the early advancements in the processes of heating and distillation. The Jewess's most remarkable and enduring achievement, though, was her discovery of hydrochloric acid. She had emerged from a hermetic tradition whose origins were largely lost in the mists of time, mostly due to the order that the Roman dictator Emperor Diocletian had given right around the end of the third century that all alchemy texts should be burned.

What is still known is that while alchemy in China was focused on healing and the creation of medicines (both acupuncture and moxibustion have their roots in Chinese alchemy), the alchemy of India had been closely associated with the development of metallurgy. The use of mercury in alchemical processes, for example, first appeared in the *Arthashastra* in the late third century and in various Buddhist texts that were written between the second and fifth centuries. The conquests of Alexander the Great were likely what made the connection between the Eastern and Western traditions of alchemy.

However it happened, the Western tradition's incorporation of the Eastern tradition had produced the next major figure in its development, the Sufi Jabir ibn Hayyan (better known in Europe by his Latinized name Geberus) who had set up a laboratory where he introduced scientific methodology and controlled experimentation into alchemy and in the process earned a reputation as the father of modern chemistry. He was also, at least in part, responsible for the reputation alchemy acquired as a dark art: Jabir's stated goal was what he called *takwin*, the artificial creation of life, up to and including human life.

Jabir's work was introduced to Europe in 1144 when Robert of Chester translated the Arabic work *Book of the Composition of Alchemy*. As it began to be practiced in Europe, what in Chinese alchemy had

been a search for the so-called grand elixir of immortality and in India
was the aim of producing a gold so pure that touching it would perfect
a man's soul, the West made into a quest for the philosopher's stone.

The alchemy of Europe was at once material and spiritual, McKaig
discovered in her reading. Given the reputation alchemy had acquired
as something either fraudulent or satanic, it was fascinating to discover
that in thirteenth-century Europe the three most notable students of
alchemy had been the Franciscan Roger Bacon, the Dominican Albertus
Magnus, and the latter's student, Thomas Aquinas. It was not until the
fourteenth century that the practice of alchemy began to leak outside
the confines of the church, and that process sped up in the fifteenth
century, when the Italian Marsilio Ficino translated the *Corpus Herme-
ticum* (along with the works of Plato) into Latin. This set the stage for
the first two major European alchemists, born just seven years apart,
the German Heinrich Cornelius Agrippa (1486–1535) and the Swiss
Philippus Aureolus Paracelsus (1493–1541).

Agrippa was the mystic, whose opus *De Occulta Philosophia* attempted
the fusion of kabbalah, hermeticism, and alchemy into something very
like a religion. Paracelsus was less interested in the occult and in the
manufacture of precious metals, focusing instead on the creation of
medicines.

John Dee followed Agrippa's tradition. For all his accomplishments
in mathematics, cartography, astronomy, cryptography, and navigation,
by far the best known and most widely read of Dee's works during his
own lifetime was his 1564 work on alchemy, *Monas Hieroglyphica*. In
it, Dee had been the first to describe alchemy as a kind of terrestrial
astronomy, coining the axiom: "As above, so below."

"And of course Betty McKaig discovered that it was John Dee who
had been Francis Bacon's instructor in the art and science of alchemy,"
Dawkins told me.

Historians have had little to say about Bacon's involvement with
and practice of alchemy. As Dawkins had it, this was because Sir Francis
had kept it well hidden during his lifetime. "But through this doctor's

collection, Betty had access to materials that aren't commonly known," he explained. "She found that his practice of alchemy, in the manner described by John Dee, was at the center of Francis Bacon's work."

Bacon's connection to the flowering of English alchemy in the seventeenth century has not gone entirely unrecognized. Lauren Kassell, a professor of history and philosophy of science at Cambridge, named Bacon as one of the three principals responsible for that occurrence. Though started by John Dee, English alchemy was "codified by Francis Bacon in the early decades of the seventeenth century, and implemented by Samuel Hartlib in the 1650s."

In the histories I read, Hartlib was regarded as the most significant figure in English alchemy after John Dee and the one who did the most to take it mainstream. The "Hartlibean improvers," as Kassell called them, had made alchemy the basis of a grand scheme for the combined investigation of nature's secrets and the reform of society. Hartlib's circle was a precursor to the formation of the Royal Society, and the man himself openly and repeatedly acknowledged Bacon as his inspiration. In fact, he had modeled his vision of the Royal Society on the research institute Bacon had called Salomon's House in his great work *New Atlantis*. Two of the Royal Society's earliest fellows, Robert Boyle and Elias Ashmole—"both Baconians," as Dawkins, through McKaig, had it—were proponents of alchemy who openly stated their belief that the philosopher's stone might be used for, among other things, communicating with angels.

Alchemy's ascendance in Britain, however, was also its downfall. More and more alleged practitioners of the recondite science were selling their services to kings and queens, lords and ladies. Many of them were con men or stage magicians, like Betruger, whose combination of sleight of hand and swindling had resulted in a public trial by the Holy Roman Empire. Those who preferred to be called scientists began to distance themselves from the practice, and the pressure to do so only increased as science and materialism began to merge. As early as 1720 chemists began to insist on a firm distinction between themselves and alchemists, and by the 1740s alchemy was almost totally associated with gold making and the various flimflammers that claimed they could accomplish it.

The works authored by the pseudonymous Philalethes (Greek for "lover of truth") would provide the most enduring descriptions of alchemical processes, and it was the Philalethes books that had most captivated Betty McKaig, Dawkins told me. There were actually two Philalethes who had authored published books on alchemy in the seventeenth century I would learn in between conversations with Dawkins, and neither of them was ever identified as Francis Bacon. The one with the more interesting story was Eirenaeus Philalethes ("peaceful lover of truth"), who historians almost universally believe was George Starkey, born in 1628 two years after Bacon's death. Starkey, who had been born George Stirk, was a colonial American physician who for reasons not entirely clear had immigrated to London at twenty-two. Most believe the motive for the move was his wish to have greater access to materials and equipment and, especially, teachings that would further his alchemical experiments. In London, he changed his name and continued his medical practice while at the same time working tirelessly to develop what he called sophic mercury, the amalgam of antimony, silver, and mercury that he believed would dissolve gold into a mixture that when heated would produce the philosopher's stone. He was enormously respected in his day for both his laboratory expertise and the formal scientific methodology he developed. Many credit him as the forerunner to and teacher of Robert Boyle, who is today regarded as the first modern chemist. Starkey was plagued throughout his life by the debts he accumulated in pursuit of his alchemical research, actually went to debtor's prison twice, and died in the Great Plague of London in 1655, at just thirty-seven. The works he left behind, though, especially *Introitus Apertus Ad Occlusum Regis Palatium*, were enormously influential with readers who included not only Boyle, but also John Locke, Gottfried Wilhelm Leibniz, and Isaac Newton. Newton was so taken with the Philalethes texts that he devoted much of the rest of his life to the study of alchemy and in fact produced many more pages on that subject than he did on his study of physics.

The other Philalethes was Thomas Vaughan, a Welshman who made his living as a royalist clergyman and wrote under the name Eugenius Philalethes. He was a near contemporary of Starkey's, born in 1621, seven years before the American, while Francis Bacon was still alive. Vaughan's alchemy was more along the lines laid out by Paracelsus and he applied his skills mainly to the preparation of medicines, though he, too, was ultimately dedicated to producing the philosopher's stone. While Vaughan's personal story is less cinematic than Starkey's, the Welshman was much more open about the sources of inspiration and knowledge, which was what, Peter Dawkins told me, had helped him and Betty McKaig to connect both of the Philalethes authors to Francis Bacon. Their mutual association with Samuel Hartlib was the key, Dawkins explained, because Hartlib was a devotee of Bacon's who had joined the Invisible College created by Sir Francis as a young man and been instructed by him personally. That Starkey was also a member of what became known around the middle of the seventeenth century as the Hartlib Circle is one of the few things known about the man. Vaughan, though, was much more public about his association with Hartlib and also with the Rosicrucian order. The Welshman, who publicly proclaimed himself to be a member of what he called the Society of Unknown Philosophers, was the person who had produced the first English translation (in 1652) of the *Fama Fraternitatis Rosae Crucis*, the seminal Rosicrucian manifesto that was first published in Kassel, Germany, in 1614.

Through the research she was conducting with the resources acquired from her physician patron's library, Dawkins told me, McKaig had determined that both the seventeenth-century authors who had produced the Philalethes texts were disciples of Bacon who in large part had reproduced his unpublished alchemical formulas and writings. Out in California, putting all these pieces together, McKaig began to conduct her own alchemical experiments, following what she understood to be instructions that came directly from Francis Bacon. Dawkins, who first visited her in California in the mid-1970s, sounded truly moved as he described his experiences in McKaig's laboratory. "The experiments were all being done in these flasks," he recalled. "And I watched as she performed them. At one point she told me to watch this particular flask and out of nowhere, it seemed, there appeared a salamander."

Alchemical literature for centuries has used the salamander to symbolize the soul, and the production of them "in the shapes of fiery balls, or tongues of fire," as Paracelsus put it, has been an essential aspect of the search for the philosopher's stone. That they were magical creatures born of fire was a common belief for centuries. "The real truth is that the Salamander is no beast, as they allege in our part of the world," Marco Polo wrote after his visit to the Orient, "but is a substance found in the earth."

The skeptics of our materialist age would point out that salamanders are associated with fire because they tend to dwell in rotting logs from which they emerge when the logs are thrown onto fires. "I am telling you that what I saw was a creature that was—well, I'll just say what happened: Betty told me, 'Wait, in five minutes it's going to change into the Beating Heart of Jesus,'" Peter Dawkins recalled. "So I waited, and suddenly the salamander disappeared and in the center appeared a shape that didn't make a sound, but beat just like a heart. She said, 'That's gonna go on for a couple of hours or so, and then we'll go on to the next stage' . . . Betty firmly believed she was on her way to the production of the philosopher's stone. And so did I."

McKaig's alchemical experiments were not being conducted only in the laboratory, Dawkins said. The work she was doing that may have been just as important, and that led her to Oak Island, was born out of the astronomical alchemy—"as above, so below"—first advocated by John Dee and perfected, according to Dawkins, by Francis Bacon. In one of the Philalethes texts that had been created by Bacon, McKaig said, she had discovered "a star map with instructions to project it onto the world globe," as Dawkins recalled it. She was able to determine that the key marker was the star Deneb in Cygnus, which stood at the apex of a triangle—known as "God's hand," according to Dawkins—that pointed to a specific location on the face of the Earth, but the instructions about how to find the bearing that would determine this location were enciphered, McKaig explained. She spent weeks decoding that cipher, McKaig told Dawkins, and then performed the process of projection, which pointed to a spot in Nova Scotia. "But it wasn't Oak Island," Dawkins told me. He asked McKaig which star map—"star catalogues," they were actually known as in the sixteenth and seventeenth centuries—she had used as the basis of her projection. The Tycho Brahe star map published in 1602, of course, McKaig replied; it was by far the most accurate and respected of its time. No, no, Dawkins told her, he was fairly certain that Bacon had used an earlier star map, one created decades before Brahe's. So McKaig performed a second projection, this time using the older star map, and this time God's hand pointed to a tiny spot of land off the mainland of Nova Scotia in Mahone Bay—Oak Island. "Which Betty had never even heard of," Dawkins told me.

After reading everything she could find on the subject of Oak Island—and being especially impressed by Leary's slim volume, *The Oak Island Enigma*—McKaig became convinced that she had found the exact location of the spot where Bacon's followers had secreted his teachings for the benefit of those who would be living on Earth at the end of the present Great Age (there's considerable debate among astrologers about when that will be).

McKaig booked a flight to Montreal to meet with David Tobias, the man who seemed to control what happened on Oak Island. Her timing was not good. Tobias was invested in other ideas and associated the Bacon theory with Gilbert Hedden. Tobias and the Triton partners "either were not interested or did not believe her sufficiently," Dawkins wrote to me in one email; he honestly wasn't sure which.

Discouraged, McKaig returned to California to press forward with her quest for the philosopher's stone. "This was, like, the late 1980s," Dawkins said. By then, people affiliated with the Francis Bacon Foundation in Claremont, California, had become interested in McKaig's work and someone affiliated with that group—Peter told me he didn't know who—had arranged for her to receive a monthly stipend from what Dawkins knew only as "a company." He believed it might have been a pharmaceutical company, but Betty was secretive about her financial dealings.

"Betty really believed she was getting close" to the alchemical breakthrough she sought, Dawkins told me, "but then her house burned down, which destroyed not only her laboratory, but nearly all of her papers and records as well." I asked him how the fire started. "Someone set it intentionally," he answered. When asked who might have done it, he said, "Betty believed, and so do I, that it was a rival company that was concerned about how close she might be to success." This sounded a lot like a conspiracy theory, I thought, but did not interrupt.

After a brief period of reeling, McKaig had attempted to restart her work, Dawkins told me, but was feeling pressure from her benefactors to produce something useful. The reason he believed it was a pharmaceutical company is that her focus seemed to be on producing medicines. "Unfortunately, she began to use herself as a guinea pig, and I knew that was dangerous. I was concerned about her." In 1990 or perhaps early 1991, McKaig had called him, sounding frightened, Dawkins remembered. "She told me, 'Peter, I think I may have overdosed on mercury.' She died just a few weeks later."

At almost that exact time, David Tobias began an extensive correspondence with the Francis Bacon Foundation in Claremont and the Francis Bacon Society in Surrey, England. Word of McKaig's death and of her commitment to her work seem to have been the trigger. It was actually this correspondence that had gotten Tobias onto the idea that Francis Drake was the one who had supervised, on Francis Bacon's behalf, the original works on Oak Island. How that would have worked, I'm not certain; Drake died thirty years before Bacon did. And I couldn't ask David, because he had died in 2012.

Still, through his contacts with the Bacon groups, Tobias did make connections to a pair of mining engineers who have become tied up in various Oak Island theories. One was Joachim Gans, a Bohemian engineer who Tobias said had been shipped across the Atlantic by Drake in the late sixteenth century, making him the first Jew to touch North American soil. That last part was true, but according to the histories I consulted Gans had actually been brought to Virginia in 1584 by Sir Walter Raleigh, as part of the group that founded the first English settlement in colonial America, on Roanoke Island off the coast of North Carolina. That settlement only lasted two years, however, before Gans and the other settlers, increasingly fearful of the native tribes, accepted an invitation from Drake to sail them back to England. So there was a Drake connection, but no record that I could find of the great seaman taking Gans to some other part of North America. Somehow, though, a story had grown up that Gans had been sent by Drake (or someone) with a company of Cornish miners that landed on the Bay of Fundy and made its way to Nova Scotia. The miners had not been heard from for two years, according to this story, and were supposedly on Oak Island during that period. Tobias clearly had been fascinated with the tale and so was I when Tony Sampson, the diver associated with *The Curse of Oak Island* with whom I enjoyed a couple of meals, first told me about it. Tony said he had read about it at the O'Dell House Museum in Annapolis Royal, Nova Scotia. When I phoned the museum, though, I was told by the public information officer that she had never heard the story before. She put me in touch with a woman she described as the foremost historian in the entire Bay of Fundy, who said that this story only existed, insofar as she knew, in some "fanciful histories" written about Oak Island.

What's known of Joachim Gans is that he joined the Royal Mining Company and moved to Bristol, England, where he gave Hebrew lessons to local gentlemen who wanted to read the Bible in its original tongue. Then the bishop of Chichester paid a visit to Gans, and on learning he was a Jew, demanded, "Do you deny Jesus Christ to be the Son of God?"

"What needeth the almighty God to have a son?" Gans replied. "Is he not almighty?"

His resulting trial for blasphemy made him famous—or infamous—and inspired Francis Bacon to use him as the model for the heroic Jewish scientist Joabin in *New Atlantis*. So there were connections of a sort between the men, but David Tobias was probably following a more promising path when he became interested in the engineer most often cited in Oak Island theories, Thomas Bushell.

Bushell, who served as Britain's chief mining engineer during the reign of Charles I, was famed for his expertise in the construction of underground water channels used in the flooding and pumping out of mine shafts. He was also a protégé of Francis Bacon's. There is ample record of Bacon cultivating the mystic in Bushell, encouraging him to various esoteric pursuits that probably included alchemy, and sharing both his scientific knowledge and his experimental research with the young engineer. According to Bushell's diaries, Bacon also ultimately entrusted him with his "dearest secret." What that secret may have been is not certain, but it seems likely that it involved Bacon's plan for the creation of a research institute modeled on Salomon's House in *New Atlantis*. There are also references to "treasures" being entrusted to Bushell in the diaries.

What's known for certain is that shortly after Bacon's death in 1626, Bushell was said to have spent three years as a religious hermit on a remote island off the west coast of England. According to certain Baconians, Peter Dawkins among them, what Bushell was actually doing during much of that time was supervising the construction of the works on Oak Island, in service to the memory of Francis Bacon. This seemed vanishingly unlikely, but again I didn't interrupt Peter.

It was unfortunate that Tobias had missed his chance with Betty McKaig, Dawkins told me, and more unfortunate still that he had lost interest in the Bacon theory in favor of one that involved Spanish gold. The loss he mourned most, though, was of Betty McKaig's research and experimental notes. Those that hadn't been lost in the fire, along with the new ones Betty had generated, Peter told me, disappeared after her death. He had never been able to learn what happened to these materials.

All that McKaig had left behind was a single article written in 1985 for *Baconia*, a publication of the Francis Bacon Society. It was about Oak Island.

I found McKaig to be an intelligent writer, but the subject matter was so arcane it was a struggle to stay with her. Part of this may have been that she was summarizing what had been an exorbitantly complex process of deciphering "Bacon's subtle plan for marking out the boundaries of his *New Atlantis*," as she described it. She had relied mostly on what were described in the article as "a number of discontinuous sequences couched in a mythological matrix featuring the classical deities so dear to Bacon's heart" that she had found in the great man's "masque works," McKaig wrote, in particular the Philalethes texts. Many of these had correlated to various heavenly bodies, at least in McKaig's reading. For instance, a line about how "the Red man and the White woman must be wed in the West" was interpreted as referring to the planets Mars and Venus "in a conjunction [a marriage] of Spica in Virgo" in the western sky.

Eventually, using the star map Dawkins had suggested, she followed the other lines referenced in Bacon's works to their connecting points and found she was looking at "three overlapping triangles resembling the sails of a ship, with the original hermaphrodite line serving as mast, and the curved line of the elliptic resembling the sails of a ship."

Once she had the various points that provided a bearing for the pointer of Deneb, it was a "simple mathematical formula" that had led her to the precise latitude and longitude of the "target," as she called it, "a minuscule speck of land on the south coast of Nova Scotia called Oak Island."

To me, the most interesting part of the article had come near the end, when McKaig made reference to the stone triangle, which she described as "a great stone arrow, laid out in ancient beach boulders" that duplicated Bacon's "celestial arrow" precisely, "including a 7-degree westward slant in the vertical 'hermaphrodite' line!" McKaig promised in her "next article" to explain what she had discovered about the stone triangle, but to my knowledge no such article had ever been written; it certainly had not been published.

While it was difficult for me to fathom a mind that could have designed such a fantastically intricate scheme as the one McKaig described, I found it even more difficult to imagine the thinking of a person who believed she had unraveled it all. Still, it somehow had led Betty McKaig to Oak Island, a place Peter Dawkins said she had only discovered existed when she found that Deneb was pointing to it. If true, that was pretty astounding. I wondered if Peter, by suggesting a particular star map, had helped guide her to Oak Island, perhaps even without being aware of it, but he insisted that wasn't so.

When I had finished my Baconian research I felt certain that if nothing else I had fresh material for *The Curse of Oak Island*'s cast and producers. I would lay it all out for them in my War Room scene, which was to be the summation of my appearance on the show. To register the magnitude of Francis Bacon, I quoted the famous historian Will Durant, who had written: "The whole tenor and career of British thought have followed the philosophy of Bacon."

I used the star map Peter Dawkins had created for me as my main illustration and went through the story of Betty McKaig in considerable detail, explaining how widespread encryption and secret societies were in Elizabethan England, a time when the power of the Crown and the church were absolute and a man could easily lose his head for saying or thinking the wrong thing. As historian Michael Taylor had written, "Bacon resurrected the Rosicrucian Mystery School and the Freemasons, and injected new life into these secret fraternity societies so they became vehicles for the new Baconian philosophy of reason and scientific enquiry." Peter Dawkins had pointed me to something Bacon had written under one of the "masque names" identified by Betty McKaig that involved using a treasure hunt as a form of spiritual instruction, turning the search for material wealth into the discovery of inner riches.

Extraordinary, outlandish even, as the Bacon theory of Oak Island might seem, he was one of the few men in the history of the human race who might have been capable of imagining and accomplishing what had been done on the island, and in fact some of his published work came close. We had to at least consider it.

I described the ways in which Bacon had been connected to the New World and to the Atlantic coast of Canada in particular. Sir Francis had been a partner in private enterprises that had established early North American colonies in Newfoundland and Virginia. Newfoundland, in fact, had in 1910 issued a stamp that commemorated the three hundredth anniversary of Bacon's role in the founding of the province's first colony, printed with a salute to Sir Francis as "the guiding spirit in the Colonization Schemes in 1610." One of Bacon's closest associates had been Sir William Alexander, the Scottish poet and philosopher who had given Nova Scotia its name.

Then I finished by explaining that I had first started thinking seriously about the Bacon theory when I considered something Dan Blankenship had said to me back in 2003, and that I had used in the *Rolling Stone* article: "The people who did the original work on this island were the most brilliant sons of bitches in the history of the world." Francis Bacon may very well have been *the* most brilliant, I said.

I felt afterward it had gone well. At the least, I'd brought hard evidence and solid research into the more esoteric elements of the second most popular theory about the mystery of Oak Island.

Several cast members approached me to say they thought they knew pretty much all there was to know about Oak Island and were amazed by how much I'd told them that they didn't know. They found the Betty McKaig story especially powerful.

So naturally it came as a surprise to me when the show used absolutely none of it.

Weeks would pass before I learned that this hadn't been because of me or even because of the fairly arcane details of the Bacon theory. It had all been about the Norwegian Shakespeare researcher who'd first visited the island back in 2003, Petter Amundsen.

CHAPTER TWENTY-THREE

Petter Amundsen had come back to Oak Island in 2014, during season one of *The Curse of Oak Island*, to follow up on excavations he had done with Fred Nolan's permission eleven years earlier. While on the island, he had helped the producers build the platform that launched what was arguably the most dramatic moment of the show's first three seasons.

In 2003, Amundsen would explain to me, his entire focus was on the Cabalistic Tree of Life that he believed extended from Nolan's Cross. The Tree of Life was an intrinsic aspect of the kabbalah, the ancient Jewish mystical tradition of Bible interpretation. The cabala was a Christian reconfiguration of the kabbalah that linked Jesus to the ten Sephirot (divine emanations) that formed the branches of the Tree of Life. The Rosicrucians had adopted it, according to Amundsen, and of course the leader of the Rosicrucian movement had been Francis Bacon.

When Amundsen, who made his living as the organist at the Evangelical Lutheran chapel in the Holmenkollen section of Oslo, Norway, tried to explain how he had arrived at his Tree of Life theory, his process sounded so abstruse that it made Betty McKaig's seem succinct by comparison. It was rooted in the same basic Baconian theory, though, and included the belief that Sir Francis had been the actual author of the Shakespeare plays. Amundsen also had used a sky-to-land projection that involved the Northern Cross in the Cygnus constellation.

When I asked if he felt he owed a debt to McKaig, however, Amundsen's denial was suspiciously circuitous. While he would concede that McKaig had "introduced me to the possibility that the stone triangle could have an astronomical significance" and that a projection from the sky to the earth might be the key to solving the Oak Island mystery, and he had included McKaig's work in a pamphlet he provided to Triton Alliance in 2003, he had "since come to disregard her input," Amundsen told me. He had not had his own star map interpreted until 2005, Amundsen noted.

So Amundsen was contending he had no star map in 2003? "When I was at Oak Island in 2003 I only had the Tree of Life element in my pocket," he replied, "and the observation that the Northern Cross part of Cygnus resembles Nolan's Cross, which I linked to the Sweet Swan of Avon [Shakespeare], not knowing that this is 'New Temple of God' read backwards with the Greek-Latin cipher."

When I heard this I shook my head and smiled, imagining how Fred Nolan—and Dan Blankenship especially—must have reacted to Amundsen's theory. It was clear, however, that Dan at least had been mightily impressed by the way the Norwegian had gone about confirming his ideas.

After Amundsen conducted a survey that overlapped the one by which Nolan had found his cross, he announced that they should dig at the exact spot on Oak Island where he believed the Kingdom Sephirot of the Tree of Life lay. They needed to scrape away only about five centimeters of soil, Dan Blankenship had told me, before discovering a "very unusual red granite rock." That rock was curved like a seashell on one side, with a nearly perfect flat edge that was ideal for placing it in an upright position. Amundsen had pointed out three dots on the rock that may or may not have been man-made, Blankenship said, that did seem to form an almost perfect isosceles triangle.

This had been enough to win Amundsen the continuing cooperation of both Dan and Fred Nolan (and getting Fred to cooperate, as everyone who had dealt with the man knew, was never an easy task), who would allow Amundsen to film on his Oak Island property during the production of a documentary that in 2009 would run in four episodes on Norway's main national television channel, NRK. "Shakespeare's Sweet

Swan of Avon," was the title's English translation. I thought Shakespeare *was* the Sweet Swan of Avon, I told Amundsen. "Yes and no," he told me, declining to elaborate.

By the time Amundsen returned to Nova Scotia to appear on *The Curse of Oak Island* in 2014, his theory had grown even larger and more complex. It still centered on Francis Bacon, but now it included the "coded map" he had created from the ciphers found in the Shakespeare plays. He had relied on the *First Folio*, in which the misspellings and the misordered pages were the key to unraveling the code, Amundsen explained, and revealing the map that "takes you up in the sky and brings you down on Oak Island." After describing the Tree of Life and the ten Sephirot (Crown, Wisdom, Intelligence, Mercy, Justice, Beauty, Victory, Glory, Foundation, Kingdom), Amundsen explained to the Laginas that his calculations had convinced him that the Mercy Point was the key location where access to the Oak Island treasure might be found. The Mercy Point turned out to be in the island's swamp, which was the beginning of the continuing comic relief on the show provided by Marty's abhorrence of the foul-smelling marsh.

First Amundsen had the Laginas dig for the Kingdom Stone he had found in 2003. The first rock the brothers dug up was not right—"too small," Amundsen said—but then Marty had spotted a larger stone, flat on one side. That was it, Amundsen declared, pointing out the three "slightly carved" triangle-point indentations. The brothers then rented an airplane for a flyover of Oak Island where they saw that if the "Kingdom" stone was added to the other stones that comprised Nolan's Cross, a diamond shape was formed that aligned perfectly with the place where Amundsen said the Mercy Point would be found.

Back on the ground, as the Laginas said goodbye to Amundsen, the brothers promised him they were committed to searching the Mercy Point and seeing what might be found there. This had led to the climactic scene of *The Curse of Oak Island*'s first-season finale. The drama was all built on whether they would continue the Oak Island treasure hunt (and of course the show). Rick was inclined to keep going, but Marty was beginning to wonder what the point of it all might be. They needed to find something to keep him with them, Marty told the rest of the cast.

An expert named Steve Zazulyk was brought in to operate his Lorenz Deepmax X6, an advanced piece of high-tech metal detection equipment that would probe the area where Petter Amundsen had said the Mercy Point would be found. Zazulyk's machine found nothing at first; the display screen on which the presence of nonferrous metals would register in orange or red was blank. Then suddenly the screen filled with what Craig Tester's stepson, Jack Begley, called "mountains of red."

Minutes later, as Zazulyk and Marty Lagina were probing the bottom of the swamp with their hands, up to their necks in the mucky water, they had simultaneously felt the object that Marty lifted out into the open air. It was a copper coin with an 8 inscribed on it, a Spanish *maravedi* ("piece of 8") from the 1600s. On camera, Marty would call it "probably the most valuable thing ever found on Oak Island."

This was not true. Back in the mid-1960s, Peter Beamish, the teacher who'd revived Andy DeMont and Edward White after they were pulled from the shaft where the Restalls had died, had led a party of nineteen students from Phillips Academy through an electromagnetic survey of Oak Island that had produced, among more than three hundred other metal objects, a maravedi coin dated 1598. Any number of other old coins also had been found on the island over the years.

Still, it was an affecting moment when Marty presented the coin from the swamp to Dan Blankenship, who had choked up on camera as he turned the maravedi in his gnarled fingers. "That's the first thing I've held in my hands," in forty-eight years. "The real evidence," he declared.

That final episode of season one, titled "The Find," had been the determining factor in the decision to film a second season of *The Curse of Oak Island*. The last scene was shot in the War Room, where the implications of the coin's discovery were discussed. Dan, of course, felt it confirmed his suspicion that the Spanish had done the original work on the island. But there were other possibilities. In the seventeenth century, coins crossed borders far more easily than today. The English used Spanish coins, and the Spanish used French coins. Pirates had called the maravedi "the treasure coin." Wasn't it even possible that a Spaniard could have dropped the coin while digging in the Money Pit to find the Templar treasure long before the Pit's 1795 "discovery?" the show's narrator asked.

While almost everyone agreed they wanted to keep the treasure hunt going, it came down to Marty, who as the man with the money would have the final say. "Well, I was sort of playing this in my mind," he said on camera. "There's a bunch of these guys, they go out, they spend a bunch of money, they bust their asses, they're up to their necks in the swamp, then at the end of their summer quest, they find a pirate coin. And then they quit." As the others laughed with relief, Rick raised Marty's hand, making the vote to continue unanimous.

It had been a rousing conclusion to the first season of the show, made better by the History Channel's decision to order a second series of episodes. Only when I arrived on Oak Island during the shooting of season four did I learn that both of the Lagina brothers were nagged by the suspicion that the maravedi had been planted at the Mercy Point by the producers of *The Curse of Oak Island*.

It was the only subject on which I heard both the brothers speak with one voice. Without me bringing it up, Rick and Marty had each, in separate conversations, told me that they'd intensely questioned Kevin Burns and the other producers about their suspicions. "It just seemed a little too convenient," Marty said. The producers had adamantly denied it and the Laginas had accepted those denials, but they had also told Burns that if they ever found out the coin *had* been planted, the show would end immediately. I told them that what I knew of the producers had convinced me they would never go along with such a deception, and both brothers appeared happy to hear it.

A second Baconian theorist arrived from Scandinavia during the show's second season. He was a Swede named Daniel Ronnstam who asserted that the message carved onto the inscribed stone actually bore two messages: "a double cipher." After explaining how his cipher disk worked, Ronnstam had undertaken a revisionist critique of the dubious translation performed by Dr. Ross Wilhelm in 1971; the main mistake Wilhelm had made, according to Ronnstam, was failing to use the Spanish alphabet rather than the English. Then Ronnstam revealed his own translation of the more deeply encrypted message on the inscribed stone: "At 80FT Guide Corn, Long Narrow Sea Inlet Drain: F." It was very nearly identical to the message Wilhelm had found, the only real difference being that Wilhelm had said the *F* stood for Felipe, king of Spain, while Ronnstam said it stood for Francis Bacon. The similarities between Wilhelm's decryption and Ronnstam's went unmentioned on the show but it did add to the sense that the production was committed to running the Bacon theory alongside the Templar one.

What I didn't know when I was watching the Ronnstam scenes was that he had been invited at the last minute to replace Petter Amundsen, who had become persona non grata across the entire production. Amundsen's "betrayal" (as one producer called it) had arisen out of his relationship with a politically connected Nova Scotia marine biologist named Wynand Baerken. Very early in the production of the first season of *The Curse of Oak Island*, Baerken had become concerned about the cultural and environmental impact on the island and had taken that concern to the Member of Parliament who represented the Chester–St. Margaret's District, Denise Peterson-Rafuse. She responded by writing a bill that called for placing Oak Island under the same "heritage protection" statutes that prevailed in the rest of Nova Scotia. "Then she and Wynand contacted me, hoping to seek my support," Amundsen would explain to me more than two years later "Which I gladly provided."

Amundsen told me he hadn't offered to assist the passage of the legislation because he distrusted the Laginas and couldn't have cared less about anything the brothers chose to do in the Money Pit area, "which is totally ruined anyway from earlier explorers." His concern was for the mideastern part of the swamp, "because I believe in my rather fantastic theory," he explained. "If they should accidently ruin such artifacts as

I describe, then the consequences would be dramatic to say the least." All Amundsen was hoping for was that an archeologist be consulted each time new operations were begun on the island. "In Europe, this is totally normal." It certainly seemed reasonable to me.

The Laginas, however, saw Amundsen's cooperation with Canadian activists as an impediment to the progress of their work on Oak Island. Amundsen had stepped way over the line in their view when he obliged Baerken by encouraging a letter-writing campaign to Minister of Culture Tony Inces, who was blocking the Peterson-Rafuse bill. Amundsen contacted some "Norwegian Oak Island enthusiasts who supported the legislation," he said, and "Rick was very unhappy when he found out about that." Amundsen sent an email to Kevin Burns and Joe Lessard acknowledging that he had been lobbying for the bill. "I also expressed my understanding, should they need to prevent me from appearing in season two, to which I had been invited."

The dispute became moot when the Peterson-Rafuse bill was defeated in Parliament, and the special permission to dig on Oak Island remained intact.

THERE WAS SOME IRONY at least in the fact that all of the most notable finds the Laginas had made during those earlier seasons had come from the swamp. Early in season one Dan Blankenship had explained to Rick and Marty that while there'd been a lot said about the metal stakes and wooden posts that he and Fred Nolan discovered in the swamp, the most significant thing they'd found were the stumps of old oak trees. What this suggested was that the swamp had at one point been dry land and was man-made, most likely by holding back the water with a cofferdam, digging out the triangle shape, then letting it fill with freshwater. It had always been an intriguing notion. Fred Nolan had been advancing a related theory in these past years: He believed that Oak Island probably had been two close but separate islands in the past and that at some point someone had sailed a ship between the two islands, then allowed it to founder and sink, before joining the two landmasses with what became the swamp. It tied in to Fred's other theory that the Money Pit was a deliberate distraction and that the treasure was buried closer to the surface someplace else on the island. An arborist was brought in to examine one such stump that the Laginas and their team managed to pull from the swamp. He could only say that it was hardwood and that he found it highly unlikely that it could have grown in water. Eventually the stump would be dated to between 1450 and 1640 by another expert who was absolutely convinced that the swamp was man-made.

All of that had given the others enough leverage to overcome Marty's objections and arrange for the swamp to be pumped out—or rather down. Pumping in the swamp truly was dangerous work; the pockets of hydrogen sulfide that produced the swamp's rotten egg stench were highly flammable and running motors near them could have caused an explosion. Luckily, it didn't, but unluckily the search for something of value in the swamp yielded no results—until the maravedi was discovered in the final episode of season one.

Season two had begun with a trip to Global Marine Exploration in Tampa, Florida, a company that salvages coins from shipwrecks. The coin they'd found was no treasure—closer in value to a copper penny than a silver dollar, in point of fact, Global's experts said—but after cleaning it they had been able to find a date on the maravedi: 1652.

This information led to the only winter scenes of the show ever shot, with Rick and Marty dragging a sled loaded with the Deepmax X6 across the ice and snow to the swamp, accompanied by the machine's operator, Dave Spencer. When Spencer began to get hits, they were of nonferrous metals, which meant possibly gold and silver but also copper. His graph was showing him a chamber or container of some sort about the size of the War Room tabletop, about 15 to 20 feet below the surface, Spencer said. It was either right at or very near the spot Petter Amundsen had selected as the Mercy Point.

The Laginas were back in the spring, this time to use caissons to isolate and drain the Mercy Point. It was fairly compelling drama up to the point they found absolutely nothing. At that point, it seemed like the right decision to abandon the swamp for the time being.

I wanted the show to stay in the water, though. To me, the most promising line of inquiry *The Curse of Oak Island* had pursued was in its offshore explorations. These had been limited, however, and the lack of follow-up was terribly disappointing. Diving about 300 feet off the south shore, Tony Sampson had found two triangular rocks pointing in a line straight at the Money Pit. I had the feeling there would be others, but I also knew, having paddled through the thick beds of kelp just offshore, that it would become increasingly difficult to find them. Still, I thought they should have tried. The show had acknowledged that Blair's 1898 dye test proved that the flood system that had been for two-hundred-plus years the main obstacle to exploring the Money Pit was connected to the south shore. There'd been an attempted replication of that test, but the dye being used in 2015 instead of red was a very difficult-to-see green that was dropped down 10X rather than into the Money Pit. That effort fizzled, but I began pushing for another try within a couple of days of arriving in Nova Scotia. Almost certainly, it seemed to me, the south shore was the main source of the water that now saturated the east-end drumlin. Blair's results, after all, had been confirmed by the second dye test conducted by Hamilton in 1938. And a connection between 10X and the ice holes Dan Blankenship had spotted off the south shore in the harsh winters of 1979 and 1987 left little doubt that openings in the seabed off the south shore were sending most of the water into the flood system. Those openings likely hadn't been in the seabed but rather on the beach, probably near the high tide line, at the time the Money Pit had been dug.

Back in 2003, Fred Nolan told me about an offshore survey of Oak Island that had been conducted in the early 1960s by a group of Nova Scotia divers. David Tobias later confirmed that Fred was right about this. I'd lost interest when Fred told me the diver leading the survey, Eric Hamblin, had believed Oak Island was where the treasure of Tumbes had been buried. I was pretty sure even back then that was about as unlikely a theory of Oak Island as had ever been put forward. But now, in 2017, it occurred to me that Fred had also told me that the most interesting thing those divers had found all those years earlier was a hole in the seafloor off the south shore that they were convinced was man-made. The first chance I had to talk to Dan Blankenship, I mentioned this to him and he stared at me for a moment, his eyes wide in surprise. "I think I know what you're talking about," he said. He had found just such an opening off the south shore himself back in the late sixties, Dan said. He'd actually used an air hose to blow away the debris around the opening, and had showed it to his son, David, but he had become distracted by other things and forgotten all about it. "Today's the first time I've thought of it in almost fifty years," he told me. Dan was ninety-three now and hard of hearing, but his mind was still remarkably acute; I was pretty sure his recollection could be trusted. Armed with his story, I made the case to the producers for more exploration off the south shore; maybe Dan and David together could remember approximately where the hole in the seafloor could be found. But neither the production team nor I could locate any documentation of the early sixties survey or any divers who'd participated in it, Eric Hamblin included. I asked my diver friend Tony Sampson to make some inquiries and he did, but he came up with nothing. Not surprising, considering it had taken place more than a half century earlier. I suggested consulting Fred Nolan, and it was then that I learned that Fred was no longer with us.

CHAPTER TWENTY-FOUR

One of my favorite parts of the show had been the relationship that developed between Fred Nolan and Rick Lagina. I was quite familiar with how difficult Fred could be and how hard he made people work to get any kind of information about Oak Island out of him. Rick, though, had won him over as thoroughly as anyone ever had. Part of this transformation was that Fred had finally begun to face his mortality. He was eighty-seven when Rick met him, and far more gaunt and frail looking than he'd been even back in 2003. I came to realize that it was Rick's enthusiasm for the treasure hunt combined with his respect for those who had conducted it that largely made the relationship with Fred work. Rick's demeanor was entirely genuine and a big part of what contributed to his winning personality, onscreen and off. Honoring those who'd come before him was to Rick an important reason for the show's existence and his participation in it. Fred had come to acknowledge that, and some of the frost on the old fellow had melted. "I don't want to be an obstacle anymore," he had told Rick at one point. "I'm too old for that now."

This didn't mean, of course, that Fred was prepared to share everything he knew. I was amazed that Rick had been able to get Fred to confess during one of their off-camera conversations that just as Dan Blankenship suspected, he had moved many of the objects and markers he'd found on Oak Island over the years. Their original locations, though, were all recorded on his map of the island, Fred said. That map was Nolan's life's work, a chart on which he'd recorded more than fifty years of discovery on Oak Island. After weeks of back and forth, he had finally agreed to share it with Rick, on camera, and that was no small thing. To my knowledge, Fred had never let another living soul see his map. The scene in which this was supposed to happen, though, was a complete fiasco. First, Fred had presented Rick with what he said was his map but turned out to be something else. Rick told me it was the only time he'd ever lost his temper with Fred. After Fred more or less confessed to what he'd done, he agreed to let Rick, and Rick alone, see his map at his house on Joudrey's Cove. When Rick arrived at the appointed time, however, there was no answer to his knock. He didn't know if Fred was inside pretending not to be home or had actually left, but he'd never gotten to see the map.

Now Rick was concerned that he never would. Fred had died at age eighty-nine on June 6, 2016, about six weeks before my arrival in Nova Scotia. It wasn't until the show aired the following November that I saw the scene where Rick went to Dan Blankenship's house to tell him Fred had passed. Recalling how Dan had cursed Nolan for the things he'd done to conceal or disguise his discoveries over the years, it was strangely moving to hear him observe that while Fred was "a little bit on the secretive side," so were most treasure hunters, himself included.

Rick was struggling now with his concern that all of Nolan's research might never be seen, at least by him. Fred's son, who felt he had already lost his father to Oak Island many years earlier, was said to be despondent about facing that this loss was now permanent, and he was nowhere near ready to make decisions about how to dispose of the enormous collection of objects and documents Fred had accumulated in more than fifty years on Oak Island. Promises that had been made to Rick but never put in writing were just whispers in the wind now and it seemed inevitable that the son would soon realize his father's research was worth money—perhaps a lot of money—to someone somewhere.

The older Lagina brother sounded sincere, though, when he observed that what pained him most was that Fred had not lived until the end of this year. Because in the summer of 2016 he and Marty and the rest of them were poised to make a search of the island that would be more comprehensive than all they'd done in the previous three seasons of *The Curse of Oak Island*. That sounded a trifle grandiose to me, until I paid my first visit to the Money Pit since 2003. It was a different place.

The production had kept me away from the Money Pit for my first week on Oak Island, preferring to shoot scenes of me doing research at the Genealogical Society, among other locations. I knew something major was happening at the east-end drumlin, though, because of the steady stream of big trucks that were carrying loads of gravel in that direction. Rick—and Marty especially—seemed very excited about what was going on, but all the details were withheld from me so my initial reaction to the changes taking place could be caught on camera. Both my astonishment and mixed emotions were genuine when Rick and Marty walked me to the high spot that provided an overview of what had once been the crown of the east-end drumlin but was now an acre-sized, three-foot-thick platform of gravel. It was utterly unrecognizable as the place I had first seen thirteen years earlier. In 2003, in spite of all that had been visited on the east-end drumlin in the previous two centuries, the Money Pit area still had the quality of a living history. This was mainly due to all the wrecked, broken or abandoned machinery and other equipment that had been pushed to the side each time a new expedition arrived on Oak Island, offering mute testimony of what had taken place. The ghosts of Frederick Nolan, Gilbert Hedden, Melbourne Chappell, Robert Restall and, yes, even Robert Dunfield had haunted the place. They were gone now.

The enormous pad of gravel, which was still being built up with dump truck load after dump truck load, then spread by bulldozers, would be necessary to support the three-hundred-ton crane that would hoist the caissons (steel chambers, air locked at the top, whose air pressure would repel the water below the work area) that were then to be driven into the ground by an oscillator that itself weighed five tons. One location where the first 40-inch-wide metal cylinder would be put down was called C1 because it had been chosen by Charles Barkhouse as his best guess as to the location of the original Money Pit. That seemed appropriate; Charles knew as much or more than anyone about the history of Oak Island and his guess was likely to be an informed one.

The prep work had been going on for weeks already, beginning with the construction of a new road that had been built to accommodate the enormous rigs required to carry the two cranes (the second was a mere hundred-ton model) that would be used to lift, lower, and place the caissons. While the pad was being created, the Laginas and the rest of the cast had been spending a good deal of their time in one of the two other locations that had been selected as the focus of this season's efforts on Oak Island. That, of course, was the swamp, which the Laginas had obtained permission from Fred Nolan, before his death, to drain as much water from as possible.

The stated goal of that summer's work in the swamp was to determine whether it had formed naturally centuries earlier or was man-made, and whether Nolan's theory that a ship had been deliberately sunk there to conceal the treasure it carried held any water. "Why are there stumps in the swamp?" Marty asked. "Because trees grew there once, obviously."

They had already spent $2 million in the Money Pit area that summer, but what they were doing in the swamp was costing even more, Marty told me. The first find they had been rewarded with was the 18-foot-long wooden plank Tony Sampson brought up from just below the surface of the water. It had to be either deck or side planking from a masted ship all agreed. Considering how thin the plank was, it seemed almost certain it was from the ship's deck. A company called Beta Analytic ran carbon-dating tests and came back with a report that the ship had been built sometime between 1680 and 1735, with 90 percent likelihood. As this was being explained to me I had the feeling for the first time that the search was actually getting somewhere.

Once 90 percent of the water in the swamp had been pumped out (and, for environmental reasons, into the Cave-in Pit), the backhoe was brought in to lift out bucket upon bucket of foul-smelling muck that would be dumped into an enclosure made of hay bales and sandbags that the crew called the cattle pen. Jack Begley, my favorite by far among the younger people on the show, in part because he was always willing to take on a dirty job, was literally covered with the filth of the cattle pen as he swept it with a metal detector. Then the man who had been chosen as the best at locating metal objects in this kind of slimy mess, Gary Drayton, arrived to take over, scanning the cattle pen with his own, more high-powered detector. Drayton was a sturdy Brit with a piping voice and a charming sense of humor who wore a billed cap to cover his bald dome. He had made his bones as a "mud larker" (a scavenger in river mud) back in Lincolnshire, England, but was better known these days for searching shipwrecks out of his home base in Florida. Drayton had not taken long to locate a heavy lead spike—he called it a nail—in the spoils from the swamp. He recognized it immediately as the type of nail that was used to hold down the deck planks of old ships; he said he had found a number of identical nails on Spanish galleons from the 1600s.

A decision was made to seek confirmation from an antiques appraiser. Dr. Lori Verderame, better known as Dr. Lori, was a familiar face on television from her appearances on the Discovery Channel's *Auction Kings* and the Fox Business Network's *Strange Inheritance*. After examining the spike-size nail, Verderame identified it as a wrought iron deck nail called a *barrote*, which in Spanish meant simply "iron bar." She dated it to earlier than 1652, meaning it was made before the coin that had been found in the swamp at the end of the show's first season. The barrote, the length of planking, along with the scuppers Fred Nolan had earlier pulled out of the swamp, all added support to Nolan's theory that a Spanish galleon had been sunk where the swamp now lay.

Gary Drayton, though, was making finds on another part of the island that seemed to point away from Spain and toward the British. With Charles Barkhouse in tow, Drayton was using his metal detector to scan much of Oak Island's lot 24, owned during the early 1800s by Samuel Ball. I noticed that when these scenes aired later in the year, there was no mention of the fact that there had been many metal detector searches of the island in previous years, most notably the exhaustive one conducted by Peter Beamish and his students from Phillips

THE CURSE OF OAK ISLAND

Academy. Knowing how picked over the island already was, I found it fairly impressive that Drayton was able to come up with what he at first thought was a coin, then decided must be a "dandy button" of the sort used on the cuffs of British military officers during the eighteenth century. Drayton also found a British coin on lot 24, one engraved with the name and likeness of King George II, which would have placed it in the mid-1700s, and a lead ingot like the one British soldiers had used for making musket balls in the same time frame. All of this suggested to Drayton that there had been a British military encampment on Oak Island at some point prior to 1795. Or, I thought to myself, all of it could have belonged to Samuel Ball himself, who after all had served with the British army during the Revolutionary War.

Still, there *was* something exhilarating about this accumulation of small discoveries and the giddy speculation that they could add up to more confirmation of Fred Nolan's theory that the treasure of Havana had been secreted on Oak Island. I realized that beneath a veneer of detachment I was as susceptible to the wish to believe as any of the others involved with *The Curse of Oak Island*. Unlike them, though, I had to consider the possibility that the finds made by Drayton might support what everyone associated with the island regarded as their least favorite theory, the one that had been proposed by a woman from Sydney, Nova Scotia, named Joy Steele.

IT SOUNDED PLAUSIBLE when I first heard it described, and even in the brief introduction of it that I read in Joy Steele's book, *The Oak Island Mystery Solved*. Steele described herself as a longtime member of various Oak Island forums who had been more or less obsessed with various theories associated with the place, until she got seriously ill and while convalescing realized that "Oak Island was the site of naval stores installation, part of a mercantilist scheme engineered between the British government and a company of English merchants in the early part of the 18th century." By "stores," Steele meant tar, raw turpentine, pitch, and rosin, all made by cooking down the crude gum oleoresin that comes out of pine trees. The Money Pit, Steele contended, "was none other than a ground kiln constructed to produce naval stores for use of either the British Admiralty and/or use by the South Sea Company in its triangular slave trade."

Steele had done an extraordinary amount of research into the British naval stores industry in the Americas that thrived between 1713 and 1720, as a result of the Act for the Encouraging of the Importation of Naval Stores of 1705. Most of her book in fact was derived from various records and documents associated with the production and transport of naval stores by the South Sea Company at the behest of the Crown. There were detailed accounts of businesses created for the production of tar among Virginia's Jamestown colonists and the Palatine Germans of New York. It made for tedious reading, but the curious thing was that absolutely none of it made any direct connection to Oak Island. That alone spoke a good deal about the weakness of Steele's theory: the fact that both the British government and the South Sea Company kept such detailed records of their naval stores, and yet there was not a single mention of any such operation on Oak Island was a strong indication that there had been none.

What Steele had done, I realized, was to take a slender implied connection to the island and built her entire case on it. This was a letter written by a member of the British Parliament named Thomas Harley in 1720 in which, speaking of Nova Scotia as a possible source of naval stores, he stated, "They are likewise to have some pretty island in those parts, which is not yet peopled, and therefore more valuable." Really, that was all she had, aside from the fact that also in 1720 Colonel Richard Phillips had sailed into Annapolis Royal with orders that vast tracts of forest in Nova Scotia should be set aside as Crown reserves. That order specifically cited that the white pine trees in those forests should be used for "masts and timber." It probably wasn't unreasonable to assume that some of those trees, or their stumps at least, might have been used to cook tar and turpentine, but Steele had no evidence of it. She did think it was quite important, though, that one of those tracts—one among dozens—was set along the LaHave River, which emptied into Mahone Bay. It might have been enough to establish a thesis, but it was far from the proof Steele implied when she wrote, "All evidence weighted, Oak Island strongly appears to be the island Thomas Harley talked about in his letter."

Steele also tended to cherry-pick the written record—often including highly dubious sources to buttress her claim. She cited what Edward Rowe Snow had written in *True Tales of Buried Treasure* about "tales" of men silhouetted against fires on the island that had been seen in the early eighteenth century, whom she asserted were the operators of the "ground kiln." Any reasonable person would have read Snow's account as apocryphal. He cited not a single source, other than "tales" he claimed to have heard from people he didn't identify. Worse was the enormous fuss Steele made over the fact that one of the pieces of wood that Robert Dunfield had pulled out of the Money Pit had been white pine. She seemed completely oblivious to the fact that nearly every treasure-hunting team attempting to get to the bottom of the Pit had built or rebuilt the cribbing reinforcing it. Almost certainly, the piece of pine was a fragment of that cribbing. Steele used the inconclusive Woods Hole Oceanographic Institution dye test as evidence that there was no flood system on the east-end drumlin, and echoed Captain Henry Bowdoin's claim that the water was simply "percolating" not pouring into the Money Pit. I was certain there was no way she wouldn't have known about the Money Pit dye tests conducted by Frederick Blair and Edwin Hamilton. It was possible that Steele didn't know about the ice holes Dan Blankenship had spotted in 1979 and 1987, but it was impossible that she could be unaware of the various tests that had established water poured into the Money Pit at a rate of between four hundred and eight hundred gallons a minute. And Captain Henry Bowdoin's false claims had clearly been a form of extortion or vengeance.

It took me longer than it should have to realize that what Steele had offered as the strongest pieces of evidence for her theory actually

disproved it. It was a line at the end of her naval stores narrative that
did it. The South Sea Company "bubble burst" in 1720, she had written, and "Oak Island and the naval stores produced there was but one
casualty among many ruined and abandoned enterprises." The one piece
of evidence on which Steele's thesis rested was that letter from Thomas
Harley about "some pretty island" in Nova Scotia (which has literally
thousands of pretty islands). The Harley letter, though, had been written
in December 1720, just as the bubble, as Steele described it, was bursting.
No more such facilities were set up in Nova Scotia after that date, at
least not by the South Sea Company or its partners in the British navy.

The other "aha!" piece of evidence Steele had offered was a set of
instructions for constructing a tar kiln used by Jonathan Bridger, surveyor general of His Majesty's Woods in America, dated 1706. Those
instructions stated that one should begin by digging a pit "eight feet
deep, twenty foot wide at top, sloping towards bottom." The Money
Pit was more than 100 feet deep, which is to say at least twelve times
as deep as Bridger's instructions called for, and more deep than wide,
which would have severely limited the supply of oxygen to feed the fire
at the bottom.

Steele had, however, done considerable research, making a good
case to defeat the claim that the Money Pit was a natural sinkhole, the
favorite theory of the most determined Oak Island skeptics. And Steele
had discovered some interesting documents related to the South Sea
Company's involvement in the slave trade, which included human trafficking in Nova Scotia. In Lunenburg, during the years when it was
becoming a major shipbuilding center, most of the well-to-do in town
had owned slaves, Steele found. While there was no actual evidence to
support her claim that those slaves had been manufacturing naval stores
on Oak Island, her research did support the possibility that slaves might
have been involved in the excavation of the Money Pit and the construction of the artificial beach on Smith's Cove. Steele had devoted a good
deal of research to the inscribed stone. Like me, she had concluded
after looking at all the evidence that the stone must have existed. But

she had accepted without reservation that the inscription on the stone was the rows of symbols that had been translated to read: "Forty feet below, two million pounds lies buried." Those 2 million pounds, Steele asserted, were the capital allotted to the naval stores operation on Oak Island, and the inscription was a sardonic epitaph on that operation, written for some reason in code.

Steele did help me find new information about the inscribed stone, however, in her mention of the long-out-of-print 1929 article "The Oak Island Treasure" by Charles Driscoll. Trying to find the Driscoll piece had led me to a research group headed by the Swedish Baconian Daniel Ronnstam that was attempting to locate the inscribed stone.

The Ronnstam group had obtained a bit more information about Jothan McCully, finding records of his birth on January 19, 1819, in Truro and his death on September 9, 1899, also in Truro, where he had fathered ten children and worked at a train station when he was not employed on Oak Island. Ronnstam was convinced by the story (told by Charles Driscoll and subsequently repeated by others) that McCully in the early 1860s had taken the inscribed stone to his own home after the Smith family sold the house where it had been part of the fireplace, and that it was from there that the stone had been moved to Creighton and Marshall in Halifax. Ronnstam also had accepted the description of the rock as 1 foot thick, roughly cut into a 2-foot square. He and his team were pursuing the theory that the stone was today part of the foundation of a home on the south shore. They'd had no luck in locating it.

During season two the production had undertaken a brief but quickly abandoned inquiry into the whereabouts of the stone that largely involved using Charles Barkhouse's connections to Nova Scotia's Masonic Grand Lodge, where the librarian agreed to scour the archives looking for information on Jothan McCully. The librarian reported back that there was no mention of the man, but he had found that a James Pitblado, whose profession had been listed as "drilling engineer," had been a lodge officer at one point. But there was nothing further and no record of where the mysterious Pitblado and whatever he had plucked from that drill bit back in 1849 had gone. I suggested to the producers of *The Curse of Oak Island* that I could hook up with this group and join their search.

The producers told me they already had their own team searching for the inscribed stone and I was told they had produced the first real leads to what had happened to the stone after the closing of Creighton and Marshall in the 1930s. That wasn't a complete exaggeration, although most would date the last recorded sighting of the stone to 1909, when Henry Bowdoin had seen it. The two principals of Blockhouse Investigations, Doug Crowell and Kel Hancock, had obtained permission to explore the building on Upper Water Street that had once housed the bookbindery. With Charles Barkhouse and Marty Lagina's son Alex in tow, they had joined up with Dr. Allan Marble, the former president of the Royal Nova Scotia Historical Society. After a search of the building's basement, where the only really interesting thing they found was a boarded-up military tunnel, Dr. Marble revealed a recent conversation with the son of a former member of the nearby Halifax Club, who said his father had told him he believed a stone set into the floor of the club's headquarters was the "90-foot stone" from Oak Island. The Halifax Club had been formed in 1862 and continued to operate as a hub of social activity among Halifax's most prominent businessmen and women. It certainly seemed possible that some lore connected to the Oak Island stone might have been passed down through the decades. The group's visit to the Halifax Club building, though, produced absolutely nothing. They not only found no one familiar with the story of the stone being built into the club's floor, but they also discovered that the building was in the midst of a remodeling project. The construction supervisors had suggested looking in the basement, where a good many items had been removed for storage, but there was no sign of the stone.

What we all were certain of was that the stone still existed; crushing it would have been pointless and because it was so dense that job would have been a difficult one, anyway. Even if it was found, though, I doubted the stone would reveal much; Harry Marshall's 1935 description of the inscription as worn away by the bookbindery's leather workers rang true. The chances were infinitesimal that we were ever going to know for certain what the inscription on the stone had been. It was one more mystery of Oak Island that no one was likely to solve.

Accepting the fact that after more than two centuries of search and exploration there was still more about Oak Island we didn't know than we did made it difficult to issue definitive statements about anything connected to the island. I was prepared to say, for instance, that I thought Joy Steele's theory was extremely unlikely, but I wasn't prepared to say that it absolutely was not true, and likewise with the inscription on the stone. In one of our conversations, Rick Lagina had characterized Steele as "one of those people who really need to believe they're right, and can't consider any other possibilities. For people like you and me, though, it's impossible to rule anything out, until we know we have the answer. And the only way to get that is to bring up whatever's down there."

CHAPTER TWENTY-FIVE

The first time I ever spoke at any length with Rick, he told me that the only way he would continue with the show for another season "is if we find something significant this summer." Only a day later, Marty ended a conversation with me about the endless stream of theories about Oak Island by saying: "The only thing that really matters is what we can find, see with our own eyes, and hold in our own hands."

I wondered if Rick would feel they had hit the mark of "something significant" with the maravedi and the coin and button found by Gary Drayton. I doubted it. And I knew Marty would say that all they had actually seen or held that summer were more clues that pointed in multiple directions. The younger brother in particular seemed to need verification of claims from the past, a sense that the stories they had been told could be trusted. Marty even refused to accept without reservation what had been written for more than a century and a half about the drainage system connected to Smith's Cove. He and Rick and the others had all agreed that a search for some remaining evidence of that system, something that hadn't been torn apart by Dunfield and those who preceded him, should be one of the summer's major projects.

They had begun with the same first step as so many others before them, the installation of a cofferdam that would block the tide from entering the cove and permit it to be drained. The Laginas and their partners, though, had access to equipment and technology that the members of the Onslow and Truro companies couldn't have begun to imagine. In this case, that was an enormous system of inflatable rubber bladders that completely enclosed Smith's Cove and gave the brothers 9,000 square feet below the high tide line that could be excavated and searched.

A good deal of the digging was by hand and Jack Begley did a lot of it, not only without complaint, but with genuine enthusiasm. Jack was dealing with a medical condition that had forced him to drop out of college and spend the entire winter and spring recuperating, so I was pleased that he was the one to find the first coconut fibers beneath the sand and clay on Smith's Cove, and it was gratifying as well when Dan Henskee looked at the fibers and announced this was the place to dig deeper. Henskee was supervising the excavation at the cove, owing to his memory of the undisturbed drainage system from thirty years earlier. Henskee's elevated role was also due to Rick Lagina's faith in him, one more thing I liked about the older Lagina brother. During one of our conversations, Rick and I each described cringing at the way Dan Blankenship sometimes spoke to "the other Dan" as if he were a simpleminded servant. Henskee sometimes struggled to express himself, but Rick and I agreed that he knew Oak Island as well as anyone alive and maybe better.

The digging in the spot Henskee had selected gradually revealed stratified layers of soil that according to the consulting archeologist, Laird Niven, could only have been created by human beings. Niven also agreed with Henskee that the clay they were digging in was not native to the cove. When the shovels hit blackened wood, it was obvious the excavation had reached the remains of a wooden structure of some sort, most likely the one that Robert Restall had reported finding in his notes from 1964.

Eventually, at a depth of about 5 or 6 feet below the surface, the digging had begun to expose what looked like a rock wall. When he saw that the stones were also in layers, stones of one size above and of another size below, Rick, who had constructed a number of rock walls back in Michigan, said the rocks looked fitted to him. Laird Niven was brought in to take a look and agreed that the wall was man-made. Eventually it became clear that the stones were the sides and the bottom of a long trench. Dan Blankenship came to take a look and declared that it was a French drain. The atmosphere was jubilant. Finding "original work" was the aim of every search effort made on *The Curse of Oak Island*, and Rick announced that he was certain that this *was* original work. No one, including me, was going to argue with him.

During the work at Smith's Cove, Robert Restall's daughter Lee Lamb had made a return trip to Oak Island, presenting the "1704 stone" for inspection. "This *is* the Oak Island treasure," Rick told her as he took the stone into his hands.

Rick's sentimentality had proven to be a key ingredient of *The Curse of Oak Island*'s winning formula, in large part because he wasn't faking his feelings. References to "Rick's big heart" were a refrain among the members of the show's crew, who all respected him immensely. Rick had told me himself that he believed the emotional connections being made among the people involved in the production and in the treasure hunt itself "might be the real purpose of all this." Rick also treated every person who approached him with a theory of Oak Island, even the most agitated crackpots, with unfailing courtesy. He said that since no one really knew what Oak Island was about he felt an obligation to listen with an open mind to whatever ideas people brought him.

This was also, however, how Rick explained being open to what some would regard as fringe histories often featured on *The Curse of Oak Island*. There, he and I parted ways. I could see that Rick was a bit hurt and slightly offended by my rejection of the Templar theory. Within a couple of weeks of arriving in Nova Scotia I had given up arguing the case, but I truly had to bite my tongue when the La Formule cipher showed up.

THE SHEAF OF DOCUMENTS and the map of Nova Scotia and Oak Island that included the La Formule cipher had been presented to the Laginas by Doug Crowell of Blockhouse Investigations. Crowell and his partner, Kel Hancock, were amateur historians who had spent twenty years investigating the various loose ends associated with the Oak Island treasure hunt. Though often the object of their investigations was obscure stuff that ultimately went nowhere, some of it, especially what had been culled from long-dead Nova Scotia newspapers more than a century old and public records from remote municipalities, provided rich texture to what had been bare-bones tales and legends. But when Crowell presented the Laginas with the story of a lady in New York whose investigation had followed the Templars from Jerusalem to France to Scotland to the New World, I reacted with a skepticism that bordered on suspicion. The woman, Zena Halpern, described the papers in her possession, claiming an associate of hers had discovered them tucked into the back pocket of a book she had been given several years earlier.

These documents, Halpern said, were dated from 1178 to 1180 and described a Templar voyage to the northeast part of the North American continent, where their ship made landfall on "an island of oaks." Then, "when I found the map, which is dated 1347, I began to put the pieces together," Halpern explained to the Laginas. The mystery of the island, she revealed, was connected to African gold that had been under the protection of King David's army commander Joab. How exactly the Templars had gotten hold of it, Halpern didn't say.

Halpern was best known up to that point for her association with the Burrows Cave, a purported hole in the ground that a man named Russell Burrows claimed to have stumbled upon—or into—while taking a walk through the Illinois countryside one April day in 1982. I say "purported" because in the thirty-five years since Burrows's alleged discovery, he hasn't allowed other people to take a look at his cave, out of fear, he has insisted, that it would be ruined by looters if its exact location were ever known. What Burrows *has* done is present hundreds of the thousands of carved stones that he professed to have found in the cave to various archeologists and epigraphers (inscription scholars) including former Harvard zoology professor Barry Fell,

RANDALL SULLIVAN

whose studies of other stone artifacts have made him perhaps the most famous diffusionist in the United States, if often considered an outlier by his colleagues. Zena Halpern had herself become one of those who traffic in theories about the ways in which cultures all over the planet have been communicating and sharing since much further back in time than mainstream historians believe. Halpern was also among those who have embraced the claim that the Burrows Cave was filled with inscriptions written in Egyptian, Sumerian, Greek, Etruscan, and other ancient languages that were never spoken in North America. University-affiliated historians, on the other hand, including Barry Fell, have not only rejected but also openly derided Burrows's claims. Fell publicly denounced the carved stones Burrows had given him as fakes and observed that one of them, the so-called elephant stele, had obviously been copied from his own book, *America B.C.* Halpern, though, had written extensively in defense of the Burrows Cave artifacts, publishing alleged translations of what some peer-reviewed scholars dismissed as gibberish.

What most excited the Laginas when they took a look at Halpern's "1347 map" were the various notations written in French on it. The body of land depicted was, as Marty correctly stated, "clearly Oak Island." Written alongside various markings on the map were identifiers that included: "The Basin," "The Marsh," "The Dam," "The Anchor," "The Valve," and, most intriguing, "The Hatch."

People had been searching for the "walk-in tunnel," as R. V. Harris had described it, since the nineteenth century. Fred Nolan and Dan Blankenship had between the two of them stepped across just about every inch of ground on Oak Island without ever finding this entrance to the treasure chamber, but both men had continued to believe it existed. I also believed it likely existed, though I had a feeling it might now be underwater. For those who didn't hold Zena Halpern's involvement in the Burrows Cave theory against her, the possibility was tantalizing that the map could show them the way into the Oak Island treasure vault.

I have to admit my heart skipped a beat when Jack Begley pointed out that the location of the Hatch on Halpern's 1347 map was on the west side of Oak Island near where the Blankenships lived, and then Dave Blankenship said he had stumbled into a "depression" in the ground right near there while out trailing a deer one day. Dave showed the others that depression, which Marty characterized as "a square hole chiseled into bedrock by humans," because there was no geological explanation for it. Laird Niven was summoned and agreed with Marty that it was "strange" and "odd," not a natural formation. Jack Begley probed the bottom and sides with a shovel, striking only rock under the soil, but suggested the wooden door to the Hatch might have rotted away. It was Jack who had made an overlay of the 1347 map on a current map of Oak Island and determined that the depression near the Blankenships' homes was almost exactly where the 1347 map placed the Hatch. Despite what I suspected about the map, I was rooting for Jack and Rick as they dug and chiseled in the depression to see if it contained an opening that led someplace. It didn't.

Kevin Knight, a professor of computer science at the University of Southern California, was contacted to test Halpern's claims. Knight's reputation as perhaps the leading authority in the world on "machine translation and decipherment," as a *Los Angeles Times* article put it, had been cemented by what was widely viewed as a successful translation of the famous Copiale Cipher, a 105-page, 75,000-character cipher that the professor's computer program had proved to be the work of a secret society from the 1730s called the High Enlightened Occultist Order. The producers of *The Curse of Oak Island* had given Knight the La Formule cipher provided by Zena Halpern, written on a page that had been torn away at the edges, so that pieces of it were missing. When Knight reported back, he said his computer program had determined that French was the main language behind the cipher, which it had translated to read as follows (with some words missing at the ends or beginnings of lines):

> *Halt. Do not burrow/dig to*
> *Forty foot with an angle of forty*
> *five degree the shaft of five hundred*
> *twenty two foot you enter the*
> *corridor of one thousand sixty-five foot*
> *reach the chamber*

Knight's critics said his computer program was capable of finding meaning where there was none. Still, I felt that speck of doubt inside me become a drop of wonder.

When the production made a quick pivot to follow the Templar trail from Zena Halpern to the village of New Ross in the rugged northeast corner of Lunenburg County, about twenty-two miles inland from the Atlantic Ocean on the banks of the Gold River, however, it was further than I could go. How the remains of a nineteenth-century blacksmith shop have been transformed into the ruins of the castle that Henry Sinclair/Glooskap built nearly five hundred years earlier is one of more bizarre skeins that runs through the Oak Island story. It goes back to the 1970s and a woman named Joan Harris who married delusions of grandeur to extreme gullibility and gave birth to the whole idea.

Not long after Joan Harris and her husband, Ron, bought their property on high ground just outside New Ross in 1972, the couple began to landscape their yard and discovered the relatively modest remains of stone walls along with artifacts that she decided were evidence that the property had been home to first a Viking castle with seven towers, and second a Scottish mansion with twelve marble pillars and a golden dome. Her most sensational find, Harris would maintain, was an iron implement that was described as the tip of an ancient Viking sword that had been made with a "blood channel."

Eventually Joan Harris would author and self-publish *A Castle in Nova Scotia*, in which ghosts and aliens in UFOs are added to the story as guardians of a property where "Phoenicians, Celts, Mi'kmaqs, Norsemen and other Europeans" had lived and practiced various religions over the years. Harris, who claimed to regularly commune with the ghosts who haunted her property, said that some of them were members of a cult of phallic worship.

Before the book, Harris had written letters, dozens and dozens of them, many directed to Canada's national Minister of Environment, who eventually dispatched an archeologist from Parks Canada, Charles Lindsay, to investigate. Lindsay visited the property, interviewed Harris, and examined the artifacts and other evidence on display. In his subsequent report to Parks Canada, Lindsay wrote that nothing he had been shown predated the nineteenth century, and that the walls of foundations of the supposed castle and mansion were mostly just linear piles of stones from field clearing, plus some rough stone foundations of modest outbuildings that had been constructed later. The supposed Viking sword was actually the blade of a scythe, Lindsay wrote, and probably dated to the twentieth century.

Lindsay had actually tried to be nice about it, at least publicly. Interviewed by a local newspaper called the *Lighthouse*, the archeologist diplomatically described Harris's claims as "wild and wonderful," but added that neither he nor the colleague who had accompanied him to the property, Birgitta Wallace, believed they "have any credibility at all." Harris described Lindsay's remarks as "offensive and derogatory," and filed a lawsuit that was eventually thrown out of court. The uproar she created, however, attracted the attention of author Michael Bradley, who interviewed Joan Harris, then made use of her claims for his own purposes in *Holy Grail across the Atlantic*. Bradley not only made New Ross famous, but he also cast Joan Harris (whom he called Jeanne MacKay in his book) as the heroic victim of a vast government conspiracy to suppress what she had discovered. In spite of this, Harris came to despise Bradley, mainly because he had discarded most of her theories about the New Ross property in order to turn it into the place where Henry Sinclair had lived as Glooskap when he came to Nova Scotia in the late fourteenth century, as described in the Zeno narrative.

In the years since, various sane and earnest scholars had attempted to set the record straight, pointing out, for example, that the British documents that Judge Mather DesBrisay had relied on in *History of Lunenburg County* establish that New Ross had first been settled in 1816 by Captain William Ross and a company of 172 soldiers recently discharged from the Nova Scotia Fencibles regiment to clear the forest and prepare it for habitation. British surveys as far back as 1815 made no mention of any sign that nonnative people had ever lived there. Finally, historian Brian Culbertson had found an 1817 letter from the surveyor general of Nova Scotia, Charles Morris, suggesting that Captain Ross should find a suitable location for the blacksmith shop of a Mr. Daniel McKay. Culbertson then produced an 1860 survey map that showed a property allotted to McKay in the same location later occupied by the Harrises. What Joan Harris had found, obviously, was what was left of McKay's old blacksmith works.

Harris never accepted that, nor did the tens of thousands who read Michael Bradley's book as a work of history. When the Harrises left their New Ross property in 1990 it was swiftly purchased by Alva and Rose Pye, who had continued to perpetuate—for fun and profit, apparently—the majority of Joan Harris's claims. Now a new couple, researcher and author Alessandra Nadudvari and her partner, Tim Loncarich, had purchased the property and were invited to discuss its "amazing story" on *The Curse of Oak Island*.

Nadudvari and Loncarich were an amiable pair who quite possibly believed their claims about New Ross. Nadudvari was convinced she had seen the Templar cross carved onto what Jean Harris had claimed was a "burial stone," while Loncarich directed the group to the stone well that Harris had imagined was built centuries before it actually was. Loncarich called it the holy well, saying it was known to possess curative powers. The well *was* beautifully made, with four-foot-thick walls of fitted stones from the shores of the Gold River and a level flagstone floor. Tony Sampson was sent down first in a bosun's chair rigged to a pulley that allowed him to rotate 360 degrees. He became excited by a rock that appeared to have a triangle carved on it, with what might be an eye in the center. Later, when he went down in a dive helmet and wet suit, Tony discovered a "broad arrow" carved onto another rock. His claim these were Masonic symbols could have been correct; the well was probably built by stonemasons after all. But none of it meant that New Ross had been a Templar outpost.

Far more compelling to me than the visit to New Ross was the trip to the Franklin D. Roosevelt Presidential Library and Museum in Hyde Park, New York. Doug Crowell's friend Paul Troutman led the expedition and had combed through FDR's personal letter collection, tedious and difficult work that had turned up at least a couple of items I was unaware of. One was a letter to Roosevelt from his former classmate Duncan Harris, who had joined him on those trips to Oak Island in the summer of 1909. The Harris letter didn't say much, but it provided an opportunity for the show's narrator to remind people that FDR had been a Mason and that "many" had suggested a Masonic/Knights Templar connection. The other thing Troutman turned up was a fact of which I had been completely unaware, which was that Henry Bowdoin's notion that the crown jewels of France that were buried on Oak Island had come from FDR, who got them from his maternal grandfather, Warren Delano, a wealthy maritime trader who had invested in the Truro Company back in the middle of the nineteenth century. That nugget of new knowledge, though, did nothing to legitimate the story that the crown jewels had disappeared after Marie Antoinette's lady-in-waiting had been assigned to smuggle them out of France, nor that she had emigrated to Canada, as one account had it, and in the last years of her life told people the crown jewels were buried in Mahone Bay.

Weeks earlier, I had made a point of telling Marty Lagina that the story of the crown jewels being smuggled out of Paris by the servants of the king and queen had been thoroughly discredited long ago, that a mob had stolen them from the Royal Storehouse at the height of the revolution in 1792 and that afterward every single piece of the collection had been recovered, except for the Blue Diamond of Louis XIV, which

covered with silt, not easy for a diver, even Chatterton, to detect in what was basically a zero-visibility environment. Dan Blankenship offered the closing argument. Rick finally made it into Dan's basement, along with his brother and the others, where Blankenship put on the same show-and-tell he had done for me thirteen years earlier, laying out the materials that had come out of 10X back in the early 1970s. What they were looking at was more than anyone had ever brought up out of the Money Pit, Dan stated.

Marty remained reluctant. Their budget was already strained and going back into 10X would limit their operations in the Money Pit area. When Craig Tester agreed with his partner Marty, Rick said he and Dave Blankenship would do the work in 10X themselves. That put Marty on the spot and in the end he announced that he owed it to Dan to do as the old man asked and take another look at 10X. He wouldn't accept any cutback in the work at the Money Pit site, though, so that meant going deeper into his pocket.

THE CAISSONS WERE ALMOST IN PLACE at the first shaft being dug at the Money Pit site by then. The enormity of the three-hundred-ton crane used to lift the caissons was astounding. When work had paused for the weekend, I had Jack Begley take a photo of me standing on the base of that gargantuan rig and could barely make myself out as a tiny dot on the giant object when I brought the picture up on my iPhone.

Both the Lagina brothers believed—or at least hoped—that this first shaft was more or less directly above the Chappell vault. But almost immediately a new dispute arose between Rick and Marty about the pace of the operation. Marty wanted to dig as fast and as deep as possible, because this was their one and only chance at an excavation of the Money Pit and he wanted to accomplish as much as he could, while Rick insisted that they proceed cautiously, for fear of damaging the precious artifacts he believed might be inside the vault. The vault had been breached more than a century earlier, and whatever was in there was long-since soaked with saltwater, Marty pointed out. Rick argued that it might be wet but also intact; he wasn't going to agree to anything potentially destructive. Matters came to a head when the ribbed teeth on the bottom of the caisson began to scrape against what the operator said were horizontal pieces of wood.

Things didn't really begin to get interesting until the crew was ready to send the "hammer grab" down the shaft. This was a long cylinder with what looked like metal jaws at the bottom. After Rick convinced Marty they should lower the hammer grab just 2 inches at a time once they made contact with the wood in the shaft, the apparatus was lifted out, its jaws clutching a large chunk of wood. "We bingoed it!" Marty exulted. Rick was slightly despondent at the amount of damage they might be doing to the vault. More timbers were lifted out of the shaft, but the excitement onsite was soon quieted by the discovery that the wood had been cut with a circular saw, a tool that wasn't used in North America until the late nineteenth century. This certainly wasn't part of the original work. Dan Blankenship was of the opinion they had brought up part of the Chappell shaft, most likely timbers that had shored up the 10-foot stub of a lateral tunnel that had been abandoned because of the cave-ins caused by flooding.

The decision was made to move to the second "target site," C1, the spot chosen by Charles Barkhouse. C1 was where Charles had seen a "shiny gold object" when a camera was sent down the narrow tube of the initial borehole. Much drama was made of sending down a camera to take a look. The pictures that came back seemed to confirm that there was a 21-foot-wide cavity at the bottom of C1, and some of those aboveground thought they saw an opening at a 90-degree angle to the floor of the cavity that could be a tunnel. There was also a moment when the camera seemed to catch sight of something shiny. Craig said it was almost certainly the camera's light reflecting off anhydrite.

It was decided to send the hammer grab down C1. What it brought up, mostly, was big rocks. There were a few splinters of wood, and some of them had come from deep underground, more than 10 feet below the bottom of the stacked caissons, where the void under the bedrock lay below 160 feet. When Charles showed Dan Blankenship one of those splinters, the old man held it to his nose. Dan claimed to be able to tell the age of wood by smelling it and carbon-dating had proven him right about that more than once. This was very old, he told Charles, but most likely not enough to be original work.

JOHN CHATTERTON WAS BACK on the island, preparing for a dive down C1. Before he went into the shaft, though, a new team of sonar experts were going to use equipment from BlueView Technologies to make certain the void at the bottom of the shaft was stable enough for Chatterton to enter and explore the opening "leading off your void," as the chief technician, Blaine Carr, put it. His scans had showed, Carr would explain later, "what looks to be a corridor" opening in the wall about 10 feet from the outer edge of the caisson, about 7 feet high and 10 feet across. The reason he believed it was man-made, Carr said, was that it went at an almost perfectly perpendicular 90-degree angle to the shaft. And the void did seem safe for a diver.

Chatterton again went down wearing a helmet fed by umbilicals. After being lowered through the pipe to the water level, Chatterton quickly descended through the rest of the caisson and within seconds was standing on the bottom of the void at a depth of slightly more than 170 feet. Predictably, visibility was terrible. Chatterton churned silt up from the floor of the void with every move. Going almost entirely by feel, the diver described soft clay beneath his feet, very little water movement, and walls that were extremely irregular. When Chatterton had groped his way to what he thought was the entrance to the corridor, he reported that the roughness of the interior walls suggested to him that it was a man-made feature, something that had been chipped out, because walls worn away by water would have been much smoother.

After Chatterton came up, his partner, Mike Huntley, went down, armed with a metal detector that immediately began to deliver hits. He was fairly certain he had found a "block" of metal embedded in the wall of the void, something that felt smooth and wavy, Huntley reported, but he was unable to pry it loose. He had gotten two more "hard hits" with the metal detector as he probed the clay floor, Huntley said after he returned to the surface. Chatterton himself went down only a short time later with the metal detector and got exactly no hits in either the wall or the floor of C1. The people on the surface looked at one another and said, "Oak Island," in unison.

After some debate about whether to continue exploring C1 or to turn to the third and last planned shaft that was to be put down that season, it was agreed to do the latter. There was considerable disagreement, though, about where to sink it. Gathered in Dan Blankenship's basement around a drawing that had been made by Mel Chappell of where he believed the Money Pit could be found, Marty voted for digging there. Rick, though, wanted to try the northeast corner of the broader target area, while mild-mannered Craig was surprisingly insistent that they should try the southeast. In the end it was decided that Craig should choose the spot for the third shaft. T1, it would be called, T being for Tester.

The probe of T1 looked promising almost immediately. For one thing, they were going much deeper than usual without finding water. Almost always, the seawater in the Money Pit area was reached at a depth of 40 feet or so. The shaft known as Valley3 was just feet away and it was full of water, but T1 stayed dry. Then, when the hammer grab was sent down to a depth of just 102 feet, it came back with a large vertical piece of wood that was clearly hand-sawn; it was the first time that summer that hand-sawn wood had been brought up from underground in the Money Pit area. Craig's speculation that they had probably hit a tunnel dug by the Truro Company rang true, given the depth.

Even more exciting was the 3-inch-diameter round piece of wood that was brought up from 122 feet. It was utterly black and to Craig looked "old-old." Dan Blankenship took a whiff of the round piece and said the odor was the foulest he had ever breathed on Oak Island. This was original work, Dan declared, and carbon-dating seemed to confirm it. The piece from 102 feet was dated to between 1670 and 1780, while the pieces brought up from below 120 feet were dated to between 1655 and 1695. What they had held in their hands, all agreed, were pieces from the original construction of the Money Pit. The hammer grab was sent down again, and the excitement was palpable as it was raised—its jaws holding nothing but chunks of anhydrite floating in clay. The hammer grab went down again and again, with the same result; not even a splinter of wood. At 156 feet they finally hit water, and bedrock was reached soon after. They were done with T1, Marty declared, and no one disagreed.

Rick, though, was not ready to quit for the season. They should try one more shaft he said, at the spot he had suggested. His logic seemed sound to me. A few weeks earlier, he had told me that he was concerned the calculations that had been done as to the exact location of the Money Pit weren't taking into account the 1861 collapse of the Pit, when the bottom hadn't just fallen out, but most likely tumbled in the direction of the tunneling that had caused the collapse, which he believed had come from the southwest. Specifically, he wanted to try 7 feet south and 4 feet west of the spot where Chappell had said the center of the Money Pit would be found.

On camera, Marty made a speech about how Rick deserved to get his wish, because nobody had sacrificed more or been less self-aggrandizing. I had the feeling I believed it more than Rick did. Marty, though, looked genuinely moved when Rick said he wanted to call this last shaft GAL1, for George and Anne Lagina, their parents. Both brothers made regular references to their mother, who sounded like a paragon of pluck, quoting her various maxims: "Forward, always forward" and that sort of thing. I asked Rick once about George and he said his father had been an almost impossibly good man. When I asked him for an example, Rick told me he had once asked his father what his greatest regret might be. George thought about it for a while, then said that he had skipped Mass a couple of times while serving in the army during World War II.

While GAL1 was being put down, there was a return to 10X, where it had been decided to try an "airlift" in which an immense compression system combined with pumps to lower the water level might bring up objects from below. At 235 feet, 10X was still the deepest hole on Oak Island and bringing up hundreds of pounds of sediment from the bottom of the borehole sounded nearly impossible to me, but in fact the operation yielded not one but two moments of suspense that would, at a minimum, carry over into the next season of the show. One of those items brought up out of the borehole offered at least the possibility of confirmation for Dan Blankenship's indefatigable conviction that there was a wealth of information at the bottom of 10X.

Jack Begley and Craig Tester had found that item while washing down the spoils sucked up from the bottom of the borehole. It was a large piece of wood that appeared to be coated with pitchblende, which would have dated it to no later than the mid-eighteenth century. When Dan gave it the smell test, he said it was very old and that he could see it had been cut with a handsaw. It was the first piece of wood cut by men that had ever come out of 10X, said Dan, who was demanding to know how it could possibly be at the bottom of the borehole if there was no tunnel connecting 10X to the Money Pit.

When the long hose connected to the equipment that was essentially vacuuming the bottom of 10X had first been dropped into the shaft, Dan called out to the operator: "Watch out for bones!" The old man was spending as much time as he could watching the airlift operation at 10X, fretting over the possibility that the activity down below could cause a collapse of the fissure in the shaft at a depth of 222 feet. If that happened, Dan knew it would mean that the hole in the ground that had consumed so many years of his life would be closed forever. The collapse never occurred but there was a moment of real drama when the airlift was stopped by an obstruction that had blocked the hose. The bangs and rattles that sounded each time the machine was restarted in an attempt to draw the obstruction through indicated it was a solid object. That was confirmed when the pipe finally cleared and a search of the spoils resulted in the discovery of a bone, whether animal or human I wasn't told.

Though not so obviously exciting, the carbon dating of the hand-sawn wood that had come out of 10X was truly significant. When those dates were reported, I felt fairly confident the search for the tunnel at the bottom of the borehole would continue.

By then the caissons in GAL1 had been driven down to 151 feet, deep enough to start sending the hammer grab into the shaft. Buckets of what appeared to be pieces of primitive cement came up first, then fragments of wood in 6-inch-by-6-inch chunks. When Gary Drayton went over the spoils from GAL1 with his metal detector, he found a piece of hammered iron with a square hole. It was for a square nail, Drayton said, the kind that were used until the end of the 1700s, hand forged with tapering square shafts. The fact that the piece of iron had been pounded flat by hand also suggested a date no later than the eighteenth century.

Larger pieces of wood, square-shaped and hand-cut timbers, began coming up next. Dave Blankenship, who knew construction, said the notches suggested to him they were roof pieces. Craig Tester thought they might be on top of the vault. Then the hammer grab brought up bigger sheets of hammered metal that weren't iron and might have been tin, but felt too heavy for that. There was speculation that they might be from a furnace that had been lowered into the shaft to draw down air.

The anticipation grew every time the hammer grab was lowered another foot, but then suddenly, at 154 feet, the drilling caisson stopped. Whatever it had hit created such friction that the oscillator couldn't turn even slightly. A chisel bit was sent down to act as a battering ram in the hopes the object could be broken or pushed aside. It made only a slight penetration, but it was enough to send down a smaller hammer grab to collect whatever had been loosened. What it came back up with was remarkable, a piece of heavy, rectangular, hand-hammered steel with holes in it that also appeared to have been cut by hand. Craig Tester at once called it a corner piece, which of course raised the possibility that it was from the corner of a chest. Marty would observe only that there was "no modern look to it," nor to the large, thick washer and nut that the smaller hammer grab also brought up from a depth of about 160 feet.

The exploration of GAL1 was brought to a halt when the hammer grab snagged on something so heavy it couldn't be pulled past it. After being lowered and raised repeatedly, the hammer grab finally came loose and was winched to the surface, but the operator and the company he worked for didn't want to send it down again, for fear of losing it. The Laginas and Craig Tester were fearful of destroying whatever it was the hammer grab had been stopped by. And now it was late October; the weather was wetter and cooler each day. Nova Scotia winters begin, for all practical purposes, in November.

The final congregation of the season in the War Room featured a Skype conference with Dr. Lori Verderame, who had analyzed the items recovered from GAL1. One was yet another gold-plated dandy button, dated to between 1775 and 1815, which almost certainly meant it had been on the cuff of either the first or second team of searchers. It was what Craig had called a corner brace, though, that was of most interest. Dr. Verderame described it as a decorative bracket "used to actually attach the metal or wooden sides of treasure chests." She dated it and the other metal pieces brought up out of GAL1 to between 1650 and 1800, which meant they were almost certainly part of the original work. It was arguably, along with the piece of parchment, the most significant artifact ever brought up from underground on Oak Island. And, of course, a good cliffhanger.

CHAPTER TWENTY-SEVEN

Just inside the entrance to the Oak Island Museum, the main display greets visitors with a blowup of my 2003 article, printed on both sides of a framed 8-foot-wide panel. The cast and crew of the show shooting on the island are in and out of the museum daily, and whenever one of them would ask a question or make a remark about the article it was almost always about the title: "Do you really believe Oak Island's cursed?" I do, I'd say. Well, if not cursed, at least haunted.

I had found Oak Island to be a spooky place almost from the moment I'd seen it. In those dreary, sodden days of my 2003 visit, I would stand on the mainland shore and watch the island filter through mists and loom out of fogs in a perpetually fluctuant gloom. The voice of Edgar Allan Poe whispered to me from somewhere deep in adolescent memory, as if I were looking at the remains of a world that had fallen alongside the House of Usher. When I crossed the causeway, there was the sense that time was a wheel spinning me through decades and past centuries. The depredations of Robert Dunfield and the others who had attempted to plunder Oak Island were at once visible and concealed, ugly scars softened by the mosses and vines that flourish in this dank climate. Driving alone or with Dan Blankenship along the broken road that led to the Money Pit, I passed the panorama of what seemed an epic battle of man and nature, most visible in the broken equipment and failed machine parts that lay in the weeds, covered with rust and lichen.

The overwhelmingly eerie sensation of being watched by ghosts and evil spirits had deepened after my meeting with Dan Henskee. In the course of describing what he alternately referred to as "my two nervous breakdowns" and "my spiritual experiences," Henskee had occasionally looked imploringly into my eyes, as if he hoped I would tell him which were the right words. All I knew is that he was talking about the same two incidents, no matter how he categorized them, and that when I listened to Dan's story "spiritual experience" and "nervous breakdown" sounded to me like "cause" and "effect."

Henskee said his troubles had begun in 1973, after Dan Blankenship persuaded him to try dowsing in the vicinity of 10X. Blankenship had told him repeatedly that dowsing worked, even if he didn't know *how* it worked, and within moments of taking the divining rod in his hands he was convinced his mentor had been right. He had "felt an energy" coming up through the ground and entering him. It was an overwhelming experience and not in any way a good one, Dan said. He was so shaken that he handed the rod back to Blankenship, wondering what was happening to him.

The only time I ever saw Dan Blankenship show anything like fear—or at least trepidation—along with what seemed true remorse, was when he described to me what happened after he took Henskee back to his house. "Dan was in my kitchen when he lost it," Blankenship recalled. "All of a sudden it was like something took him over. He said, 'I had to kill you! I had to kill you!' I said, 'Who? What?' He said, 'You lost a chest in the water. I had to kill you.'"

He felt himself being "possessed" by the spirit of a slave who had worked underground on Oak Island. Henskee told me: "One of the other slaves had lost a chest in the water, so they chained him to a post. I knew they were going to torture him to death, so I cut his throat, to let him die quickly. I saw and felt it all with perfect clarity, then I blacked out."

Henskee had been removed from Blankenship's home in a straitjacket and spent the next two weeks in a Halifax psychiatric ward. He returned to Oak Island to work once more alongside Blankenship, but struggled constantly with the fear that something truly dark lay buried beneath the ground he was digging in. Dan told me the entire time he was haunted by things that had been said to him in separate conversations by Fred Nolan and Fred's former associate Ray Nutt. First, Fred had told him that when he let Blankenship talk him into dowsing, what he had taken into his hands was not a "divining rod" but "the Devil's stick," Henskee recalled. Later, Fred advised him that "there are good spirits and there are evil spirits" and that both might be found on Oak Island. Dan sounded as if he had been as surprised as I was to hear of such words coming out of Fred Nolan's mouth; neither of us had imagined that Fred held even the slightest belief in the supernatural. Henskee said not long after that Ray Nutt described experiencing the "presentation of messages or information" on Oak Island. The suggestion was that these had been dark in nature.

Something I didn't tell Dan at the time—or tell anyone else, either—was the mad thought that had come into my own mind the first time I'd gone to the Money Pit area alone. I was standing above 10X, looking down on the ladder whose rungs descended into that black hole, when out of nowhere it struck me that what had been done on Oak Island wasn't designed to keep men out, but to keep something else, something terrifying, in. I shook the idea out of my head, but it returned when Dan Henskee told me about his second nervous breakdown.

Dan said a thought had come to him soon after his return to Oak Island from the psychiatric ward, but he "tried not to think it" and to carry on, and this had worked, sort of, for almost a quarter century. In February 1998, though, his strategy of suppression was overwhelmed by a growing conviction that the Money Pit was the entrance to hell.

"I was raised in an almost completely 'Christian' small town and rural culture in which almost everyone truly believed in the existence of angels, at least one Deity and perhaps also in the existence of 'ghosts' of dead humans," Dan would explain to me by email in the spring of 2017, after I had asked him to reflect on what happened to him on Oak Island in 1998. As a boy, he had heard sermons on and even read passages from the Bible's book of Revelations and he knew that there were at least four references in it to "the bottomless pit. . . . I have checked a couple of dictionaries for definitions of 'metaphysics' and 'metaphysical,'" Dan wrote to me, "and the meanings are not exactly clear. It appears that most people are using these words to refer to vague and perhaps mysterious entities." To him it had seemed obvious back then and still did "that Oak Island is the sort of place where such 'entities' would gather in large numbers." So that was perhaps a sort of explanation for why, in February 1998, he had become convinced that Oak Island was one of several places referred to by the word "Armageddon."

"I felt that 'the final battle' would be a battle for people's minds rather than a physical battle, and that Oak Island might be a sort of focal point," Dan explained in his 2017 email. Back in 2003, though, all Dan had told me was that one frigid February day at dusk he had been stricken with the absolute certainty that evil spirits were about to erupt into the world out of the ground on Oak Island. He tried to escape by stripping off all his clothes and diving into the icy waters of Mahone Bay, then swimming to the shore wearing only a yellow hardhat. He was discovered the next day curled up naked on the floor of a mainland house, and once again he was removed to the psychiatric ward.

One of the ways Dan Henskee had coped—stayed sane, it might be said—was by becoming increasingly religious, although Dan's religion was definitely idiosyncratic rather than doctrinaire. "I decided that the best choice for me was to become a conduit for 'the Holy Spirit,'" he explained in his 2017 email. "As such, my means of 'praying' would be to set aside other things in order to merge my individual spirit with the Holy Spirit." However it had happened, his practice had made Henskee into an extraordinarily kind, humble, and generous person. He had lived meagerly his entire adult life (often aided by Nova Scotia's generous social welfare system), and yet regularly he gave money to an assortment of acquaintances who were worse off than he was. "Some of these people really depend on me," Dan told me on the August day in 2016 when we were watching them sink the first caisson at the Money Pit. People could call Henskee crazy if they wanted to, but what I knew for certain was that he was a good man.

And I believed he really did know things. Back in 2003, Dan told me that he had never stopped believing Oak Island was haunted by the souls of those who died there. "Something about that place makes everything go wrong that can go wrong," he had said.

Not a single person who has worked on *The Curse of Oak Island* would disagree with that statement. Inexplicable equipment failures have become one of the show's recurring themes. "You may not be used to this, but we are," Craig Tester would tell the young man whose inflatable dam burst at Smith's Cove. Many others have happened off camera. Rick Lagina told me about a geophysicist who had come to the island with an apparatus he had used all over the world, most recently in a search for mineral deposits in Zaire. As soon as he attempted to use the machine on Oak Island, though, it failed. He had listened when the geophysicist, very upset, called the manufacturer in France and was told that the machine was incapable of malfunctioning because of the number of redundancies that had been built into it as default systems. "The geophysicist said, 'Maybe it can't fail, but it has,'" Rick recalled with a laugh. Tony Sampson described a man who nearly broke down into tears when a machine that provided underwater propulsion broke down just off the south shore of Oak Island. "He kept saying, 'This has never happened before, anywhere, ever,'" Tony recalled. "We tried to tell him how many times we've heard people speak exactly those words on Oak Island, but the poor bloke was inconsolable."

More interesting to me were the stories I head from the television crew about the failures of their own equipment. The soundmen in particular said their microphones cut out and in and back out again constantly in certain places on the island, mainly the eastern corner of the swamp and in the vicinity of 10X. They and the rest of the crew seemed to have become almost inured to such experiences. Every time something broke down or got lost, they would simply look at one another and say with a shrug: "Oak Island." Marty Lagina, a confirmed skeptic on the subjects of the supernatural or the paranormal, told me he had no explanation for the number of equipment malfunctions and electrical failures he's witnessed on Oak Island. "It happens so much more often here than anyplace else I've ever been that it's not even close," he admitted. When I tried to keep him on the subject, Marty said that maybe we should perform a "magnetic survey" of the island that summer. It never happened.

Like Marty, the crew were reluctant to talk about the spooky things they'd experienced on Oak Island. It was as if they believed giving the subject any air would increase the likelihood of it happening again or draw the darkness to them. Marty, though, did tell me about the first time he was alone at the Money Pit area after the sun had set. "First, I don't believe in any of this stuff," he said. "But I was there not even ten minutes when I heard this blood-curdling shriek, and I admit it, I was terrified. I got out of there as fast as I could." Had he ever gone back alone after dark? I asked. "Never have," Marty told me.

I became a good deal more interested in Oak Island's scary stories after I talked to Jim Kaizer's grandson Tim. Countless people had claimed to have seen ghosts or specters on the island. The most often reported of the latter was a big black dog with fiery-red eyes, though there were a good number who claimed that they had encountered the spirits of dead men who appeared as crows or ravens. Anthony Graves's son, William, claimed on his deathbed in the 1850s that while he was out in his boat spearing lobster one evening, a man with a long white beard had called to him from the shoreline: "Come here and I will give you all the gold you can carry." He had been so frightened, William Graves declared with some of his last breaths, that he had immediately started rowing for home. In 1868, E. H. Owen had written an essay for a Lunenburg newspaper about the legend that the treasure could be found by anyone willing to throw a baby into the Money Pit. Jack and Charlotte Adams, who were working as caretakers for Edwin Hamilton in the 1940s, said they were haunted by the story their four-year-old daughter had told of coming upon a group of men wearing red jackets and pants with broad yellow stripes sitting on the timbers of the old wharf at Smith's Cove.

Probably the last person I expected to tell me a spooky story was Dave Blankenship, but out of nowhere one afternoon Dan's son began to describe the day he and a couple of men who were visiting the island had seen flames rising over the treetops on the east end of the island. They had hurried over, afraid the blaze might be already out of control, Dave said, but when they got to where they had seen the fire, there was nothing. "I *saw* a fire!" Dave told me. "Nobody can tell me I didn't. But there was no fire. Damnedest thing."

When I kept asking questions about these sorts of occurrences, members of the crew started telling me: "You should talk to Becky."

Becky Parsons was an Englishwoman who had worked as a camera operator on the show for two summers before I arrived. When I finally got hold of her, she told me that she had grown up hearing about Oak Island, because her father was fascinated by the place. He was a student of history with a special interest in the age of piracy. She hadn't heard much if anything about the purported paranormal activity on the island, but she considered herself sensitive to such things. "And when I first came to the island, I got very strong feelings about one of the places there, a spot just past 10X on the edge of the wooded area."

One afternoon she was shooting B-roll—the visual filler that all nonfiction television shows use—Becky said, "and I just sort of started exploring in that area, just looking through the camera and kind of letting the camera system lead me toward that wooded area on the left of 10X. All of a sudden I had a strong sensation that there was someone behind me. I thought it was my assistant. I put the camera down and turned around to talk to him but . . . there was no one there. But there was this depression in the ground right at that spot, one I hadn't seen before. And, I don't know, I just felt very strongly as though I had encountered something."

Some weeks later, a psychic visited the island and stayed late into the evening. After dark, the woman invited her to go on what Becky called "a ghost walk." She was carrying a psychometry instrument the psychic had brought, Becky said, a device that was supposed to measure "energy." "I sort of made a beeline for that spot by 10X, because I was very curious about it. I walked into the woods and all of a sudden the energy on this instrument goes off the charts. I stepped onto the pathway there and I felt this flush of energy. It was a sensation, like something is entering my body. It happened very, very strongly, and I'm looking at the needle and it's still off the charts. I just sort of pushed it away, the energy that was trying to enter me. I didn't feel the presence of evil, didn't feel any danger, I just didn't want it to come any closer to me." Then she heard the psychic screaming from the clearing behind her and came back out toward 10X, Becky said, "and she was really freaked out. She said she had seen what she called 'a black mass' follow me into the woods. And I felt like I knew what she was talking about."

Later that same night, the psychic had held what Becky called a sort of séance. "She tried to call up some energy and I experienced this manifestation right in front of me. Of a man. But I only saw his legs, like he was being built in front of me, in this transparent light kind of way." Somehow, she had known this was the spirit of someone who had been "killed there and left to guard the place." Becky said. I brought up the legend of the slave who had supposedly been killed and thrown into the Money Pit so his spirit would guard the treasure, and Becky swore she had never heard about it before. By the excitement in her voice I believed her. Later during the séance, a date had come to her, and she knew it was connected to the spirit that had tried to "enter her" earlier, Becky said. She couldn't remember the date exactly, other than that it was in the 1700s. "I wrote it down and put it in a teacup in a cupboard in the Blankenships' kitchen," Becky said. I later asked Dan Henskee to look for that note in Dan Blankenship's kitchen cupboard; he couldn't find it.

WHEN I RETURNED TO OAK ISLAND in 2016, I had to consider the possibility that my view of the island as a place steeped in darkness was based mostly on atmospherics. Could my perceptions have been shaped by something as obvious as the weather? I wondered.

Most of the clothes and gear I'd packed were for the sort of cool, damp climate I'd experienced back in 2003. But Nova Scotia was in the middle of the warmest summer anyone could remember, day after day of sunny skies and temperatures in the upper seventies and eighties that felt a lot hotter than that in the high humidity of Canada's Atlantic coast. And the island was far from the lonely place I'd first visited thirteen years earlier, when the only people on it beside myself were Dan and Jane Blankenship. The success of *The Curse of Oak Island* had resulted in by far the largest crew I'd ever seen working on a reality show, and the island buzzed with activity as big trucks came and went across the causeway constantly. It was no longer a scary place, at least in daylight hours. Only when I walked off to explore alone or stayed on the island after dark did that sensation of free-floating dread come back to me.

As the days passed, I began to understand better that when I'd written about the "curse" of Oak Island it wasn't based mainly on stories of ghost sightings or diabolical possessions. The largest part of the island's haunted aspect, in my eyes, was the way it swallowed up people's lives. That included the six who had died, of course, but to their number I added the dozens of others who had sunk their time, their money, and their dreams into Oak Island. Fred Nolan's death brought it home. I'd only read about the obsessions of Frederick Blair and Gilbert Hedden, of the bankruptcies of T. Perley Putnam and Captain John Welling. But I had met Nolan, spoken with him, listened to the voice of a man whose compulsion had consumed six decades of his life. Dan Blankenship, who was approaching his midnineties, had been on the island for more than five decades.

The passage of time had changed Blankenship, but so, I believed, had Fred Nolan's death. There was a deeper melancholy about the man. Dan had admitted to me even thirteen years earlier that he brooded over the possibility that death would find him before he found the Oak Island treasure. "What I find most frightening is the thought that what I know might die with me," he said. The arrival of the Laginas on the island had provided Dan with a repository for his knowledge, but he seemed to be finding very little consolation in the process of sharing it. I could see in his eyes and hear in his voice that Dan was now certain he would be gone before the treasure hunt was finished. I think he had begun to wonder, finally, if the treasure hunt on Oak Island *ever* would be finished. Every time I saw him, I would recall what Dan told me in 2003 about the many hours he had invested in contemplating the mind, or minds, that directed the work on Oak Island. He wondered if they had any idea that the riddle they created would rob so many men of their lives, their wealth, and their sanity.

"Sometimes," he told me, "you begin to believe that they understood exactly what they were doing to us, and you start to despise the sons of bitches."

Postscript

The summer of 2017—season five of *The Curse of Oak Island*—would yield discoveries that rivaled any made during the previous century. Many of these were pulled from a shaft dug in the east drumlin that had been designated as "H8." Marty Lagina believed that H8 was centered on the original Money Pit. His brother Rick wasn't "quite there," but considered it entirely possible.

Whether Marty was right or not, he and Rick and their fellow treasure hunters had brought up "an extraordinary amount of stuff" out of H8, as the executive producer of *The Curse of Oak Island*," Kevin Burns, put it. Easily the most startling of that "stuff"—found at a depth of one hundred ninety feet under ground—were the bones of two separate human beings, one of European origin and the other Middle Eastern, according to DNA testing. In his opinion, these fragments of human skeletons were "the best finds ever" made on Oak Island, Marty told me from the island's "War Room" when I spoke to him and Rick on a conference call in June of 2018. "Even for a skeptic like me it's hard to find a plausible reason for them being so deep underground," he explained.

Carbon dating, as always, could only answer the question of when these two people had lived with what Marty called "a probability window." The fact that this window was centered in the late seventeenth century offered more support for some theories than for others, however fragile it might be. It comported quite well, for example, with the theory of Francis Bacon's involvement in the works on Oak Island. So did the scraps of what appeared to be leather bookbinding material brought up out of H8. Rick described the pieces of leather and the apparent specks of parchment attached to them that had been found in H8 as the most "scary discovery" he and his brother had made on Oak Island, because it suggested that their excavation might have destroyed centuries-old volumes of incalculable value.

At the same time, Rick was circumspect in his assessment of the leather scraps and the parchment flakes found with them, acknowledging the possibility that these had "migrated in" to H8. "We know how highly disruptive the Money Pit area is," he explained. Also, unlike his brother, he continued to harbor doubts about whether they had hit the heart of the Money Pit with H8, Rick added. "The question for me is, 'Where's the wood?'" Records indicated that 10,000 board feet of timber had dropped into the ground during the 1861 collapse of the Money Pit, Rick pointed out. "Where is it?"

"I thought we pulled a lot of wood out of there," Marty said. Not enough to be convincing, Rick countered, "but that could be addressed again by the idea of migration in and out of the area." Records indicated that the cribbing in the Money Pit had fallen in a southwesterly direction, and that it most of it might have come to rest some distance from the center of the shaft.

The Laginas acknowledged being almost as fascinated by an object Gary Drayton had found at Smith's Cove with his metal detector as he was by the bones brought to the surface in the Money Pit area. This was a "very strange medieval cross," as Kevin Burns described it, that Drayton had discovered only about six inches under the rock on the beach at Smith's Cove. Made of hand wrought lead with details that suggested a human body—legs, toes, fingers—the cross had been dated to somewhere between 900 and 1300 A.D. by antiquities experts and forensic testing.

What made the discovery of the cross "extraordinarily weird," Kevin Burns told me, was that Rick's immediate response when he was first shown it had been to say, "I've seen this recently." The producers looked through all the photos of the crosses Rick might have observed during trips to England and France that summer and "nothing matched," Burns recalled. "We thought Rick wasn't remembering properly."

On his European trip, Rick had examined a purported "underground Templar cave" in the north of England and the prison at Domme in the French department of Dordogne where the Knights Templar had been locked up by King Philip in 1307. Rick had been guided at Domme by a descendant of the Rochefort family, who showed him the prison walls that the Templars had covered with a graffiti of geometric figures they used as a coded language: An octagon represented the Holy Grail; a square represented Solomon's Temple; a triangle with a cross planted in it stood for Golgotha, the Jerusalem hill where Jesus had been crucified. Only in a close examination of their footage of the graffiti at Domme had the producers of *The Curse of Oak Island* discovered a cross carved in a wall of the prison that was a near perfect match for the cross found at Smith's Cove, with the same esoteric details that suggested a rood formed from a human body.

"How likely is it that someone in the 1600s would be wearing a cross from the 1300s or earlier?" asked Burns, who was delighted by Marty's reaction when he saw the image of the cross carved into the wall at Domme. "It energized Marty's interest like nothing ever has," Burns said. "He's always been the toughest nut to crack, but the discovery of the cross at Smith's Cove and of its match at Domme Prison convinced him that there *is* a treasure on Oak Island, not necessarily gold or silver, but a historical treasure at the very least."

He wasn't making any connection between the bones pulled from H8 and the medieval cross found at Smith's Cove, Marty told me from the War Room, but in combination the two discoveries had led him to "the conclusion that something extraordinary happened here."

An event from season five of *The Curse of Oak Island* that had fascinated me involved a pair of cameras lost in the T1 shaft. The cameras had been sent down in an attempt to examine the "shiny gold object" that Charles Barkhouse had first observed the previous summer. After the cameras slipped loose from their tethers and fell into the hole, a diver with a metal detector was sent down to locate them, but found no trace. The show's producers and crew had been suitably impressed by the vanishing cameras, as was I, but Rick and Marty more or less shrugged it off as one more inexplicable phenomenon of the island. "Sloughing currents" might have explained the disappearance of the cameras, Marty suggested. "Or it could just be a technically challenging dive and we just didn't know where to point the detector," Rick added, then chuckled. "Or maybe leprechauns."

"It might have just been equipment failure," Marty said then. "As you know, Randall, it happens all the time out here." I asked about the "magnetic survey" Marty and I had talked about in the summer of 2016. "As a matter of fact, we discussed doing that just today," Marty told me.

The Laginas' schedule for the summer of 2018 was already packed, Kevin Burns advised me. Smith's Cove would be their main focus. A "massive" excavation was planned, Burns said. Its main goal would be to locate and explore the manmade "U-shaped structure" that Dan Blankenship had discovered decades earlier, but the brothers and their cohort would also be searching for the two "round mineshafts" described in the Robert Restall records. They had "some plans for the swamp" as well, Burns said, and would be exploring the Money Pit area with the particle physics theories and technology that had resulted in the discovery of a hidden chamber inside Egypt's Giza Pyramid during October of 2017. At Giza, scientists had tracked subatomic particles known as muons as they descended from space into the earth to locate and explore a hall nearly a hundred feet long and seventy feet wide. "We really want to see what the same technology might find on Oak Island," Burns told me.

There would be a further exploration of the C1 shaft as well, said the show's creator, who admitted being continually surprised by viewers' obsessive fascination with Oak Island. It had even infected the show's crew, Burns said: "I have to actually admonish them not to get involved in trying to solve the mystery. That's how invested they get just by being on the island."

Through season four, *The Curse of Oak Island* had continued to be the most popular reality show on cable television, and often the most popular cable show of any kind on the Tuesday nights when its episodes aired. "The possibility of an extraordinary find" was what kept viewers coming back, Burns said.

When the Laginas asked me about the theories I "embraced" or had ruled out, I admitted that the most perplexing thing about Oak Island was how difficult it was to either hold close or outright dismiss any one of the dozens of propositions I had heard or read about. I recalled the old television show *Columbo*, in which the detective played by Peter Falk, in episode after episode, would conclude his questioning of a suspect, begin to step away, then turn back to say, "One more thing." On Oak Island there was always one more thing.

"It's maddening," Marty agreed. "Like the story of the five men and the elephant. You only get bits and pieces."

Rick's view was predictably more romantic: "An Island of what if's and possibilities," he called Oak Island, and sounded as if that was what he most loved about the place.

Kevin Burns compared Oak Island to a slot machine in Las Vegas. "You get just enough to keep you coming back. You want to walk away, but you're afraid the next person's going to pull the lever and hit the jackpot."

Certainly, the Laginas said, they had collected enough in the summer of 2017 to support an enthusiastic search in 2018. After that, well, he wasn't sure, Marty said. His brother Rick, though, was never going to let the treasure hunt go, and Marty knew it. So did Burns: "For Rick, it's a quest, a mission, a tribute to the dreams of those who came before." And in spite of the demurrals he offered, Marty had been ineluctably drawn into that quest. "He's hooked," Burns said, "even if he doesn't want to admit it."

Afterword

I anticipate that there will be complaints that I have failed to mention some of the many theories of Oak Island that have been put forth over the years. I'd like to consider a few briefly.

There are those who have suggested the native people of Nova Scotia, the Mi'kmaq, were responsible for the works on Oak Island. The idea is dubious. There is absolutely nothing that connects the tribe to Oak Island other than that they were living in what would become Nova Scotia long before even the earliest Europeans arrived. The Mi'kmaq themselves have no stories or legends associated with Oak Island, which one would expect if this had occurred.

Some theories sound plausible at first, but they fall apart upon even a cursory examination. A number of investigators, for instance, have energetically promoted the idea that the works on Oak Island were done by the British army during the Revolutionary War in the years between 1776 and 1783. After the British evacuated Boston in March 1776, they had good reason to fear that their New York command post was next, these theorists point out. The New York garrison contained several million pounds for the payment of troops and the purchase of supplies. Also, there were rumors that George Washington intended to attack Halifax (something Washington is known to have considered). The theory goes that to protect its assets, the British sent engineers to Oak Island to supervise the construction of a repository for its colonial treasure that would not be threatened with seizure by the upstart Americans.

There is also a sort of opposite theory that it was the American revolutionaries who created the works on Oak Island as a weapons cache to be used when the War of Independence spread north into Canada's Atlantic coast. Some other theorists have suggested that the pits on Oak Island were used as a part of a smuggling operation run by those who supported the American cause. The problem with both of these—as with the theory that the French army buried a Louisbourg treasure on the island—is obvious. By the middle of the eighteenth century, Mahone Bay was increasingly populated with Europeans who would have been well aware of any major operation on Oak Island. Along with the fact that the carbon-dating points strongly to the late seventeenth or early eighteenth century, this makes these scenarios extremely unlikely.

Even when one has to be impressed by the time and energy an investigator has devoted to the problem of Oak Island, one does not have to treat it with great regard. George Young of Queensland, Nova Scotia, was the project manager for an engineering firm that in 1975 installed a sewage disposal system for the community of Western Shore on behalf of the city of Chester. Part of this work involved constructing a pumping station for the Oak Island Inn, on the mainland about three thousand feet across the bay from Oak Island. During that work, an excavator bucket broke through the earth into a 10-foot wide cavern that was 52 feet deep. From this discovery, Young developed an elaborate theory that hundreds of years before the birth of Christ, Mediterranean peoples were operating a number of trading settlements on the Atlantic coast of North America and that one group of them—people from the coast of Libya who were of mixed Phoenician and Greek blood—were using the cave he had found along with others, including some on Oak Island, as living quarters. This arrangement was ended by the Punic Wars, circa 260 BC, and at that point, Young would assert, those who had been living in the caves were integrated into the Mi'kmaq tribe. Later a group of Copts from Egypt inhabited the abandoned caves, Young's theory went on, then around 1384 AD a large party of Copts arrived on Oak Island with something of extraordinary value that they wished to conceal (Young doesn't claim to know what) and converted the old living quarters on Oak Island into what would become the Money Pit. He doubted they ever intended to reopen the vault they created. Young speculated that they may have been "interring one of exalted rank," which for him was an explanation of the flood tunnel system. It's every bit as outlandish as the theory that Oak Island holds the lost secrets of Atlantis—and one hell of a lot more complicated.

A couple of former miners have proposed theories of Oak Island that probably don't deserve to be dismissed out of hand. The first was John Steadman, a New Brunswick man who had worked at Oak Island with the Truro Company. His claim was that the Money Pit was an old mine that had been dug by the earliest French inhabitants of Nova Scotia. The major problem with that claim is that there is no evidence that valuable minerals were ever on Oak Island to be mined. A former miner named John O'Brien did an extraordinary amount of research in support of a book he titled *Oak Island Unearthed! A Miner's Investigation into the Enigma of Oak Island, the Mesoamericans, and the Treasure Buried Within*. O'Brien at least claimed that the Money Pit was dug to mine something that actually exists on Oak Island, the strata of blue clay found deep underground. It was the ancient Mayans who first dug the mine, O'Brien claimed, and the Aztecs who came later, after the Spanish conquest in the fifteenth century. There is evidence that the Maya were maritime traders whose reach extended as far north as the coastal lagoons of Mexico, Belize, and Guatemala. Their only watercraft, though, is believed to have been the dugout canoe. No intact Mayan canoes have ever been discovered, but there are depictions in Mayan art of royal figures being ferried about by canoe. Also, Christopher Columbus's son Ferdinand wrote a fairly detailed description of seeing the Mayans paddling offshore in their canoes. There is absolutely no evidence, however, that the Maya ever got as far north as even Florida, and the notion that they paddled all the way to Nova Scotia to mine blue clay strains credulity to the breaking point.

A fringe theorist who got to make an on-camera presentation to the Laginas for *The Curse of Oak Island* is Gary Clayton, a former Baptist minister from Arizona, who had acquired Little Mash Island, a tiny blot of sand very near Oak Island. He had found evidence of tunnels and chambers connecting Oak Island to Little Mash, claimed Clayton, who asserted that a treasure that included several hundred tons of gold bullion had been deposited in those chambers following a 1740 voyage from England by a group with "ties" to the Freemasons and Templars. He was there to offer a consulting contract, Clayton told the Laginas, for which he would receive 15 percent of any treasure found.

What was not mentioned but I knew was that Clayton had been claiming to know exactly what was buried on Oak Island and where since the 1970s, when he and two partners put together a theory that involved the Aztecs and Mayans. As late as 2004, Clayton was boasting that he had invested "forty-five thousand hours' research" to the problem of Oak Island and had figured it out completely by breaking the various clues and codes that had been left on the island by the original depositors and was ready to prove beyond all doubt that the Aztecs or Maya had had engineered the Oak Island works. He had "mathematical proof," asserted Clayton, who was equipped with elaborately drafted engineering blueprints of the various vaults, passageways, flood tunnels, and underground living quarters he claimed were on Oak Island. Now, forty-four years after he started, Clayton had left the Aztecs and Maya behind and was claiming he had absolute proof instead of a Freemason/ Templar treasure.

I WAS FAIRLY CERTAIN when I left Nova Scotia at the end of August 2016 that the Laginas would continue their treasure hunt and their television show for at least another year. In the months that followed, though, a disturbing thought struck me: Now that the treasure hunt and the television show had become not just intertwined, or even symbiotic, but had merged to the point of being completely indistinguishable, what would happen when the show ended? When the show was cancelled, might the treasure hunt be as well?

That the show would go on wasn't completely confirmed in my mind until November, when the fourth season began to run on the History Channel. Shortly after the season debut, Kevin Burns called me to talk about my work on the show. Early in the conversation he told me that this first episode of the new season had been the highest rated program on cable that week. At some point we got on the subject of another season. I mentioned Rick Lagina's remark about not continuing unless they made a breakthrough discovery that summer. Was he sure there would be a fifth season of *The Curse of Oak Island*? I asked Burns. Of course there would be a fifth season. I thought, answering my own question. I just wouldn't be part of it.

Even as I was putting myself at the distance from the show that would be required to write a book about Oak Island, I knew I would be rooting for the Laginas and their cohort to find the "game changer" Dan Henskee had written to me about. I told those who inquired that I was content to watch from the sidelines with the rest of the audience. What I didn't say was that while I was certain the mystery of Oak Island would be solved someday, I doubted it would be any day soon. I would be long gone by then. The most I could hope for, probably, was that someone who read what I wrote about Oak Island would carry the search forward and allow me some small contribution to the end of the story.

Oak Island Time Line

1497	John Cabot becomes first European known to have set foot on Nova Scotia; claims territory for England
1602–1614	Career of pirate Peter Easton, based on island of Oderin off coast of Newfoundland
1604	Samuel de Champlain establishes Port Royal on Bay of Fundy, laying the first French claim to Nova Scotia
1605	Acadians begin settling in Nova Scotia
1632	French establish LaHave settlement at entrance to Mahone Bay
1670	Henry Morgan sacks city of Panama; treasure haul is never accounted for
1680–1699	Career of privateer and pirate William Kidd; Kidd buries part of treasure seized from *Quedegh Merchant* on Gardiners Island in 1699
1687–1694	Career of privateer William Phipps; Phipps sacks Acadian city of Port Royal in Bay of Fundy in 1690
1685	Huguenots persecution begins in France; many sail to and settle in Nova Scotia
1700	French governor invites Atlantic Coast pirates to make LaHave their "depot"
1713	French found fortress of Louisbourg on Cape Breton; Louisbourg pay ships begin sailing Atlantic
1745	Louisbourg falls to British

1746   D'Anville fleet sails from France to take back Louisbourg; many ships lost at sea

1756   Governor Cornwallis expels Acadians from Nova Scotia

1759   Shoreham Grant brings influx of settlers to Mahone Bay from New England; Chester Township established

1763   Treaty of Paris permits Acadian return to Nova Scotia

1765   What will become Oak Island designated as Island No. 28 by Charles Morris, surveyor general of the Nova Scotia province; Morris divides island into thirty-two four-acre lots

1768   Anthony Vaughan Sr. immigrates to Mahone Bay area of Nova Scotia

1781   Two Vaughan brothers purchase lots 13 and 14 on Oak Island

1783   Freed slave Samuel Ball arrives in Canada and settles in Mahone Bay

1784   Donald Daniel McGinnis, father of Money Pit discoverer, awarded a Crown grant of one hundred acres near Chester Township

1786   Eleven-year-old John Smith moves onto Oak Island with family

1787   Samuel Ball purchases first of nine lots he will own on Oak Island

1788   Vaughans petition province of Nova Scotia for permission to cut and mill pine trees on the mainland

1795   Putative year of discovery of Money Pit by Daniel McGinnis, John Smith, and Anthony Vaughan; initial excavation of the Pit

1795   John Smith purchases lot 18 on Oak Island; whether this was before or after the discovery of the Money Pit is not known

1795   Daniel McGinnis marries Maria Barbara Saller in Lunenburg

1797   Daniel McGinnis's son Johan baptized in Chester

1804   Onslow Company sails to Oak Island, begins second and more extended excavation of Money Pit; discovery of lot platforms, charcoal, coconut fiber, blue clay, and inscribed stone follow, as does flooding of Money Pit

1805   Onslow Company returns to Oak Island; unable to solve flood system problem

1827   Daniel McGinnis dies on Oak Island

1845   Truro Company formed

1849   Truro Company begins operations on Oak Island; discoveries include the chain "links" brought up by a pot auger from the Money Pit; also claim to have passed through "metal in pieces" while drilling at a depth of more than 100 feet in Money Pit; dig shaft no. 2 on the island's east-end drumlin

1849   Anthony Vaughan gives his account of Money Pit's discovery to Robert Creelman

1849   Truro Company drill operator James Pitblado disappears from Oak Island and Mahone Bay area, supposedly after having removed some unknown object from drill tip

1850   Truro Company returns to Oak Island, barging out a "two-horse gin"; digs shaft no. 3; after failing to solve flood system, company explores Smith's Cove, where they discover man-made beach and five-fingered drain system

1857   John Smith dies

1857   Geologist Henry Poole observes and describes the Money Pit area

1861   Oak Island Association begins operations on Oak Island with sixty-three workmen; by the time they finish there are six shafts in Money Pit area; digging and tunneling results in collapse of Money Pit; burst boiler results in first death of Oak Island treasure hunt, name of victim not known

1862   Jothan McCully writes first article about discovery of Money Pit for *Liverpool Transcript*

1863   Andrew Learmont Spedon's *Rambles among the Blue-Noses* published, the first mention of Oak Island to appear between hard covers

1863   Inscribed stone is removed from Smith home to home of Jothan McCully

1863   Treasure hunter James McNutt writes a description of the early search for treasure on Oak Island; it is never published and only fragments of the manuscript are recovered

1864   Oak Island Association locates what they believe is the "flood tunnel" but operations on the island soon abandoned; by this point there are nine shafts in Money Pit area

1864   Jothan McCully (most likely) writes first published full account of Money Pit's discovery for the *Colonist*

1865   Inscribed stone is removed from McCully home to be displayed in window of A. and H. Creighton in Halifax

1866   Oak Island Eldorado Company (soon to be the Halifax Company) formed; begins operations on Oak Island

1867   Halifax Company gives up treasure hunt on Oak Island

1870   Judge Mather Byles DesBrisay's *History of the County of Lunenburg* originally published, the first description of the Money Pit's discovery to appear between hard covers

1878   Sophia Sellers's team of oxen falls into what will become known as the Cave-in Pit

1885   Ivory or bone boatswain's whistle found at Smith's Cove

1893   Frederick Blair establishes Oak Island Treasure Company in Boston

1894   Treasure Company begins operations on Oak Island; excavates the Cave-in Pit; digs shaft no. 12

1896   Second edition of *History of the County of Lunenburg* published; in it DesBrisay replaces Samuel Ball with Anthony Vaughan as one of the Money Pit's original discoverers

1897   Blair and Treasure Company dig shaft no. 13; Maynard Kaiser becomes second to die during treasure hunt on Oak Island; Captain John Welling and Treasure Company crew find man-made tunnel flowing with saltwater to Money Pit; scrap of parchment with writing in India ink pulled from bit of drill bit probing

Money Pit; Treasure Company sinks six more shafts on east-end drumlin, bringing the total to nineteen; A. Boake, Roberts and Company of London identify substance removed from drill bit as primitive man-made cement

1898   Captain John Welling is first to discover stone triangle and drilled boulder; Treasure Company besieged by creditors and collapses, with many investors declaring bankruptcy

1900   Frederick Blair buys out all other shareholders in the Treasure Company

1904   Through an agent, Blair acquires forty-year lease on Money Pit under Nova Scotia Mines Act

1909   Captain Henry Bowdoin announces in a series of interviews with New York newspaper that he is taking over the Oak Island treasure hunt after striking a deal with Frederick Blair, forms Old Gold Salvage and Wrecking Company, sells only five thousand of 250,000 shares offered, ten to Franklin Delano Roosevelt; first claim made (in *New York Times*) that what is buried on Oak Island are the French crown jewels; Bowdoin begins operations on Oak Island, doing little of what he promised, quits the island in November, promising to return before end of 1911

1911   After failing to make a deal with Frederick Blair to continue work on Oak Island, Bowdoin takes revenge by writing article for *Collier's* magazine in which he claims there has never been any treasure on Oak Island and that flooding of the Money Pit is a naturally occurring phenomenon

1912   Blair answers Bowdoin's article with one of his own written for the *Amherst Daily News*

1912   Professor S. A. Williams proposes solving Money Pit problem with Poetsch method but is unable to raise adequate funds

1913   Blair acquires eight-year lease on Money Pit lot from Sophia Sellers

1919   Creighton and Marshall bookbinding business closes and inscribed stone disappears, never to be seen again

1921	Blair makes deal with engineer Edward Brown to excavate the Money Pit, but Brown never gets deeper than 7 feet
1922	Blair posts advertisement in *Boston Journal of Commerce* for a partner in the treasure hunt
1931	Blair signs partnership agreement with William Chappell, the drill operator who brought up the parchment scrap; William's son Melbourne helps him organize operations on the island; they sink shaft no. 21, broadest hole ever dug on Oak Island; among the artifacts they recover are an anchor fluke, an Acadian axe and seal-oil lamp; storms end work in October
1932	Blair loses lease on Money Pit property and it is acquired by engineer John Talbot on behalf of investor group headed by New York heiress Mary B. Stewart; Talbot accomplishes little, but does take the boatswain's whistle to Stewart in New York, and it is never seen again
1933	Thomas Nixon, the first to suggest that the treasure of Tumbes is buried on Oak Island, signs deal with Blair to enclose Money Pit in steel pilings in order to excavate; instead he drills fourteen boreholes to bring up fragments oak and china
1935	Gilbert Hedden signs deal with Blair to take over the Oak Island treasure hunt, buys Money Pit property from Sophia Sellers's heirs
1936	Hedden's crew, under supervision of engineer Frederick Krupp, begins operations on Oak Island, opening and draining shaft no. 21, known as the Chappell shaft, find what they believe to be an original flood tunnel at a depth of 93 feet
1936	Exploring the island on his own, Hedden discovers the timbers of a structure built before the early 1700s at Smith's Cove
1937	*Captain Kidd and His Skeleton Island* by Harold Wilkins published, containing what becomes known as the Mar Del map; Hedden writes to Wilkins, noting similarities to Oak Island
1937	Hedden and crew return to Oak Island, begin work on shaft no. 22, to be twice the size of Money Pit; Blair tells Hedden about stone triangle and drilled boulder discovered by Captain Welling

in 1897; Hedden orders his men to search, and one of them, Amos Nauss, finds the triangle; Hedden also finds not just one drilled boulder, but a second as well; Charles Roper is brought to the island to conduct a survey using the reference points written on the Mar Del map; Roper discovers that medial line of stone triangle is pointing due north and right into the center of the Money Pit

1937   Hedden writes to President Roosevelt to inform him of the discoveries, then sets sail for England to meet Harold Wilkins; Wilkins confesses he created the Mar Del map but says he may have based it on the Captain Kidd treasure charts he saw at the British Museum

1938   Hedden is sued by the Internal Revenue Service, effectively ending his direct involvement in the Oak Island treasure hunt

1938   Professor Edwin Hamilton signs a deal with Blair and Hedden to take over the treasure hunt on Oak Island, begins boring operations that summer, putting down fifty-eight holes in Money Pit area, bringing up "very old oak" and what he believes are connections to the flood tunnel system; establishes that seawater is pouring into Money Pit area at rate of 800 gallons per minute; also establishes that Chappell shaft and Money Pit are just a few feet apart

1939   Professor Burrell Ruth writes to Hedden, making the first known claim that what is buried in the Money Pit are the manuscripts of William Shakespeare

1940   Hamilton and crew find Halifax Company tunnel

1943   Hamilton gives up efforts on Oak Island, having proved mostly how difficult the previous work on Oak Island makes any future progress

1944–1946   Blair negotiates failed deals with Anthony Belfiglio and Edward Reichert

1947   System of tunnels and vaults reportedly found on Haiti by engineer Albert Lochard

1948   Hedden agrees to sell his property on Oak Island to Colonel
            H. A. Gardener, who proposes to explore the Money Pit with a
            radio scanner developed by US military; Blair blocks the sale

1949   Hedden does sell his Oak Island lots to petroleum engineer John
            Whitney Lewis; Lewis, however, learns that Frederick Blair has
            reacquired treasure trove rights and agrees to sell the same lots
            to Melbourne Chappell

1951   Frederick Blair dies after more than a half century of involvement
            in the Oak Island treasure hunt, leaving behind the documents
            that establish the history of operations on the island; Mel Chap-
            pell acquires Blair's treasure trove license, making him the first
            to both own the Money Pit property and the right to search for
            treasure there

1951   Edward Rowe Snow's *True Tales of Buried Treasure* is published,
            includes first claim of translation of inscribed stone by an Irish
            schoolmaster and first account of men "silhouetted against bon-
            fires" being seen on Oak Island before the Money Pit's discovery

1953   Thomas Penn Leary self-publishes his book *The Oak Island
            Enigma*, arguing that Francis Bacon or his followers were behind
            the works on the island

1955   George Greene makes deal with Mel Chappell to apply oil drill-
            ing methods to probe of Money Pit area; locates a large under-
            ground cavity at 45 feet belowground, finds that 100,000 gallons
            of water won't fill it

1956   Greene writes to Chappell that he won't be able to return to Oak
            Island that spring as promised; he never sets foot on the island
            again

1957   Robert Restall and Mel Chappell exchange letters, nearly make
            an agreement, but Chappell changes mind

1958   Chappell makes a deal with Harman brothers, professional drill-
            ers who begin probing Money Pit, bringing up oak and spruce
            fragments, coconut fiber, and ship's caulking; Chappell refuses
            to renew their lease

1958	R. V. Harris's *The Oak Island Mystery* is published
1959	Chappell signs first of several one-year agreements with Robert Restall, who along with son Bobbie sets up camp on Oak Island
1960	Restall's wife, Mildred, and younger son, Ricky, move onto the island; Robert Restall and Bobbie explore south shoreline where Bob finds "1704 stone"
1961	Restall searches for "mystery box" in swamp, cannot locate it, also discovers the triangle of piled stones on slope of island's east-end drumlin
1962	David Tobias becomes a Restall investor
1962	Fred Nolan completes first survey of Oak Island, approaches Chappell with offer to lease search rights in Money Pit area; Chappell refuses
1963	Nolan acquires seven disputed lots on Oak Island, reapproaches Chappell, offering to trade his lots for right to excavate Money Pit; Chappell refuses; Nolan excavates two shafts on own property
1965	Robert Dunfield becomes Restall investor
1965	Restall and crew open new shaft between Cave-in Pit and Money Pit; on August 17, Robert Restall, Bobbie Restall, Cyril Hiltz, and Karl Graeser die in that shaft
1965	Robert Dunfield takes over operations under the Restall contract; Mildred and Ricky Restall are moved off the island to house on mainland; Dunfield builds causeway connecting Oak Island and mainland, uses it to haul across the seventy-ton digging crane he will use to perform massive excavations at the Money Pit area and at Smith's Cove
1965	Dan Blankenship joins treasure hunt as Dunfield investor, begins research at Nova Scotia Archives
1965	*Reader's Digest* publishes article on Oak Island
1966	Nolan purchases quarter acre of land next to causeway entrance at Crandall's Point

1966   Robert Dunfield abandons operations on Oak Island

1967   Dan Blankenship assumes control of operations on Oak Island, in association with David Tobias; Blankenship and Tobias make deal to include Fred Nolan; on island's south shore, Blankenship finds handwrought nail and washer

1967   Tobias persuades Chappell to permit Becker drilling program that will establish basic facts of Oak Island's underground structure; Canada Cement LaFarge identifies cement pulled from belowground as type common in sixteenth and seventeenth centuries; wood brought up is carbon-dated to be at least two and a half centuries old; beneath Hedden shaft, Becker drill finds holes filled with layers of small stones and blue clay putty; on basis of Becker program, Blankenship and Tobias announce they have proved the existence of man-made tunnels at depths of more than 200 feet beneath the surface of Oak Island

1967   Fred Nolan opens his Oak Island museum at Crandall's Point

1969   Tobias, Blankenship, and investor group form Triton Alliance; Fred Nolan accuses Blankenship and Tobias of breach of contract, blocks entrance to causeway, forcing Triton to build a bypass; Triton retaliates by blocking causeway access to Oak Island, forcing Nolan to travel by boat; Nolan retaliates by blocking roadway through his property to Money Pit

1969   Borehole 10X is first drilled; cofferdam at Smith's Cove permits Triton to expose a huge U-shaped wooden structure offshore; carbon-dating establishes structure was built prior to 1720; Blankenship also discovers the "G stone" near the Cave-in Pit

1970   Steel Company of Canada issues report stating that metal pulled from 10X is pre-1700 wrought iron

1970   Professor Ross Wilhelm produces his translation of inscribed stone and claims that Oak Island was used as a depot for storm-damaged Spanish ships in sixteenth century

1970   Tobias sends Blankenship to Haiti to find the pirate bank Albert Lochard claimed to have found in 1947; Blankenship can't locate it

1971   Borehole 10X is widened and lined with 27-inch diameter casing; Steel Company of Canada reports that new metal fragments removed from 10X are case-hardened steel, most likely pre-1750

1971   Fred Nolan acquires his own treasure trove license; Triton responds by making a new agreement with Nolan for a share of any treasure found on his property in exchange for Nolan's right to drive across causeway and a promise not to challenge his ownership of disputed lots

1972–1976   Blankenship makes a series of dives to bottom of 10X

1973   Jane Blankenship moves to Mahone Bay

1975   Blankenships acquire lot 23 on Oak Island, begin building home there

1975   Engineering operation supervised by George Young finds cavern 52 feet deep at Western Shore, directly across from Oak Island

1976   Dan Blankenship nearly crushed by collapsing casing in 10X

1976   Blankenship and Tobias form Oak Island Tours

1977   Mel Chappell sells all of his land on Oak Island to David Tobias

1978   Blankenship begins using railroad tank cars to case 10X, assisted by Dan Henskee

1979   Blankenship first discovers "ice holes" off the south shore of Oak Island; dispute opens between Blankenship and Tobias about trying to seal south shore holes and about continued exploration of 10X

1981   Fred Nolan first finds the five cone-shaped boulders that constitute what will become known as Nolan's Cross

1983   Triton files a lawsuit against Fred Nolan, alleging he is not legal owner of the disputed seven lots on Oak Island

1985   Triton/Nolan lawsuit goes to trial; Nolan prevails with ruling he is legal owner of seven lots on Oak Island